D1598039

Today's Social Issues

Today's Social Issues

Democrats and Republicans

TIMOTHY W. KNEELAND

Across the Aisle

 ABC-CLIO™

An Imprint of ABC-CLIO, LLC
Santa Barbara, California • Denver, Colorado

Library of Congress Cataloging-in-Publication Data

Names: Kneeland, Timothy W., 1962- author.
Title: Today's social issues : Democrats and Republicans / Timothy W. Kneeland.
Description: Santa Barbara, California : ABC-CLIO, 2016. | Series: Across the aisle | Includes bibliographical references and index.
Identifiers: LCCN 2015051075 | ISBN 9781610698351 (hardback) | ISBN 9781610698368 (ebook)
Subjects: LCSH: Democratic Party (U.S.) | Republican Party (U.S. : 1854-) | Political parties—United States—Platforms. | BISAC: POLITICAL SCIENCE / Political Process / Political Parties. | POLITICAL SCIENCE / Political Ideologies / Democracy.
Classification: LCC JK2316 .K64 2016 | DDC 324.273/13—dc23
LC record available at https://lccn.loc.gov/2015051075

ISBN: 978-1-61069-835-1
EISBN: 978-1-61069-836-8

20 19 18 17 16   1 2 3 4 5

This book is also available on the World Wide Web as an eBook.
Visit www.abc-clio.com for details.

ABC-CLIO
An Imprint of ABC-CLIO, LLC

ABC-CLIO, LLC
130 Cremona Drive, P.O. Box 1911
Santa Barbara, California 93116-1911

This book is printed on acid-free paper ∞

Manufactured in the United States of America

Contents

Introduction

Both the Democratic Party and the Republican Party claim that they have the best interests of the nation and its people at heart, and they are equally adamant that they have the best policy solutions to address America's problems and challenges. This volume in ABC-CLIO's *Across the Aisle* series examines the proposals and positions of the two parties—from profound disagreements to areas of common ground—in the realm of social policy.

Today's Social Issues: Democrats and Republicans sorts through the rhetorical clutter and partisan distortions that typify so many disputes between Republicans and Democrats in the 21st century in order to provide an accurate, balanced, and evenhanded overview of the parties' respective policy positions and attitudes on the most important and divisive social issues in the United States. Coverage also details instances in which the rhetorical positions staked out by Democrats and Republicans are inconsistent with their voting records and policy priorities.

Finally, in addition to explaining the differences between the two parties on today's hot-button social issues, this volume also documents significant differences of opinion *within* the parties where present. After all, neither Republicans nor Democrats march in complete lockstep on a wide range of issues, from immigration to legalizing marijuana to sentencing reform. Nor do the policy positions of Republican and Democratic politicians always reflect the views of Republican and Democratic voters.

Throughout this volume, the text features actual quotes from conservative and liberal party leaders, think tanks, and media figures, public opinion poll results, and other valuable, authoritative information to enhance its coverage. This information serves as the foundation for the volume's summaries of the philosophies and records of the two parties in such diverse realms as abortion, gun control, the death penalty, the minimum wage, reparations, unions, income inequality, and privacy rights.

Entry Features

Each essay in *Today's Social Issues: Democrats and Republicans* begins with an At a Glance summary of the prevailing sentiments and policies of the two parties on the issue being discussed. This section also includes reader-friendly "bullet points" listing the most important views of each party.

Each essay then provides an Overview section on historical trends, events, and attitudes displayed by both Republicans and Democrats regarding the issue in question. This section explores party attitudes toward key pieces of legislation, details their political alliances, and tracks evolutions in party thought over time.

From there each essay moves into a deeper exploration of the history and attitudes of the two parties on the social issue in question. Every essay features two special sections—one devoted to the Democratic record on the issue, the other concerned with the Republican record. As with the At a Glance and Overview sections, these sections are carefully crafted to provide both an accurate and an impartial overview of the parties' respective positions.

Every essay in this collection is further supplemented with sidebars featuring illuminating excerpts from speeches, court decisions, and editorials from liberal and conservative presidents, senators, pundits, and justices on the issue being studied. Each essay then concludes with a helpful Further Reading section to direct users to other information sources. The collection is also enhanced with a helpful Glossary of social policy terms, programs, and organizations mentioned in the book, as well as a comprehensive Bibliography.

Abortion

At a Glance

The abortion debate divides Democrats and Republicans over three critical issues: the right to privacy, the right to life, and how to regulate abortion without creating an undue burden on women. Most Democrats believe that a woman has a fundamental right to privacy and that her choice of whether or not to terminate her pregnancy is one she alone should make. The great majority of Republicans believe that abortion on demand terminates the life of an unborn child and should be outlawed or strictly regulated.

Many Republicans . . .

- Are pro-life.
- Believe they need to protect the right of unborn infants by restricting abortions.
- Oppose abortion on demand.
- Reject the Court's decision in *Roe v. Wade*.
- Support the so-called Hyde Amendment that bans the use of federal funds for abortion.
- Want a pro-life amendment to the Constitution to ban abortion.
- Want to pass legislation to mandate waiting periods with counseling for women seeking abortions.
- Seek to protect the right of people to have free speech that opposes abortion.
- See themselves as champions of women and families.
- Often have the backing of conservative and evangelical voters.

Many Democrats . . .

- Are pro-choice.
- Believe that a woman has a fundamental right to control medical decisions about her own body.
- Believe that the right to privacy includes the right to choose whether or not to have children.
- Support *Roe v. Wade* as the law of the land.

- Oppose a Human Life Amendment to the Constitution that would ban abortion.
- Oppose attempts to end the funding of family planning activities and abortion overseas.
- Support a Freedom of Choice Bill that protects a women's right to choose.
- Seek legislation to protect medical staff and women entering and leaving abortion clinics.
- See themselves as champions of a woman's right to choose.
- Often have the backing of feminist groups.

Overview

The issue of whether a woman should have the legal right to voluntarily end her pregnancy through abortion has increasingly divided the two major political parties since the Supreme Court legalized abortion in 1973 with its *Roe v. Wade* decision. Proponents of a woman's right to choose an abortion call themselves pro-choice and have found strong support for their position in the Democratic Party, which added a pro-choice statement to its party platform in 1980. Opponents of abortion call themselves pro-life, believe that personhood begins at conception, and see abortion as unjustified killing. Pro-life groups have found strong support in the Republican Party, which added antiabortion language to its party position at their national convention in 1980. The public attitude toward abortion is evenly divided. A 2013 Gallup Poll found that 48 percent of Americans labeled themselves pro-life and 45 percent described themselves as pro-choice. Fifty-two percent of Americans surveyed in the poll believed that abortion should be "legal under certain circumstances," 26 percent supported abortion in all circumstances, and 20 percent thought it should be illegal in all circumstances.

Abortion was legal from the 18th century until the late 19th century in the United States, but only up to the point when the mother could feel the fetus move in her womb. This changed after the American Medical Association (AMA) determined that abortion should only be medically used to preserve the life of the fetus or the mother. The AMA and other opponents lobbied against abortion in the mid-19th century, and by the 1870s they had convinced most states to adopt laws against the practice. Thus, for the first half of the 20th century, abortion was illegal across the United States.

This changed after the 1950s when organized advocates for abortion such as the Planned Parenthood Federation of America lobbied for liberalizing abortion laws. Planned Parenthood was soon followed by members of the medical, legal, and women's rights communities (McBride 2008).

For the three decades leading up to *Roe v. Wade*, Alan Guttmacher led the medical community in calling for legal abortion. At a meeting of Planned Parenthood in 1942, Guttmacher proposed changing the law to make abortion legal. Members of the legal profession weighed in on this issue in 1959 when the American Law Institute proposed model legislation for creating a legal right to an abortion. In 1967 the National Organization for Women (NOW) endorsed the idea that abortion was a decision best left to a woman and not to male doctors and legislators and since that time the issue has been at the forefront of debates surrounding women's rights. In 1969, the pro-choice group National Abortion Rights Action League (NARAL) was created to actively lobby for women's reproductive rights.

Throughout the 1960s, pro-abortion proponents changed public opinion about abortion with little or no organized opposition. In 1967, Colorado became the first state to legalize abortion in cases of rape, incest, risk to maternal health, and fetal deformity. By 1970, a dozen states had followed Colorado's example. New York repealed its abortion law in 1970 and made abortion on demand legal throughout the entire time of a woman's pregnancy. This was a significant turning point for those who opposed legal abortion and triggered organized opposition to the procedure. Opponents lobbied the New York state legislature to repeal the on-demand abortion law in 1971 but were dismayed when Governor Nelson Rockefeller, a Republican, vetoed it. Meanwhile they began to oppose efforts to legalize abortion in other states; in 1972, they successfully defeated a pro-abortion referendum in Michigan.

The abortion debate became nationalized in 1973 when the Supreme Court ruled in *Roe v. Wade* that abortion was an issue of privacy and that a woman had a "fundamental right" to choose whether or not to terminate her pregnancy. Dividing pregnancy into trimesters, the Court said that states could not regulate an abortion until the fetus was viable outside the mother's womb, usually after the second trimester. In *Doe v. Bolton,* the Court ruled that any state laws regulating abortion must provide exceptions for late-term abortions when they were medically "necessary to save life and health of mother" (*Roe v. Wade* 1971).

Prior to the *Roe v. Wade* decision in 1973, abortion was not an issue that divided the political parties. As we have seen with the case of New York state, within each of the two main political parties there were advocates for and against abortion. However, pro-life groups organizing after 1970 increasingly drew support from men and women with children in traditional marriages, conservative Christian groups such as the Moral Majority and the Christian Coalition, and members of the Republican Party. Antiabortion groups were able to secure a pro-life antiabortion plank in the GOP platform in 1980. Women's rights groups such as NOW and NARAL responded by joining with other progressive groups to sponsor pro-choice language in the Democratic Party platform in 1980. Since 1980, candidates in both parties have been subjected to a litmus test on their views of abortion, and views on the issue have increasingly served to divide people and lawmakers into one party or the other.

Republicans on Abortion

The Republican position on abortion has evolved to become staunchly antiabortion since the 1973 decision in *Roe v. Wade*. In the 1970s, pro-choice Republicans included New York Governor Nelson Rockefeller, who vetoed an antiabortion law in 1971, and future president George H. W. Bush, who was pro-choice until his presidential bid in 1980. What turned the tide for the Republican Party were demographic changes in its makeup and the rise of politically active Christian conservatives. Economic and social conservatives within the GOP allied in the 1970s to bring southern and western voters into the Republican Party, which meant drawing on evangelical and pro-life voting blocs that wanted a so-called "Human Life" amendment to the U.S. Constitution to end abortion on demand and protect the unborn. After 1980, pro-choice candidates for federal office within the Republican Party found it increasingly difficult to raise money and to receive official support from the National Republican Committee or votes from Republican rank and file.

The national GOP platform in 1976 was a curious mix of compromise between pro-choice Republicans and pro-life Republicans and called for more public dialogue on the issue. This changed with the nomination of Ronald Reagan in 1980 and the crafting of a GOP platform that called for "a constitutional amendment to restore protection of the right to life for unborn children." Since that time, the GOP platform has been solidly antiabortion, and antiabortion policies have been asserted by Republicans at the national and state level.

From 1973 until 1989 the Supreme Court struck down most state restrictions and reiterated states could not interfere with a woman's right to choose. This changed in large part because of the election of Ronald Reagan, who suggested "abortion on demand now takes the lives of up to one and a half million unborn children a year. Human life legislation ending this tragedy will someday pass the Congress, and you and I must never rest until it does" (Reagan 1983).

However, judicial appointments by Reagan, which included Sandra Day O'Connor, Antonin Scalia, and Anthony Kennedy to the Supreme Court, and elevation of Justice Rehnquist to chief justice on the Supreme Court, created a federal judiciary that was more open to allowing states to regulate abortion practices. President Reagan's nomination of pro-life judges to the federal courts echoed the party platform of the Republican National Committee (Kinsley 2012). Reagan's judicial nominees did not overturn *Roe v. Wade,* as many pro-life supporters had wanted, but they allowed more regulation of the procedure in such cases as the pivotal 1989 U.S. Supreme Court decision in *Webster v. Reproductive Health Services*— which successfully upheld a Missouri law restricting state funding of abortions.

In 1992, the Court abandoned the rigid trimester criteria created in *Roe v. Wade* in the case of *Planned Parenthood of Southeastern Pa. v. Casey,* which adopted a less restrictive standard for state regulation of abortions—the so-called "undue burden" standard. The Supreme Court allowed states to impose a waiting period before a woman could obtain an abortion. This new standard allowed some legislative interference in the first trimester in the interest of women's health, and permitted parental consent requirements for minors seeking abortions.

Republicans in Congress and Republican presidents also worked together to stop public funding for abortions. President Reagan used his executive authority

Pro-life and pro-choice demonstrators outside of the U.S. Supreme Court building in Washington, D.C., on July 3, 1989. The protests came after the court ruled on the Missouri abortion case which gave states greater power to limit abortion. (AP Photo/Ron Edmonds)

to impose a "gag rule" that stated any agency receiving federal funds for family planning could not discuss abortion in any circumstances; instead they were to discuss only abstinence or adoption. Pro-choice groups challenged these policies in court but Reagan's use of executive power was upheld in 1991 in *Rust v. Sullivan*. Reagan again used executive power when he ordered that all nongovernmental agencies that received any funding from the United States Agency for International Development (USAID) refrain from performing abortion services, including counseling a woman, even if they used their own resources to pay for this service. All Republican presidents since Reagan have reiterated this policy, while all Democratic presidents have rescinded the executive order when occupying the Oval Office (McBride 2008).

Congressional Republicans have also enacted policies to restrict publicly funded abortion services. In 1976, Congress passed the Hyde Amendment to stop Medicaid funding for abortion. This amendment was named for Illinois Republican congress member Henry Hyde and congressional Republicans have kept this ban in place. Republicans in Congress have been less successful in their efforts to enact a Human Life Amendment to the Constitution. Since 1973, there have been annual proposals for a constitutional amendment, but the issue was brought up for a vote only once in 1983, when Senator Orrin Hatch was able to get the Senate Judiciary Committee to bring the amendment to a full Senate vote. It failed with 49 senators in favor, 50 opposed, and 1 senator voting present, although a bill has been offered every year since (National Committee for a Human Life Amendment).

The Republican-led Congress passed the Partial Birth Abortion Ban of 2003, which outlawed the practice of dilation and extraction of the fetus (a.k.a. partial birth) during late-term pregnancies. Four years later, the Supreme Court, in a 5–4 split along ideological lines, voted to uphold the partial birth abortion ban in *Gonzales v. Carhart*.

Republican opposition to abortion has been reflected in their official party platforms as well. In 2012, for instance, the GOP platform stated that

> We assert the sanctity of human life and affirm that the unborn child has a fundamental individual right to life which cannot be infringed. We support a human life amendment to the Constitution and endorse legislation to make clear that the Fourteenth Amendment's protections apply to unborn children. We oppose using public revenues to promote or perform abortion or fund organizations which perform or advocate it and will not fund or subsidize health care which includes abortion coverage. We support the appointment of judges who respect traditional family values and the sanctity of innocent human life.

The party's platform language, however, insisted that its opposition should not be construed as suggesting support for criminal prosecutions of women who have abortions. "We oppose abortion, but our pro-life agenda does not include punitive action against women who have an abortion. We salute those who provide alternatives to abortion and offer adoption services, and we commend congressional Republicans for expanding assistance to adopting families and for removing racial barriers to adoption" (Republican National Committee 2012).

At the state level, Republicans have crafted laws aimed at restricting Medicaid funding for abortion, created parental notification laws, imposed mandatory waiting periods, passed partial birth abortion bans, and, increasingly since 2010, introduced laws imposing a variety of regulations on abortion providers. The latter TRAP (Targeted Regulation of Abortion Provider) laws have effectively limited the number of abortion providers in Republican-controlled states (Medoff 2011). These laws may require a certain size facility for performing abortions or providing medication, specific qualifications or college degrees for individuals who assist in abortion procedures, and specific qualifications such as hospital admission privileges for physicians performing abortions. As Arian Campos-Flores and Cameron McWhirter reported in the *Wall Street Journal* in 2015, nearly 250 state laws have been passed since 2010 to limit abortions, including a Tennessee referendum to amend the state constitution to limit the procedure. Pro-choice advocates believe these laws are meant to restrict abortions and that in the Republican-controlled states where these have been enacted, the number of abortions has fallen (Medoff 2013).

Republicans who openly support abortion rights are rare and find themselves isolated from funding from such organizations as the National Evangelical

Association, Family Research Council, Pro-Life Action League, and the Christian Coalition. Earlier in his political career, Mitt Romney, who received the Republican nomination for president in 2012, was pro-choice. Over time, however, his view of abortion changed. Not every Republican is socially conservative, though. At least one group, Republican Majority for Choice, has its own political action committee and seeks to support Republican candidates who adhere to a limited government view, in this case leaving the choice of an abortion not to the government but to the individual. Although pro-choice Republicans are uncommon, some members of the Republican Party have expressed concerns that attacks on GOP abortion policies as "anti-women" may hinder election fortunes in the future. As reported by Scott Conroy in a story for Politico on June 6, 2014, some in the GOP have called for more willingness to embrace the views of local and state elected officials who have a pro-choice mind-set.

Democrats on Abortion

Prior to the 1973 Supreme Court decisions covering *Roe v. Wade* and *Doe v. Bolton,* Democrats had both pro-life and pro-choice advocates within the party. In the past four decades, however, the Democratic Party became ideologically committed to the pro-choice position on abortion and the majority of Democratic voters and elected officials oppose restrictions and limitations on a woman's right to choose (Keefe and Hetherington 2013). Under President Jimmy Carter, the Democratic Party was willing to recognize that there were deep religious and ethical convictions about abortion. As a group, however, Democrats have supported the Supreme Court decision that made abortion rights "the law of the land" and have vigorously opposed the Human Life Amendment that sought to overturn *Roe v. Wade* (Democratic National Committee 1980).

Since 1980 Democrats have embraced a solidly pro-choice stance, to the point that they barred the pro-life Democratic governor of Pennsylvania, Bob Casey, from speaking at the 1992 Democratic National Convention. Since 1992, the official stance of the Democratic Party has been that there needs to be a law to protect a woman's right to choose and that the government should provide abortion funding for poor women to have access to abortion procedures. In 2012, many speakers at the Democratic National Convention suggested that the Republican agenda, including their pro-life stance, was tantamount to a "war on women." The 2012 Democratic Party platform also reflected the party's dominant position that abortions should be legal, safe, and rare. The party's platform on abortion also framed the issue as a profoundly personal decision for women. "The Democratic Party strongly and unequivocally supports *Roe v. Wade* and a woman's right to make decisions regarding her pregnancy, including a safe and legal abortion, regardless of ability to pay," declared the party platform. "We oppose any and all efforts to weaken or undermine that right. Abortion is an intensely personal decision between a woman, her family, her doctor, and her clergy; there is no place for politicians or government to get in the way. We also recognize that health care and education help reduce the number of unintended pregnancies and thereby also reduce the need for abortions" (Democratic National Committee 2012).

Democrats recognize that the courts are a key battleground in the struggle over abortion. After Ronald Reagan reshaped the federal judiciary in the 1980s, Democrats in the White House sought to uphold a woman's right to choose by appointing pro-choice judges, by passing legislation to support women, or through executive orders. Democratic President Bill Clinton used his executive power to rescind the "Mexico City Policy" so that USAID could fund nongovernmental organizations (NGOs) that provided abortion services and he lifted the gag rule. Clinton appointed pro-choice judges to the federal courts as well, including Supreme Court justices Ruth Bader Ginsburg and Stephen Breyer. President Barack Obama made women's reproductive care a feature of his Affordable Care Act and appointed pro-choice judges Sonia Sotomayor and Elena Kagan to the Supreme Court and many pro-choice judges to lower courts.

Democrats have also championed a range of pro-choice legislation. When anti-abortion violence, including murder, arson, attacks on property, attacks on people, and harassment of women and staff entering facilities providing abortions, erupted in the 1980s and 1990s, congressional Democrats passed the Freedom of Access to Clinic Entrances Act (FACE), and this legislation led to a decline in some types of clinic violence. Congressional Democrats were less successful in enacting pro-choice legislation in the form of the "freedom of choice" bill in 1993. The bill declared that every woman had the "fundamental right to choose to bear a child; terminate a pregnancy prior to fetal viability; or terminate a pregnancy after viability when necessary to protect her life or her health." It prohibited any federal, state, or local government from passing laws restricting or denying this right and authorized anyone denied this fundamental right an opportunity to find relief through civil action (Freedom of Choice Act 2004).

Nationally, abortion rights formed a critical aspect of President Barack Obama's 2012 campaign for reelection. Using the phrase, "the Republican war on women," Democrats supporting President Obama successfully targeted unmarried women between 18 and 29 in their efforts to champion the rights of women and their right to choose. Exit polls from the 2012 presidential race showed that President Obama outpolled Republican Mitt Romney by 11 points among women. Further analysis shows that unmarried women and minorities were the critical factor in this effort (CNN 2012).

States with Democratic majorities in their legislatures and Democratic governors have also passed legislation to protect against abortion clinic interference. These might include "bubble zones" that protesters or antiabortion activists are not allowed to enter. The Supreme Court upheld an eight-foot limit as constitutionally protected in *Hill v. Colorado* (2000) but struck down a 2007 Massachusetts law, which had created a 35-foot buffer zone around abortion clinics, calling it an infringement of free speech in the case of *McCullen v. Coakley* (2014). Pro-choice advocates have also attempted to advance state versions of the freedom of choice bill, but unclear bills rarely come to a vote and largely serve to symbolize Democratic support for women's right to choose.

The Democrats for Life of America was founded in 1999 and seeks to keep the party open to a pro-life agenda. In 2010 this group supported Michigan Democrat Bart Stupak and seven of his Democratic colleagues in the House of Representatives who tried to keep abortion services from being included in President Obama's Affordable Care Act. Although they claimed victory, President Obama's secretary of health and human services later interpreted the law so that abortion services were mandatory under the law.

Further Reading

Campo-Flores, Arian, and Cameron McWhirter. 2015. "Abortion Restrictions Pick Up Steam in GOP-Led States," *Wall Street Journal,* January 11. Accessed January 12, 2015: http://www.wsj.com/articles/abortion-restrictions-pick-up-steam-in-gop-led-states-1421010036.

CNN Election Center. 2012. Exit Polls. Accessed June 20, 2014: http://www.cnn.com/election/2012/results/race/president.

Conroy, Scott. 2014. "Christie's Choice in New Hampshire is Pro Choice," *Politico,* June 6. Accessed June 17, 2014: http://www.realclearpolitics.com/articles/2014/06/06/christies_pick_in_nh_primary_is_pro-choice_122877.html.

Democratic National Committee. 1980. "Democratic Party Platform of 1980," August 11. Online by Gerhard Peters and John T. Woolley, "The American Presidency Project." Accessed June 20, 2014: http://www.presidency.ucsb.edu/ws/?pid=29607.

Democratic National Committee. 2012. "Democratic National Platform: Moving America Forward." Accessed April 17, 2015: http://www.democrats.org/democratic-national-platform.

Derr, Mary Krane, and Rachel M. MacNair. 2006. *Prolife Feminism.* New York: XLibris.

Freedom of Choice Act. 2004. The Library of Congress THOMAS. Accessed June 20, 2014: http://thomas.loc.gov/cgi-bin/bdquery/z?d108:s.02020.

Gould, Lewis. 2003. *Grand Old Party: A History of the Republicans.* New York: Random House.

Greenhouse, Linda. 2006. *Becoming Justice Blackmun: Harry Blackmun's Supreme Court Journey.* New York: New York Times Books.

Hendershott, Anne. 2006. *The Politics of Abortion.* New York: Encounter Books.

Hull, N. E. H., and Peter Charles Hoffer. 2010. *Roe v. Wade: The Abortion Rights Controversy in American History,* 2nd edition. In *Landmark Law Cases and American Society* series. Lawrence: University Press of Kansas.

Keefe, William J., and Marc J. Hetherington. 2013. *Parties, Politics, and Public Policy in America,* 9th edition. Washington, D.C.: CQ Press.

Kinsley, Michael. 2012. "Republicans and Abortion: A Brief History," August 30, *Bloomsburg News.* Accessed June 13, 2014: http://www.bloomberg.com/news/2012-08-30/republicans-and-abortion-a-brief-history.html.

McBride, Dorothy. 2008. *Abortion in the United States: A Reference Handbook.* Santa Barbara: ABC-CLIO.

Medoff, Marshall H. 2011. "TRAP Abortion Laws and Partisan Political Control of State Government," *American Journal of Economic Sociology*, 70 (4): 951–973.

Medoff, Marshall H. 2013. "Social Policy and Abortion: A Review of the Research," *The Open Demography Journal*, 6: 18–27. Accessed June 14, 2014: http://www.benthamscience.com/open/todemoj/articles/V006/18TODEMOJ.pdf.

National Committee for a Human Life Amendment. Accessed June 17, 2014: http://www.nchla.org/datasource/idocuments/HLAhghlts.pdf.

Reagan, Ronald. 1983. "Speech in Orlando," March 8. Accessed June 21, 2014: http://www.ontheissues.org/celeb/Ronald_Reagan_Abortion.htm.

Republican National Committee. 2012. "We the People: A Restoration of Constitutional Government." Accessed April 17, 2015: https://www.gop.com/platform/we-the-people/.

Roe v. Wade. 1971. The Oyez Project at IIT Chicago-Kent College of Law. Accessed June 13, 2014: http://www.oyez.org/cases/1970-1979/1971/1971_70_18.

Solinger, Rickie. 2002. *Beggars and Choosers: How the Politics of Choice Shapes Adoption, Abortion, and Welfare in the United States*. New York: Hill and Wang.

Weingarten, Karen. 2014. *Abortion in the American Imagination: Before Life and Choice, 1880–1940*. Rutgers: Rutgers University Press.

Witcover, Jules. 2003. *Party of the People: A History of the Democrats*. New York: Random House.

Affirmative Action

At a Glance

Is affirmative action necessary in the 21st century? Democrats believe that, yes, it is. They say that because of systemic and individual prejudice, policies are needed to ensure that all people, regardless of race, sex, national origin, and sexual orientation, have equal opportunity. Many Republicans would say no. They believe that individual merit, not categorical assistance, is the key to success in the United States and oppose affirmative action. Some Republicans even believe that affirmative action policies create reverse discrimination that unfairly targets white males.

Many Democrats . . .

- Believe that systemic racism, sexism, and ethnocentrism are barriers to success for women and people of color.
- Support legislation to end discrimination.
- Support affirmative action programs to end discrimination in hiring and college admissions.
- Promote actions and policies to provide equal opportunity for all people.
- Support legislation to amend, not end, affirmative action.
- Practice affirmative action in their party structure by requiring proportionate representation.

Many Republicans . . .

- Are concerned that affirmative action programs lead to quotas in hiring and education.
- Believe that affirmative action practices result in "reverse discrimination."
- Believe that identifying people based on their membership in a specific group undercuts individual initiative and merit.
- Argue that affirmative action programs are no longer needed since there are sufficient laws that punish discrimination in employment, housing, and education.

- Have sought to mitigate or end affirmative action programs.
- Successfully ended affirmative action programs in several states by asking voters to approve referendums banning the use of affirmative action by state officials.

Overview

The term *affirmative action* refers to federal and state programs created to redress past discrimination in the workplace and higher education. These programs consist of actions or policies aimed at providing equal opportunity to people based on, among other things, their membership in a particular group. Affirmative action was one method federal courts used as they sought to desegregate educational institutions following *Brown v. Board of Education* (1954) (Martin 1998). Presidents Franklin Roosevelt, who served in the White House from 1933 to 1945, and Harry Truman, who succeeded Roosevelt from 1945 to 1953, issued executive orders in hiring aimed at ensuring that minorities were included in New Deal programs. The term *affirmative action* was first used by John F. Kennedy, who was president from 1961 to 1963. Kennedy used the term in executive order 10925, which he used to end discriminatory employment practices. Since 1963, affirmative action has expanded to include more protected classes of individuals including women, Latinos, people with disabilities, veterans, and the aged. Affirmative action remains controversial, as critics assert that it challenges long-standing American beliefs about individual effort and achievement.

Affirmative action was a key factor in the Civil Rights Act of 1964. The legislation protected individuals from discrimination in housing, public accommodation, and employment. Title VII of the Civil Rights Act called for equal employment opportunity and prohibits discrimination in hiring on the basis of race, color, religion, sex, and national origin. The law also spawned the creation of the Equal Employment Opportunity Commission (EEOC). The EEOC sets guidelines for American companies with over 15 employees on how to train, hire, and promote women, minorities, the elderly, and the handicapped.

In the 1960s the federal government began the practice of "set asides" for "socially and economically disadvantaged" businesses to ensure that the federal procurement process would include minority and women business owners. Following the example set by African Americans during the civil rights era, other underrepresented groups such as women, Hispanic Americans, and Native Americans mobilized to lobby for extending affirmative action programs to include their members.

Affirmative action faced a backlash after the Supreme Court unanimously ruled in 1971 that employers could be found guilty of discrimination under Title VII if their hiring procedures excluded a protected class of workers, even if there was no clear intent to discriminate. This is called "disparate impact" and focuses on the negative impact of the hiring practices rather than the motives for such practices

National Organization of Women

Women wanted gender included in the Civil Rights Act of 1964, but after Lyndon Johnson rejected the addition of the word sex, women's rights advocates organized the National Organization of Women (NOW) in 1966. After organizing, NOW's immediate agenda included amending the U.S. Constitution by passing an Equal Rights Amendment (ERA). An ERA had been offered in Congress every year since 1923. Finally, through organized pressure the amendment passed both the House and the Senate and was sent to the states for ratification in 1972. The states did not ratify the amendment within the proscribed time limit, however.

1972 was a banner year for NOW, which created and launched *Ms.* magazine and helped secure the passage of Title IX as a portion of the United States Education Amendments of 1972. Title IX reads "No person in the United States shall, on the basis of gender, be excluded from participation in, be denied the benefits of, or be subjected to discrimination under any education program or activity receiving federal financial assistance." The impact of Title IX has been widespread in gender equity in public and college sports programs.

NOW continues to redress gender and sexual preference discrimination and wage and employment discrimination and to urge the government to allow women the right to choose their own contraceptives and when to start a family.

(*Griggs v. Duke Power Company* 1971). Fearful of lawsuits, corporations and elite academic institutions created affirmative action programs that included quotas to remediate historical discrimination and to achieve compensatory justice. Set asides, quotas, and hiring and firing practices that ended seniority systems in order to protect less senior minorities led some whites to feel that they were being targeted by "reverse discrimination." These groups claimed that white males were being excluded from hiring, job promotions, and college admissions based on their race and gender (Patterson 2005).

Opponents of affirmative action were emboldened by the work of Harvard sociologist Nathan Glazer. Glazer argued in his book *Affirmative Discrimination* that the use of racial preferences was discriminatory to all other groups. In 1978, Allan Bakke, who had been denied entry into the UC Davis Medical School twice even though he had higher test scores and grades than minority applicants who were admitted, sued on the premise that his rights were being violated because of his race. The Supreme Court ruled 5–4 that quotas violated the Fourteenth Amendment and ordered UC Davis to admit Bakke. The Court upheld affirmative action practices that did not include quotas and ruled that race could be used as one of several criteria for granting admission to students at colleges and universities. This decision was reaffirmed 25 years later in the 2003 Supreme Court case of *Grutter v. Bollinger* (Dale 2002).

Political opposition to affirmative action coalesced in the Republican Party in the 1970s. Affirmative action programs were dismantled or saw their funding cut

Allan Bakke is trailed by news and television reporters after attending his first day at the Medical School of the University of California at Davis on September 25, 1978. Bakke sued the university for reverse discrimination after his application was rejected in 1973 and 1974. (AP/Wide World Photos)

by Republican presidents in the 1980s. Both Ronald Reagan, who sat in the Oval Office from 1981 to 1989, and his successor in office George H. W. Bush, who was president from 1989 to 1993, reshaped the political landscape by appointing federal judges and members of the Supreme Court who were more skeptical about affirmative action and who rejected quotas and set asides as potentially discriminatory actions. After the Republican Party won control of the U.S. House of Representatives and many state legislatures in 1994, attempts were made to end affirmative action programs. In 1996, California voters approved of Proposition 209, which ended the use of affirmative action programs in hiring, contracting, and education, and voters in Washington subsequently passed a similar measure. Since 1996, many states have banned the use of affirmative action in public life, including Arizona, Florida, Texas, Nebraska, New Hampshire, Oklahoma, and Michigan (National Council on State Legislatures 2014). Bans on affirmative action were challenged in the courts as violations of civil rights but the bans were upheld by the Supreme Court in 2014, which determined that while affirmative action programs are permissible under the Constitution, they are not mandatory.

Democrats on Affirmative Action

As the Democratic Party made clear in their 2012 party platform, their support for affirmative action is "ironclad." Democrats unabashedly declared that "we support affirmative action to redress discrimination and to achieve the diversity from which all Americans benefit (Democratic Party 2012). Democrats believe that affirmative action provides redress for inequities and historic wrongs. It has provided equal opportunity in employment and education for groups that traditionally have been denied avenues to jobs and education—namely, racial minorities and women. Democratic presidents Kennedy, Johnson, Carter, Clinton, and Obama have all vigorously pursued affirmative action policies and sought to appoint federal judges who support affirmative action.

The Democratic position on affirmative action has been solidified by the support of minority groups and women who have benefited from these programs. They form important blocs of voters who cast their ballot for Democrats in presidential elections. In the past four presidential elections an average of 90 percent of African American and 75 percent of Hispanic voters cast ballots for the Democratic candidate. Democrats have also seen a gender gap in voting patterns of men and women, and Democratic candidates have consistently won the majority of the women's vote since the 1990s.

In light of the long history of discrimination against African Americans, President John F. Kennedy moved to establish hiring practices that would remediate discrimination by issuing executive order 10925 on March 6, 1961. This order established the President's Committee on Equal Employment Opportunity and also enjoined government contractors to take affirmative action to ensure that hiring decisions would not be influenced by race, creed, color, or national origin. This was followed by the 1964 Civil Rights Act, which addressed discrimination in public and private hiring practices and access to public or private educational institutions.

National Association for the Advancement of Colored People

Founded on February 12, 1909, the National Association for the Advancement of Colored People (NAACP) is the nation's oldest, largest, and most widely recognized grassroots-based civil rights organization. The NAACP led the fight to end segregation and the organization's legal counsel, Thurgood Marshall, played a pivotal role in ending this practice in public education in the case of Brown v. Board of Education in 1954. In the 1960s, the NAACP played an integral role in the civil rights movement across the United States.

Social justice and economic opportunity became critical in the organization's campaigns in the 1970s and 1980s, and it remains an important voice on those issues in the 21st century. In 2014, for example, the NAACP was a leader in the protest against police actions in the shooting deaths of Michael Brown in Ferguson, Missouri, and the chokehold death of Eric Garner in New York City.

Today, the NAACP has more than a half-million members and supporters throughout the United States, and it remains the premier advocate for civil rights in many communities, campaigning for equal opportunity and antipoverty initiatives and conducting voter mobilization.

Johnson followed the Civil Rights Act with executive order 11246, which set hiring goals for firms of a certain size that did business with the federal government. This order was later modified to include discrimination by sex (Leiter 2011).

Democratic presidents also demonstrated a concern for diversity. President Johnson, who served from 1963 to 1969, appointed the first African American to the Supreme Court in 1967. Thurgood Marshall was former chief counsel for the National Association for the Advancement of Colored People (NAACP) and lead counsel in the *Brown v. Board of Education* cases in 1954 before being appointed by Johnson. Jimmy Carter, who was president from 1977 to 1981, appointed the first African American woman to the U.S. cabinet, Patricia Harris, who served first as secretary of health and human services and later as secretary of housing and urban development. Carter appointed Andrew Young, a colleague of Dr. Martin Luther King Jr. as the first African American U.S. ambassador to the United Nations. President Clinton, who served two terms from 1993 to 2001, sought to create a cabinet that was as diverse as the U.S. population, with Hispanics, Asian Americans, African Americans, and women assuming key positions (Bergmann 1997).

Elected officials within the Democratic Party found themselves forced to defend the gains made by affirmative action programs in the 1980s and 1990s, rather than expanding these programs. Opposition to affirmative action programs in the 1990s became so strong that President Clinton made an impassioned speech in favor of affirmative action entitled "Amend It Don't End It" in 1995. Opposition to affirmative action by conservatives and Republicans led many minority and women's groups to adhere even more loyally to the Democratic Party, which continued to advocate for affirmative action programs. This support from Latinos, African Americans, and women has been significant to the successes of Democrats in national and statewide elections since the 1990s.

The 2008 election of Barack Obama, the first African American president in U.S. history, was a signature moment for the party. Obama's rise to the presidency is seen by many as the direct result of the civil rights movement of the 1960s and of affirmative action programs that provided greater educational and professional opportunities to people of color (Ifill 2007). President Obama appointed the first black attorney general, Eric Holder, who vigorously endorsed affirmative action as a means to redress past and present discrimination. Obama also appointed Sonia Sotomayor, the first Hispanic member of the Supreme Court. Sotomayor has stated that she believes that she was only admitted to Yale Law School because of affirmative action programs. Thus, she strongly defended affirmative action in her blistering dissent in *Schuette v. Coalition to Defend Affirmative Action* (2014), the Supreme Court case upholding the right of states to ban affirmative action programs. In her dissent, Sotomayor castigated the Supreme Court for abandoning those who most rely on the Court to protect them against discrimination.

Despite strong support by elected leaders, affirmative action remains controversial and is at times a wedge issue between the elected leaders of the party and rank and file members. A 2009 Pew Poll showed that, while most Americans support affirmative action in a generic sense, when it comes to giving preferential treatment to minorities only 22 percent of whites polled support this. In 2014, California voters were asked to support a referendum restoring affirmative action programs in California. Opposition from Asian Americans, who have tended to support the Democratic Party, has been cited as a critical factor in the measure's defeat.

Republicans on Affirmative Action

Many Republicans believe that affirmative action is in itself discriminatory and unjust because it thwarts individual efforts by supporting specific groups. As stated in their 2008 party platform, "Precisely because we oppose discrimination, we reject preferences, quotas, and set-asides, whether in education or in corporate boardrooms. The government should not make contracts on this basis, and neither should corporations." In 2004, they even suggested that affirmative action led to a reaction against successful minorities: "We reject preferences, quotas, and set-asides based on skin color, ethnicity, or gender, which perpetuate divisions and can lead people to question the accomplishments of successful minorities and women (Republican Party 2004).

Conservative Southerners, who had opposed civil rights, began the slow process of realigning with the Republican Party in the 1970s, encouraged to do so by Richard Nixon who was president from 1969 to 1974. Nixon's "southern strategy" was an attempt by the president to woo disaffected conservative Democrats into the Republican Party by stalling efforts at ending segregation in the South. He nominated federal judges to the bench with weak records on civil rights, and he gave little support to the EEOC and Office of Federal Contract Compliance (OFCC). His so-called Philadelphia Plan was, on the surface, an attempt to address issue of minority workers in cities that had large minority populations but were underrepresented in labor unions. To obtain federal contracts unions were required to increase over a set period of time the percentage of minority members with the quotas based on the percentage of minorities living in the metropolitan area, the larger the number of unrepresented minorities in a city the higher the quota for union membership was set. The Philadelphia Plan effectively created a wedge issue between labor unions, which generally supported the Democratic Party but rejected quotas, and leaders of the Democratic Party who supported affirmative action.

The election of Ronald Reagan in 1980 proved to be a watershed for those opposed to affirmative action. Reagan cut funding to the EEOC, which was charged with overseeing compliance on affirmative action laws. Reagan appointed Clarence Thomas, a conservative African American, to direct the program. Thomas, who was later appointed to the Supreme Court, was the longest serving chair of the EEOC and often disagreed with the liberal/progressive view of affirmative action (Williams 1987). Reagan also reshaped the Supreme Court by making three new appointments to the Court when vacancies appeared. Reagan's appointees began to chip away at affirmative action gains in such cases as *Wards Cove Packing Co. v. Antonio* (1989). President Reagan and his successor George H. W. Bush remade the Supreme Court by appointing more conservative judges who were much more skeptical about affirmative action. In the case of *City of Richmond v. J.A. Croson Company*, the majority determined that affirmative action standards required strict scrutiny as to whether the purpose was in line with historical discrimination and narrowly tailored to remediate the situation. They determined that in this case it had not. The same Court went on to apply strict scrutiny to federal set asides in *Adarand Constructors, Inc. v. Pena*. The Court also eroded the ability of employees who felt they were discriminated against to sue. When Congress passed the Civil Rights Act of 1990 to rectify this, President George H. W. Bush vetoed the bill but signed a weaker version of the legislation in 1991.

Opposition to affirmative action in the states was also led by or endorsed by Republicans such as Ward Connerly (2007). Connerly is an African American businessman and registered Republican who was appointed to chair of the California Board of Regents by Republican Governor Pete Wilson in 1990. Connerly used his position on the Board of Regents to oppose affirmative action and became the chief spokesman for Proposition 209, a ban on using affirmative action in California public life. After Connerly and his allies won the referendum with 54 percent of the vote in California he created a nonprofit organization called the American Civil Rights Institute (ACRI) to spearhead a campaign to end affirmative action in

---

Supreme Court Justice Sandra Day O'Connor

Sandra Day O'Connor was the first woman appointed to serve on the U.S. Supreme Court. Born in 1930, O'Connor attended Stanford University as an undergraduate and then went on to law school there. She received her JD then passed the bar in 1957 and set up her own firm. Later she worked in Republican political circles in Arizona, including service on Barry Goldwater's presidential campaign in 1964. She was subsequently elected to the Arizona state senate and became the first female majority leader in the history of that body. In the 1970s, she supported the Equal Rights Amendment but later demurred when the national GOP turned against the amendment. She went on to become state court judge and was appointed to be an associate justice on the Supreme Court by President Ronald Reagan in 1981.

On the Court she was considered a swing vote, although her general inclination was to side with the conservative wing of the court on cases such as *Planned Parenthood of Southeastern Pennsylvania v. Casey* (1992). Still, her moderate instincts led her to write opinions narrowly tailored to the specifics of each case at hand. On the issue of affirmative action, O'Connor wrote the majority opinion in *Grutter v. Bollinger* (2003), which upheld the use of race as a means to admit underrepresented groups that supported educational diversity. As part of her opinion she opined that "we expect that 25 years from now, the use of racial preferences will no longer be necessary to further the interest approved today."

the United States. As reported by Dan Frosch in an article in the *New York Times,* November 8, 2008, the ACRI led the fight to pass similar referendums that end affirmative action in Michigan, Washington, Nebraska, Arizona, and Oklahoma.

The Republicans have also received support from black intellectuals such as Thomas Sowell, Walter Williams, Shelby Steele, Glenn Loury, and Stephen Carter, as well as other scholars from underrepresented groups including Dinesh D'Souza and Linda Chavez. In general, their argument suggests that affirmative action erodes intellectual initiative, is a disguise for "soft-racism" or the belief that minorities could not compete without affirmative action programs, and empowers civil rights groups that make empty promises. In turn, civil rights leaders have roundly denounced these individuals and suggest they are promoting the white backlash against affirmative action programs (Hardisty 1999).

Despite opposition to affirmative action, Republican presidents—like their Democratic counterparts—have made judicial and cabinet appointments that are diverse in ethnicity and gender. Richard Nixon appointed the first director of the Congress of Racial Equality (CORE), James Farmer, to be assistant secretary of health, education, and welfare. Ronald Reagan appointed Sandra Day O'Connor, the first female to sit on the Supreme Court. George H. W. Bush appointed African American Clarence Thomas to succeed the retiring Thurgood Marshall on the Supreme Court. George W. Bush appointed Colin Powell to be the first African American secretary of state; Powell's successor was Condoleezza Rice, the first female African American to hold the post.

Further Reading

Bergmann, Barbara. 1997. *In Defense of Affirmative Action.* New York: Basic Books.

Connerly, Ward. 2007. *Creating Equal: My Fight against Race Preferences,* 2nd edition. New York: Encounter Books.

Dale, Charles. 2002. *Affirmative Action Revisited: A Legal History and Prospectus.* Accessed June 30, 2014: http://digitalcommons.ilr.cornell.edu/cgi/viewcontent.cgi?article=1012& context=key_workplace.

Democratic Party. 2012. "Democratic Party Platform." Online by Gerhard Peters and John T. Woolley, "The American Presidency Project." Accessed August 3, 2014: http://www .presidency.ucsb.edu/ws/?pid=101962.

Glazer, Nathan. 1987. *Affirmative Discrimination: Ethnic Inequality and Public Policy.* Cambridge: Harvard University Press.

Griggs v. Duke Power Company. 1971. The Oyez Project at IIT Chicago-Kent College of Law. Accessed July 29, 2014: http://www.oyez.org/cases/1970-1979/1970/1970_124.

Hardisty, Jean. 1999. *Mobilizing Resentment: Conservative Resurgence from the John Birch Society to the Promise Keepers.* Boston: Beacon Press.

Ifill, Gwen. 2007. *The Breakthrough: Politics and Race in the Age of Obama.* New York: Anchor Books.

Leiter, William. 2011. *Affirmative Action in Antidiscrimination Law and Policy: An Overview and Synthesis.* Albany: State University of New York Press.

Martin, Waldo E., Jr. 1998. *Brown v. Board of Education: A Brief History with Documents.* New York: St. Martin's/Bedford.

National Conference of State Legislatures. 2014. "Affirmative Action: State Action." Accessed August 3: http://www.ncsl.org/research/education/affirmative-action-state -action.aspx.

Patterson, James T. 2005. *Restless Giant: The United States from Watergate to Bush v. Gore.* New York: Oxford University Press.

Republican Party. 2004. Republican Party Platform. Accessed July 4, 2014: http://www .presidency.ucsb.edu/papers_pdf/25850.pdf.

Williams, Juan. 1987. "A Question of Fairness," *The Atlantic*, February. Accessed August 3, 2014: http://www.theatlantic.com/magazine/archive/1987/02/a-question-of-fairness/306370/.

Animal Rights/Animal Welfare

At a Glance

Do animals have rights? Democrats are more likely to say, yes, and Republicans more likely to say, no, to this idea. The issue is more than philosophical, as many Democrats have urged legislation to carefully regulate scientific testing, hunting, farming, and the animal entertainment business, as well as concentrated animal feeding operations (CAFOs). Many Republicans have responded by asserting that although animals need to be treated humanely, burdensome regulations all too often interfere with the right of hunters, farmers, scientists, and others to use animals for food, research, and entertainment.

Many Democrats . . .

- Believe that animals have fundamental rights that must be protected by law.
- Want to stop the practice of using animals in laboratory research in ways that cause suffering or death.
- Want to see more laws protecting farm animals from inhumane industry practices.
- Want to regulate hunting to provide greater protection to endangered or vulnerable species.
- Want to regulate the use of animals in zoos, circuses, and the entertainment industry.

Many Republicans . . .

- Want to ensure the welfare of all animals.
- Reject the proposition from some animal rights activists that animals and humans are morally equivalent.
- Support the use of animals in laboratory testing.
- Champion the right to farm using traditional practices.
- Reject attempts to restrict or ban hunting and fishing.

Overview

The animal rights movement is founded on the belief that animals should have the same rights as humans, especially those animals with superior intelligence such as chimpanzees, orcas, dolphins, and elephants. The animal welfare movement consists of those who believe that all animals should have freedom from cruel treatment or unnecessary pain and that protection of species and habitat is legitimate and necessary. For much of U.S. history there has been bipartisan support for federal and state animal protection laws that include regulation and restrictions on the care, treatment, and use of animals (McLeod 2014). However, the issues of animal rights and animal welfare, like so many other issues in American culture and society, create division between those who support the Democrat Party and those who support the Republican Party.

Ethical concern for animals is not new. In 1866, the American Society for the Prevention of Cruelty to Animals (ASPCA) was established. A few years later the American Humane Association was founded to protect children and animals, and, in 1954, the Humane Society was spun off to focus on protecting animals. The Humane Society is best known for their work in protecting animals used on television and in motion pictures. They were successful in forcing regulation on these businesses that now proclaim at the end of their productions that "no animals were harmed" during filming (Unti 2004).

In the 20th century, the ASPCA and Humane Society successfully pushed for federal legislation to protect animals, which led directly to the 1966 Animal Welfare Act. The Animal Welfare Act directs the secretary of agriculture to regulate the transport, sale, and handling of small animals including dogs, cats, nonhuman primates, guinea pigs, hamsters, and rabbits that are used in research or for other purposes. The law requires licensing and inspection for dealers in pets and humane handling of animals at auction sales.

The contemporary animal rights movement was sparked by *Animal Liberation,* published in 1975 by Peter Singer. In this book Singer declared that animals have rights similar to those of human beings. Singer's book developed the concept of "speciesism," the idea that the way people treated animals in the past was analogous to racism, sexism, and other forms of prejudice. Singer predicted that someday people would look back at the way society treated animals with the same revulsion we now hold for human slavery (ProCon.org). Singer inspired the belief that animals have an inherent worth not associated with their usefulness to humans and had a right to live free from pain and suffering. His book inspired the evolution of an animal rights movement that has been marked by such milestones as the passage of the 1977 Universal Declaration of Animal Rights, the creation of the Animal Legal Defense Fund (ALDF) in 1979, the establishment of People for the Ethical Treatment of Animals (PETA) in 1980, and the Farm Animal Rights Movement (FARM) in 1981.

In the 1980s, the animal rights movement began to explore ways to engage the public and draw in more support for the recognition of animal rights. PETA has been the most media savvy organization and its campaigns have been controversial and successful. In 1981, PETA sent a member of their organization undercover to a medical research laboratory, where they took photographs of stressed monkeys engaging in self-mutilation. One notorious photo showed a monkey in a harness with all four limbs restrained. This photo became an icon for those pushing for animal rights and has often been a poster image of animal cruelty. PETA has also been successful in shaping consumer behavior in the United States. Their 1990 campaign "I'd rather go naked than wear fur" showed celebrities and others either nude or seminude, in a dramatic show of their opposition to the use of fur in fashion. The campaign led directly to a decline in fur sales in the United States. PETA also launched a successful campaign in the 1990s aimed at teenagers to promote vegetarianism. More recently, studies have found that 10 to 30 million Americans may be following a vegetarian lifestyle.

Animal rights activists also have targeted zoos, aquariums, and circuses that confine animals, whether for profit or education. They successfully called for a ban on exotic animals held by private owners, and their opposition to curtail so-called puppy mills resulted in the U.S. Department of Agriculture (USDA) implementing rules for dog breeders. Activists also succeeded in ending the sale and ownership of exotic animals in 31 states. A list of banned animals includes bears, big cats, primates, constrictors, and alligators. More recently, campaigns initiated by PETA and other groups against SeaWorld for alleged mistreatment of animals in its shows

PETA protesters urge to vote "No" on SeaWorld's proposed new orca prisons at Long Beach Convention Center in Long Beach, California, on October 8, 2015. (Photo by Earl Gibson III/ Getty Images)

has been cited as a direct factor in that company's losses in revenue and visitors (Guither 1998).

The regulation of agriculture and the environment has led some to push back against regulating livestock and food industry practices and hunting and fishing activities. Those who fear overregulation is diminishing their right to farm, fish, or hunt are supported by agribusiness, some business groups, and individual farmers and retailers. This coalition has found support within the Republican Party. Farmers and their supporters have organized to pass right-to-farm laws in all 50 states. Advocates say that right-to-farm laws protect farmers who use traditional farming methods from nuisance lawsuits and regulatory interference. In 2014, voters in Missouri even amended their state constitution to include the right to farm largely because they were concerned that animal rights activists might use the courts to overturn legislation (Baur 2008).

The animal rights movement also faces opposition from the medical testing community and their argument for treating animals as humans has been rejected by the courts. Proponents of animal testing include corporations engaged in pharmaceutical and medical device development, scientific groups, as well as individual scientists and academic units. Although concerned about the welfare of animals, they do not believe that animals are equal to human beings and insist that animal testing is necessary for the health and safety of human beings. Steven Wise, who founded the Center for the Expansion of Fundamental Rights in 1996 (later renamed the Nonhuman Rights Project in 2007), filed a constitutional challenge to extend the status of personhood to nonhuman primates. The case was heard by New York's Supreme Court in 2013 but was rejected by the court. Wise then appealed the case to the State Court of Appeals, which held that unlike human beings, chimpanzees do not have the capacity to assume legal duties, submit to societal responsibilities, or be held legally accountable for their actions.

Democrats on Animal Rights and Animal Welfare

The Democratic Party, in general, rejects the notion that laws protecting endangered species and animals held in captivity and regulating agribusiness and hunting are inimical to a healthy economy. Most Democrats believe that these laws help preserve habitats and species, and they support animal welfare laws and legislation to regulate farming, hunting, animal use in sports, and animal testing as well as the criminal prosecution for violations of those laws. Elected Democrats are often supported by animal rights activists but do not necessarily march in lockstep with activists on issues of hunting, fishing, animal testing, zoos, and wearing fur. Elected Democrats from states or districts with significant rural populations where hunting is an important part of the culture, such as Alaska and West Virginia, are less likely to support regulation of these activities or animal rights campaigns in general (Jaspers and Nelkin 1991).

The first federal law to regulate industry and to protect animals was passed by a Democrat-controlled Congress and signed into law by a Democrat, President

Lyndon Johnson, who served in the White House from 1963 to 1969. In 1966, Congress passed the Laboratory Animal Welfare Act, later simply known as the Animal Welfare Act. In a June 3, 2009, story for Slate, Daniel Enberger relates the story of congress member Joseph Y. Resnick. Resnick was asked to intervene after a Pennsylvania family's pet dog was kidnapped and sold to medical researchers in New York. Dognapping had already been popularized in such films as Disney's *Lady and the Tramp* and *101 Dalmations* as well as in a series of articles in *Sports Illustrated* and *Life* magazine. Resnick suggested a federal law to regulate the way medical labs procured and cared for animals. The law has been amended several times in Democrat-controlled Congresses to expand the number of animals protected, outlaw animal fighting, and increase the fines assessed for violations (Evans 2014).

In the 1970s, a series of environmental laws pertaining to animal welfare were passed with strong Democratic support. These included the Endangered Species Act (ESA) of 1973, which protects both endangered and threatened species by regulating or restricting human activity in their habitats. The act has been continually updated to expand the endangered or threatened species.

The ESA, which received support from Republicans as well, has proven to be controversial. Protecting species meant regulating or prohibiting development in certain habitats and in some cases undercut private property rights. In the 1980s and 1990s, there were widely publicized battles pitting those who wanted development projects for dams or industry against those who supported animal rights. One such controversy involved the development of the Tellico Dam in Tennessee under the auspices of the Tennessee Valley Authority (TVA); citing the ESA, the dam was challenged for threatening the habitat of the endangered snail darter. The case went all the way to the Supreme Court, which ruled in *TVA v. Hill* (1978) that the ESA protected all species irrespective of cost. Congress immediately amended the law to allow Congress to intervene when the cost of habitat preservation may outweigh its benefits (Murchison 2007).

Controversies continued into the 1980s, when Democratic efforts to expand the protection of animals and the environment faced stiff opposition from Republicans in Congress and in the administration of President Ronald Reagan, who served two terms from 1981 to 1989. President Bill Clinton, a two-term president who served from 1993 to 2001, was hamstrung by a Republican majority in the U.S. House and Senate. It was not until the election of Barack Obama in 2008 that animal rights and welfare advocates gained a sympathetic ear in the White House. President Obama has signed international conventions to protect animals: Sharks were protected when President Obama signed the Shark Conservation Act in 2011, which banned vessels from carrying into the United States shark fins not "naturally attached" to corresponding carcasses. And in 2014, the U.S. government stopped imports, exports, and the resale of ivory in the United States except pieces certified as at least 100 years old.

Despite a lack of attention in the nation's capital, animal rights activists and their allies have been successful in shaping state laws to protect animal rights. Democrats in California have taken a lead in the animal protection and regulation

---

Animal Welfare Controversy at SeaWorld

Founded in 1959, SeaWorld Parks and Entertainment, is one of the largest and best-known animal entertainment corporations in the United States. The company owns Busch Gardens in Florida and Virginia, and SeaWorld parks in San Diego, California; San Antonio, Texas; and Orlando, Florida. It also operates a theme park based on the popular children's program *Sesame Street*. Animal rights activists have agitated against SeaWorld and their holding of animals in captivity and its use of animals for entertainment for years, but the controversy became a national issue after the documentary *Blackfish* (2013) was released. The fallout from the film, which accused the company of mistreating its famous orca whales, led to a decline in attendance, proposals to ban the use of orcas in California, and a lawsuit from investors who claimed the corporation had underreported its decline in attendance. The park responded by initiating new standards for the care and maintenance of orcas and in highlighting its contributions to animal welfare programs.

Sources

Blackfish Official Film Site. Accessed June 18, 2014: http://blackfishmovie.com/.

Kirby, David. 2012. *Death at SeaWorld: Shamu and the Dark Side of Killer Whales in Captivity.* New York: St. Martin's.

Norton, Brian G., Michael Hutchins, Elizabeth F. Stevens, and Terry L. Maple, eds. 2012. *Ethics on the Ark: Zoos, Animal Welfare, and Wildlife Conservation.* Washington, D.C.: Smithsonian Institution.

---

of key industries. In 2008, over two-thirds of California voters passed an initiative banning certain kinds of housing for egg-laying chickens, veal calves, and pregnant pigs. Californians also banned the use of foie gras. After viewing the 2013 documentary *Blackfish*, which decries the conditions in which orcas are held at SeaWorld, California Assemblyman Richard Bloom introduced a bill banning the holding of killer whales in captivity for entertainment purposes, punishable by six months in jail and/or a $100,000 fine.

New York City Mayor Bill de Blasio, a Democrat noted for his progressive agenda, ignited a furor when he pledged to end the use of horse drawn carriages in the city. His campaign received support from animal rights activists who formed Clean Livable and Safe Streets (CLASS). As reported by Trevor Kapp in the *New York Daily News* on June 6, 2011, the mayor promised to make good on his pledge but faces resistance from those who feel the 165-year-old tradition is safe and already well regulated. Many of those in the carriage trade belong to the powerful Teamsters Union, which traditionally supports the Democratic Party.

Republicans on Animal Rights

Republicans, in general, believe that human beings are stewards of nature and animals, but they scoff at claims of human–animal equivalency. Elected Republicans

People for the Ethical Treatment of Animals

People for the Ethical Treatment of Animals (PETA), founded in 1980, is a nonprofit organization that seeks to end the use of animals for clothing, food, and experimentation. The organization was strongly influenced by the idea that animals should have recognized rights just as human beings do. Based in Norfolk, Virginia, the group claims membership of over 1.6 million and has a budget of nearly $30 million.

PETA uses direct action protests such as people stripping off their clothes in public to declare, "I would rather go naked than wear fur." Their sensational ads were iconic and eye catching and pushed the envelope in the pre-Internet era. In addition to publicizing the plight of animals they also lobby for legal protection of animals; protest industries, agribusinesses, and scientific laboratories that use animals; and promote a vegan diet, which is free of any animal products including eggs and milk.

mostly oppose across-the-board animal rights legislation and express skepticism of the tactics and ideals of many of the animal rights groups. They favor human need over animal rights and are pro-hunting, pro-agricultural business, and in favor of medical testing using animals. Animal rights activists tend to lump all Republicans in the category as opposed to animal rights and help perpetuate the myth that the GOP opposes animal welfare and safety issues, but there is little difference between self-identified Democrats and Republicans when it comes to issues surrounding animal welfare (Gallup 2010). Animal rights activists also promote the myth that Republicans are cruel to animals. Mitt Romney, the GOP candidate for president in 2012, admitted that in the 1980s he once put his dog Seamus in a dog carrier on top of his station wagon and drove for 12 hours. Animal rights activists used this information to promote the idea that the GOP is cruel toward animals and the incident solidified an image, popular among liberals, that the GOP is out of touch with ordinary Americans.

The clash between animal rights activists such as PETA and the Republican Party began in the 1980s, during Ronald Reagan's presidency. Ronald Reagan sought to reduce the influence of environmental laws that restrained economic development. Reagan appointed Anne Burford to head the Environmental Protection Agency (EPA) and James G. Watt to head the Department of the Interior. Both of these individuals were noted for challenging environmental protection laws that stifled development. Using their power to administer these agencies, they interpreted environmental laws to be more favorable to industry and economic development. The Office of Management and Budget (OMB) was also given new powers to write regulations that would curtail the power of environmental regulation. The last Republican in the White House, George W. Bush, who served two terms from 2001 to 2009, revised some of the protections offered in the Endangered Species Act, removed grizzly bears and wolves from the endangered species list, endorsed commercial whaling, and signed executive orders to allow more oil companies, miners, loggers, and other industries to work without consultation with government wildlife experts when they open up new areas for commercial development.

Republicans are generally supportive of agribusiness complaints about regulation of large-scale hog farming, chicken hatcheries, veal farming, and the like. One of the most vocal supporters of these activities is Representative Steve King of Iowa. King sponsored an amendment to the House Farm Bill in 2012 that thwarted attempts by animal rights advocacy groups to regulate large-scale farming. The so-called King Amendment prohibited federal and state governments from interfering with agricultural practices that are recognized as traditional and acceptable within a state. The legislation was a direct response to a proposition in California that demanded all chickens bought and sold in that state have a cage that had larger dimensions than was standard in the Midwest.

King is not alone in his opposition to animal rights activists. In some states Republicans have offered bills to make it more difficult for organizations like PETA

An Ally of Agribusiness in Congress

Steve King is a member of the House of Representatives representing Iowa's Fourth District, which is one of the leading agricultural districts in the United States, ranking near the top as the center of production of eggs, pork, corn, and soybeans. Thus, King's constituents are farmers, agribusinesses, and those who work in associated industries.

Born in 1949, he ran his own construction firm before being elected to the House in 2002. "King was a member of the Tea party before there was a Tea Party," said one political science professor who has studied King's career. In the House, King is a member of the Tea Party Caucus and disparages the size of government and its increasing need for taxes and fees to run the system. King often takes controversial stances. He has depicted Islam as religion that breeds terrorists. He opposes amnesty and the Dream Act for illegal immigrants. He opposes gay marriage and led a successful recall effort to oust three Iowa state judges who voted in support of it. He claimed the belief in global warming was more a religious conviction than a scientific one. King is a supporter of cock fighting and dog racing, which has angered animal rights supporters.

King serves on the Agricultural Committee and is chair of the Subcommittee on Department Operations, Oversight and Nutrition where he works to keep animal welfare and animal rights activists from regulating traditional farm practices. In fact, King is recognized by animal rights activists as one of their most implacable opponents in Congress. King opposed a bill to end the practice of horse slaughter, took offense at a federal proposal to assist in recovering and caring for pets after a natural disaster, and unsuccessfully tried to block an amendment that would have made it a crime for an adult to bring a child to a dog fight.

Source

Stewart, James B. 2013. "In Rural Iowa, Spending, Not the Shutdown, Raises Worry," *New York Times,* October 4.

to go undercover in certain animal industries by requiring that all evidence of potential animal abuse be reported to authorities within a limited time frame. Failure to do so would lead to the arrest of the undercover operative and not those involved in the initial offense. To thwart animal rights activists who might try to harass farmers, Republican Party platforms in most states contain language supporting the right to farm and exempting agribusiness from existing animal cruelty laws. In addition to protecting farmers from interference, Republicans have sought to protect hunting and fishing as a lifestyle choice (Smith 2012).

Historically, however, Republicans have been sympathetic to concerns about animal welfare. President Richard Nixon who was in the White House from 1969 to 1974, signed the Endangered Species Act in 1973. President George H. W. Bush, who served from 1989 to 1993, appointed the first environmentalist to the EPA and signed both the Clean Air Act and the Clean Water Act, which had the effect of protecting various animal habitats. Congressional Republicans have also worked in favor of animal welfare over the years. Vin Weber, a Republican congress member in the 1990s, attempted to create an Animal Welfare Caucus in the House that opposed animal rights but supported animal welfare. In the 1990s, Senator Robert Smith created Humane USA, a political action committee (PAC) that supports candidates who espouse the values of the Humane Society. According to the Humane Society, all the Republicans seeking to be the GOP nomination in the 2012 presidential election held a mixed record on animal rights, but all supported some form of animal welfare.

Republicans can cite evidence that support for animal rights remains low in the United States. Gallup polls from 2003 to 2012 consistently showed support for giving animals the same rights as humans remained around 25 percent, while support for protecting the welfare of animals while maintaining the right of humans to benefit from animals is much higher at 72 percent. The national GOP platform in 2012 stated that "we believe people are the most valuable resource, and human health and safety are the most important measurements of success. A policy protecting these objectives, however, must balance economic development and private property rights in the short run with conservation goals over the long run. Also, public access to public lands for recreational activities such as hunting, fishing, and recreational shooting should be permitted on all appropriate federal lands" (Republican Party 2012).

Further Reading

Baur, Gene. 2008. *Farm Sanctuary: Changing Hearts and Minds about Animals and Food.* New York: Touchstone.

Evans, Kim Master. 2014. *Animal Rights*. Detroit: Gale Cengage Learning.

Gallup. 2010. "Four Moral Issues Sharply Divide Americans," May 26. Accessed August 7, 2014: http://www.gallup.com/poll/137357/Four-Moral-Issues-Sharply-Divide-Americans .aspx.

Guither, Harold D. 1998. *Animal Rights: History and Scope of a Radical Social Movement.* Carbondale: Southern Illinois University Press.

Jaspers, James M., and Dorothy Nelkin. 1991. *The Animal Rights Crusade: The Growth of a Moral Protest*. New York: Free Press.

McLeod, Ethan. 2014. "Animal Rights," *CQ Researcher*, June 13. Accessed August 7, 2014: http://0-library.cqpress.com.libra.naz.edu/cqresearcher/cqr_ht_animal_rights_2014.

Murchison, Kenneth. 2007. *The Darter Snail Case: TVA v. the Endangered Species Act*. Lawrence: University of Kansas Press.

People for the Ethical Treatment of Animals (PETA). Accessed August 7, 2014: http://www.peta.org/.

ProCon.org. "Should Animals Be Used for Scientific of Commercial Testing?" Accessed August 6, 2015: http://animal-testing.procon.org/#background.

Republican Party. 2012. Republican Party Platform. Accessed August 7, 2014: https://cdn.gop.com/docs/2012GOPPlatform.pdf.

Singer, Peter. 1975. *Animal Liberation*. New York: Ecco Press.

Smith, Kimberly K. 2012. *Governing Animals: Animal Welfare and the Liberal State*. New York: Oxford University Press.

Unti, Bernard. 2004. *Protecting All Animals: A Fifty-Year History of the Humane Society of the United States*. New York: Humane Society.

Birth Control

At a Glance

Much like the debate over abortion, the debate over whether companies, religious organizations, and health insurance plans must cover contraception has divided Democrats and Republicans along the line of religious freedom versus the right to privacy. Republicans have sided with those who believe that requiring health insurers, religious organizations, and businesses to provide contraception to all women as part of the Affordable Care Act violates the religious belief of those who hold that certain kinds of contraception are tantamount to abortion. Democrats have sided with women's rights groups who believe that women should not be burdened with the cost of this preventive health aid. They believe a woman's right to choose includes whether or not to use contraceptives to avoid unplanned pregnancies.

Many Democrats . . .

- Are pro-choice.
- Believe that a woman has a fundamental right to control her own body.
- Believe that the right to privacy includes the right to choose whether or not to have children.
- Believe that a woman's health care should include contraceptives.
- Support the Affordable Care Act mandate that contraceptives should be available for free to women as part of preventive medicine.
- Oppose attempts to provide religious exceptions for corporations that claim a religious exemption from the mandate.
- Are concerned that attempts to switch contraceptives from prescription medication to over-the-counter medication will place an undue cost on women.

Many Republicans . . .

- Are pro-life.
- Dislike government programs that dispense contraceptives to teens and the poor.

- Opposed the contraception provisions in the Affordable Care Act passed in 2010.
- Support religious exemptions from the Affordable Care Act mandate on contraceptives.
- Favor switching birth control from a prescription medication to an over-the-counter drug because, under this arrangement, organizations would not be legally mandated to provide it for free.
- Support the Supreme Court's 2014 decision in *Burwell v. Hobby Lobby*.

Overview

The debate over contraception or birth control—and government regulation thereof—divides those who support a woman's right to privacy and to shape their own reproductive decisions and those who support the right of individuals to express their religious convictions about birth control, including concerns that easy access contributes to irresponsible and immoral sexual behavior.

Prior to the 1970s, there was little debate between the parties over birth control. In 1873, Congress passed the Comstock Law, an "Act for the Suppression of Trade in, and Circulation of, Obscene Literature and Articles for Immoral Use," which prohibited the sale and distribution of, among other things, contraceptives. The law was challenged by Margaret Sanger, who created the American Birth Control League in 1921, which later evolved into the Planned Parenthood Federation of America. Sanger's attempts to promote birth control were frustrated until 1932 when a federal judge struck down the ban on mailing such items in the case of *United States v. One Package*. Although contraceptives were then available through mail order, many states still banned the sale of contraceptives in pharmacies. This was overturned when Planned Parenthood sued and won against the state of Connecticut in the 1965 landmark case of *Griswold v. Connecticut*, which struck down a state law denying contraceptives to married women and also established a woman's right to privacy. The Court expanded this right in 1972 in the case of *Baird v. Eisenstadt* which legalized birth control for all citizens irrespective of marital status (Engelman 2011).

President Lyndon Johnson, a Democrat, and President Richard Nixon, a Republican, both urged family planning legislation that included assisting poor, married women in obtaining birth control. Debates became more heated in the 1970s, though, over whether unmarried women and teenagers should have access to birth control. Framing the issue as one of the right to privacy and as an issue of health care, many Democrats and their allies in organizations such as Planned Parenthood sought to make contraceptives readily available. Those who opposed this expansion of birth control included conservative Republicans who framed the issue instead as one about parental rights and the harmful psychological and health risks associated with sexual activity in teens, which included greater risk for sexually transmitted diseases (STDs) and cervical cancer.

Estelle Griswold, left, and Mrs. Ernest Jahncke pose with a newspaper article heralding the Supreme Court decision in *Griswold v. Connecticut* (1965). Griswold, the executive director of the Planned Parenthood League of Connecticut, had been convicted of giving instruction and medical advice to married people about the ways to prevent conception. In *Griswold*, the Supreme Court overturned the Connecticut statute of 1879 that made the use of any birth control device illegal. (Bettmann/Corbis)

Generally, elected Democrats who held office in federal or state governments urged schools, health departments, and nongovernmental organizations such as Planned Parenthood to provide free or low-cost contraceptives to the poor and the young. Thus, Lyndon Johnson, who was president from 1963 to 1969, created government programs in 1966 to provide low-cost contraceptives and free family planning material to poor, married women. In 1970, the Democrat-controlled Congress passed Title X of the Public Health Service Act, which made contraceptives available regardless of income and provided funding for educational programs and research in contraceptive development. Congress expanded Title X's mandate to provide community-based sex education programs and preventive services to unmarried teenagers at risk of pregnancy. In the 1970s, the U.S. Agency for International Development (USAID) worked with Planned Parenthood to export family planning and birth control to developing nations. Some of the momentum of this movement was thwarted after Republicans gained control of the White House in the 1980s and Congress in the 1990s (Merrick 2003).

In general, elected Republicans in state and federal office have opposed using state or federal money to pay for contraceptives and have supported efforts to provide parents with information about birth control use among their teenage children. During the 1980s, the Reagan administration joined with Republican allies in Congress to cut funding for birth control and impose parental notification requirements. The administration also imposed a so-called gag rule on family planning and abortion for agencies working with USAID. Many of these efforts to constrain the expansion of contraceptives were later overturned by American courts, however.

After the year 2000, the birth control debate became focused on the "morning after pill." In September 2000, the Food and Drug Administration gave final full approval to the drug RU486, a drug that was an effective early abortifacient. Abortion rights activists celebrated the decision as one that would empower women. "Today's decision is not about politics, but the health and safety of American women and a woman's fundamental right to choose," said Al Gore, the Democratic candidate for president that year. His opponent, George W. Bush, called the decision wrong. "I fear making this abortion pill widespread will make abortions more and more common," he said (Leonard 2000). Despite opposition by conservative Republicans, RU486 became common and readily available to women.

Contraceptive politics also divided the parties after passage of the Affordable Care Act in 2010. One provision of this legislation mandated that all companies cover all contraceptive methods. As expected, this mandate sparked a political debate that lasted for the next four years and continued to influence politics going into the 2016 presidential election cycle.

Democrats on Birth Control

Lawmakers and officials in the Democratic Party generally side with women's rights groups such as the National Organization of Women (NOW) and Planned Parenthood, who believe that birth control should be regarded as preventive health care, and who believe that a woman's right to privacy extends to whether or not to use contraceptives to avoid unplanned pregnancy. The party has deep roots in its support for birth control. In 1965, President Lyndon Johnson created a government program to provide contraceptive services to low-income married women as part of his Great Society War on Poverty. Congress expanded this program in the early 1970s. Democrats also opposed attempts by conservatives to limit funding for family planning programs during the Reagan years (Jutte 2008).

Democrats have frequently framed Republican attitudes about birth control as emblematic of part of a wider "war on women" being waged by the GOP. To support these claims, Democrats cite Republican stances on such issues as the government mandates for contraception coverage contained in the Affordable Care Act, which became law in March 2010. The law included a contraception coverage exemption for "religious employers," but this term was aimed almost explicitly at churches and excluded religiously affiliated organizations such as colleges, K-12 schools, and health care service organizations. Nor did it allow companies owned by religious individuals to apply for an exception to the law. Many Democrats and their supporters believed that providing an exception for all of these organizations would unduly burden women. "Ninety-nine-percent of women use contraceptives at some time in their lives," said Judy Waxman, a vice president of the National Women's Law Center, which supported the Affordable Care Act (Bronner 2013). Many Democrats rejected the claim by Republicans that the First Amendment protected religiously affiliated organizations from having to comply with the law and noted that the Supreme Court did not routinely provide institutions exemptions from neutral laws of general applicability. As a result of the Affordable Care Act and the FDA decision, birth control became a divisive issue in both electoral and judicial politics.

Women's rights advocates and their Democratic allies were pleased with the August 2011 decision by the U.S. Department of Health and Human Services (HHS) to require that insurance plans provide all FDA-approved contraceptive methods as part of women's preventive health service, making them available without copays under the Affordable Care Act. These included "contraceptive methods and sterilization procedures," including the "morning after pills" and intrauterine devices.

Republicans and their evangelical and Catholic supporters were displeased, however, and they continued to fight the law by offering amendments in Congress and taking the government to court. Democrats protested the attempt to limit the health care law. "Millions of women work for colleges, hospitals and health care systems that are nominally religious, but these folks use birth control and need coverage," said Diana DeGette, a Colorado Democrat and leader of the Congressional Pro Choice Caucus (Pear 2011). Liberal-leaning media voices also signaled their support for the Democratic position. In February 2012, for example, the *New York Times* Editorial Board expressed strong support for the contraceptive provisions of the Affordable Care Act: "Churches are given complete freedom by the Constitution to preach that birth control is immoral, but they have not been given the right to laws that would deprive their followers or employees of the right to disagree with that teaching . . . [Religious institutions] cannot simply opt out of society or claim a special exemption from the law" (*New York Times* Editorial Board 2012).

In early 2012, Congress held hearings on the issue. One witness called to testify was Sandra Fluke, a third-year law student at Georgetown, a Jesuit college that due to its Catholic beliefs did not provide contraceptives in its student health care plans. She praised the Democratic health care plan and criticized moves by several Republican senators to strip the contraceptive mandate from the Affordable Care Act: "Ours is not a war against the church. It is a struggle for access to the health care we need." Fluke's testimony led to a firestorm of criticism that included comments by conservative talk radio host Rush Limbaugh who cast aspersions on her character. In response, Democrats framed the criticisms of Fluke from conservatives as part of a wider Republican "war on women." The Democratic National Committee made this a signature theme at the 2012 Presidential Nominating Convention and even invited Sandra Fluke to speak. This strategy may have contributed to the Democratic Party's 67 percent share of the unmarried female vote in the 2012 elections ("Exit Polls How the Vote Has Shifted" 2012). Democrats were suspicious when Republican candidates for the Senate and House in the 2014 midterm elections began urging the sale of contraceptives over the counter. The Republican idea was labeled "a cynical attempt to mask their larger efforts," said the Planned Parenthood Action Fund, referring to the GOP attempts to end the Affordable Care mandate (Babington 2014).

Democrats were dismayed in 2014 when the Supreme Court ruled in favor of Hobby Lobby, a family owned for-profit company that objected to the contraceptive mandate on religious grounds. The ruling was along ideological lines, with Republican appointees to the Court siding with Hobby Lobby and Democrat appointees to the Court dissenting. Justice Ginsburg who wrote the dissenting opinion, reiterated the Democratic position, which is that religious beliefs must not impinge on the rights of third parties, as the sought-after exemption would do to women seeking contraception in this case. Almost immediately, Democrats in the Senate offered legislation to reverse the Court's decision. Senator Patty Murray, a Democrat from Washington, declared, "Your health care decisions are not your boss's business. Since the Supreme Court decided it will not protect women's access to health care, I will" (Pear 2014). The bill was not offered in the Republican-controlled House, however, so as of 2015 the Court's Hobby Lobby decision stands.

Democrats continued to urge the expansion of contraceptive coverage for women by offering the Access to Contraception for Women Servicemembers and Dependents Act of 2015. Under this proposed legislation, military service members and their families would receive the same contraception coverage that federal employees have had for a decade and civilians have had since the Affordable Care Act, which would include FDA-approved items including RU486.

Republicans on Birth Control

Republicans do not necessarily oppose using birth control; to the contrary, many Republicans have relied on various forms of birth control. As a party, however, the GOP has consistently proposed government policies that have made access to birth control easy and sometimes free for teens. The Republicans assert that such programs obviate the parent's rights to raise their children as they see fit and encourage sexual activity among teens. They also object to government mandates that force people with strong religious convictions to provide contraceptive coverage in their employer-based health care plans.

This was not always the case within the GOP. In 1970, for example, Republican President Richard Nixon put family planning into his budget proposal and stated, "It is my view that no American woman should be denied access to family planning assistance because of her economic condition" (Nixon 1969). In the 1980s, however, conservative Republicans urged President Ronald Reagan to limit or end these programs and to affirm the importance of abstinence from sex for teens. The Reagan administration issued regulations in 1982 ordering the nation's 4,000 government-funded public health clinics to notify parents when teens were issued prescription contraceptives. Advocates for free birth control sued and a federal court overturned the ruling (Gordon 2007).

Conservative Republicans were pleased with the actions taken by President George W. Bush during his eight years (2001–2009) in the Oval Office. Bush stripped funding from a plan that would have required insurance companies to supply contraceptives to all nine million federal employees. The Bush administration promoted in-school sexual education for teens that featured abstinence only and rejected teaching teens about birth control methods.

Republicans also see the birth control issue as one of religious freedom. Across the United States, conservatives in dozens of state legislatures have introduced bills and passed laws giving pharmacists the legal right to refuse to fill prescriptions for birth control on religious grounds. Six states under Republican control had implemented these laws as of 2012—Arizona, Arkansas, Georgia, Idaho, Mississippi, and South Dakota.

The argument for religion dominated the debate about birth control coverage mandated by the Affordable Care Act passed in March 2010. Some companies, religious organizations, and health plan administrators objected to the Affordable Care Act mandate, citing the First Amendment protection of an individual's right to free exercise of religion. Representative Joe Walsh, Republican of Illinois, insisted: "This is not about women. This is not about contraceptives. This is about religious freedom" (Pear 2012).

In August 2011, Sylvia Burwell, Secretary of the Department of Health and Human Services (HHS) in the Obama administration, issued regulations that indicated that in the view of the HHS, contraception included all FDA-approved methods of birth control, including RU486. This announcement sparked a negative reaction from many religious conservatives who view the "morning-after pill" as tantamount to abortion. President Obama subsequently offered a compromise whereby insurance companies would provide this coverage to clients free of charge, thus making it so the birth control coverage would not actually be "covered" by the religious organizations. Conservatives, however, were unimpressed. Senator Roy Blunt, Republican of Missouri, described the proposal as nothing more than "an accounting gimmick" (Pear 2012). Blunt offered an amendment to the Affordable Care Act that would have allowed employers to refuse to cover contraceptives on moral grounds (Morone and Ehlke 2014).

Mandatory birth control coverage was a hot button issue in the 2012 presidential election. Conservative talk show host Rush Limbaugh, who has been an unofficial spokesman for conservative Republicans since 1989, disparaged the Democratic plan to mandate contraceptive coverage for women. Limbaugh called Georgetown University law student Sandra Fluke a slut and a prostitute for claiming that she knew of many of her fellow law school students who could not afford to purchase birth control pills or other devices that were not covered by the Jesuit college. His comments led to backlash by women's groups and the departure of a number of important advertisers from his program. Ultimately, the condemnation proved so strong that the radio host made a rare, formal apology for his attacks on Fluke.

After Republicans lost the 2012 presidential contest, they took the issue to the Supreme Court, following a flood of lawsuits by Roman Catholics, evangelicals, and Mennonites who said the law requiring employers to cover birth control in employee health plans violated their religious rights. The Supreme Court took the case of *Burwell v. Hobby Lobby*, in which the owners of the company argued that the requirement that the employment-based group health care plan cover contraception violated the Free Exercise Clause of the First Amendment and the Religious Freedom Restoration Act of 1993 (RFRA). Along ideological lines, conservative Republican appointees to the Court held in a 5 to 4 decision that forcing closely held corporations to provide contraceptive coverage for female employees was unlawful because it violated RFRA.

The latest move by Republicans who were concerned about being called "anti-women" but who wanted to support their conservative constituencies was to remove the issue from the courts and the ballot box by suggesting that some contraceptives be relabeled from controlled substances that need a prescription to over-the-counter items. The idea had the support of some major medical groups such as the American Academy of Family Physicians and has been the focus of Republican legislators in Colorado, North Carolina, Minnesota, and Virginia. "One of the most rational ways for Washington to break this gridlock is to approve oral contraception for over-the-counter purchases by adults," wrote Republican Cory Gardner in the midst of his successful 2014 campaign for one of Colorado's U.S. Senate seats. "When treatments go over-the-counter, two things happen: they get dramatically cheaper and consumers save time and hassle by avoiding unnecessary doctors' appointments just to get the pharmaceuticals they already know they need . . . The inevitable cost savings from a switch to OTC status should not be underestimated. Almost all therapies that move to OTC drop in price dramatically" (Gardner 2014).

Further Reading

Babington, Charles. 2014. "Senate Races: Democrats Decry Birth Control Plan," *The Washington Times,* September 18. Accessed October 10, 2014: http://www.washingtontimes.com/news/2014/sep/18/senate-races-democrats-decry-birth-control-plan/print/.

Bronner, Ethan. 2013. "A Flood of Suits Fights Coverage of Birth Control," *New York Times,* January 26. Accessed June 1, 2014: http://www.nytimes.com/2013/01/27/health/religious-groups-and-employers-battle-contraception-mandate.html?pagewanted=all.

Engelmann, Peter. 2011. *A History of the Birth Control Movement in America.* In *Healing Society: Disease, Medicine, and History* series. New York: Praeger.

"Exit Polls How the Vote Has Shifted," 2012. *The Washington Post,* November 8. Accessed June 3, 2014: http://www.washingtonpost.com/wp-srv/special/politics/2012-exit-polls/table.html.

Gardner, Cory. 2014. "Women Should Be Able to Buy the Pill without a Prescription," *Denver Post,* June 19. Accessed June 6, 2014: http://www.denverpost.com/opinion/ci_25995739/women-should-be-able-buy-pill-without-prescription.

Gordon, Linda. 2007. *The Moral Property of Women: A History of Birth Control Politics in America.* Urbana: University of Illinois.

Jutte, Robert. 2008. *Contraception: A History.* New York: Polity.

Leonard, Mary. 2000. "Bush, Gore Split over FDA's Decision to Approve Sale of Abortion Pill in U.S.," *Boston Globe,* September 29. Accessed June 1, 2014: http://go.galegroup.com/ps/i.do?id=GALE%7CA121963207&v=2.1&u=nysl_ro_nazareth&it=r&p=ITOF&sw=w&asid=a1fae8285dedb274784114da599e5847.

Merrick, Janna, and Robert H. Blank. 2003. *Reproductive Issues in America: A Reference Handbook.* Santa Barbara: ABC-CLIO.

Morone, James A., and Dan Ehlke. 2014. *Health Politics and Policy.* New York: Cengage Learning.

New York Times Editorial Board. 2012. "The Freedom to Choose Birth Control," *New York Times,* February 12. Accessed June 6, 2014: http://www.nytimes.com/2012/02/11/opinion/the-freedom-to-choose-birth-control.html.

Nixon, Richard. 1969. "Special Message to the Congress on Problems of Population Growth," July 18. Online by Gerhard Peters and John T. Woolley, "The American Presidency Project." Accessed July 18, 2014: http://www.presidency.ucsb.edu/ws/?pid=2132.

Pear, Robert. 2011. "Democrats Urge Obama to Protect Contraceptive Coverage in Health Plans," *New York Times,* November 19, 2011.

Pear, Robert. 2012. "Passions Flare as House Debates Birth Control Rule," *New York Times,* February 16. Accessed July 20, 2014: http://www.nytimes.com/2012/02/17/us/politics/birth-control-coverage-rule-debated-at-house-hearing.html?_r=0.

Pear, Robert. 2014. "Democrats Push Bill to Reverse Supreme Court Ruling on Contraceptives," *New York Times,* July 8. Accessed July 20, 2014: http://nyti.ms/1n4D1LP.

Bullying

At a Glance

Democrats and Republicans may agree that bullying is a serious problem that needs to be addressed, but overall they disagree on whether or not special status should be accorded to certain victims of bullying, for example, people who are lesbian, gay, bisexual, or transgender (LGBT). Whereas, for the most part, Democrats would like federal policies aimed at protecting LGBT individuals who they see as more vulnerable to victimization, Republicans would prefer to treat all victims the same and to focus on the perpetrators. Many Republicans fear that focusing on a particular class of victims might endanger the right of free speech for those who oppose the LGBT lifestyle and also reject the intervention of the federal government into a social policy they claim is best left to state or local authorities.

Many Democrats . . .

- Believe that bullying is a serious problem in American schools.
- Believe that bullying is expanding into the military, sports, and the workplace.
- Believe that bullying is used to reject pluralism and diversity.
- Would like the federal government to do more to protect individuals from being bullied.
- Want to create new state laws regulating the conduct of individuals in schools, workplaces, and sports.
- Want strict laws to punish those who use social media as a form of cyberbullying.
- Support courts that uphold anticyberbullying laws.
- Want schools to collect data on the kinds of individuals harassed by bullies.

Many Republicans . . .

- Believe that bullying is a serious problem in American schools.
- Are skeptical of Democratic policies that would enumerate a special class of victims.

- Believe that any policies governing bullying should focus on the behavior of the bully, not the identity of the victim.
- Reject that the federal government should create antibullying policies.
- Believe that bullying is an issue that is best addressed by state and local authorities.

Overview

Democrats and Republicans may agree that bullying is a social problem that needs to be addressed. What, overall, they do not agree upon is how to define bullying and the proper response to curtail the practice. According to the federal government, "Bullying is unwanted, aggressive behavior among school aged children that involves a real or perceived power imbalance. The behavior is repeated, or has the potential to be repeated, over time. Bullying includes actions such as making threats, spreading rumors, attacking someone physically or verbally, and excluding someone from a group on purpose" (Stop Bullying 2014). The definition has been expanded recently and the term is now applied to harassment of adults in the workplace, military, and college and professional sports.

While bullying has been an ongoing social problem for decades, the development of the Internet and social media exacerbated existing problems and made public humiliation more visible and more likely for the victims of bullying. Internet harassment has its own classification and is called cyberbullying. Cyberbullying is defined as "willful and repeated harm inflicted through the use of computers, cell phones, and other electronic devices" (Hinduja and Patchin 2011). In the past decade there have been a number of incidents in which individuals were either filmed being bullied or have committed suicide as a direct result of bullying, especially when it takes social media forms. This has spurred public health officials, education policy makers, experts in management, and elected representatives to craft new laws and strengthen existing regulations protecting people from being harassed. The political parties, while both expressing opprobrium at this antisocial behavior, are divided over the question of what constitutes bullying, the severity of bullying, and the appropriate role of government in regulating social behavior (Bazelon 2014).

Liberals, many of whom are Democrats, in general believe that the surge in bullying, harassment, and hate crimes has risen in resistance to diversity and pluralism in the United States. Democrats overall see some groups—such as LGBT individuals, people with disabilities, and socially isolated youths—at increased risk of being bullied and want to strengthen laws protecting these individuals from speech or actions that are discriminatory. Conservatives, many of whom are Republicans, in general believe that bullying is a serious social crime but raise concerns that antibullying laws might restrict the free speech and religious rights of individuals and groups who see the LGBT lifestyle as sinful or deviant. They are also concerned that any punishment, especially within the context of K-12 and college education, be proportionate with the crime and not excessive.

Political scientists call specific incidents that lead to policy change "focusing events." National attention was focused on school bullying after the mass murder at Columbine High School in 1999 (Gerdes 2012) in which bullying was implicated as a potential underlying cause for the psychotic behavior of the two high school attackers (Stuart-Cassel et al. 2014). This led to a spate of antibullying laws across the United States and the rise of specific antibullying organizations such as the National Bullying Prevention Center, which sponsors national bullying prevention month and Stop Bullying Now.

President Barack Obama "On Bullying"

President Barack Obama made bullying a national issue when he called for the first ever bullying prevention conference at the White House. In his remarks he enumerates characteristics of victims that are often identified by Democrats and civil rights advocates as those needing the most protection:

> As adults, we all remember what it was like to see kids picked on in the hallways or in the schoolyard. And I have to say, with big ears and the name that I have, I wasn't immune. I didn't emerge unscathed. But because it's something that happens a lot, and it's something that's always been around, sometimes we've turned a blind eye to the problem. We've said, "Kids will be kids." And so sometimes we overlook the real damage that bullying can do, especially when young people face harassment day after day, week after week. So consider these statistics. A third of middle school and high school students have reported being bullied during the school year. Almost 3 million students have said they were pushed, shoved, tripped, even spit on. It's also more likely to affect kids that are seen as different, whether it's because of the color of their skin, the clothes they wear, the disability they may have, or sexual orientation. And bullying has been shown to lead to absences and poor performance in the classroom. And that alone should give us pause, since no child should be afraid to go to school in this country . . . We've got to make sure our young people know that if they're in trouble, there are caring adults who can help and young adults that can help; that even if they're having a tough time, they're going to get through it, and there's a whole world full of possibility waiting for them. We also have to make sure we're doing everything we can so that no child is in that position in the first place. And this is a responsibility we all share—a responsibility we have to teach all children the Golden Rule: We should treat others the way we want to be treated.

Source

The White House. 2011. "President Obama and the First Lady at the White House Conference on Bullying Prevention," March 10. Accessed April 17, 2015: http://www.whitehouse.gov /blog/2011/03/10/president-obama-first-lady-white-house-conference-bullying-prevention.

In the past five years, a series of high-profile workplace bullying incidents led the public to expand the issue beyond school-aged children. In 2014, the National Football League investigated claims of bullying within the Miami Dolphins organization. A 144-page report commissioned by the NFL condemned the team for allowing the use of sexual innuendo, harassment, and coercion of players, which the report stated was "a classic case of bullying, where persons who are in a position of power harass the less powerful." One bullying victim, Jonathan Martin, quit the team, thought about quitting the sport altogether, and contemplated suicide as a result of being bullied (Shpigel 2014). In the military, the death of Danny Chen led the Army to investigate whether bullying by his peers led the soldier to kill himself. Chen's death resulted in the implementation by the U.S. military of a zero tolerance policy for hazing as well as for other forms of harassment. In another high profile case, Tyler Clementi, an 18-year-old Rutgers University freshman, jumped to his death from the George Washington Bridge in September 2010 after discovering that his roommate had secretly used a webcam to stream Clementi's sexual liaison with another man. Meanwhile, statistics show that about 35 percent of the workforce reporting psychological and/or physical abuse on the job (Workplace Bullying Institute 2015). This indicates that bullying has expanded well beyond the school yard and is a serious social problem (Lipinski 2013;

New Jersey senator Barbara Buono, D-Edison, stands with other lawmakers in Trenton, New Jersey, on October 25, 2010, as she answers a question about a bill they introduced to toughen the state's anti-bullying laws after the widely publicized suicide of Rutgers University student Tyler Clementi. The bipartisan group of lawmakers touted the "anti-bullying bill of rights" targeting public schools and colleges. (AP Photo/Mel Evans)

Nathan 2014). Despite this, much attention remains on the youngest and most vulnerable of victims.

Democrats on Bullying

Democrats, in general, see bullying as a response to diversity and pluralism in the United States and see some groups, such as LGBT youths, youths with disabilities, and socially isolated youths, as more vulnerable to being bullied. They are likely to support laws to protect individuals from being harassed verbally, physically, and online. Since 1999, states have passed over 150 laws to specifically address bullying in schools (Stuart-Cassel et al. 2014). Advocates for new legislation have pushed for the inclusion and enumeration of specific victims in state laws in order to protect lesbian, gay, bisexual, and transgender youths. LGBT youths have experienced high rates of bullying but in some cases they are not legally protected under federal civil rights laws. Proponents in favor of listing specific victims say that such a directive is needed so schools will safeguard the children who are most vulnerable to bullying (Coloroso 2009).

Organizations such as Stomp Out Bullying point to the positive effects when antibullying policies contain explicit protections. Specifically, studies have shown that there is lower prevalence of bullying behavior and increased propensity to report threats or bullying acts against LGBT students when specific protections are covered under school bullying policies (Stomp Out Bullying 2014). Other antibullying proponents want this legislation as counterweight to religious leaders whose "antigay rhetoric" may encourage conservative students to harass those who are openly gay. Many congressional Democrats have also taken up the call to protect victims of bullying. Senator Tom Harkin was the Democratic chair of the Committee on Health, Education, Labor, and Pensions from 2009 to 2014, and he regularly used his position to push antibullying legislation. Harkin held hearings on school bullying in 2012, and, in 2013, he sponsored a bill in the Senate, which was introduced in the House by Bruce Braley. "This bill . . . will help ensure that all students, regardless of gender identity or sexual orientation, are treated fairly and afforded equal opportunities to succeed in the classroom. The legislation aims to reduce future bullying cases by gathering data on the incidence and prevalence of violence, including harassment and bullying, and uses that information to implement evidence-based programs to ensure our kids have a safe and healthy school environment." As reported in the *Cedar Rapids Gazette,* March 28, 2014, the Braley/Harkin bill, entitled The Successful, Safe and Healthy Students Act, sought to establish grant programs so schools could bring in experts and train students and teachers on how to stop or prevent bullying. One grant was earmarked for states that were to distribute the money to school districts that improved learning conditions, increased opportunities for physical activity and nutrition learning, prevented drug use and violence, and promoted mental health all of which were useful in combating the rise of bullying. Opposition from the

Republicans, who held a majority in the House, kept the bill tied up in committee and it was never enacted.

Since taking office in 2009, President Barack Obama has urged new policies on bullying. He held the first ever bullying prevention conference at the White House where he said, "Almost 3 million students have said they were pushed, shoved, tripped, even spit on. It's also more likely to affect kids that are seen as different, whether it's because of the color of their skin, the clothes they wear, the disability they may have, or sexual orientation."

Under Obama, the Centers for Disease Control and Prevention (CDC) crafted a new definition of bullying that they released in January 2014. The CDC states that bullying is "any unwanted aggressive behavior(s) by another youth or group of youths who are not siblings or current dating partners that involves an observed or perceived power imbalance and is repeated multiple times or is highly likely to be repeated." Obama's secretary of education, Arnie Duncan, issued a 10-page letter to school districts across the United States, calling on them to comply with federal law by preventing harassment. After a yearlong review of federal statutes and case law covering racial, sexual, and other forms of harassment, the Department of Education created model legislation for states and policy guidelines for schools. Citing federal civil rights laws, Duncan suggested that policies and laws specifically include the following list of characteristics to be protected against harassment: race, color, weight, national origin, ethnic group, religion or religious practice, disability, sexual orientation, and gender or sex. Duncan's guidelines were only fully enacted in states with Democratic majorities in the legislature or in control of the executive branch such as Colorado, Hawaii, Massachusetts, New Jersey, and Rhode Island.

Anticyberbullying legislation and policies have led to partisan splits in the federal courts. Policies that punish students for their activities online have been challenged on the premise that they violate the right of free speech for students outside of school. The Fourth Circuit Court of Appeals has 15 active judges, 11 of whom were appointed by Democratic presidents. This court heard the case of Kara Kowalski, who was suspended under the antibullying policy for creating a Myspace page that successfully invited others to make offensive comments and bully a student. After being suspended for this, Kowalski sued the school district, but the Fourth Circuit Court supported the school district's discipline of Kowalski, citing *Tinker v. Des Moines Independent Community School District,* and upheld the school's interest in regulating speech that interferes with or disrupts the work and discipline of the school. However, decisions in the Third Circuit Court, which had six Republican and seven Democratic members, upheld students' free speech rights over school policy. The Supreme Court has so far refused to hear cyberbullying cases.

Bullying, while once a term associated only with children and teens, has developed into a general term for harassment, and Democrats in 19 states have offered legislation to protect employees from workplace harassment and bullying. The legislation follows the model established for school legislation by enumerating certain protected classes of individuals. The legislation is often opposed by Republicans who say that stronger enforcement of existing antidiscrimination laws is sufficient to address the problem.

Republicans on Bullying

Republicans generally recognize the severity of bullying but are critical of Democratic efforts to control it through strict government regulation. They worry that such legislation only adds more mandates on schools that already have policies in place to deal with behavioral problems in the classroom. Overall, Republicans in Congress are opposed to creating federal antibullying laws, which they see as a federal overreach into an area that is the sole responsibility of state and local governments. When liberal Democrat Tom Harkin introduced legislation in the Senate in 2013, Republican Senator Chuck Grassley stated, "If it makes money available to schools to discourage bullying without any policy established at the federal level, then it might be doable. But if it's any more than that, I want to reserve judgment" (McDermott 2012).

Republican critics have said some antibullying laws impose overly strict punishments and carry language that unfairly favors certain groups of students based on factors such as race, sexual identity, and religion, and they argue bullying should be defined solely based on behavior and not on the characteristics of students who are bullied. They fear that such language will silence people with religious objections to homosexuality or force them to embrace liberal beliefs about sexuality and gender or face punishment under strict antibullying policies. Conservative pro-family groups have argued that preaching tolerance of homosexuality is tantamount to encouraging an immoral lifestyle. "Making schools safe for 'gay' kids means indoctrinating impressionable, young minds with homosexual propaganda," Laurie Thompson, a spokesperson for the Parent's Action League, stated in an article for the *International Business Times* on March 7, 2012. In Michigan, the Republican majority drafted an antibullying law, "Matt's Safe School Law," which included language noting that the bill "does not prohibit a statement of a sincerely held belief or moral conviction" of a student or school worker (Strauss 2011). The amendment met disdain from Democrats and civil rights workers who believe the law will only encourage further bullying of gay students. In 2012, conservatives objected to West Virginia's antibullying policy, saying the measure limited free speech and unfairly allowed teachers to crack down on students who spoke out against homosexuality. "[The policy] is not appropriate. It's not equitable. It's not fair," said Jeremy Dys, president of the Family Policy Council of West Virginia, after West Virginia adopted the guidelines issued by the Department of Education under Arne Duncan. Dys was quoted in an article written by Eric Eyre for the *Charleston Gazette* on November 27, 2012: "This new law has a chilling effect on speech," Dys said. "We should be working to increase speech, not limiting it."

Some Republicans express the concern that some legislation and school policies effectively undermine the constitutional guarantee of free speech. Representative Michelle Bachman asked, "What will be our definition of bullying? Will it get to the point where we are completely stifling free speech and expression?" Their claims are backed by some legal experts, who also caution against limiting definitions of bullying to behavior. Some conservatives complain that anticyberbullying laws encroach on the right of free speech. While the Fourth Circuit has upheld schools' rights to stop online harassment, the more ideologically balanced Third Circuit Court of Appeals tends to favor free speech. In case after case, judges found that school districts failed to demonstrate it could reasonably forecast that the students' words would cause substantial disruption in school and, therefore, the "bullying" student's suspension was a violation of the First Amendment right to free speech. In one opinion the court wrote that schools cannot punish students "for expressive conduct which occurred outside of the school context" (Stone 2013).

Some Republican opponents of antibullying laws worry that broader state supervision and detailed reporting requirements threaten the ability of schools to handle bullying incidents internally. All 50 states now have antibullying laws, including Montana, where Republican lawmakers had opposed a state law on the grounds it would disempower local school districts but in the face of public support, GOP legislatures made no objection when Democrats sponsored a bill in February 2015.

Further Reading

Bazelon, Emily. 2014. *Sticks and Stones: Defeating the Culture of Bullying and Rediscovering the Power of Character and Empathy*. New York: Random House.

Coloroso, Barbara. 2009. *The Bully, the Bullied, and the Bystander: From Preschool to High School—How Parents and Teachers Can Help Break the Cycle*. New York: William Morrow.

Gerdes, Louise. 2012. *The Columbine School Shooting*. New York: Greenhaven Press.

Hinduja, Sameer, and Justin Patchin. 2011. "Cyberbullying: A Review of the Legal Issues Facing Educators," *Preventing School Failure*, 55 (2): 71–78.

Lipinski, John. 2013. *Bullying in the Workplace: Causes, Symptoms, and Remedies*. New York: Routledge.

McDermott, Kevin. 2012. "Illinois House Passes New Anti-bullying Measure," *St. Louis Post Dispatch*, March 28. Accessed June 1, 2014: http://www.stltoday.com/news/local/illinois/illinois-house-passes-new-anti-bullying-measure/article_e2abedb2-7906-11e1-b84a-001a4bcf6878.html.

Nathan, Randy. 2014. *Bullying in Sports: A Guide to Identifying the Injuries We Don't See*. New York: Pearson.

Shpigel, Ben. 2014. "'A Classic Case of Bullying' on the Dolphins, Report Finds," *New York Times*, February 14. Accessed June 1, 2014: http://www.nytimes.com/2014/02/15/sports/football/investigation-finds-pattern-of-harassment-in-dolphins-locker-room.html?_r=0.

Stomp Out Bullying. 2014. "Anti-Gay Bullying." Accessed June 1, 2014: http://www.stompoutbullying.org/.

Stone, Carolyn. 2013. "Cyber Bullying: Disruptive Conduct or Free Speech?" School Coun-
selor, May–June. Accessed June 1, 2014: https://www.schoolcounselor.org/magazine
/blogs/may-june-2013/cyber-bullying-disruptive-conduct-or-free-speech.

Stop Bullying. 2014 "What Is Bullying." Accessed June 1, 2014: http://www.stopbullying
.gov/what-is-bullying/.

Strauss, Valerie. 2011. "Anti-bullying Legislation Attacked for Allowing Bullying," *The
Washington Post,* November 5. Accessed June 1, 2014: http://www.washingtonpost
.com/blogs/answer-sheet/post/anti-bullying-legislation-attacked-for-allowing-bullying
/2011/11/05/gIQARflapM_blog.html.

Stuart-Cassel, Victoria, Ariana Bell, and J. Fred Springer. 2014. *Analysis of State Bullying
Laws and Policies.* Folsom, CA: EMT Associates.

Workplace Bullying Institute. 2015. http://www.workplacebullying.org/individuals/problem
/definition/.

Climate Change

At a Glance

Is climate change being driven by human action? Many Democrats claim that global climate change is occurring due to the release of greenhouse gases into the atmosphere as a by-product of human activity. To address this trend, which they view as potentially catastrophic, they have expressed support for imposing new regulations on industries and products that produce greenhouse gases. They have also championed heavy investment in renewable energy sources and asserted that the United States needs to take an international leadership role in combating this threat. Many Republicans, on the other hand, are much more skeptical that the climate is changing, and they generally reject the notion that human action is the sole cause of climate change. They believe that the American economy is more fragile than the planet and seek to protect American businesses from unnecessary regulations meant to address climate change.

Many Democrats . . .

- Believe that climate change is occurring, citing the almost universal scientific consensus on the issue.
- Believe that climate change is caused by anthropogenic (human) activities.
- Believe that climate change is a national security threat.
- Blame recent increases in the frequency of extreme weather events on climate change.
- Advocate fundamental changes in U.S. energy policy to reduce the use of carbon fuels such as coal and oil.
- Favor increased investment in renewable energy resources such as solar and wind power.
- Support government regulation to reduce America's carbon footprint.
- Support international agreements to limit carbon emissions worldwide.
- Are willing to tax corporations that exceed government imposed limits on greenhouse gases.

Many Republicans . . .

- Insist that the science of climate change is unsettled.
- Reject the idea that human action is the primary cause of climate change.
- Oppose government regulation to limit greenhouse gases.
- Oppose energy policies that limit U.S. production of carbon fuels.
- Support greater drilling for oil.
- Support hydrofracking.
- Support the use of clean coal for energy use.
- Reject international agreements that place limits on U.S. carbon use.
- Argue that the United States should not commit to greenhouse gas reductions without receiving the same level of commitment from industrializing nations like China.

Overview

Global climate change refers to a change in the average global temperature, which has risen by nearly 1.5 degrees Fahrenheit since the 19th century. Most scientists agree that the temperature increase, which they warn will continue to escalate without major changes in human behavior, is due to the concentration in the atmosphere of certain gases generated by industrialization and other forms of human action (Weeks 2014). These gases are called Greenhouse Gases (GHGs) and consist of carbon dioxide, methane, chlorofluorocarbons, and nitrous oxide, which collectively trap the sun's energy in the stratosphere, preventing infrared energy from escaping the Earth's surface and slowly increasing the global temperature.

Although most scientists accept the evidence of global warming, not everyone has accepted the claim that the rise in temperatures is due to human activities, sometimes called anthropogenic climate change. Democrats generally side with scientific organizations such as the Intergovernmental Panel on Climate Change (IPCC), which asserts that climate change is due to industrialization and the release of greenhouse gases like CO_2. Republicans are much more skeptical of the claim of global warming, and those who do accept that climate change is happening may dispute there is one singular cause. They are generally opposed to proposals to combat climate change by reducing consumption of fossil fuels like oil and coal.

The United States played a pioneering role in the study of climate and in taking action to mitigate the damage caused by human-produced atmospheric gases. The leading figure in the development of the idea of global warming was geophysicist Roger Revelle. In the 1960s, Revelle was the first to scientifically demonstrate that carbon dioxide levels in the air had increased as a result of the use of fossil fuels. Revelle joined President Lyndon Johnson's Scientific Advisory Committee on Environmental Pollution, and this group held hearings on the subject and published findings suggesting CO_2 might lead to global warming. The group produced a report in 1974 that pointed to changes in the ozone layer of the atmosphere caused by chlorofluorocarbons (CFCs), which were then widely used as coolants in air conditioners and refrigerators, in the process of dry cleaning, and as propellants in common household items such as hairspray and deodorant. Following debate on the topic, it was during the administration of Jimmy Carter, president from 1977 to 1981, that Congress responded by banning all nonessential use of CFCs. That year also brought Roger Revelle back into the public eye, as he led a widely publicized National Academy of Science study warning of global warming. This spurred Congress to pass the National Climate Act in 1978. This legislation established the National Climate Program Office and charged it with documenting and researching the effects of greenhouse gases (Sarewitz and Pielke 2000).

Research on climate change was dismissed by President Ronald Reagan, who served from 1981 to 1989, and at times even those engaged in studying climate change reached different conclusions about the severity of the problem. However, a widely held belief among conservatives that many scientists and environmentalists of the 1970s and 1980s were actually warning about impending "global cooling" is a myth. In actuality, however, reviews of the scientific literature from that period indicate that contrary to claims from Republicans and some news media, "even a cursory examination [of the peer-reviewed literature of the 1970s] reveals that global cooling was never more than a minor aspect of the scientific climate change literature of the era, let alone the scientific consensus" (Peterson et al. 2008).

In contrast to Reagan, Democratic Senator Al Gore Jr. who had taken a class with Revelle, was convinced that this was an unheralded environmental crisis and held a series of congressional hearings on the matter. At one such hearing, on June 23, 1988, National Aeronautics and Space Administration (NASA) scientist James Hansen testified to Congress that scientists were "ninety-nine percent" confident that the "greenhouse effect has been detected, and it is changing our climate now." Hansen's proclamation was the front-page story and headline in every major newspaper and television station. Ever since this dramatic declaration, the issue has been the preeminent environmental concern for politicians and public alike, dividing conservatives, who refute the findings, and liberals, who see the issue as a threat to human life everywhere (Pielke 2014).

The U.S. and global response since 1988 has been the center of debate between Democrats and Republicans. In 1992, the United Nations hosted the Earth Summit in Rio de Janeiro. This two-week conference on global warming was attended by all major American news outlets, which reported on how the conference nations endorsed the UN Framework Convention on Climate Change (UNFCCC) that committed nations to reduce greenhouse gas emissions, based on the premise that global warming existed and was caused by man-made CO_2 emissions. This was followed in 1997 by a meeting in Kyoto, Japan, where delegates from 150 nations met to endorse the Kyoto Protocol, the idea that since developed countries were primarily responsible for global warming due to their 150-year history of emitting greenhouse gases as part of industrialization they had a greater responsibility to cut or stop these emissions under the principle of common but differentiated responsibilities. Despite the global acceptance of this platform, the United States rejected the Kyoto Protocol (Downie 2009).

In 2006, the British government issued a 700-page report on the *Economics of Climate Change,* also known as the Stern Review. This comprehensive report was widely read and cited as the most detailed discussion of how climate change would change the global economy and called on developed nations to begin investing in ways to combat climate change. Many Democrats saw this as a blueprint for the future, while many Republicans sought to discredit its contents by emphasizing that it had not been peer reviewed. In 2009, under the direction of President Barack Obama, who was elected in 2008, the United States accepted the Copenhagen Accord, which merely recognized the Kyoto Protocol and called on signatories to consider mitigation and adaptation to climate change, which was officially recognized. As a result of this accord Obama issued a series of reports on action taken by the U.S. federal government to combat climate change (U.S. Department of State 2014). During Obama's presidency, his administration has also launched programs and initiatives to reduce GHG emissions from automobiles and coal-fired power plants and to increase the percentage of America's energy needs met by renewables. Democrats have been largely supportive of Obama's moves to address climate change, while Republicans have largely condemned them as economically destructive and unnecessary.

Democrats on Climate Change

Since the 1980s, the issue of climate change has been a permanent feature of environmental debates between Democrats and Republicans. Republican presidents Ronald Reagan and George H. W. Bush rejected taking dramatic action on the issue without further study, but many environmental interest groups hoped that the election of Bill Clinton in 1992 would change this. They were especially encouraged by his choice of a running mate, noted climate activist and Senator Al Gore of Tennessee (McKibben 2012).

Gore persuaded Clinton to endorse a "Climate Change Action Plan," which committed the United States to reducing emission of greenhouse gases to better mitigate the effects of climate change. The climate plan was stymied when Republicans took control of the House and Senate in the 1994 midterm election. The election interjected new conservative voices into the climate debate and the tone of those who disagreed with the theory of anthropogenic climate change grew more strident. President Clinton was unwilling to expend political energy on this issue, given that opponents controlled both houses of Congress. Rather than strive for a dramatic regulation of greenhouse emissions, Clinton found bipartisan support for improvements in energy efficiency and revisions to automobile emissions (Weart 2015).

In the early 1990s, the international community created the IPCC under the auspices of the UN. In 1992, 154 nations gathered at a conference in Rio de Janeiro to agree upon a plan sponsored by the UNFCCC. Five years later, the international community negotiated a treaty to limit greenhouse gas emissions at a meeting in Kyoto, Japan. The Kyoto Treaty, as it came to be called, set limits for 37 industrialized countries and the European Union (EU) to reduce their output of greenhouse gases to 5 percent below 1990 levels by the year 2012. However, the U.S. Senate declared by a vote of 95–0 that it would reject any treaty that did not set greenhouse gas limits for developing nations, which included at that time China and India. Given the unanimous Senate vote, the Kyoto Protocol clearly did not enjoy any meaningful support from Democrats on Capitol Hill (Hillstrom 2010).

During the early 2000s, Democratic leaders began talking with greater urgency about the need to take climate change seriously, most importantly by reducing GHG emissions both domestically and around the globe. After the Democrats regained control of the House and Senate in the 2006 midterm elections, however, they were frustrated by the refusal of Republican President George W. Bush to embrace international climate change agreements. Democratic action on the issue would have to wait for the election of a Democrat to the White House. Obama had often spoken of the need to combat climate change on the campaign trail, and upon entering the White House he declared that his administration understood the necessity of curbing greenhouse gas emissions to mitigate global warming. With a Democratic majority in both House and Senate during his first two years in office, however, Obama prioritized health care reform and economic stimulus packages over climate change legislation (Weart 2015).

Nonetheless, climate change legislation did come up for consideration. Groups such as the U.S. Climate Action Partnership, a coalition that gathered conservationist organizations like the National Resources Defense Council and the Environmental Defense Fund together with corporations like Shell, General Electric, and DuPont, called for congressional action on the issue. In 2009, the Democrat-led House of Representatives managed to pass, by a slim majority, a bill to institute a "cap-and-trade" program to restrict emissions. The bill would have given key industries a limit, or cap, on the amount of greenhouse gases they could emit with gradual reduction of this amount over a 10-year period. Large companies that could not meet the standards could buy or trade with smaller companies that had exceeded these limits. This "Waxman-Markey" bill, so named because its chief sponsors were Democrats Henry Waxman and Ed Markey, died in the Senate, where the Republican minority was able to kill it by threatening a filibuster, which would have stopped all business in the Senate. This was a maneuver that had bedeviled Democrats interested in climate change policy since the 1990s.

President Obama passed his health care reform bill in 2010, and following his reelection in 2012, the president signaled a new interest in climate change policy. In his second inaugural address in January 2013, Obama called for action and said that failure to do so "would betray our children and future generations." He took a swipe at his Republican opponents by stating that "some may still deny the overwhelming judgment of science, but none can avoid the devastating impact of raging fires and crippling drought, and more powerful storms" (Pielke 2012).

From left, Senators Tom Udall (D-N.Mex.), Bill Nelson (D-Fla.), Gary Peters (D-Mich.), Brian Schatz (D-Hawaii), and Ed Markey (D-Mass.), conduct a news conference in the Capitol's Senate studio to urge Republicans to acknowledge climate change and to work with Senate Democrats to address the issue, on December 8, 2015. The news conference came ahead of a hearing held by Senator Ted Cruz (R-Tex.), where witnesses were expected to refute that climate change exists. (Photo by Tom Williams/CQ Roll Call)

In Obama's State of the Union address in February 2013, he indicated that if Congress did not act to reduce GHG emissions, he would use his executive power to direct federal agencies to develop policies without passing new laws, such as regulating greenhouse gas emissions from coal-fired power plants (Obama 2013).

Following through on his promise, President Obama used his executive power to order the Environmental Protection Agency to use its authority to order a reduction in greenhouse gases in both the auto industry and the coal-fired power plants. Obama also vetoed legislation for a Keystone XL Pipeline that had been proposed to transport heavy oil and sand deposits from Alberta, Canada, all the way to refineries on the U.S. Gulf Coast.

Frustrated by this gridlock at the federal level, Democrats and environmental groups have worked in concert in many states and cities under Democratic control to pass climate control legislation. California led the way in 2006 when the California legislature passed the Global Warming Solutions Act of 2006. The California law called for reducing greenhouse gas emissions to 1990 levels by 2009, and to 80 percent of the 1990 level by 2014. Other states followed suit, including Connecticut, Hawaii, Maine, Minnesota, North Dakota, and New Jersey. In 2014, in advance of the U.S. Climate Summit in New York City, Mayor Bill deBlasio,

A Democratic Senator on Climate Change

Lawmakers in the Democratic Party are far more likely than their Republican counterparts to view human-caused climate change as a major issue. Following is a representative sample of Democratic thought on the issue from a 2013 speech by Democratic Representative Peter DeFazio of Oregon:

Today I rise as a member of the Safe Climate Caucus to talk about an important new report on climate change . . . Last week, scientists from Oregon State University, including two constituents of mine, Shaun Marcott and Alan Mix, joined with our colleagues from Harvard University and published a study in the journal Science, peer reviewed, that provides new context on today's climate and rising temperatures . . . [This report states that] we have experienced almost the same range of temperature change over the last 100 years, coinciding with the invention and widespread use of engines and turbines powered by fossil fuels, as over the previous 11,000 years of Earth history. I want to repeat that for emphasis. Rising temperatures over the last century have been greater than the temperature increases over the previous hundred centuries combined.

It shows that human activity reversed a cooling pattern of 5,000 years of 1.3 degrees Fahrenheit in 100 years. It is extraordinary. And their projections for the future are also very sobering.

Climate deniers are running out of excuses. They said, 118 years not enough, 2,000 years not enough. Well, how about 11,300 years of certified research? They say it is biased by region. This was done in 73 sites around the entire planet.

. . . [this report] confirms what those of us who believe in science already know: manmade climate change is real, it is progressing quickly, and we must take action. It's time to stop the nonsense and the blather and get serious about climate change. The evidence is in. The only question is whether the [Republican-led] United States House of Representatives will listen and act.

Source

Congressional Record. 2013. March 12. Accessed June 14, 2015: https://www.congress.gov/congressional-record/2013/03/12/house-section/article/h1333-4/?q=%7B%22search%22%3A%5B%22Inhofe+calls+climate+change+a+hoax%22%5D%7D.

a leading progressive Democrat, announced an ambitious plan to reduce greenhouse gases by 80 percent in New York City by the year 2050. As reported by the *New York Times* in a story by Matt Flegenheimer on September 20, 2014, the plan aimed to make all public buildings more energy efficient and to use incentives and taxes to encourage private landlords to follow suit.

Climate change is also seen by Democrats as a critical election issue, as Carl Hulse and Michael Shear reported on June 20, 2014, in the *New York Times*, some Democrats believe that the younger generation will continue to support Democratic candidates who call for reforms to reduce greenhouse gas emissions. In the 2014 midterm elections, many Democratic candidates running for election touted their support for strong EPA emissions standards. Climate change deniers have also been targeted by California billionaire Tom Steyer, who created a political action committee (PAC) called NextGen Climate and pledged $50 million of his own money to target Republican climate change skeptics.

Republicans on Climate Change

Ronald Reagan, elected president in 1980, was skeptical about the climate claims of the scientific and environmental community. Furthermore, Reagan preferred private and voluntary action on social and environmental issues rather than government intervention, and warned the public in his first Inaugural Address that "government isn't the solution, government is the problem" (Reagan 1981). Reagan found support from groups such as the American Enterprise Institute, which opposed the "radical environmental movement." Climate change, they believed, was an alarmist, anticapitalist, and collectivist attempt to impose new lifestyle choices on the American public. The opposition generally denied that environmental threats were real and were especially dismissive of global warming.

President George H. W. Bush was more receptive to environmental issues than Reagan. During his campaign for the presidency, Bush pledged to be an environmental president who would take action to combat the greenhouse effect. Bush signed amendments to the Clean Air and Clean Water Acts, and, in 1990, also accepted The Global Change Research Act of 1990, which provided billions of dollars to study the effects of climate change. Despite his promise, however, Bush never made global warming a major policy priority. The Bush White House displayed greater concern about the negative effect regulating greenhouse gases might have on the American economy. Bush's rhetoric on the issue changed to emphasize scientific uncertainty about climate change and the potential negative economic impact of various climate change mitigation proposals. Such organizations as the Heartland Institute, the Heritage Foundation, and the American Association of Petroleum Geologists argued that human-generated greenhouse gas emissions were too small to substantially change the Earth's climate. The Bush position on climate change became notorious to environmental groups after a White House memo was leaked to the press that suggested the best way to deal with global warming was "to raise the many uncertainties" about its existence (Giddens 2011).

During George W. Bush's presidency (2001–2009), Republican hostility to the idea of climate change further intensified. Bush was urged by some members of his cabinet and many foreign leaders to take steps against climate change, but he was also subject to pressure from industries that emitted greenhouse gases, as well as conservatives who rejected government regulatory action and/or believed that climate change was a hoax. Bush, much as his father had done, rejected action on climate change and repudiated the Kyoto Protocol. Rather than attack climate change head on, he chose to offer energy conservation reforms (Ball 2014).

Republicans in Congress have been some of the most vociferous opponents of climate change policy, and many seem to take their cues from conservative talk radio. Conservative talk became a dominant fixture of AM radio after the FCC set aside the Fairness Doctrine in 1987. Syndicated conservative talk show hosts such as Rush Limbaugh, Glenn Beck, Sean Hannity have tens of millions of daily listeners, many of whom are antigovernment conservatives who see climate change as a hoax perpetuated by liberals who seek to redistribute the wealth of the rich nations to the poor nations. These opponents of climate change often cite reports issued by conservative think tanks or organizations that analyze and study the impact and implications of government policy (Mooney 2012). These think tanks have typically rejected proposals for emission restriction, either by asserting that the science surrounding climate change is unproven or by claiming that measures to reduce emissions of GHGs would be too injurious to the economy. Matt Ridley, in an article in the *Wall Street Journal,* September 4, 2014, noted that among other things, conservatives declared that such action by the government would increase energy costs in the United States by replacing cheap coal-fired and oil-dependent power plants with more expensive renewable energy.

As the UNFCCC, environmentalists, and Democratic politicians urged drastic action, Republican hostility became even more entrenched. In January 2005, Senator James Inhofe made a speech on the Senate floor condemning the idea

---

A Republican Senator on Climate Change

Some elected members of the Republican Party have claimed anthropogenic climate change is a fraud. Others have accepted that climate change is a reality but are resistant to GHG-mitigation policies they fear will hinder American economic growth. Senator James Inhofe of Oklahoma is one of the most famous of the Republican deniers of human-caused climate change in Washington. Here is a sample of his viewpoint from a January 2015 speech on the Senate floor:

> Climate has always changed. If we go back and read history, look at archeological findings, and read the Scriptures, it has changed since the very beginning of time. We know it is real. The hoax is that somehow there are people so arrogant who are going to go along with the President's program to say: Yes, if we spend enough money we, the human beings, can stop the climate from changing. I think people do understand that is not going to happen . . . The hoax I have referred to since 2002 is that man is going to be in the position to change climate. That is not going to happen.

Source

Congressional Record. 2015. January 22, 114th Congress, 1st Session Vol. 161 (11). Accessed June 14, 2015: https://www.congress.gov/congressional-record/2015/01/22/senate-section/article/s370-4/?q=%7B%22search%22%3A%5B%22Inhofe+calls+climate+change+a+hoax%22%5D%7D.

of global warming as the greatest hoax ever perpetrated on the American people (Inhofe 2012). And, in 2015, virtually all of the Republican candidates for their party's presidential nomination either denied that climate change was occurring or insisted that any temperature changes had not been proven to be of anthropogenic origins.

Not all congressional Republicans have denied climate change. Republican Senators John McCain, Lindsey Graham, and Lisa Murkowski have all suggested addressing climate change policy, but their efforts have been rejected by Republican colleagues. Generally, talking about climate change is not appealing to Republicans, many of whom have addressed the issue only after leaving Congress.

Thus far, however, the Republican position on this issue has not seemed to hurt them politically. Polls show that while a narrow majority of Americans accept the fact of climate change, action on the issue is always near the bottom of their list of policy priorities (Davenport 2014).

Further Reading

Ball, Tim. 2014. *The Deliberate Corruption of Climate Science*. Mount Vernon, WA: Stairway Press.

Davenport, Coral. 2014. "Political Divide Slows U.S. Action on Climate Laws," *New York Times*, April 15, 1.

Downie, David L., Kate Brash, and Catherine Vaughan. 2009. *Climate Change: A Reference Handbook*. Santa Barbara: ABC-CLIO.

Giddens, Anthony. 2011. *The Politics of Climate Change*, 2nd edition. New York: Polity.

Hillstrom, Kevin. 2010. *U.S. Environmental Politics and Policy: A Documentary History* Washington, D.C.: Congressional Quarterly Press.

Inhofe, James D. 2012. *The Greatest Hoax: How the Global Warming Conspiracy Threatens Your Future*. Los Angeles: WND Books.

McKibben, Bill. 2012. *The Global Warming Reader: A Century of Writing about Climate Change*. New York: Penguin Books.

Mooney, Chris. 2012. *The Republican Brain: The Science of Why They Deny Science—and Reality*. New York: Wiley.

Obama, Barack. 2013. "State of the Union Message." Accessed September 10, 2014: http://www.whitehouse.gov/the-press-office/2013/02/12/remarks-president-state-union-address.

Peterson, Thomas C., William M. Connolley, and John Flick. 2008. "The Myth of the 1970s Global Cooling Scientific Consensus," *Bulletin of the American Meteorological Society* (*BAMS*), 89 (9), September. Accessed September 2, 2014: http://journals.ametsoc.org/doi/pdf/10.1175/2008BAMS2370.1.

Pielke, Roger, Jr. 2012. "Hurricanes and Human Choice," *Wall Street Journal,* October 31. Accessed September 10, 2014: http://online.wsj.com/news/articles/SB10001424052970204840504578089413659452702.

Pielke, Roger, Jr. 2014. *The Rightful Place of Science: Disasters and Climate Change*. Consortium for Science, Policy, and Outcomes. Tempe: Arizona State University.

Reagan, Ronald. 1981. "Inaugural Address," January 20. Online by Gerhard Peters and John T. Woolley, "The American Presidency Project." Accessed September 10, 2014: http://www.presidency.ucsb.edu/ws/?pid=43130.

Sarewitz, Daniel, and Roger Pielke. 2000. "Breaking the Global-Warming Gridlock," *The Atlantic,* July 1. Accessed September 2, 2014: http://www.theatlantic.com/magazine/archive/2000/07/breaking-the-global-warming-gridlock/304973/?single_page=true.

Stern Review. The Economics of Climate Change. Accessed September 2, 2014: http://mudancasclimaticas.cptec.inpe.br/~rmclima/pdfs/destaques/sternreview_report_complete.pdf.

U.S. Department of State. 2014. "Fact Sheet 2014 U.S. Climate Action Report." Accessed September 4, 2014: http://www.state.gov/e/oes/rls/rpts/car6/219259.htm.

Weart, Spencer. 2015. "Discovery of Global Warming." Accessed July 1, 2015: http://www.aip.org/history/climate/Govt.htm.

Weeks, Jennifer. 2014. "Climate Change," June 15. *CQ Researcher.* Accessed September 2, 2014: http://0-library.cqpress.com.libra.naz.edu/cqresearcher/.

Death Penalty

At a Glance

Is the death penalty cruel and unusual punishment? Is it a deterrent for future crime? Does the death penalty too often fall on poor and minority offenders? After years of relatively even support for capital punishment between Democrats and Republicans, the two parties have diverged markedly on this issue. A growing majority of Democrats now oppose the death penalty, a shift that has been attributed to concerns that it is applied disproportionately to minorities and the poor, to reports of innocent people being released from death row, and to botched execution procedures. Republicans, on the other hand, remain generally supportive of the death penalty, whether as a deterrent to serious crimes or as morally justified punishment.

Many Republicans . . .

- Believe that the death penalty is not cruel and unusual.
- Believe that some crimes that are inhumane and barbaric justify the use of the death penalty.
- Believe that the death penalty is a deterrent for future crimes.
- Worked to reinstate the death penalty when it was removed by federal and state judges.

Many Democrats . . .

- Believe that the death penalty is a barbaric practice that should be banned under the Eighth Amendment's prohibition of cruel and unusual punishment.
- Believe that capital punishment is disproportionately applied to the poor and minorities.

Overview

The death penalty is a punishment given to certain individuals convicted of selected federal or state crimes. Procedures for administering the death penalty have changed from the days when hanging was a common form of execution until today when the most common practice is the lethal injection. Lethal injections consist of a concoction of drugs in combinations that include an anesthetic, a paralytic, and a drug to stop the heart.

For much of the nation's history, the death penalty was a relatively uncontroversial form of punishment for crimes deemed by American society to be particularly heinous, such as murder and treason. Relative unanimity among Democrats and Republicans changed modestly in the mid-1950 when a series of exposés on people sent to the gas chamber were published and made people ponder this ghastly form of execution. Gaps between liberals and conservatives on this issue widened after the execution of Julius and Ethel Rosenberg. The couple sentenced to death after being convicted of treason against the United States for passing on atomic secrets to the Russians in 1953.

Opponents of the death penalty have been able to make a case against the practice by using the human face of those convicted and questioning the proportionality of the sentence (Prejean 1994). In the late 1950s, a handful of states passed laws ending the death penalty, including Alaska, Hawaii, and Delaware. Those who opposed the death penalty found support in the Supreme Court, which, beginning with the case of *Furman v. Georgia* (1972), began to place constitutional restraints on the use of the death penalty. In *Furman* the Court found that the application of the penalty was in that particular case unconstitutional because it was arbitrary and suggestive of an institutional bias against minorities—particularly black defendants. In the wake of this decision, state and national lawmakers scrambled to pass new statutes that would ensure that their capital punishment laws were not discriminatory, thus allowing capital punishment to continue.

Since the Court had not held that the application of the death penalty was in and of itself "cruel and unusual," opponents of capital punishment worked to eliminate the practice for certain crimes and its application to certain persons whose mental capacity made it impossible for them to be fully responsible for their actions. In *Coker v. Georgia* (1977), the Court banned its use in rape cases; in *Ford v. Wainwright* (1986), the Court banned the execution of insane prisoners; and in *Atkins v. Virginia* (2002), the Court forbade the execution of offenders with intellectual disabilities (although it left it up to the states to define intellectual disability). In a controversial move, the Court banned the application of capital punishment for those under the age of 18 in the 2005 case of *Roper v. Simmons* (Latzler 2010).

From the mid-1970s to the 1990s attempts to end the death penalty were stalled by public opinion, which favored strict sentencing and harsh penalties for criminals. After the Supreme Court struck down the death penalty, 35 states seeking to restore the practice rewrote their laws to conform to Court mandates about its application. In 1976, the Court reaffirmed the constitutionality of capital punishment in *Gregg v. Georgia* (Kronenwetter 1993).

The debate over capital punishment intensified in the 1990s, as critics gathered evidence using the new forensic technique of DNA analysis to show that some individuals had been wrongfully convicted and put on death row. Concerns over wrongful convictions led Illinois Governor George Ryan, a Republican, to declare a moratorium on the state's use of the death penalty in 2000. A statistical study subsequently published in the *Proceedings of the National Academy of Sciences* suggested that at least 4.1 percent of death-penalty convicts may have been falsely accused (Johnson 2014).

As a result of these developments, support for the death penalty has undergone considerable attrition. In the 1990s, about four out of five Americans polled were in favor of the death penalty, but an ABC News–*Washington Post* poll issued in June 2014 found that that number had dropped to 43 percent (Ergun 2014). Significantly, however, polls suggest that most of this decline in support for the death penalty is due to erosion among Democrats; Republican support has declined much more modestly.

By 2014, 18 states had banned capital punishment and in the 32 states where it was allowed, it is seldom used. The 39 executions carried out in 2014 occurred in the nine states with a majority of Republican voters.

Republicans on the Death Penalty

The Republican Party has a long history of championing the rights of victims of crime and calling for harsher punishments for criminals. Their "tough on crime" stance has been seen by scholars as a critical factor in their success in winning national elections in the 1980s and 1990s. The Republican Party platform officially endorses the death penalty.

Beginning with the administration of Richard Nixon (1969–1974), the Republican Party has consistently advocated for stronger criminal sentencing. In March 1973, President Nixon made a "State of the Union on Law Enforcement and Drug Abuse Prevention," and told the public he would ask Congress to modernize the law (Banner 2003). He made it perfectly clear that "when I say 'modernize,' I do not mean to be soft on crime; I mean exactly the opposite" (Nixon 1973). In response to the Supreme Court's 1972 ruling that certain applications of the death penalty violated the Eighth Amendment's protection against cruel and unusual punishment, Nixon called for new statutes to restore the federal death penalty. He cited his belief that it acts as a deterrent in specific crimes: "The potential criminal will know that if his intended victims die, he may also die," Nixon declared (Nixon 1973).

Nixon was unable to get the Democrats in Congress to restore the federal death penalty but the GOP advocated for its return in their 1980, 1984, and 1988 party platforms. Ten days after Republican candidate George H. W. Bush defeated anti–death penalty Democrat Michael Dukakis in the 1988 presidential election, Republicans in Congress mustered the necessary votes to restore the death penalty in the

Anti-Drug Abuse Act of 1988. Democrats in many parts of the country subsequently became reluctant to make the death penalty a campaign issue, either because they themselves supported capital punishment, or because of concerns that opposition would leave them vulnerable to "soft on crime" attacks from political opponents. During the presidency of George W. Bush, the GOP remained largely unified in their support for capital punishment. The party's official 2004 platform, for instance, stated that "the Republican Party and President Bush support a federal Constitutional amendment for victims of violent crime that would provide specific rights for victims protected under the U.S. Constitution. We support courts having the option to impose the death penalty in capital murder cases" (Republican Party 2004).

Republican governors are more likely than Democratic governors to support the death penalty, and their stances are strongly supported by rank-and-file Republicans. In 2015, a Pew Research Center poll found that 77 percent of Republicans favor the death penalty (Pew Research Center 2015). Not surprisingly, then, the death penalty is more frequently used in Southern states with conservative Republican governors and legislatures. Governors in these states are resistant to clemency or commutation of the death sentence. For example, in 1998 the first woman since the Civil War was executed in Texas. Karla Faye Tucker's execution in Texas made national headlines, not only because of her gender but also because Tucker converted to Christianity in prison and many believed that she was a different person than the convicted murderer who brutally bludgeoned another person to death. Despite enormous pressure from the left, and even from some conservative Christian groups, then Governor George W. Bush refused to grant clemency.

After it took 40 minutes to perform an execution using lethal injection in Oklahoma in April 2014, the death penalty once again became a focal point of public debate. Oklahoma's Republican Governor Mary Fallin, however, unapologetically defended the practice in a series of public statements and press interviews. Fallin argued that the death penalty was meted out fairly to the prisoner, Clayton Lockett: "Lockett had his day in court. The state lawfully carried out a sentence of death. Justice was served," she told the *New York Times*.

Republican governors have also worked to reinstate the death penalty in cases where it has been ended. Such was the case in New York state, which abolished the death penalty in 1977. In 1995, George Pataki, New York's first elected Republican governor since Nelson Rockefeller, reinstated the death penalty in his first year in office in 1995 (Palmer 2013).

Not all Republicans favor the death penalty, however. In 2000, George Ryan, the Republican governor of Illinois, troubled by reports that DNA evidence was showing that a number of people convicted of capital crimes were actually innocent, imposed a moratorium on the death penalty in that state, and then just before leaving office in 2003 commuted the death sentences of 157 people on death row across the state. Other conservatives and Republicans have come to question the expense (in terms of litigation) and efficacy of the death penalty. In 2013, for example, a group of conservatives in Montana began urging the repeal of the death penalty in

Governor Mary Fallin Defends the Execution of Clayton Lockett

Mary Fallin (1954–) is the first female governor in the history of Oklahoma. A 1977 graduate of Oklahoma State University, Fallin is a Republican who first ran for state office in 1990. She served in the state legislature from 1990–1994 and was then elected lieutenant governor, a position she held until 2006. She served in the U.S. House of Representatives for two terms, 2007–2011, before running and winning the gubernatorial race in 2010.

In April 2014, Fallin came under the glare of the national media spotlight after the execution of an Oklahoma inmate named Clayton Lockett, who had been sentenced to death by lethal injection for his crimes, went awry. His execution turned into a prolonged ordeal of more than 40 minutes, during which time Lockett was in evident pain. But when opponents of the death penalty decried the incident as a grim example of the barbaric nature of capital punishment, Fallin responded with the following blog post:

> Last week, the state of Oklahoma conducted the lawful execution of Clayton Lockett, a man who was convicted of first degree burglary, assault with a dangerous weapon, kidnapping, robbery by force and fear, forcible oral sodomy, rape and first degree murder. A timeline released by the Department of Corrections shows what witnesses to the execution knew immediately: the process of death by lethal injection took too long. To avoid a repeat of last week's prolonged execution, I have asked Department of Public Safety Commissioner Michael Thompson to conduct a thorough review of the events leading up to Lockett's death. I have also asked the commissioner to develop a set of updated and improved execution protocols, and Department of Corrections Director Robert Patton to implement those protocols. While that process is taking place, the state of Oklahoma will delay its upcoming executions. It is obvious that Lockett's death has reignited a national debate over the death penalty. Some anti-death penalty advocates have even gone so far as to say that all Oklahomans have blood on their hands . . . The people of Oklahoma do not have blood on their hands. They saw Clayton Lockett for what he was: evil. His execution means he will never again harm or terrorize another person.

Source
Fallin, Mary. 2014. "In Death Penalty Debate, Remember the Victims," May 5. Accessed September 1, 2015: http://www.ok.gov/triton/modules/newsroom/newsroom_article.php?id=223&article_id=14158.

that state. Their organization, Conservatives Concerned about the Death Penalty, seeks to align the death penalty with small government conservative values.

Democrats on the Death Penalty

In the 1990s, Democratic candidates were largely supportive of capital punishment. In some cases, this stance may have reflected genuine convictions about the death penalty's legitimate role as a deterrent or instrument of justice. Others, however, were worried that they would be labeled "soft on crime" or even pro-criminal if they expressed opposition to the death penalty. They had good reason to be concerned, for, in the 1980s, the Republican Party had successfully targeted many leading Democrats as too liberal on crime. The GOP's greatest success came in 1988, when Michael Dukakis, a Democratic governor from Massachusetts who opposed the death penalty, became his party's presidential nominee. In a series of ads, Dukakis's stance on crime was compared to that of the Republican candidate George H. W. Bush. One specific ad, controversial for its racial overtones, depicted Dukakis as having signed off on a state law that allowed an African American convicted killer named Willie Horton to have a weekend furlough away from prison. Horton left prison only to kidnap a couple, kill the man, and then violate and torture the woman. Dukakis was subsequently asked during a presidential debate with Bush whether he would continue to oppose the death penalty if his own wife were raped and murdered. Dukakis responded that "I don't see any evidence that it's a deterrent and I think there are better and more effective ways to deal with violent crime." Political pundits thought that this unemotional response further hurt

Oklahoma City bombing suspect Timothy McVeigh is escorted by law enforcement officials from the Noble County Courthouse in Perry, Oklahoma, on April 21, 1995. The April 19 bombing of the Alfred P. Murray Federal Building claimed the lives of 168 people. McVeigh, who was found guilty in the Oklahoma City bombing trial, received the death penalty from the jury in Denver, Colorado, on Friday, June 13, 1997. (AP Photo/David Longstreath, File)

Dukakis with voters. When Dukakis lost decisively to Bush in the 1988 election, his "soft on crime" image was cited as one of the factors responsible, and he was the last Democratic presidential contender to oppose the death penalty. Elected Democratic leaders began to toughen up their image by advocating for the death penalty (Ogletree and Sarat 2006).

After Democrat Bill Clinton stepped into the Oval Office in 1993, Democrats in Congress rigorously supported a crime bill that created 60 new federal crimes for which the death penalty could be imposed. By the end of the 1990s offenses for which the federal death penalty might apply included any large-scale drug trafficking, terrorist homicides, the murder of federal law enforcement agents, as well as drive-by shootings and carjackings that resulted in a death. Democrats boasted in their 1996 party platform that "we established the death penalty for nearly 60 violent crimes, including murder of a law enforcement officer, and we signed a law to limit appeals" (Democrat Party 1996). After the Oklahoma City bombing by homegrown terrorist Timothy McVeigh, President Clinton signed into law the Anti-Terrorism and Effective Death Penalty Act of 1996 (Melusky and Pesto 2014).

President Barack Obama, who was elected to office in 2008, has expressed cautious support for the death penalty as well. As he stated in his 2006 book, *The Audacity of Hope*, "While the evidence tells me that the death penalty does little to deter crime, I believe there are some crimes—mass murder, the rape and murder of a child—so heinous, so beyond the pale, that the community is justified in expressing the full measure of its outrage by meting out the ultimate punishment" (Obama 2008).

As fears about crime diminished and as public opinion swung against the use of the death penalty, however, the Democratic Party has become was more measured in its support for this punishment (Bedau and Cassell 2005). Their 2012 platform cautioned that the death penalty "must not be arbitrary. DNA testing should be used in all appropriate circumstances," and "defendants should have effective assistance of counsel" (Democratic Party 2012). And after the botched April 2014 execution in Oklahoma, President Obama called the incident "deeply troubling"

Sister Helen Prejean's Battle against Capital Punishment

A Sister of the Catholic congregation of St. Joseph, Helen Prejean (1939–) is one of the best-known opponents of the death penalty in the United States. She attributes her activism against the death penalty to her theological commitment to her Roman Catholic faith and also to the relationship she developed with Patrick Sonnier, a convicted death row inmate. Her experiences led her to write the national best-seller *Dead Man Walking: An Eyewitness Account of the Death Penalty in the United States* (1993). The book inspired a critically acclaimed film in 1995 of the same name starring Susan Sarandon and Sean Penn. Prejean went on to establish the Ministry against the Death Penalty, a nonprofit located in New Orleans.

and asked the attorney general to analyze problems surrounding the application of the death penalty in the United States. The Justice Department then issued a statement, reported by the Associated Press, that it had begun reviewing the execution protocol used by the federal Bureau of Prisons and would expand that review to include "a survey of state-level protocols and related policy issues."

Meanwhile, a new generation of Democratic politicians have expressed opposition to the death penalty. This comes at a time when Democratic rank-and-file support for capital punishment has fallen dramatically. A 2015 poll conducted by the Pew Research Center, for example, found that Democratic support for the death penalty fell by more than 30 points from 1996 to 2015, from 71 percent to 40 percent (Pew Research Center 2015). This sea change has had a measurable real-world impact. Democratic administrations have successfully ended the death penalty in 2011 in Illinois, 2012 in Connecticut, and in 2013 in Maryland.

Further Reading

Banner, Stuart. 2003. *The Death Penalty: An American History.* Cambridge: Harvard University Press.

Bedau, Hugo Adam, and Paul Cassell, eds. 2005. *Debating the Death Penalty: Should America Have Capital Punishment? The Experts on Both Sides Make Their Case.* New York: Oxford University Press.

Democratic Party. 1996. "Democratic Party Platform of 1996," August 26. Online by Gerhard Peters and John T. Woolley, "The American Presidency Project." Accessed September 29, 2014: http://www.presidency.ucsb.edu/ws/?pid=29611.

Democratic Party. 2012. "2012 Democratic Party Platform," September 3. Online by Gerhard Peters and John T. Woolley, "The American Presidency Project." Accessed September 29, 2014: http://www.presidency.ucsb.edu/ws/?pid=101962.

Ergun, Damla. 2014. "New Low Preference for the Death Penalty," ABC News. Accessed September 29, 2014: http://abcnews.go.com/blogs/politics/2014/06/new-low-in-preference-for-the-death-penalty/.

Johnson, Michelle. 2014. "Death Penalty." *CQ Researcher,* May 13. Accessed September 29, 2014: http://0-library.cqpress.com.libra.naz.edu/cqresearcher/cqr_ht_death_penalty_2014.

Kronenwetter, Michael John. 1993. *Capital Punishment: A Reference Handbook.* In *Contemporary World Issues* series. Santa Barbara: ABC-CLIO.

Latzler, Barry. 2010. *Death Penalty Cases: Leading U.S. Supreme Court Cases on Capital Punishment,* 3rd edition. Burlington, MA: Butterworth-Heinemann.

Melusky, Joseph, and Keith Alan Pesto. 2014. *The Death Penalty: Documents Decoded.* Santa Barbara: ABC-CLIO.

Nixon, Richard. 1973. "Radio Address about the State of the Union Message on Law Enforcement and Drug Abuse Prevention," March 10. Online by Gerhard Peters and John T. Woolley, "The American Presidency Project." Accessed September 29, 2014: http://www.presidency.ucsb.edu/ws/?pid=4135.

Obama, Barack. 2008. *The Audacity of Hope: Thoughts on Reclaiming America's Dream.* New York: Vintage.

Ogletree, Charles, and Austin Sarat, eds. 2006. *From Lynch Mobs to the Killing State: Race and the Death Penalty in America.* In *The Charles Hamilton Houston Institute Series on Race and Justice.* New York: NYU Press.

Palmer, Louis. 2013. *The Death Penalty in the United States: A Complete Guide to Federal and State Laws,* 2nd edition. Jefferson, NC: McFarland.

Pew Research Center. 2015. "Less Support for Death Penalty, Especially Among Democrats." Pew Research Center online, April 16. Accessed June 1, 2015: http://www.people-press.org/2015/04/16/less-support-for-death-penalty-especially-among-democrats/.

Prejean, Helen. 1994. *Dead Man Walking: The Eyewitness Account of the Death Penalty That Sparked a National Debate.* New York: Vintage.

Republican Party. 2004. Republican Party Platform 2004. Accessed September 15, 2014: http://www.ontheissues.org/celeb/Republican_Party_Crime.htm.

Disability Rights

At a Glance

Democrats and Republicans agree that Americans with disabilities should be provided with equal opportunities to participate in U.S. society. They disagree in three critical ways in which such policy should be enacted. They cannot agree on what equal opportunity means, they disagree on how much of the cost of providing such opportunities should be paid for by private funds or taxpayer dollars, and they disagree on whether the United States should embrace the UN Convention on the Rights of Persons with Disabilities.

Many Democrats . . .

- Support legislation to guarantee the inclusion of all Americans in everyday life.
- Approve of the Americans with Disabilities Act (ADA).
- Supported the amendments to the ADA.
- Approve of the Individuals with Disabilities Education Act (IDEA).
- Would like to see more federal funding for IDEA.
- Support ratification of the UN Convention on the Rights of Persons with Disabilities.

Many Republicans . . .

- Support the inclusion of all Americans in all aspects of American society.
- Support legislation that will assist people in becoming independent and economically self-sufficient.
- Oppose unfunded mandates.
- Oppose laws that disempower state laws.
- Express reservations about the economic and legal costs imposed on business and local government by the ADA.
- Oppose ratification of the UN Convention on the Rights of Persons with Disabilities.

Overview

Following on the heels of the civil rights struggle waged by minorities and women in the 1960s, advocates for disability rights began urging the U.S. government to adopt laws to protect individuals who were disabled. For many years, disabled Americans felt marginalized in U.S. society. They faced a wide array of discriminatory barriers when they sought employment, wanted to use public accommodations, or looked to rent houses and apartments. Since the 1970s, Republicans have been more likely to champion the rights of employers, business owners, and local governments who express concern that overly broad disability legislation may lead to "excessive" economic and legal burdens. Democrats have been less sympathetic to these claims and have been more likely to pursue disability rights legislation. As with many social issues, however, there is crossover from both parties on this subject.

In the 1970s, attempts to pass new legislation to protect the disabled was initially thwarted by President Richard Nixon, who served from 1969 to 1974. Nixon twice vetoed legislation designed to buttress the rights of disabled people, explaining that the proposed laws would be too costly for businesses. In his veto message, Nixon said "supporters would have the American public believe that each of these bills would further an important social cause, but they neglect to warn the public that the cumulative effect of a Congressional spending spree would be a massive assault upon the pocketbooks of millions of men and women in this country" (Nixon 1973). A few months later, though, compromise between President Nixon and congressional Democrats led to the Rehabilitation Act of 1973. This legislation contained nondiscrimination language in sections 501 and 503, barring employment discrimination and requiring affirmative action programs for any entity doing business with the federal government. Section 504 covered all aspects of discrimination with language drawn from the Civil Rights Act of 1964, but these provisions were never fully enacted. In 1975, advocates for disabled children persuaded Congress to enact what is now known as IDEA, which mandated that all children, regardless of ability, were entitled to a free public education (Fleischer and Zames 2011).

In the late 1970s, Democratic President Jimmy Carter created the National Council on Disability (NCD). NCD became an independent agency in 1984 and was charged with reviewing all federal disability programs and policies This agency recommended enactment of the ADA, but this proposal faced stiff opposition from the National Federation of Independent Businesses, the U.S. Chamber of Commerce, the National Restaurant Association, public transportation entities, and conservative Republicans. These opponents claimed that the legislation would lead to new entitlement programs and take a heavy economic toll on businesses and local governments who would incur the costs of meeting the new regulations of any such law. Grassroots advocates for disability rights worked with Senator Tom Harkin (D-Iowa) and Representative Steny Hoyer (D-Md.), however, to skillfully guide the ADA through Congress. And the ADA did enjoy support from many

Jessica Delarosa, center, and her dog Mayim participate in the inaugural Disability Pride Parade in New York City, on July 12, 2015. The parade grand marshal was former U.S. senator Tom Harkin, the Iowa Democrat who 25 years ago sponsored the Americans with Disabilities Act. (AP Photo/Seth Wenig)

Republicans, including conservatives who touted the bill as a means of moving people from welfare to employment.

The signing of the ADA marked a new era for people with disabilities in the United States. Advocates were heartened by the law's broad definition of disability as "a physical or mental impairment that substantially limits a major life activity." It prohibited discrimination against the disabled in employment, public services, and public accommodations and required that telecommunications be accessible to those with speech and hearing impairments through the use of special relay systems. The law applied to all public facilities, including office buildings, gas stations, airports, hotels, bars, restaurants, lobbies, sports facilities, libraries, and parks.

Once the ADA became law, however, further debate erupted. Some of this debate stemmed from the law's vague language, including the definition of disability and the requirement that businesses make "reasonable accommodation" unless it caused "undue hardship" on them. Defining these terms became the job of the Supreme Court, which took up a series of cases related to the ADA. The conservative majority on the Court narrowed the definition of disability in cases such as *Sutton v. United Air Lines, Inc.*, 527 U.S. 471 (1999) and *Toyota Motor Manufacturing, Kentucky, Inc. v. Williams*, 534 U.S. 184 (2002).

Disability advocates claimed that the more narrow view of disability espoused by the Supreme Court allowed discrimination against those with disabilities to continue. They sought new legislation to rewrite the law and expand the definition of disability, in effect upending the Court's ruling. After the Republicans lost the House and Senate in the midterm elections of 2006, disability rights groups were in a position to secure passage of the ADA Amendments Act (ADAAA) in 2008. Although Republicans voted for ADAAA, they later unsuccessfully attempted to shield businesses from lawsuits related to the legislation. They wanted to pass a new law requiring that prior to filing lawsuits against businesses, people would be required to notify business owners of the specific incidents of ADA violation including the time and place of such occurrences.

Democrats on Disability Rights Policy

Since the 1960s the Democratic Party has been active in expanding the civil rights for all people. Philosophically, Democrats are committed to removing existing barriers and providing equal opportunity to persons with disabilities by facilitating "access of Americans with disabilities to the middle class, employment opportunities, and the ability to lead full, productive, and satisfying lives" (Democratic Party Platform 2012). In keeping with this practice, liberal Democrats in the legislature have been more likely than their conservative Republican counterparts to champion disability rights legislation.

In the late 1960s, civil rights activists found a sympathetic supporter for their goal of protecting people with disabilities from discriminatory practices in former Democratic vice president and presidential candidate Hubert Humphrey. Beginning in 1972, Humphrey took the lead in moving the Rehabilitation Act of 1973 through Congress. Vetoed twice by Richard Nixon, who thought it too burdensome on businesses, Humphrey rallied Democrats who passed the bill and granted protection from employment discrimination for the disabled. President Jimmy Carter, who served in the White House from 1977 to 1981, created the NCD to monitor federal programs and ensure compliance with the needs of people with disabilities (Berkowitz 1987). In the 1980s, the NCD suggested new legislation, the Americans with Disabilities Act, to broaden the protections for those with physical and mental disabilities from discrimination outside of the workplace (Benfer 2009). The ADA was sponsored and led by Democrats Tom Harkin, a senator from Iowa, and Steny H. Hoyer, a representative from Maryland. The ADA was passed in final form by the House on July 12 and by the Senate on July 13. It was signed into law at a White House ceremony on July 26, 1990. Adam Amdor quoted Harkin's farewell speech in a story for KWWC in Iowa, "Not one nickel or dime in the ADA is given to a person with a disability. But we broke down barriers, opened doors of accessibility and accommodation, and said to people with disabilities—Now go on, follow your dreams, and in the words of the Army motto, 'be all you can be,'" said Harkin.

Some provisions of the ADA were successfully challenged by corporations in federal court, and congressional Democrats were dismayed when the Supreme Court narrowed the definition of disability in two critical cases involving workplace discrimination, *Sutton v. United Airlines* 527 U.S. 471 (1999) and *Toyota Mfg. v. Williams* 534 U.S. 184 (2002). In each of these cases the Court focused on the question of what constituted a major impairment and reasonable accommodation. Following the unanimous Supreme Court decision in the Toyota case, the National Council on Disability (NCD) issued the report "Righting the ADA" and recommended new laws to broaden the definition of disabled. Advocates for the disabled once again worked with Senator Tom Harkin and Representative Steny Hoyer to prepare new legislation. After opposition by the business community and the Department of Justice, Republicans and Democrats crafted compromise legislation that was signed into law on September 25, 2008. The legislation favored the disabled over business interests and required an expansive reading of the term disability and the phrase major life activities. Advocates for disability rights are quick to note that even with current legislation, two out of three individuals with a disability have difficulty finding full-time employment. They have worked with President Barack Obama, who took office in 2009 and who has pledged to help disabled Americans through an affirmative action hiring program. Obama also provided more money for high school programs that assist children with disabilities in preparing for the workplace.

Related to the civil rights for the disabled is another piece of legislation, the IDEA, passed in 1975. The law guaranteed all children access to a free, appropriate, public education in the least restrictive environment. This created the modern classroom in which students of all abilities learn together. Conservative Republicans rejected aspects of the IDEA as being overly burdensome on local school districts and an attack on state's rights. Liberal Democrats appointed to the Supreme Court were critical to rejecting these claims in the case of *Cedar Rapids Comm. Sch. Dist. v. Garret F. and Charlene F.* (5 26 U.S. 66 1999). John Paul Stevens, a Republican appointee who voted with the liberal wing of the Court, sided with those who saw the outcome of educating children with disabilities as a preferred right over the issues of cost or state rights. Despite this victory, elected Democrats have long argued that the federal government has failed to keep its end of the bargain on IDEA, which they claim would be to pick up 40 percent of the cost of ensuring access and education for those with disabilities.

Elected Democrats have also found themselves in disagreement with advocates for the disabled over the issue of physician-assisted suicide. Many Democrats have been active in proposing or supporting legislation to allow death-with-dignity laws. They even included stipulations in the Affordable Care Act to pay physicians who talked to terminally ill or elderly patients about end-of-life decisions. Sarah Palin, the GOP vice presidential candidate in 2008, was often ridiculed by Democrats for decrying these so-called death panels, but her concerns reflected those of some disability rights advocates who saw in the language a move toward euthanasia for the most vulnerable and medically expensive populations, which include those with lifelong disabilities.

Many Democrats have strongly supported ratification of the UN Convention on the Rights of People with Disabilities in the Senate, which is closely modeled on the ADA. But Republicans have been able to block ratification—a stance that has earned the party condemnation from treaty supporters like the *New York Times* Editorial Board: "Contrary to critics, national sovereignty is in no way compromised in the treaty's declaration that all people, regardless of ability, deserve to live in dignity, safety and equality under the law" (*New York Times* Editorial Board 2013).

Other policy debates surrounding disability rights include the rising number of service animals in use by people with emotional or physical disabilities. The use of these animals on public transportation and in restaurants has led some people to suggest restrictions in the name of health and safety. Debates over their potential disruptive role in the classroom and the meaning of reasonable accommodation will no doubt pit liberal Democrats who support the liberal use of service animals in a wide range of circumstances against conservative Republicans who would like more constraints on their use.

Republicans on Disability Rights Policy

Republicans generally believe that the rights of the disabled must be balanced against the economic and legal burdens disability rights legislation adds to the cost of doing business. Philosophically, conservative Republicans are committed to smaller federal government and lower taxes and are therefore leery about adding new entitlement programs and unfunded mandates on the states. Unfunded mandates are federally imposed laws, such as the Americans with Disabilities Act, that require modifications such as architectural changes, or new services, that have to be paid for by local and state governments. Republicans also believe that government regulation inhibits economic enterprise and autonomy, which they see as the hallmarks of American capitalism and society. Therefore, Republicans were natural allies with groups opposed to the ADA because business owners claimed that they would have to spend large amounts of money to comply with the new rules, such as provisions mandating the installation of wheelchair ramps, elevators, and telephone devices for the hearing impaired.

Even though the ADA was opposed by economic and social conservatives and business groups such as the National Federation of Independent Businesses, the U.S. Chamber of Commerce, and the National Restaurant Association, the legislation did receive support from moderate Republicans who helped it gain passage in the summer of 1990. Moreover, the president who signed the ADA into law was George H. W. Bush, a Republican.

Many Republicans who supported the ADA were persuaded to do so by arguments from supporters of the legislation who framed the purpose of the ADA as one of individual responsibility and autonomy. Republicans who endorsed the

ADA in 1990 responded to critics within their party and to outside pressure groups by describing the positive economic effects of adding more talented workers to the labor pool and by noting that the legislation moved people from being dependent on government welfare to independence as taxpayers. President George H. W. Bush elaborated on these ideas and also noted the cost savings of the legislation for all levels of government in his ADA signing statement: "When you add together Federal, State, local, and private funds, it costs almost $200 billion annually to support Americans with disabilities—in effect, to keep them dependent" (Bush 1990). Republican leaders have continued to pursue these goals in more recent years. For example, in 2012 the GOP platform specifically endorsed the movement called Employment First, a national movement developed by disability rights groups to move those with major disabilities from dependence on entitlements to working in jobs in the mainstream of the American workforce (Republican Party Platform 2012).

Once signed into law, advocates and opponents of the new law used the federal courts to remedy what they thought were ambiguities in the law, especially phrases such as "major impairment," "undue burden," and "reasonable accommodation." Business groups and some Republicans were pleased when the Supreme Court narrowed the definition of disability and shielded the states from protracted lawsuits from individuals with disabilities. For example, in the case of *University of Alabama v. Garrett* (2001), the Supreme Court found that the plaintiffs had not brought sufficient evidence of disability discrimination to justify applying the Equal Protection Clause of the Fourteenth Amendment to those with disability, which in many ways limited the scope of the law (Krieger 2003).

The base of the Republican Party contains conservative Christian voters who oppose euthanasia as being immoral. Citing the right to life as fundamental to American liberty, these groups are at the forefront of opposing right-to-die laws and physician-assisted suicides. Thus, Republicans are natural allies with disability rights advocates who are likewise opposed to euthanasia laws. Not Dead Yet is a national organization dedicated to opposing legalization of assisted suicide and euthanasia as deadly forms of discrimination against old, ill, and disabled people. Although a secular organization, their concern about terminating life aligns with similar concerns articulated by evangelicals, Roman Catholic leaders, and conservative Christians, many of whom are Republican. Thus Republicans stated in their 2012 party platform that they "oppose the non-consensual withholding of care or treatment from people with disabilities, including newborns, as well as the elderly and infirm, just as we oppose euthanasia and assisted suicide, which endanger especially those on the margins of society" (Republican Party Platform 2012).

On the issue of global rights for the disabled, there has been division within the GOP. Specifically, there is strong disagreement among party members over whether the United States should ratify the UN Convention on the Rights of Persons with Disabilities (UNCRPD), which is largely modeled on the U.S. ADA. On the one hand, former Republican secretaries of state and GOP presidential candidates Bob

Dole, who ran in 1996, and John McCain, who ran in 2008, have lobbied fellow Republicans in the U.S. Senate to affirm this charter. On the other hand, there are Republicans who fear that the treaty gives UN bureaucrats the power to make decisions about the needs of disabled children that would trump state laws and the rights of parents concerning people with disabilities. Walter Olson of the conservative Cato Institute expounded on this fear in 2013: "The treaty is full of language mandatory on ratifying states, not advisory: the word 'shall' appears more than 150 times over its 50 sections." Olson pointed out that the language of the UNCRPD specifically stipulates that ratifying states must "eliminate discrimination on the basis of disability by any person, organization or private enterprise" (Olson 2013).

Further Reading

Benfer, Emily. 2009. *The ADA Amendments Act: An Overview of Recent Changes to the Americans with Disabilities Act.* Washington D.C.: American Constitution Society for Law and Politics. Accessed July 9, 2015: http://www.law.georgetown.edu/archiveada /documents/benferadaaa.pdf.

Berkowitz, Edward D. 1987. *Disabled Policy: America's Programs for the Handicapped—A Twentieth Century Fund Report.* New York and London: Cambridge University Press.

Bush, George. 1990. "Statement on Signing the Americans with Disabilities Act of 1990," July 26, Online by Gerhard Peters and John T. Woolley, "The American Presidency Project." Accessed June 30, 2015: http://www.presidency.ucsb.edu/ws/?pid=18712.

Democratic Party Platform. 2012. "Democratic Party Platform," September 3, 2012. Online by Gerhard Peters and John T. Woolley, "The American Presidency Project." Accessed June 30, 2014: http://www.presidency.ucsb.edu/ws/?pid=101962.

Fleischer, Doris, and Frieda Zames. 2011. *Disability Rights Movement: From Charity to Confrontation,* 2nd edition. Philadelphia: Temple University Press.

Krieger, Linda Hamilton. 2003. *Backlash against the ADA: Reinterpreting Disability Rights.* Ann Arbor: University of Michigan Press.

New York Times Editorial Board. 2013. "A Second Chance for the World's Disabled," *New York Times,* July 17. Accessed June 30, 2015: http://www.nytimes.com/2013/07/18 /opinion/a-second-chance-for-the-worlds-disabled.html.

Nixon, Richard. 1973. "Veto of the Vocational Rehabilitation Bill," March 27. Online by Gerhard Peters and John T. Woolley, "The American Presidency Project." Accessed June 30, 2105: http://www.presidency.ucsb.edu/ws/?pid=4154.

Olson, Walter. 2013. "U.N. Disabled-Rights Treaty Is Back—And So Are Its Myths," Cato Institute Web site. Accessed June 30, 2015: http://www.cato.org/blog/un-disabled-rights-treaty-back-so-are-its-myths.

Republican Party Platform. 2012. "Republican Party Platform," August 27. Online by Gerhard Peters and John T. Woolley, "The American Presidency Project." Accessed June 26, 2014: http://www.presidency.ucsb.edu/ws/?pid=101961.

Education

At a Glance

Although Democrats and Republicans acknowledge that many schools in the United States operate at a high level, they also believe that the American education system is failing millions of children. They disagree on the reasons for this, however. Many Democrats cite inadequate school funding and social inequities built into the fabric of American society as major contributors to education problems. Republicans are more likely to believe that problems with the education system stem from poor teachers, poor administration, and wasteful spending.

Many Republicans . . .

- Are worried that American education is failing.
- Believe that failures in education are created by the current system of education, which needs closer measurement and assessment.
- Have tried to enhance U.S. education by adopting assessment practices originally created in the business realm.
- Support annual assessments to measure student progress and teacher effectiveness.
- Support closing failing schools.
- Believe parents should have more choice over schools.
- Are more likely to support charter schools and homeschooling.
- Have disparaged Common Core as "Obamacore."
- Are critical of teachers' unions.
- Believe teacher tenure is part of the problem in public education.

Many Democrats . . .

- Are worried that American education is failing.
- Believe that the failure is a reflection of high concentrations of poverty in urban and rural America.
- Have tried to enhance U.S. education through more funding and enhanced teacher training.
- Support equity or parity of funding for all schools across the United States.

- Attribute the disparity of urban and suburban students on standardized tests to structural inequalities embedded in U.S. society.
- Reject the use of annual testing to evaluate learning outcomes.
- Disparage what they call "high stakes" testing to evaluate teachers.
- Have changed their view on the No Child Left Behind Act.
- Support aspects of the Common Core.
- Support teachers' unions.

Overview

As the cost of public education has grown and the measurable competency of student proficiency on standardized tests has diminished, public and political debate over the best method of reforming public education has become a hotly contested issue in the United States. Everyone agrees that public education is critical for a democratic society and most would argue that the first concern should be for the children. Debate remains over how to fund public education, the proper role of the federal government in setting assessment goals such as No Child Left Behind or Common Core, whether school choice enhances educational opportunity for children or merely siphons away necessary resources from public schools, and whether teachers' unions and teacher tenure serves to protect teachers or are detriments to educational reform.

Throughout most of U.S. history, education policy remained firmly in the domain of state and local governments. The Constitution gave the federal government no authority to interfere in this aspect of state power. This changed during the struggle for civil rights. In 1954, the Supreme Court unanimously declared in *Brown v. Board of Education* that states and local schools had no right to allow segregation in public education and this decision established a firm federal presence in protecting the rights of all children. Federal influence in public education was expanded when Democratic President Lyndon Johnson increased federal financing of education in the Elementary and Secondary Education Act (ESEA) of 1965.

In the 1960s and 1970s, political issues surrounding public education most often pivoted about expanding minority access to schools. Federal courts continued the work begun under *Brown v. Board* to desegregate schools by mandating busing or taking other actions to enforce the decree that schools desegregate. The government was also able to force compliance with educational policy by threatening to cut off federal funding for schools and to sue schools on behalf of a protected class of children. One example of this is Title IX of the Civil Rights Act. This provision explicitly promoted the educational rights of women, stating that "no Person in the U.S shall, on basis of sex be excluded from participation or denied the benefits of, or be subjected to discrimination under any educational program or activity receiving federal aid."

The federal government expanded educational opportunities for differently abled children in 1975, when Congress passed the Education for All Handicapped

Children Act. This law, which required states to developed free educational opportunities for all children, was later renamed the Individuals with Disabilities Education Act (IDEA) in 1990 (it was reauthorized in 1997). In 1988, the federal government reauthorized ESEA and added the Jacob Javits Gifted and Talented Students Education Act, which was passed to support and coordinate grants and other programs for gifted and high-achieving students. Another indication of the increased federal role in education policies and programs was the creation of the cabinet-level Department of Education in 1979 (Urban and Wagoner 2013).

In the 1980s and 1990s, much of the discussion and debate about education in the United States shifted to questions about quality (Gouwens 2009). This shift in focus was prompted in large part by studies suggesting that American students might be falling behind some of their international counterparts in mathematics, science, and other subjects. Bipartisan legislation to rectify this perceived problem was common. Nonetheless, both parties saw each bill as an opportunity to push their own specific goals. Republicans generally wanted to reform education by creating and then assessing national standards. They also wanted to change or end the teacher tenure system so school districts could more easily remove underperforming teachers from the classroom. Democrats generally were in favor of creating voluntary standards for assessment but wanted more funding for schools, especially urban schools, to attract good teachers, address infrastructure problems, and invest in new educational resources and technology.

Education and tenure reform became national issues when the administration of Republican President Ronald Reagan released "A Nation at Risk," a 1983 report by his National Commission on Excellence in Education. The report found that "the educational foundations of our society are presently being eroded by a rising tide of mediocrity that threatens our very future as a Nation and a people." The report led Republicans to call for reforming teacher tenure and strengthening educational standards. To measure these outcomes Republicans wanted to impose standardized tests across the nation so schools and districts could be compared to a national average.

The National Governors Association issued their own report in 1986, "Time for Results," which called for better pay for teachers, assessment of public schools, closing or privatizing schools that failed to meet assessment standards, options for parental choice when schools failed, longer school years, pre-K school readiness programs, and assessment of colleges to see if higher education enhanced student learning after high school (Alexander 1986). Republican George H. W. Bush, who was elected in 1988 for one term, and Democrat Bill Clinton, who served two terms from 1993 to 2001, created commissions to set voluntary standards for excellence in schools. Bush created the National Education Goals Panel to set and assess national standards for public education. President Clinton signed GOALS 2000 Educate America, an act that provided funding to public schools to ensure that students reached their full potential by 2000.

Concern over public education sharpened in the 21st century and led to two significant and controversial attempts to standardize and assess K-12 education: the

No Child Left Behind Act of 2001, which was one of President George W. Bush's highest domestic priorities upon taking office, and the Common Core State Standards initiative, a concerted effort (first championed by the National Governors Association in 2008 with the help of a task force composed of school officials, education experts, and business executives) to establish nationwide baselines for academic achievement at every grade level (Ravitch 2011). As of 2015, 45 states and the District of Columbia had adopted Common Core State Standards.

In addition to these major initiatives, new legal challenges to teacher tenure emerged, new federal and state legislation expanded school choice options for parents through voucher systems and charter schools, and court challenges and legislation expanded state and federal financing of education to make it more fair and equitable.

Republicans on Education Policy

The Republican Party overall has been preaching national standards and assessment since the administration of Ronald Reagan. With the election of George W. Bush to the White House in 2000, GOP reformers were able to enact the most stringent federal education assessment program in U.S. history, with provisions that tied federal funding to test scores. These standards were part of the bipartisan reauthorization of the Elementary and Secondary School Act in 2001, which was renamed the No Child Left Behind (NCLB) Act. Under provisions of NCLB, schools receiving federal funding had to administer an annual statewide standardized test with an emphasis on reading, math, and science. Schools were assessed by Annual Yearly Progress (AYP) standards. Schools that failed to meet these requirements had to provide parents with options for placing their students in other schools. If a school consistently failed to meet national standards they might be closed, turned into charter schools, or taken over by the state or a private enterprise. The legislation was met with skepticism by educators, however, and their criticism was soon echoed by school administrators, parents groups, politicians, and the wider public (Duncan 2012).

When the Obama administration urged adoption of the Common Core standards in 2009, which had been drafted with the overwhelming support of Republican governors, there was little resistance. This changed after the conservative resurgence in the 2010 midterm elections, in which the Democratic Party lost 64 seats in the House of Representatives, 6 seats in the Senate, and control of several state houses. Many attributed the change in power to the influence of the Tea Party, a new coalition of deeply conservative voters within the Republican Party. Tea Party members labeled the Common Core "Obamacore" despite its roots in Bush-era education policies and dismissed it as another example of government overreach. They claimed it was a clear violation of the Constitution, which placed education in the domain of state and local government. "States and local communities better know how to design standards based on their students' and

Teachers' Unions

The National Education Association (NEA) is the largest teachers' union in the United States with over three million members. The NEA has affiliate organizations in both state and local communities. Founded in 1857, the organization merged with the American Teachers Association in 1966. The NEA lobbies elected and government officials on everything from government funding of education to school safety to teacher pay. According to the nonpartisan Center for Responsive Politics the NEA is one of the top 10 political campaign contributors and provides millions in campaign finance to support Democrats and oppose Republicans. While the NEA has been highly critical of No Child Left Behind it has taken a stand in support of the Common Core.

The American Federation of Teachers (AFT) is the second largest teacher's union in the United States and is associated with the powerful union the AFL-CIO. With over 1.6 million members, the AFT lobbies for more funding and safer schools and opposes privatization of public education. According to the nonpartisan Center for Responsive Politics, the AFT is one of a handful of powerful campaign contributors in national and state elections and gives millions to support Democratic candidates. The AFT has been cautiously supportive of Common Core.

parents' needs," argued one conservative contributor to the conservative advocacy group Freedom Works (Clemmitt 2014). Obama administration statements defending Common Core principles further deepened conservative antipathy, and several states led by conservative GOP governors and legislatures moved to withdraw from the Common Core. Indiana was the first state to do so but Oklahoma and South Carolina followed. Objection to the Common Core was nearly universal among potential candidates for the 2016 Republican nomination for president. Not all Republicans oppose the Common Core standards, however; former Florida Governor Jeb Bush, whose brother signed NCLB into law, is a public advocate for Common Core standards.

Republicans have also been outspoken supporters for privatizing education or creating competition through charter schools, an idea first offered by the National Governors Association in 1991. Thus, many Republicans supported President Obama's initiatives that led to a doubling of charter schools since 2008. Senator Lamar Alexander, who was head of the National Governors Association in 1991 and later served as secretary of education in George H. W. Bush's administration, introduced legislation in January 2014 to allow states to use a portion of their federal education funds to provide vouchers to families who could use this to defray all or part of the cost of sending their students to private schools, schools outside of their assigned school district, or charter schools. Alexander's bill never made it to the Senate floor (Rasmussen and Schoen 2010).

Republican lawmakers also frequently characterize teachers' unions and teacher tenure as stumbling blocks to reform (Goldstein 2014). Republican Governor

Scott Walker of Wisconsin pushed for legislation that prohibited public workers, including teachers, from bargaining over anything except wages and ended the practice of automatic dues deduction from workers' paychecks. Wisconsin unions must now hold an annual vote by members who may decide to leave the union. This resulted in a decline of membership in teachers' unions across Wisconsin. Walker's legislation outraged progressives and union leaders, but their efforts to recall Walker and overturn the law in court both failed. Following Wisconsin's lead, Republican lawmakers in Ohio, Tennessee, and Idaho passed laws that cut back bargaining rights for public schoolteachers, although the Ohio law was later struck down through a public referendum.

Teacher tenure is not popular among the general public. Respondents to a nation poll given in 2014 indicated by 2:1 margins that they favored ending tenure. Republican opposition to tenure stems from a belief that this special job protection makes the removal of teachers with tenure time consuming and expensive, leading school districts to retain underperforming teachers. They also believe that tenure serves no significant purpose since federal laws already protect against job discrimination. In states where Democratic legislative majorities make passing laws ending or restricting teacher tenure impractical, conservative groups have challenged teacher tenure laws in court. A group called Students Matter, funded by a wealthy donor, sued California over its teacher tenure laws claiming that they deprived students of the right to a high-quality education guaranteed by that state's constitution. On June 10, 2014, a Superior Court judge in Los Angeles ruled in *Vergara v. California* in favor of the plaintiffs. The case was immediately appealed by Democratic Governor Jerry Brown and teachers' unions. However, emboldened by their success, the group then launched a similar challenge to New York state tenure laws.

Democrats on Education Policy

Barack Obama, who took office in January 2009, called for revision of the NCLB legislation. NCLB had become unpopular with educators, students, and parents and was seen by many Democrats as another failure of the Bush administration. Prior to the 2008 election, a significant number of Democratic senators had called for repeal of NCLB and the majority of Democrats in the Senate agreed that NCLB needed to be reformed (Klein 2007).

Critics of NCLB typically focused on several alleged problems. They charged that the high-stakes testing in select areas such as literacy and mathematics led school districts to neglect other subjects. They also asserted that the standards punished the poorest schools while rewarding high achievers in more wealthy school districts. Some also claimed that the high-stakes testing, mandated by NCLB, hurt student achievement while enhancing the bottom line and political clout of a few corporations involved in creating and marketing the testing material, such as McGraw-Hill, Houghton-Mifflin, and Pearson (Hess 2007).

Obama's Controversial Secretary of Education

Arne Duncan (1964–) has served as the only secretary of education in the administration of President Barack Obama. Duncan graduated from Harvard University in 1987 and went on to play professional basketball in Australia from 1987 until 1991. He then ran the Ariel Foundation, an organization dedicated to finding pathways to college for inner-city children, from 1992 through 1998. The Foundation also created and ran an elementary school that was founded to enhance literacy education. In 2001, Duncan was appointed to run the Chicago public school system, a position he held until 2008. During his tenure in Chicago he was known as a bold reformer, willing to close underperforming schools, encouraging the development of charter schools, and unafraid of high-stakes testing.

He continued his reformist tendencies as secretary of education in the Obama administration, helping launch and publicize the Race to the Top grant-making program and several other initiatives that seek to boost academic achievement, especially in poor and minority communities. "Duncan has injected an unusual amount of federal influence into traditionally local decisions about public education," summarized the *Washington Post.* "The result is that most Americans now accept public charter schools as an alternative to neighborhood schools, most teachers expect to be judged in some measure on how well their students perform on standardized tests, and most states are using more demanding K-12 math and reading standards."

But as the *Post* also noted, Duncan's prescriptions for improving public education have rankled progressives and conservatives alike. "Conservatives say those closest to students—local communities—lost power to decide what's best for them. Liberals complain about an unhealthy focus on math and reading and about overtesting, leading to an 'opt-out' movement that saw hundreds of thousands of students boycott tests this spring." On the Democratic side, teachers are Duncan's fiercest critics, at least partly because of his frequent criticisms of teacher tenure. In 2014, in fact, the National Education Association (NEA), the country's leading teachers' union, issued a formal call for Duncan's resignation.

Sources

Layton, Lindsey. 2015. "Even as Congress Moves to Strip His Power, Arne Duncan Holds His Ground," *Washington Post,* July 8. Accessed September 9, 2015: https://www.washingtonpost.com/local/education/as-congress-moves-to-strip-his-power-duncan-is-staying-until-the-final-buzzer/2015/07/08/cb0c9d28-15d4-11e5-9ddc-e3353542100c_story.html.

Staiti, Chris. 2014. "Teacher Tenure Is a 'Broken Status-Quo,' Secretary Duncan Says," Bloomberg Business, June 6. Accessed September 9, 2015: http://www.bloomberg.com/news/articles/2014-06-16/teacher-tenure-is-a-broken-status-quo-secretary-duncan-says.

Charter schools have also come under attack from progressives. They insist that the "for-profit" companies that run charter schools in states such as Michigan undercut the collective bargaining and tenure rights that are available to teachers in public schools, siphon taxpayer money away from public schools that need every cent that they can get, and in many cases do not deliver promised educational performance results.

After President Obama was unable to gain congressional support for revising NCLB, he implemented his own educational reforms. To remove the onerous burdens of NCLB, the Obama administration offered waivers to states that accepted the new initiatives, one of which was the Race to the Top, a $4 billion grant program meant to encourage states to innovate and reform their curricula (Clemmitt 2014). In some ways the Race to the Top replicated the outlines of NCLB (Spring 2013). To receive the money, states adopted new federal standards that set accountability systems that linked teacher evaluations to student standardized test scores, adopted new standards known as the Common Core, and accepted an expansion of charter schools. These goals retained the emphasis on testing but allowed states to create their own methodologies. While requiring teacher evaluations, the program allowed states to design their own mechanisms to achieve this. Finally, it retained the idea of school choice despite the opposition of teachers and administrators who saw charter schools as either deeply flawed or a threat. In the end, as reported by Valerie Strauss in an April 28, 2013, story in the *Washington Post,* most states signed on for these reforms, although only a dozen states and the District of Columbia ultimately received shares of the grants.

The Common Core was developed by the National Governors Association (NGA). The NGA established a task force to create a common set of learning outcomes for students in grades K-12. In 2009, most Democrats embraced the Common Core, but opposition arose from traditional supporters of the Democratic Party, including teachers' unions and educational scholars. These critics of the Common Core argued that the initiative's reliance on standardized testing to drive school improvement was detrimental to urban and rural school districts where low-achieving schools and disadvantaged students lacked the necessary resources to realize high scores. Indeed, the reforms have not addressed the question of equity, which is a central tenet of the Democratic Party view of education. Middle and upper income students do consistently better on standardized tests than lower income students, which most Democrats attribute to disparities in the social and economic systems between urban and suburban schools. Another complaint against the common core is that linking teacher and principal evaluations to standardized tests was neither reliable nor valid as teachers in some districts were evaluated for students they never had or subjects they never taught.

Progressive Democrats have also criticized the Obama administration's support for charter schools, some of which have been run by for-profit management companies. Teachers' unions and others have complained that charter schools siphon away scarce resources from public schools, which are already struggling. Opposition to charter schools is not uncommon among Democrats but the harshest criticism for the Obama administration came from the progressive wing of the party. For example, New York City major Bill de Blasio, a national figure in advocating for issues important to the progressive wing of the Democratic Party, complained

Fifth-graders in an English language arts class at Silver Lake Elementary School in Middletown, Delaware, on October 1, 2013. Silver Lake had just began implementing the national Common Core State Standards, one of the most politicized and misunderstood changes in education, for students and their teachers in grades kindergarten through high school. (AP Photo/Steve Ruark)

during his mayoral campaign that money vital to the poorest schools was being diverted to charter schools. He also noted that charter schools often undercut teacher tenure and collective bargaining rights, which they say are important in attracting and keeping good teachers.

Overall, Democrats have strong ties to teachers' unions and widely support teacher tenure laws. They argue that such laws protect teachers from being fired for personal or political reasons. They also reason that absent such laws, good, veteran teachers with higher salaries would be vulnerable to replacement by inexperienced teachers who could be paid lower salaries. The victims of such scenarios, they say, would not only include dedicated teachers, but also the schoolchildren who would be deprived of instruction from veteran teachers. Although tenure has become unpopular nationwide, California's two largest teachers' unions, the California Teachers Association and the California Federation of Teachers, filed a brief along with the California Attorney General to defend teacher tenure laws in that state. After losing the case, *Vergara v. California,* the groups filed an appeal (Clemmitt 2014).

The Democratic Party has led the way in urging money for the development of high quality preschool and prekindergarten education ever since Lyndon Johnson sponsored the first legislation creating the Head Start program in 1965. To meet the challenges faced by underfunded urban and rural school districts, the Obama administration increased spending for Teach for America, a program that sends college graduates to assist failing urban schools. The president also created a new initiative to provide health, safety, and support services to high-poverty neighborhoods through schools. To assist children in underfunded school districts, Obama has proposed expanding access to preschool and upgrading the digital infrastructure in K-12 schools and libraries. Under Obama's preschool plan, states and the federal government would share the cost of subsidizing preschool attendance for low- and moderate-income families and expanding local preschool capacities to give all children the opportunity to enroll, but preschool would not be mandatory. Obama also proposed a competitive grant program for communities to expand high-quality child care for children from birth to age three. Obama proposed spending $75 billion over 10 years for the program (Klein 2014). The idea of expanding preschool has supporters in both parties and bipartisan legislation has been introduced in Congress that echoes Obama's plan.

Further Reading

Alexander, Lamar. 1986. "Time for Results: An Overview," *The Phi Delta Kappan*, November, 68 (3): 202–204.

Clemmitt, Marcia. 2014. "Education," *CQ Researcher*, June 19. Accessed August 10, 2014: http://0-library.cqpress.com.libra.naz.edu/cqresearcher/cqr_ht_education_2014.

Duncan, Arne. 2012. "After 10 Years, It's Time for a New NCLB," Homeroom the official blog of the Department of Education. Accessed August 10, 2014: http://www.ed.gov/blog/2012/01/after-10-years-it%E2%80%99s-time-for-a-new-nclb/.

Goldstein, Dana. 2014. *The Teacher Wars: A History of America's Most Embattled Profession*. New York: Doubleday.

Gouwens, Judith A. 2009. *Education in Crisis: A Reference Handbook*. Santa Barbara: ABC-CLIO.

Hess, Frederick. 2007. *No Remedy Left Behind: Lessons from a Half-Decade of NCLB*. Washington, D.C.: American Enterprise Institute.

Klein, Alyson. 2007. "Critics of NCLB Ask Congress to Overhaul It," *Education Week*, February 23.

Klein, Alyson. 2014. "Advocates Cheer White House Spending on Early-Ed.," *Education Week*, December 22, 2014. Accessed February 7, 2016: http://www.edweek.org/ew/articles/2014/12/22/advocates-cheer-white-house-spending-on-early-ed.html?qs=obama+and+preschool.

A Nation At Risk: The Imperative for Educational Reform. 1983. Accessed August 11, 2014: http://www2.ed.gov/pubs/NatAtRisk/index.html.

Rasmussen, Scott, and Douglas Schoen. 2010. *Mad as Hell: How the Tea Party Movement Is Fundamentally Remaking Our Two-Party System*. New York: Harper Collins.

Ravitch, Diana. 2011. *The Death and Life of the Great American School System: How Testing and Choice Are Undermining Education*. New York: Basic Books.

Spring, Joel. 2013. *Political Agendas for Education: From Race to the Top to Saving the Planet*. New York: Routledge.

Urban, Wayne, and Jennings L. Wagoner. 2013. *American Education: A History*. New York: Routledge.

Entitlement Programs

At a Glance

Democrats and Republicans have each pledged to end or alleviate poverty but through different means. Democrats advocate redistribution of resources to the poor through government sponsored entitlement programs. Republicans advocate tax incentives for companies or charities that hire or assist the poor and needy. Republicans reject government solutions to poverty and have claimed that entitlement programs create a dependency on the government that diminish an individual's ability to care for him- or herself. Democrats have claimed that the Republican position shows a lack of care or sympathy with those in need.

Many Democrats . . .

- Feel that entitlement programs are necessary to support vulnerable populations of citizens.
- Oppose attempts to reduce benefits and services available through these programs.
- Support Franklin Roosevelt's assertion that Americans are entitled to economic security.
- Defend the Medicare and Medicaid programs passed by a Democratic Congress and Lyndon Johnson in the 1960s.
- Support the Earned Income Tax Credit, which was designed to lower the tax burden of the working poor.
- Supported Barack Obama's contention that health security was a basic right in passing the Affordable Care Act.

Many Republicans . . .

- Fear that entitlement programs make people excessively dependent on government.
- Believe that welfare has contributed to the destruction of the nuclear family.
- Support making states rather than the federal government primarily responsible for entitlement programs.
- Have tried to cut or check the growth of most entitlement programs.

———————

Overview

Entitlement programs, sometimes known as social welfare, come in the form of government assistance aimed at targeted groups such as the poor, elderly, disabled, and other vulnerable populations. These programs include Social Security, Medicare, Medicaid, Unemployment Insurance, Temporary Assistance for Needy Families (TANF; formerly known as Aid to Families with Dependent Children or AFDC), the Supplemental Nutrition Assistance Program (SNAP; better known as food stamps), and special supplemental assistance programs such as Women, Infants, and Children (WIC), and the National School Lunch program.

American citizens qualify for these programs if they meet certain criteria such as income, ability to work, age, and household size. Entitlement programs account for the largest expenditures in the federal budget. By law these programs fall under mandatory spending, meaning that the government is obligated to fulfill these obligations first. Discretionary spending is not mandated by law and includes funding for defense, education, highways, research grants, and all government operations.

Entitlement programs are a key fault line dividing Republicans and Democrats. Many Democrats believe that the government is obligated to provide social welfare programs that help the needy, and they oppose many GOP efforts to reduce funding for them. They suggest that Republicans turn their backs on the poor and needy even as they support "corporate welfare"—government bailouts and tax breaks for large corporations. Many Republicans, on the other hand, fear that entitlement programs disempower the individual and create a permanent underclass that becomes dependent on the government to care for them from the cradle to the grave. They also assert that heavy spending on entitlement programs threatens the economic health and stability of the country. Some have even suggested that Democratic social welfare policies are aimed at fostering dependency on government programs in order to ensure that recipients vote for their party at election time.

Prior to Franklin Roosevelt's "New Deal"—the array of social and economic programs established by Roosevelt during his presidency to combat the Great Depression—there were no federal entitlement programs (Berkowitz 1991). This was due in part to a culture that traditionally linked poverty to personal shortcomings, from lack of talent or intelligence to laziness and greed. Furthermore, it was widely held that the Constitution placed the responsibility for welfare squarely on the states, and that welfare programs violated the substantial due process doctrine and eroded basic liberties. These views underwent considerable reassessment during the Great Depression, however, when the country experienced record levels of unemployment and poverty (Coll 1995). In 1937, the Supreme Court surprised conservatives when it made a series of 5–4 decisions that upheld Roosevelt's Social Security Act. The Court abandoned the substantive due process ideal and embraced the general welfare doctrine asserted by Roosevelt (Lopez 1987). In the decades that followed the New Deal, battles over the size and scope of America's entitlement programs have been fought time and again by Republicans and Democrats in Congress, the White House, and on the Supreme Court.

Once established, entitlement programs have tended to become more generous over time. One example is the Social Security program enacted in 1935 to provide benefits to retired workers. Four years later, benefits were extended to their dependents and survivors. Later the program expanded to cover the disabled, the self-employed, and farmers. In the 1960s, legislation creating Medicare and Medicaid was signed into law by President Lyndon B. Johnson after passage by a Democrat-controlled Congress. Eligibility for Medicaid assistance was initially limited to those on public assistance but gradually was expanded to include other "poverty-related" groups such as pregnant women. For families whose income was too high to qualify for Medicaid, the government in 1997 created the Children's Health Insurance Program (CHIP), which has been subsequently renewed and expanded, most recently in 2015, with President Obama's signing of the Medicare Access and CHIP Reauthorization Act.

Since the 1960s, many Democrats have tried to enhance the benefit and expand the number of people eligible for social welfare programs. Republicans have sought to cut those programs or limit benefits and eligibility. The GOP efforts were most effective under President Ronald Reagan (1981–1989) and after they took control of Congress in the 1994 elections. Republicans led by House Speaker Newt Gingrich stopped the expansion of health care under President Bill Clinton (1993–2001) and shaped a major welfare reform act called the Personal Responsibility and Work Opportunity Reconciliation Act of 1996. Clinton has regularly touted that legislation as one of his administration's most significant accomplishments.

In 2006, for example, Clinton emphasized that, since the act's passage a decade earlier, welfare rolls had declined from 12.2 million in 1996 to 4.5 million. "At the time," he recalled in an Op-Ed for the *New York Times*, "I was widely criticized by liberals who thought the work requirements too harsh and conservatives who thought the work incentives too generous . . . Thankfully, a majority of both Democrats and Republicans voted for the bill because they thought we shouldn't be satisfied with a system that had led to intergenerational dependency. The last 10 years have shown that we did in fact end welfare as we knew it, creating a new beginning for millions of Americans" (Clinton 2006).

GOP efforts to push through major spending cuts on entitlement programs have been unsuccessful during the Obama years. In fact, Obama and Democratic colleagues created a major new entitlement program when they shepherded the Affordable Care Act into law in 2010.

There have been a few exceptions to the general trend. Republican President Richard Nixon (1969–1974) was not opposed to creating national health care and President George W. Bush (2001–2009) expanded Medicare to include prescription drugs. Democratic President Bill Clinton embraced welfare reform on the campaign trail in 1992 and signed legislation that included significant new welfare restrictions in 1996.

Democrats on Entitlement Programs

Democrats have been largely concerned about the needs of the economically marginalized since Franklin Roosevelt called for a new social contract for Americans in order to combat the ravages of the Depression (Roosevelt 1932). His New Deal proposals for supporting the aged, infirmed, and indigent led to Social Security, Unemployment Insurance, and other programs to assist families in hard economic times. Whether these were to be temporary or permanent programs was settled by Democratic President Harry Truman (1945–1953) who kept and then attempted to expand these programs in his so-called Fair Deal. Truman even called for a national health insurance program during his time in the White House, though his efforts in that regard were thwarted by Republicans (McCullough 1993).

During the 1960s, President Lyndon Johnson "declared all-out war on human poverty and unemployment" in America and exhorted Congress to pass legislation that "recognized the health needs of all our older citizens" (Johnson 1964). Aided by Democratic majorities in Congress, Johnson expanded welfare programs and increased benefits as part of his vision for a "Great Society." Some of these included new ways to support the needy such as the Food Stamp program, which has first been piloted by Roosevelt during the Great Depression and then again under President John F. Kennedy, who served from 1961 to 1963 (Short History of SNAP). President Johnson expanded Social Security by including new provisions creating health care programs for the elderly (Medicare) and the poor (Medicaid) in 1965. Acknowledging the efforts of former Democratic presidents in expanding health care coverage for vulnerable Americans, Johnson asked former president Harry Truman to the signing ceremony (Milkis and Mileuer 2005).

Concerns that welfare programs were contributing to a culture of dependency detrimental to the black family surfaced in a controversial 1965 report written by Johnson administration official, and later Democratic senator, Daniel Patrick Moynihan (Katz 2013). In 1971, Congress, with the support of President Nixon, mandated new work requirements for parents with children over the age of 6 on AFDC. To soften this action, legislation in 1975 provided additional funds for the working poor in the earned income tax credit, which redistributes taxpayer money from the wealthier to those near the poverty line (Moynihan Report 1965). Congress also passed the WIC program in 1972 to provide nutritional supplements to pregnant and new mothers and their children. In addition, Unemployment Insurance was expanded from the initial 16 weeks to 26 weeks by the 1970s.

As welfare programs expanded in size and scope, however, so too did public hostility to these programs. Conservatives increasingly expressed frustration that these programs were gradually shifting from temporary or supplemental support to permanent care. These sentiments were further exacerbated by a sluggish economy in the mid- to late 1970s, and by the Reagan administration's declarations of opposition to welfare "handouts." During this time, the stigma of receiving public assistance intensified considerably, though entitlement programs like Medicare and Social Security aimed at caring for older Americans were spared from most of this criticism (Hays 2004).

Responding to the climate of hostility regarding welfare entitlements, Bill Clinton, the Democratic candidate for president in 1992, promised that if elected he would "end welfare as we know it." As president he signed, with Republican support, the Personal Responsibility and Work Opportunity Reconciliation Act of 1996. This law replaced the Aid to Families with Dependent Children program, which had an open-ended cash benefit guaranteed to single mothers, with TANF, which carries a five-year maximum, except in hardship cases defined by states. The welfare law's work requirements include the provision that 50 percent of families receiving benefits be working or enrolled in workforce programs sounded tougher than they were and most states have been able to soften the 50 percent mandate. As reported in the *Wall Street Journal* on September 12, 2012, most states, according to author Matt Fuller, have less than 25 percent of recipients in some sort of work-related program.

President Barack Obama's efforts to combat the Great Recession, which began in 2008, prior to the beginning of his first term, included considerable expansions of various safety net programs. He was able to do so in large measure because he was working with a Democratic majority in both houses of Congress in his first two years. For example, the Obama administration temporarily waived the usual work requirements stipulated within welfare laws in response to the high unemployment rate. Obama and his fellow Democrats also increased SNAP or food stamp benefits through the 2009 American Recovery and Reinvestment Act, a massive stimulus package designed to revive the U.S. economy. Obama and leaders of his party in Congress also developed and passed into law the Affordable Care Act (sometimes also called Obamacare), a major new health care entitlement program. This new law was aimed at providing health care security to millions of Americans without health insurance.

Finally, most Democrats continue to reject initiatives by Republicans to "reform" Social Security and Medicare through funding cuts, privatization, or other means. They characterize most of these GOP efforts to reduce government spending as either callous or misguided and suggest that these programs can be fully supported through tax hikes on the wealthiest Americans, reductions in defense spending, or other means.

Republicans on Entitlement Programs

Many Republicans are concerned that welfare saps people's initiative, makes them dependent on the government, and weakens the U.S. economy by requiring higher and higher taxes from the top earners. They worry about people who cheat the system unfairly and cite data that suggests the top 5 percent of all wage earners bring in 31 percent of the income but pay 59 percent of all income taxes (Angle 2012). Money paid into government programs, they believe, could better be invested in supporting industry, encouraging entrepreneurship, or rebating money back to taxpayers. Such views have been the dominant concern of Republicans at the state and federal level since the 1960s with just a few exceptions. Republican President Richard Nixon, who served from 1969 to 1974, was not opposed to creating national health care and President George W. Bush, who served from 2001 to 2009, expanded Medicare to include prescription drugs.

GOP concerns about government entitlement programs go back to the New Deal but for many years Republicans lacked the political power in Congress to do anything about it (White 2002). Democrats controlled that body nearly without interruption from 1933 to 1995. In addition, Republicans suffered electoral defeat in the contest for the presidency from 1932 to 1952, when Republican Dwight Eisenhower ended the GOP's losing streak. President Eisenhower moderated some of the impulses of the Democratic Congress; for example, he did not deploy the food stamp program voted by Congress in 1958 (Short History of SNAP). In 1964, Republican presidential candidate Barry Goldwater made opposition to the welfare state a key tenet of his campaign. "We can deny self-indulgence," he stated. "We can restrain our pressure groups from seeking special privilege favors at the expense of the general public taxpayer" (Goldwater 1964). But Goldwater was soundly defeated by Johnson in the 1964 election.

President Reagan was more forceful in his attacks on the existing system. In 1976, he labeled some AFDC recipients "welfare queens," claiming that they garnered more money and benefits than middle-class working taxpayers. He moderated his tone somewhat when he was elected president in 1980 but continued to assert that welfare created a lifetime of dependency, broke down poor families black and white, and encouraged out of wedlock births. Reagan also consistently expressed his belief that, in too many cases, America's welfare system actually "perpetuates" rather than alleviates poverty (Reagan 1986). To end this cycle of poverty he encouraged states to create welfare-to-work programs and in 1988 enacted the Family Support Act, which mandated this. The Reagan administration also capped future increases in benefit programs and began measuring gross income, rather than net income, in evaluating eligibility for social services.

Although Republican incumbent George H. W. Bush lost the presidential contest in 1992 to Bill Clinton, the GOP won the 1994 midterm elections and control of the U.S. Congress for the first time in over a decade. Led by new Majority Leader Newt Gingrich, the House quickly pressured Clinton to approve the TANF program, which established a five-year lifetime limit for people collecting government assistance and required those collecting benefits to actively seek work or work-related training.

Members of the GOP continue to seek ways to reduce the size and scope of entitlement programs. President George W. Bush suggested privatizing social security in 2005. Congress member Paul Ryan, who supported Bush's plan, and became the House Budget Committee Chair in 2011, has prepared several budgets that he says meet the GOP goal for restraining safety net programs while also enhancing

Paul Ryan on "Expanding Opportunity in America"

On July 24, 2014, conservative Republican congress member (and 2012 vice presidential nominee) Paul Ryan gave a speech (excerpted below) to the American Enterprise Institute (AEI) delineating his ideas for reshaping America's welfare system:

> The fact is, each person's needs fit into a coherent whole: a career. And each person fits into a coherent whole: a community. So if the public and private sector work together, we can offer a more personalized, customized form of aid—one that recognizes both a person's needs and their strengths—both the problem and the potential. So I'd start a pilot program called the Opportunity Grant. It would consolidate up to eleven federal programs into one stream of funding to participating states. The idea would be to let states try different ways of providing aid and then to test the results—in short, more flexibility in exchange for more accountability. My thinking is, get rid of these bureaucratic formulas. Put the emphasis on results. Participation would be voluntary; no state would have to join. And we would not expand the program until all the evidence was in. The point is, don't just pass a law and hope for the best. If you've got an idea, let's try it. Test it. See what works.
>
> The state would get the same amount of money as under current law—not a penny less. In effect, the state would say, "Give us some space, and we can figure this out." And the federal government would say, "Go to it—on four conditions": First, you've got to spend that money on people in need—not roads, not bridges, no funny business. Second, every person who can work should work. Third, you've got to give people choices. The state welfare agency can't be the only game in town. People must have at least one other option, whether it's a non-profit, a for-profit, what have you. And fourth, you've got to test the results. The federal government and the state must agree on a neutral third party to keep track of progress.

Source

Ryan, Paul. 2014. "Expanding Opportunity in America," July 24. Accessed December 27, 2014: http://budget.house.gov/news/documentsingle.aspx?DocumentID=389033.

employment opportunities. "We have to do more to unwind the cycle of dependency on government" said Ryan, who was the 2012 Republican vice presidential nominee (Ryan 2014).

Frustrated at the federal level of government, Republicans have pursued their policy of ending dependency at the state level. In Maine, the Republican Governor, Paul LePage, cut state funding to social services in order to balance the budget and push people into the workforce. In his successful 2014 bid for reelection, LePage, was quoted in an October 6, 2014, article in the *Wall Street Journal* written by Damian Paletta, "All you able-bodied people out there get off the couch and get yourself a job." Damian Paletta and Mark Peters reported in a December 15, 2014, story for the *Wall Street Journal* that Republican governors in Indiana, Kansas, and Wisconsin are also preparing new legislation to require drug tests for recipients of welfare, requiring some to pay for their own health care, and paring away at the length of cash payments and expanding the work requirements.

But whereas Republicans regularly aim a drumbeat of criticism at many anti-poverty programs, alleging that such programs are fundamentally flawed, their criticisms of more politically popular social welfare programs like Medicare and Social Security are more muted and nuanced. In these cases, Republicans typically express support for the programs themselves but suggest that changes—whether they take the form of privatization of services, means testing, reduced payments, or increasing the eligibility age for enrollment—are necessary to keep the programs economically viable over the long term.

Further Reading

Angle, Jim. 2012. "Republicans Dispute Obama's 'Fair Share' Claims, Say Top Earners Already Pay Enough," Fox News, July 12. Accessed December 22, 2014: http://www.foxnews.com/politics/2012/07/11/obama-camp-focuses-on-answering-what-fair-share-taxes-looks-like.

Berkowitz, Edward D. 1991. *America's Welfare State: From Roosevelt to Reagan*. Baltimore: Johns Hopkins University Press.

Clinton, Bill. 2006. "How We Ended Welfare Together," *New York Times*, August 22. Accessed December 22, 2014: http://www.nytimes.com/2006/08/22/opinion/22clinton.html?module=Search&mabReward=relbias%3As%2C%7B%221%22%3A%22RI%3A9%22%7D.

Coll, Blanche D. 1995. *Safety Net: Welfare and Social Security, 1929–1979*. New Brunswick: Rutgers University Press.

Goldwater, Barry. 1964. Campaign Brochure. Accessed December 22, 2014: http://www.4president.org/brochures/goldwater1964brochure.htm.

Hays, Sharon. 2004. *Flat Broke with Children: Women in the Age of Welfare Reform*. New York: Oxford University Press

Johnson, Lyndon B. 1964. "Annual Message to the Congress on the State of the Union," January 8. Online by Gerhard Peters and John T. Woolley, "The American Presidency Project." Accessed December 22, 2014: http://www.presidency.ucsb.edu/ws/?pid=26787.

Katz, Michael. 2013. *The Undeserving Poor: America's Enduring Confrontation with Poverty*, 2nd edition. New York: Oxford University Press.

Lopez, Eduard R. 1987. "The Constitutional Background to the Social Security Act of 1935." Accessed December 22, 2014: http://www.ssa.gov/policy/docs/ssb/v50n1/v50n1p5.pdf.

McCullough, David. 1993. *Truman*. New York: Simon and Schuster.

Milkis, Sidney M., and Jerome M. Mileur, eds. 2005. *The Great Society and the High Tide of Liberalism*. Boston: University of Massachusetts Press.

Moynihan Report. 1965. Accessed December 22, 2014: http://www.dol.gov/dol/aboutdol/history/moynchapter4.htm.

Reagan, Ronald. 1986. "Radio Address to the Nation on Welfare Reform," February 15. Online by Gerhard Peters and John T. Woolley, "The American Presidency Project." Accessed December 27, 2014: http://www.presidency.ucsb.edu/ws/?pid=36875.

Roosevelt, Franklin. 1932. "FDR's Commonwealth Club Speech." Accessed December 22, 2014: http://www.heritage.org/initiatives/first-principles/primary-sources/fdrs-commonwealth-club-address.

Ryan, Paul. 2014. "A Better Way Up from Poverty," *The Wall Street Journal,* August 16–17, A11.

Short History of SNAP (Supplemental Nutrition Assistance Program). Accessed December 22, 2014: http://www.fns.usda.gov/snap/short-history-snap.

White, Edward G. 2002. *The Constitution and the New Deal.* Cambridge: Harvard University Press.

Environmental Protection

At a Glance

Environmental policy issues deeply divide voters and lawmakers of the Republican and Democratic parties. Whereas Democrats largely frame protecting the environment as a moral and ethical responsibility—and a pressing one in an age when environmental degradation is evident and widespread—Republicans, in general, are less likely to view the environment in these terms and instead view the environment through the lens of economics and individual freedom and property rights. Thus, Democrats include environmental justice as part of their agenda for social justice, and Republicans defend development of domestic fossil fuel resources—long decried by many Democrats for its negative environmental impact—as a significant part of their agenda for energy independence and U.S. self-sufficiency from overseas oil-producing nations.

Many Democrats . . .

- See themselves as environmentalists.
- See environmental protection policies as moral efforts toward being conscientious stewards of the planet's resources.
- Believe that minorities and the poor are particularly vulnerable to environmental pollution and degradation.
- Believe that climate change is occurring and must be addressed.
- Support empowering the Environmental Protection Agency (EPA), the National Oceanic and Atmospheric Agency (NOAA), and the U.S. Fish and Wildlife Services to impose regulations on businesses and individuals to preserve the environment.
- Believe that the president should use his or her executive power to impose regulations if Congress will not.
- See renewable energy resources as superior to fossil fuels for environmental, national security, and economic reasons.
- Believe that fracking causes environmental degradation.

Many Republicans . . .

- Balance their concern for the environment against the economic and property rights of individuals and businesses.
- Reject the idea that poor people and minorities have been deliberately targeted by corporations or governments for waste disposal or other environmental hazards.
- Do not believe that human-caused climate change is occurring, and warn that efforts to address the issue will damage the U.S. economy.
- Believe that environmentalists within the EPA have used "regulatory overreach" to harm businesses and trample on property rights.
- Reject the use of executive authority to impose new rules on the energy sector of the economy.
- Support hydraulic fracturing (fracking) and the coal and oil industries.

Overview

The modern environmental movement has polarized popular and political opinion in the United States since its origins in the mid-20th century. Beginning as a grassroots movement concerned with issues such as vanishing species and wilderness, pollution, and human health concerns, environmentalism became a battleground in the 1980s between economic and business interests, on the one side, and advocates for the environment and social justice, on the other side.

The modern environmental movement was influenced by two critical books, Aldo Leopold's *A Sand County Almanac* (1949) and Rachel Carson's *Silent Spring* (1962). Leopold suggested that caring for the land was a moral ethic and associated with communitarian principles and social justice. Carson connected economic activity and the use of chemicals such as DDT with the loss of species and the ruination of fragile ecosystems. Some scholars have claimed that the environmental movement is the largest social movement in U.S. history. In terms of rapid policy change, it spawned the rise of the Green Party (which first emerged in Europe) in the United States and has influenced the legislative priorities and viewpoints of Democratic lawmakers in particular.

During that decade, many of the nation's most important and far-reaching environmental laws were passed by Congress with broad bipartisan support and signed into law by President Richard Nixon, a Republican. These laws included the National Environmental Protection Act of 1970, the Clean Air Act of 1970, the Clean Water Act of 1972, and the Endangered Species Act of 1973. This legislation gave the U.S. Fish and Wildlife Services, the National Oceanic and Atmospheric Agency, and the Environmental Protection Agency unprecedented regulatory power over private and public land use, any commercial activity that might harm endangered or threatened species, and any business activity that may create pollutants, and it required setting mileage and emissions standards for all automobiles on America roads. In sum, these agencies have the potential to regulate nearly every aspect of the American economy. Controversy over these agencies and the regulations they enforce persists to this day.

Many mainstream environmentalists believe that the government does not do enough to protect the environment and wants new legislation to empower regulatory agencies and to limit action by Congress that may hinder that power. Those who believe that the government is not doing enough to protect the environment have created organizations such as the Sierra Club, which used traditional lobbying and litigation in the courts to shape policy. Greenpeace is an organization inspired by the civil rights movement and uses direct action and nonviolent confrontation against those who are harming the environment. These groups frequently denounce the Republican Party for "antienvironmental" rhetoric and policies, and many progressive media voices have leveled the same charges against the GOP. In 2015, for example, the *New York Times* issued an editorial supporting the environmental policies and priorities of President Barack Obama. In the process, the newspaper provided a clear look at how many environmentalists regard the modern GOP. "President Obama has announced or will soon propose important protections for clean water, clean air, threatened species and threatened landscapes," wrote the editorial board. "The usual complaints about 'executive overreach' and 'job-killing regulations' have been raised [by Republicans]. But beneath all the political sound bites lies a deep-seated if unspoken grievance that Mr. Obama is actually trying to realize the promise of laws that Congress passed years ago" (*New York Times* Editorial Board 2015).

Conservatives have argued that regulation by federal agencies of property rights, economic activity, and even public land use in the name of environmental protection is both unconstitutional and inimical to American society. Republicans accuse environmentalists of stifling free enterprise, abnegating personal property rights, and in some cases of sponsoring domestic terrorism. Environmentalists accuse corporations of raping the environment, ignoring climate change, and targeting politically powerless constituencies for some of their worst abuses.

The environmental policy debate, for example, has expanded in recent decades to include the idea of environmental racism. In 1987, an African American minister named Benjamin Chavis (who later became a prominent civil rights leader) claimed that people of color and their communities were being systematically targeted by corporations as toxic dumping sites. He coined the term "environmental racism," which he defined as racial discrimination in environmental policy making and the unequal enforcement of environmental laws and regulations. This accusation was even leveled at leading organizations in the environmental movement, since few of them had minorities in any meaningful positions of leadership. In 1994, President Bill Clinton recognized the issue by creating, through Executive Order 12898, the Department of Environmental Justice within the EPA (Newton 2009).

Many conservative Republicans, however, reject the idea that poor people and nonwhite Americans have been subjected to deliberate targeting. David Friedman of the American Enterprise Institute, a conservative think tank, labeled the movement a "hoax." They note that locally unwanted land uses (LULUs) such as waste treatment sites are often placed in areas where land is cheap and there is little organized resistance. Many of these sites are therefore located in districts that contain poor and minority citizens. On the other hand, when LULUs are brought into middle-class neighborhoods home values plummet and the residents who remain or move in are often poor and minorities. In other words, their contention is that such sites are not chosen to victimize the poor and minorities, but simply because that is where the land is cheapest. These conservatives assert that studies have been unable to find deliberate and systematic attempts to locate hazardous sites in communities of color (Friedman 1998).

In the 21st century, concerns about the environment expanded to include climate change (which is dealt with in another chapter in this volume) and hydraulic fracturing. This practice, also known as fracking, involves injecting water and chemicals deep into shale rock formations in order to retrieve natural gas deposits.

Supporters say that fracking has contributed to a decline in oil and gas prices worldwide and made Americans more energy independent. Environmentalists, however, claim that fracking wastes freshwater, contaminates the groundwater near fracking wells, and causes earthquakes. Many Democrats have thus called for an outright ban on fracking. Many Republicans, however, insist that links between fracking and health problems, water contamination, or earthquakes are unproven. Conservatives generally are also quick to point out that fracking is most often done in regions where oil and gas drilling has been occurring for years. They suggest that any health problem, water contamination, or earthquake might be attributed to the earlier wells.

Democrats on Environmental Policy

Many Democrats are seen as more environmentally friendly than Republicans. As Robb Willer noted in a 2015 *New York Times* article, surveys of Americans show that liberal Democrats see environmental issues in moral terms, as a right or wrong, whereas conservative Republicans do not. The majority of Democrats are more ideologically predisposed to side with environmentalists over business and energy interests in debates over environmental policy. This attitude is affirmed in key documents of the Democratic Party and statements by party members (Democratic National Committee 2015). The national platform in 2012 called for "curbing the effects of climate change, protecting America's natural resources, and ensuring the quality of our air, water, and land for future generations" (Democratic Party Platform 2012). Democrats have also tied environmental issues to civil rights and issues of race and class. Thus, Democratic leaders in Congress agree with some civil rights advocates who proclaim the existence of environmental racism and have tried to pass laws to end this practice.

The relationship between the Democratic Party and environmental groups can be measured by the amount of money provided to Democratic candidates and to efforts by elected officials to enact policies advocated by environmental groups (Open Secrets 2015). Congressional Democrats held the majority in the House and Senate when the first modern environmental legislation was proposed in the 1970s. Therefore, Democrats claim credit for initiating the EPA and passing the Clean Air Act and the Endangered Species Act. Although stymied by President Reagan in the 1980s, the Democratic environmental agenda found its way into the Clean Air Act Amendments of 1990, which were also supported by President George H. W. Bush, a Republican. Congressional Democrats have not only worked to support passage of bills to protect the environment but have also sought to hinder Republican plans that they deem inimical to the environment. For example, congressional Democrats largely (though not universally) opposed legislation that would allow completion of the Keystone XL Pipeline, a proposed pipeline that would carry crude oil from Alberta, Canada, through the United States to Nebraska where it would join existing pipelines to carry it south to the Gulf of Mexico. When the Republican majority in the Senate passed the keystone bill in 2015, President Obama vetoed it and Senate Democrats joined together to stop a GOP override of Obama's veto.

Democratic presidents have also used their executive power to protect the environment. President Clinton, who served two terms in the White House between 1993 and 2001, consulted with Benjamin Chavis before issuing Executive Order 12898 to establish an Office of Environmental Justice within the Environmental Protection Agency. Clinton also created a National Environmental Justice Advisory Council (NEJAC) and ordered all federal agencies to promote environmental justice "to the greatest extent practicable and permitted by law" (Clinton 1994). Attempts by Democratic members of Congress to codify and allow enforcement by the EPA of issues related to racial justice have been unsuccessful. Legislation was introduced in nearly every session of Congress since 1993 but failed to reach a floor vote.

President Obama, who took office in 2009, has used his executive power to cut carbon emissions on airlines, protect new wilderness areas, order tighter restrictions on emissions from automobiles, and veto the Keystone XL oil sands pipeline proposal. Under the Clean Air Act, Obama may issue new guidelines that shut down coal-fired power plants and lead to fewer new coal-powered plants in the future. Using his authority under the Clean Water Act, Obama has also proposed new limits on individual and business use of wetlands and streams, which would have far-reaching economic consequences. These stances have been applauded by environmentalists but strongly criticized by Republicans, agricultural interests, and other industries. Critics claimed that the regulations showed a clear collusion between environmental groups, the Environmental Protection Agency, and the Obama White House.

Hydraulic fracturing, or fracking, is a procedure used by oil and gas companies to extract these fuels from deep within the Earth by injecting water and chemicals. Many Democrats have been in the forefront of opposition to this process, citing environmental and public health concerns (Newton 2015). Beginning in 2009, Democrats have sought to overturn a provision of the Energy Policy Act of 2005 that grants an exception for fracking under the Safe Drinking Water Act of 1974. The Fracturing Responsibility and Awareness of Chemicals Act (FRACA) was sponsored in the House and Senate in every Congress since 2009 but has been unable to overcome Republican opposition. In frustration, many local governments, especially those led by Democrats, have pushed for local bans on fracking. Some of these votes were largely symbolic but in other areas, such as the Finger Lakes Region of New York, they thwarted efforts by oil and gas drillers to explore fracking. Local and state Democrats across the United States have worked alongside the nonpartisan Environmental Defense Fund (EDF) and other environmental groups to advocate for strict regulation of fracking. A stronger victory for antifracking environmentalists came when New York's governor, Andrew Cuomo, a Democrat, banned fracking in New York state in November 2014, citing potential health risks associated with the process.

Climate change, fracking, pesticide control, and a host of other environmental policy issues have become important issues in the Democratic Party in recent years, joining long-standing concerns about habitat and species protection, wilderness preservation, and air and water quality. Indeed, the environment has become such a core issue for many Democratic voters that it is often difficult for Democratic candidates for office to succeed if they are perceived by voters as uncaring about environmental issues.

Republicans on Environmental Policy

Many Republicans frequently provide expressions of support for conservation and preservation of the environment. However, Republicans contend that most environmental protection is flawed and too often employed without sufficient regard for its impact on economic growth and individual rights.

This conviction is affirmed in key documents and statements crafted by the Republican Party over the years. In their national platform, for example, Republicans voice support for "drilling for oil and natural gas in an environmentally responsible way. President Obama has pushed for overly restrictive EPA regulations that have cost American consumers and businesses tens of billions of dollars. Republicans have consistently voted for job creation in the energy sector through their support of the Keystone XL Pipeline and continued opposition to Obama's "war on coal" (Republican National Committee 2015).

In addressing frequent charges from Democrats and environmental organizations that they are hostile to environmental protection, Republicans often note that the first "environmental president" in American history was Republican Theodore

Roosevelt, who served 1901–1909. Roosevelt used his executive power to preserve hundreds of thousands of acres of land as federal reserves and national parks, and his speeches regularly exhorted Americans to be more conscientious in their use of the country's natural bounty. Republicans also note that Richard Nixon, another Republican, created the EPA, and signed into law the Clean Air and Clean Water Acts (Hillstrom 2010; Rosenbaum 2013).

By the 1980s, however, Republican President Ronald Reagan and other members of his party voiced growing concerns that environmental policies and regulations were harming the economy. Reagan, who served in the White House from 1981–1989, set the tone for the conservative Republican response to environmental issues. Reagan believed that the regulatory agencies established by his predecessors were undermining the power of duly elected officials, economically intrusive, and detrimental to private enterprise. He struck a blow to the federal government's regulatory power by issuing Executive Order 12291, which required that before implementation, agencies had to undertake a cost–benefit analysis and that any potential benefits to society must outweigh potential costs. In addition, the state of the economy and the impact on particular industries had to be taken into account. Many saw this as part of Reagan's antagonism toward the EPA. During his two terms in the White House, Reagan opposed or delayed many EPA policies and cut funding for antipollution enforcement by 31 percent. Democrats in Congress responded by launching a series of investigations into Reagan's appointees to the EPA and cited the director, Ann Buford, for contempt of Congress. Buford and nearly 20 other staff were forced to resign from that agency in 1983. Reagan compromised with Congress and environmental advocacy groups by appointing the well-respected William Ruckelshaus, who had served as the first director of the EPA in the 1970s.

In turn, environmentalists accused Republicans of having an "antienvironment agenda." The League of Conservation Voters (LCV), an environmental advocacy and political action group, issues an annual report card scoring members of Congress on their support for environmental legislation. For many years, their rankings have consistently placed Republican members of the House below the 50th percentile—and often far below. By contrast, most Democratic lawmakers have far higher LCV ratings (League of Conservation Voters 2014).

Many Republicans continue to argue against what they see as the "regulatory overreach" by the EPA. To thwart this, Republicans often hold hearings on the EPA's regulatory tactics and the agency's policies that impact business. In addition, they scrutinize the agency's authority to limit pollutants such carbon dioxide and ozone, limit growth of spending on EPA activities, and oppose increases supported by Democrats. When passing spending bills, they often include provisions, also known as riders, to impose limits on EPA regulations. Many Republicans also oppose aspects of the Endangered Species Act, which they believe tramples on individual and business property rights.

Many Republicans complain that President Obama's policy of using executive orders to circumvent congressional action is an example of "regulatory overreach"

William D. Ruckelshaus, the federal Environmental Protection Agency administrator, tells reporters in Los Angeles his agency is proposing gas rationing for most of southern California as an anti-smog measure, on January 15, 1973. (AP Photo/Wally Fong)

and is unconstitutional. Some have even suggested that Obama is acting as an agent for radical environmentalists. Many Republicans sought unsuccessfully to override Obama's veto of the Keystone XL Pipeline that would have allowed the completion of an oil pipeline that would have carried tar sand crude oil from Alberta to the Gulf of Mexico.

Surveys of self-identified Republicans show that nearly three out of four support fracking. Under Republican George W. Bush, the Republican-controlled Congress passed the Energy Policy Act of 2005, which excluded fracking from being regulated under provisions of the Safe Drinking Water Act of 1974. In response to challenges by Democratic legislators and mayors in cities that have banned fracking, some Republican governors and state legislators have created state laws to prohibit municipalities or counties from bans of hydraulic fracturing. Statewide bans have been enacted in Colorado, New Mexico, Ohio, Oklahoma, and Texas.

There are signs of change within the Republican Party. Not all members agree with the conservative wing of the GOP, and many younger Republicans, the so-called millennials, want environmental regulations and legislation to address climate change.

Further Reading

Carson, Rachel. 1962. *Silent Spring*. Boston: Houghton Mifflin.

Chavis, Benjamin, and Charles Lee. 1987. *Toxic Waste and Race in the United States*. New York Commission for Racial Justice United Church of Christ. Accessed June 19, 2015: http://d3n8a8pro7vhmx.cloudfront.net/unitedchurchofchrist/legacy_url/13567/toxwrace87.pdf?1418439935.

Clinton, Bill. 1994. "Federal Actions to Address Environmental Justice in Minority Populations and Low—Income Populations." Accessed June 19, 2015: http://www.epa.gov/region2/ej/exec_order_12898.pdf.

Democratic National Committee. 2015. "Environment." Accessed June 20, 2015: https://www.democrats.org/issues/environment.

Democratic Party Platform. 2012. Accessed February 7, 2016: https://www.democrats.org/party-platform.

Friedman, David. 1998. "The 'Environmental Racism' Hoax," American Enterprise Institute. Accessed June 12, 2015: http://yyy.rsmas.miami.edu/groups/ambient/teacher/env_justice/module%20segments/ib%20The%20environmental%20racism%20hoax.pdf.

Hillstrom, Kevin. 2010. *U.S. Environmental Politics and Policy: A Documentary History*. Washington, D.C.: CQ Press.

League of Conservation Voters. 2014. National Environmental Scorecard 2014. Accessed February 7, 2016: http://scorecard.lcv.org/.

Leopold, Aldo. 1949. *A Sand County Almanac*. New York: Oxford University Press.

New York Times Editorial Board. 2015. "The GOP Assault on the Environment," *New York Times*, June 8. Accessed June 10, 2015: http://www.nytimes.com/2015/06/08/opinion/gop-assault-on-environmental-laws.html.

Newton, David E. 2009. *Environmental Justice. A Reference Handbook*. Santa Barbara: ABC-CLIO.

Newton, David E. 2015. *Fracking. A Reference Handbook*. Santa Barbara: ABC-CLIO.

Open Secrets. 2015. Accessed June, 19, 2015: http://www.opensecrets.org/industries/indus.php?ind=Q11.

Republican National Committee. 2015. "Energy and the Environment." Accessed June 10, 2015: https://www.gop.com/issue/energy-and-environment/canonical/.

Rosenbaum, Walter A. 2013. *Environmental Politics and Policy,* 9th edition. New York: CQ Press.

Equal Pay for Women

At a Glance

Although there is bipartisan agreement that equal pay for women is a legitimate goal, Republicans and Democrats have long disagreed over what leads to the statistical pay gap between men and women and what remedies, if any, should be applied to create pay equality. Democrats and Republicans see the issue of the persistent pay gap between men and women very differently. Many Democrats see this as sex discrimination and have supported a variety of laws and regulations to reduce or end it. Republicans generally are more likely to see wage differences between men and women as due to a host of factors, such as education and length of time on the job, and they have generally opposed regulation of the issue as intrusive to business and economically counterproductive.

Many Democrats . . .

- Believe that people should receive equal pay for equal work.
- Assert that on average, women in America receive 77 cents for every dollar a man earns in equivalent jobs.
- Believe that women continue to be the targets of economic discrimination by employers.
- Believe that the lingering effects of sexism are undermining women's equality.
- Support new laws protecting women from wage discrimination, from the Lilly Ledbetter Equal Pay Act to the proposed Paycheck Fairness Act.
- Characterize Republican opposition to equal pay legislation as additional evidence of a GOP "war on women."

Many Republicans . . .

- Believe that people should receive equal pay for equal work.
- Reject the idea that women are systematically treated unequally in American businesses.

- Suggest that much of the gender disparity in pay is attributable to the fact that women account for a higher percentage of workers in relatively low-paying fields and industries.
- Oppose new regulations on businesses that would create new burdens in data collecting and reporting wages to the government.
- Oppose any new laws that would make businesses more liable to class-action lawsuits.
- Suggest that pay differences between men and women can often be attributed to greater reluctance by women to negotiate for raises, differences in education, and gender differences on what constitutes an appropriate work–family balance.

Overview

Many Republicans and Democrats are divided over the root causes of the gradually narrowing but still persistent wage gap between male and female workers. For decades studies have found a gap in the median pay for full-time, year-round male and female workers, although studies indicate that this gap has closed somewhat over time (Billitteri 2008). For example, in 1960 women earned 61 cents for every dollar a man earned, in the 1990s women earned 77 cents for every dollar a man earned, and in 2011 women earned 81 cents to every dollar a man earned for the same job. The gap is much wider for women of color. For example, in 2010 African American women earned 68 cents for every dollar a white male worker made, and Hispanic women earned 59 cents for every dollar a white male worker earned (Billitteri 2008).

Women's rights advocates and many Democrats believe that this gap is stark evidence of deeply entrenched gender discrimination in American workplaces. They claim that social forces including sexism and corporate paternalism explain why women have yet to achieve full pay equality. They would like to see new laws written and new regulations imposed in order to address this issue.

Business leaders and many Republicans, however, claim that the disparity reflects the different occupational choices men and women make. For example, women may choose to work less overtime, may decide to leave the workforce for a few years to raise children, and may not be as assertive when asking for raises as men. Thus, personal choice, not discrimination, is at the root of the gap (Billitteri 2008).

The first equal-pay legislation was proposed in 1945 during World War II, when many married middle-class women were encouraged to work in wartime defense industries. By 1960, a third or more of women over age 16 were working, and they pressed for equal pay for equal work. Opposition from business groups such as the Chamber of Commerce blocked any such legislation until 1963, when Democratic President John F. Kennedy signed into law the Equal Pay Act of 1963. The legislation amended the 1938 Fair Labor Standards Act and required employers to pay men and women equally for doing the same work. Essentially the Equal Pay Act mandates employers provide equal pay to workers who perform substantially equal work. The new law did allow for pay differences based on seniority, merit, quantity, or quality of production.

The Equal Pay Act of 1963 was followed by a series of laws and lawsuits that made it illegal to discriminate on wages. The 1964 Civil Rights Act outlawed employment discrimination on the basis of race, color, religion, sex, and national origin, and, in 1974, the Supreme Court ruled employers could not legally give lower wages for women for the same work.

Despite legislation and court action, many women found themselves treated unfairly in the workplace. One such woman was Lilly Ledbetter who had worked for the Goodyear Tire and Rubber Company for 19 years when she discovered she was being paid considerably less than her male counterparts. She filed suit, and in 2007 her case made it to the Supreme Court, which ruled by a 5–4 vote that the law protecting women from discrimination was not applicable in her case because she failed to file suit within six months of receiving her first paycheck, even though Ledbetter claimed that she only gradually became aware of the company's wage discrimination.

The Supreme Court decision angered women's rights activists and many Democrats. Within weeks of the decision, the Democrat-controlled House of Representatives advanced legislation to overturn the Ledbetter ruling. Republicans in the U.S. Senate, however, used procedural rules to block the legislation from coming to a vote in that body.

Barack Obama made women's pay equality a campaign issue during his run for the White House in 2008. After he was sworn into office in 2009 he joined with filibuster-proof Democratic majorities in both the House and Senate to pass the Lilly Ledbetter Fair Pay Act. In fact, the bill was the first act that Obama signed into law as president. This law, which also received support from five Republican senators (four of them women) and three of the GOP's 175 representatives, extended the time limit for employees to sue for unfair pay. Republicans claimed to oppose the measure because it would make businesses potentially liable for the actions of managers and executives who didn't even work for the company any more. Obama, though, defended the law as a statement that "there are no second class citizens in our workplaces, and that it's not just unfair and illegal—but bad for business—to pay someone less because of their gender, age, race, ethnicity, religion or disability . . . Justice isn't about some abstract legal theory, or footnote in a casebook—it's about how our laws affect the daily realities of people's lives: their ability to make a living and care for their families and achieve their goals" (Obama 2009).

The passage of this legislation, though, was seen by organizations such as the National Organization of Women (NOW) and the American Civil Liberties Union (ACLU) as only the first step in closing the gender gap in pay. They urged congressional Democrats to pass a Paycheck Fairness Act to make it easier for women to press claims of discrimination. The law would have barred retaliation by employers

President Barack Obama, surrounded by lawmakers, U.S. secretary of state Hillary Clinton, left, Senator Barbara Mikulski (D-MD), center, House Majority Leader Steny Hoyer (D-MD), center-back, and Lilly Ledbetter, 2nd right, signs the Lilly Ledbetter Fair Pay Act in the East Room of the White House in Washington, D.C., on January 29, 2009. The wage discrimination bill, which allows employees more time to file a claim, is named after Lilly Ledbetter, a retired worker at a Goodyear factory in Alabama who discovered she was paid less than her male counterparts. (Photo by Saul Loeb/AFP/Getty Images)

against workers who asked about their employers' pay practices. The bill also brought wage discrimination to the same level of other civil rights violations and provided the same protections to workers who claimed this as those who claimed employer bias based on race and ethnicity. The U.S. Chamber of Commerce and other business groups expressed fear that such legislation would lead to an explosion of nuisance lawsuits against employers, and they urged Republicans to stop the measure. As of mid-2015, GOP lawmakers in Washington have been able to do so, beating back several attempts by their Democratic colleagues to pass the bill and send it to the White House for Obama's signature.

Democrats on Pay Equity

Democratic lawmakers, officials, and activists have supported policies and laws to end the gender wage gap since the administration of John F. Kennedy, who was in the White House from 1961 to 1963. Kennedy signed the Equal Pay Act in 1963, which made gender-based wage discrimination illegal (Duerst-Lahti 1989). The law was supposed to end the pay gap between male and female workers in American industry but the gap persists. For Democrats this is proof of discrimination. Rosa DeLauro, a Democratic representative from Connecticut who has led the fight for the Paycheck Fairness Act, said, "A significant wage gap is still with us, and that gap constitutes nothing less than an ongoing assault on women's economic freedom" (Billitteri 2008). For years, women's rights groups such as NOW worked with Democrats to take action on closing the wage gap. During the presidency of Barack Obama, Republican attempts to stop new legislation led Democrats to claim that Republicans were "waging a war on women," an appeal that has been credited by some analysts with increasing the number of single women in the Democratic Party.

For many Democrats the case of Lilly Ledbetter became a defining issue for women's rights. In 1998, Lilly Ledbetter sued her employer, Goodyear Tire and Rubber, claiming that for years they had failed to provide her with pay comparable to that of her male colleagues. The case made it all the way to the Supreme Court, which threw the case out in 2007 because the existing law protecting women placed a statute of limitations on suing for discrimination. Many Democrats saw this as another case in which business interests were able to use legal loopholes to their advantage and to violate the spirit of the law. Democrats made the Lilly Ledbetter case an issue during the presidential campaign of 2008 in an effort to attract female voters, and, after President Barack Obama took office in 2009, used it to pass new legislation—the Lilly Ledbetter Fair Pay Act—to extend the time period for women to sue employers for discrimination (Ledbetter 2013).

But while this legislation expanded women's rights to seek legal redress for gender discrimination in the workplace, many Democrats remained concerned about continued problems, such as reports that corporations and other businesses were retaliating against women employees who inquired about gender pay scales at their workplace. They also wanted more specific data from each industry as to their pay practices to make them transparent for all workers. This led Democrats in the Senate to propose the Paycheck Fairness Act in 2013. This legislation was aimed at providing women with the same mechanisms to sue for pay-related discrimination as those available for other civil rights violations. In addition, it protected female employees from reprisals if they made inquiries about pay practices. After Republicans stopped action on the bill in 2014, President Obama declared that "Republicans in Congress have . . . been blocking progress" (Obama 2014). President Obama used his executive power to issue a series of executive orders extending the protections of the Paycheck Fairness Act to those under federal contract. His order banned retaliation against employees of federal contractors for disclosing or inquiring about their wages. Obama ordered the secretary of labor to collect information from federal contractors on compensation paid to employees. Democrats largely believed this would pressure federal contractors into compliance with laws against pay discrimination or face the threat of a lawsuit by women or intervention by the Department of Justice. Democrats reintroduced the Paycheck Fairness Act to Congress in March 2015, but once again the bill stalled as a result of united GOP opposition.

Nancy Pelosi Urges Passage of the Paycheck Fairness Act

Democrats believe the statistical evidence showing a gap in pay for men and women is proof of gender discrimination in the workforce. Even though there are laws banning wage discrimination, most Democrats believe that these laws do not go far enough to protect women and to punish industries that treat women unfairly. The following excerpt from a 2015 speech by Democratic House Minority Leader Nancy Pelosi provides a representative example of her party's view of the issue:

> Businesses, families, workers, and our economy benefit when all employees earn an honest day's pay for a full day's work, regardless of gender. Yet, women in the United States are currently earning only 78 cents, on average, for every dollar earned by men— while African American women earn 64 cents and Latinas make a staggering 56 cents for every dollar a man makes. Pay discrimination isn't right, it isn't fair, and it isn't how we create a robust economy. Today, under the leadership of Congresswoman Rosa DeLauro, House Democrats are again taking the lead in addressing one of the most pressing economic challenges confronting our country by re-introducing the Paycheck Fairness Act.
>
> The Paycheck Fairness Act, a pillar of House Democrats' "When Women Succeed, America Succeeds" economic agenda for women and families, is fundamental to creating a vibrant economy that works for everybody. Although Republicans have consistently voted against this measure, the promise of equal pay for equal work should not be a partisan issue. This is about commonsense, fairness, equality, and helping hardworking Americans.
>
> Securing a fair shot for women in the workplace is critical to ensuring prosperity for our nation. Rather than continue their cycle of obstruction and dysfunction, House Republicans should join with us to close the gender wage gap so we can provide bigger paychecks and better infrastructure for all Americans.

Source

Pelosi, Nancy. 2015. "Statement on the Reintroduction of the Paycheck Fairness Act," March 24. Accessed June, 20, 2015: http://www.democraticleader.gov/newsroom/pelosi-statement -on-the-reintroduction-of-the-paycheck-fairness-act/.

With pay equity measures blocked by Republicans at the federal level, Democratic leaders within states and cities have also worked on their own to prepare legislation or issue executive orders to address and close the pay gap between men and women. In 2003, for example, state legislators in New Mexico created an Equal Pay Task Force to study the problem of wage inequality between men and women. The Task Force made a number of recommendations, including a call for new legislation to punish companies that discriminated against women in terms of salary and other compensation. When Republicans in the state legislature blocked action on the bill, Democratic Governor Bill Richardson issued an executive order in 2008, establishing a second commission to create a standard for collecting data on all gender pay inequality. The systematic data gathered and publicized by the state was used to pressure employers to bring pay between men and women into alignment. In 2014, Democrats in Pennsylvania sought to address the gender gap in pay by making it harder for employers to claim that men and women's pay was unbalanced as a result of factors such as education, training, or experience. The bill banned requirements that workers keep their pay secret. State Republicans, however, were able to keep the bills blocked up in committee.

Many Democrats have also expressed concern about the low wages that are typical in careers and jobs that are primarily held by women. Some fields, such as day care workers and retail sales, attract far more women than men, and the pay in these industries is much lower than in fields dominated by men, such as construction work or truck driving. Some Democrats have cited this reality as one of their supporting arguments for increasing the minimum wage.

Republicans on Pay Equity

Many Republicans do not oppose paying women the same as men for the same work, but they have been fairly united in their opposition to specific Democratic prescriptions for making that goal a reality. These Republicans point out that as far back as 1956, Republican President Dwight Eisenhower expressed support for legislative action to address wage discrimination based on gender, stating that "the principle of equal pay for equal work without discrimination because of sex is a matter of simple justice" (Nordlund 1997). Seven years later, Republicans in Congress fully supported the Equal Pay Act of 1963. Some Republicans today point to their support for this law and the Civil Rights Act of 1964 as proof of the GOP's long-standing commitment to end wage discrimination; however, they claim that because of the Equal Pay Act of 1963 and civil rights legislation, new laws addressing pay inequality are superfluous. Wage discrimination, they say, is already illegal.

Some Republicans claim that the statistical average of women earning 77 cents for every dollar a man earns comes from faulty analysis rather than from widespread gender-based wage discrimination. The Republican National Committee issued a press release in April 2014 that disputed that number. "Women and men hold different jobs in different industries and varying levels of experience. There's a disparity [in average earnings] not because female engineers are making less than male engineers at the same company with comparable experience. The disparity exists because a female social worker makes less than a male engineer . . . The difference isn't because of their genders; it's because of their jobs" (Republican National Committee 2014).

Republicans, in general, have also argued that apparent wage gaps within the same industry are due to differences in education, length of time on the job, and the number of overtime hours or merit bonuses earned. Some have suggested that a deeper analysis of evidence incorporating such factors would show that there is no real wage difference. Therefore, Republicans oppose new regulations on businesses favored by Democrats, such as data collecting and the sharing of wage data by employees. Members of the GOP say that such regulations would add new burdens on already overregulated businesses and encourage spurious lawsuits that would cause companies embarrassment and incur unnecessary legal expenses. Conservative feminist Christina Hoff Sommers offered a representative Republican view of the Paycheck Fairness Act when she denounced it as "a special-interest bill for litigators and aggrieved women's groups . . . The legislation, built on 30 years of spurious advocacy research, will impose unnecessary and onerous requirements on employers." Sommers especially condemned a provision that would hold employers liable for the "'lingering effects of past discrimination.' What does that mean? Employers have no idea" (Sommers 2012).

As the above remark shows, Republicans are inclined to cite scholars who argue that the apparent wage gap is not due to discrimination but to the lifestyle choices made by individual women (Farrel 2005). Some studies suggest that women are less likely to negotiate for starting salaries or raises, which can deprive them of hundreds of thousands of dollars in lifetime earnings (Sandberg 2013). One study of graduate students indicated that while 57 percent of male college graduates negotiated for their starting salary, only 7 percent of women did. Linda Babcock, professor of economics, believes that this is due to gender socialization: While boys are taught to focus on themselves, girls are taught to pay attention to the needs of others first. Women, some experts claim, are forced to make choices to balance family and work obligations (Babcock and Laschever 2003). "Men and women generally have equal pay for equal work now—if they have the same jobs, responsibilities and skills," stated Diana Furchtgott-Roth, an economist who worked in the administration of President George W. Bush (Billitteri 2008). This idea has been echoed by Republican leaders who say that this creates a wage gap between men and women. "Women seek jobs that provide more flexibility for their family over more money, which is the choice that I made as a young working mom," said Republican congress member Lynn Jenkins (Lillis and Berman 2014).

Further Reading

Babcock, Linda, and Sara Laschever. 2003. *Women Don't Ask: Negotiation and the Gender Divide.* Princeton: Princeton University Press.

Billitteri, Thomas J. 2008. "Gender Pay Gap," *CQ Researcher,* March 14, 18 (11): 241–264. Accessed February 20, 2015: http://0-library.cqpress.com.libra.naz.edu/cqresearcher/cqresrre2008031400.

Duerst-Lahti, Georgia. 1989. "The Government's Role in Building the Women's Movement," *Political Science Quarterly,* 104 (2): 249–268, 251.

Farrel, Warren. 2005. *Why Men Earn More: The Startling Truth Behind the Pay Gap—and What Women Can Do about It.* New York: AMACOM Press.

Ledbetter, Lilly. 2013. *Grace and Grit: My Fight for Equal Pay and Fairness at Goodyear and Beyond.* New York: Three Rivers Press.

Lillis, Mike, and Russell Berman. 2014. "Dems, GOP Spar Over Equal Pay for Women," *The Hill,* April 8. Accessed April 7, 2015: http://thehill.com/blogs/ballot-box/202928 -dems-gop-spar-over-equal-pay-for-women.

Nordlund, Willis J. 1997. *The Quest for a Living Wage: The History of the Federal Minimum Wage Program.* Santa Barbara: Praeger.

Obama, Barack. 2010. "Remarks on Signing the Lilly Ledbetter Fair Pay Act of 2009." *Public Papers of Presidents of the United States: Barack Obama 2009.* Washington D.C.: U.S. Government Printing Office.

Obama, Barack. 2014. "President Obama Speaks about the Paycheck Fairness Act," April 12, C-SPAN. Accessed April 1, 2015: https://archive.org/details/CSPAN_20140412 _200000_President_Obama_Remarks_on_the_Fair_Equity.

Republican National Committee. 2014. "The Misleading Paycheck Fairness Act." Accessed April 8, 2015: https://www.gop.com/misleading-paycheck-fairness-act/.

Sandberg, Sherry. 2013. *Lean In: Women, Work, and the Will to Lead.* New York: Knopf.

Sommers, Christina Hoff. 2012. "The Case against the Paycheck Fairness Act," *US News and World Report,* May 4. Accessed April 12, 2015: http://www.usnews.com /debate-club/should-the-senate-pass-the-paycheck-fairness-act/the-case-against-the -paycheck-fairness-act.

Family Policy

At a Glance

Often Democrats and Republicans cannot agree on a definition of what family means, which complicates and divides their use of the term when it comes to policy. In general, Democrats embrace a broader definition of family and are more likely to enact policy crafted for individual members. Many Republicans, on the other hand, are more likely to see the family in terms of the traditional, heterosexual, two-parent nuclear family, and the GOP historically has supported policy prescriptions that address the family as a whole.

Many Democrats . . .

- Believe that social policy should support families of all kinds.
- Believe that many different forms of family units are legitimate.
- Believe in supporting "family-friendly" policies such as increases in the minimum wage, health care reform, and paid leave from full-time employment.
- Support laws to accommodate same-sex couples.

Many Republicans . . .

- Believe that the American family is under threat and needs to be protected.
- Believe that social policies should support the traditional nuclear American family.
- Wish to create laws to protect parental rights over government policies.
- Oppose laws to accommodate same-sex couples.

Overview

The definition, character, and gender roles of American families have undergone rapid changes since the 1960s under the influence of the sexual revolution, women's liberation, postindustrialization, and other factors. Since the 1960s, divorce laws have relaxed and the social stigma once attached to marital breakup has diminished. People are marrying, divorcing, and remarrying and creating blended families. The millennials, loosely defined as those born from the early 1980s through the early 2000s, are marrying later (or not at all) and having fewer children. Legal changes in the definition of marriage have created more same-sex parenting. Having children out of wedlock, once considered an immoral and shameful event, has become increasingly common. All the above factors have led to a rise in single-parent households. Some demographers have estimated that in the future, 50 percent of Americans might live in a "nontraditional" family arrangement, such as a blended family, a single-parent family, or a same-sex marriage. The Republican family policy is summed up under the phrase "family values" and aims to protect the traditional American family arrangement from further change, while Democratic family policy is summed up by the phrase "family friendly" and seeks to support individual members within the changing American family. Thus, they sponsor laws that recognize the importance of families to society and act to meet the needs of children, parents, disabled family members, and the elderly (Turner 2002).

The Republican Party platform in 2012 stated that the foremost American institution is "the American family," which they believe is under attack by Democratic policies and their constituent groups. Social conservatives, most of whom identify as Republican, have been active in the "culture wars"—the public debate between conservatives and liberals over changing social trends and government policies related to social change. Conservatives generally oppose same-sex marriage and "safe sex" educational programs and support greater religious freedom, parental rights, and censorship of media and Internet content. They oppose any policies or movements that they believe are detrimental to the traditional nuclear family values of "cooperation, patience, mutual respect, responsibility, self-reliance." Over the course of the past four decades, surveys of the electorate show a persistent concern for the decline of moral values by self-identified Republicans. Many Republicans believe that many government social policies created by Democrats, such as Aid to Families with Dependent Children (AFDC), which was launched during the New Deal and endured until the mid-1990s, undermined the traditional two-parent family by fostering a culture of dependency on government welfare and lessening the need for contributions from two adults in families. In essence, they believe that government has become a substitute for family. The GOP insists that "public policy, from taxation to education, from healthcare to welfare, be formulated with attention to the needs and strengths of the family" (Republican Party Platform 2012). It was this thinking that inspired the Republican-led Welfare Reform Act of 1996. This legislation, which was signed into law by Democratic President Bill Clinton, replaced permanent government support with Temporary Assistance for Needy Families (TANF), a program that capped welfare payments, which, according to proponents, would push people off welfare rolls and into gainful employment.

Social liberals, most of whom identify as Democrats, believe that the traditional nuclear family structure has in many instances been excessively heteronormative and patriarchal. They celebrate changes to the family structure that empower women and respect lifestyles once oppressed by prior social norms (Woods 2012). Thus, the Democratic Party platform in 2012 highlighted the need to strengthen the American community, of which family was one of several components. Polls show that individuals who identified as Democrats are far less likely to be concerned about moral decline in America and far more concerned about the economic erosion of the middle class and increasing income inequality between the richest and poorest Americans. The Democratic Party policy is aimed at increasing government intervention in society to assist people, especially the most vulnerable populations. They style their policy aims as family-friendly policies, some of which would require businesses to increase benefits for workers, including paid paternity leave, more paid sick time, and an increase in the minimum wage, all in the name of helping working families. Democrats have also called for legal sanctions and protection for nontraditional family arrangements such as same-sex marriage, the ability of same-sex couples to adopt, and protections for transgendered individuals and their families.

According to the liberal nonprofit Institute for Women's Policy Research, the benefits of Democrat-sponsored family-friendly policies include gender equality, lower infant mortality, higher fertility rates, better child health, labor force growth, and lower poverty rates. It was this thinking that led Democrats to enact the Family Medical Leave Act (FMLA) of 1993, which required employers with over 50 full-time workers to provide upward of 12 weeks of unpaid medical leave to employees, with certain restrictions. Medical and family conditions covered by the law included military family leave, pregnancy, adoption, and family or personal illness.

Debates about family continue to shape the rhetoric of candidates seeking the presidency in 2016. On the Republican side, social conservatives such as Rick Santorum, author of the book *It Takes a Family*, have continued to make a case for traditional family values. On the Democratic side, social progressives such as Hillary Clinton, author of the book *It Takes a Village,* argue for recognition of the diversity of the American family and the need for family-friendly government to protect the family from economic erosion.

Democrats on Family Policy

Although Democratic lawmakers have crafted important family policies dating back to Franklin D. Roosevelt's New Deal, many of the specific family policies supported by Democrats today originated with the Clinton administration. To support working parents, but more specifically working mothers, President Clinton and Democrats in Congress passed the FMLA in 1993 with the goal of allowing parental leave from work for medical emergencies, caregiving, or other issues without fear of losing their jobs. The law mandated up to 12 weeks of job-protected unpaid leave for qualified workers employed in companies with 50 or more employees. Democrats would like to expand on the FMLA to cover all employees. Many Democrats have argued for paid leave for workers, with the money to come from contributions into a fund from both employees and employers. This update to FMLA would provide 12 weeks of paid, job-protected leave for new parents or workers facing family medical emergencies. Paid parental leave allows women to "handle both their work and their family responsibilities and increase labor force participation." In addition, Democrats advocate the "Healthy Families Act," congressional legislation to increase the number of sick days allowed annually, from an average of 7 to 12, so workers can tend to sick children. Recognizing the complexity and demands of the changing American family, Democrats have proposed legislation to mandate or support flex-time for workers. Flex-time could mean complete freedom for workers to design their own work schedule, or having options such as choosing to work a four-day rather than a five-day week, perhaps with days off in the middle of the week rather than on the weekend, or beginning and ending the workday several hours earlier or later than normal.

Due to conflict between Democrats and Republicans over equal pay and workplace flexibility, federal action has been stalled. However, Democrats have piloted some of these initiatives at the state level. For example, Democratic legislatures established paid family leave in California, New Jersey, and New Mexico through family leave insurance, which was funded by a special payroll tax. Vermont passed an equal pay law that included protection from retaliation by employers for workers requesting flexible work hours. Democratic legislators and governors through the United States are also working on proposals to add paid leave so that individuals who have family emergencies will not have to choose between staying in a job or taking time off to care for family members.

Democrats support child-rearing practices through federal tax policy by advocating for increasing the Child Tax Credit available to all parents with children, the Earned-Income Tax Credit for working families, and the Child and Dependent Care Tax Credit for families that use day care. Democrats have also suggested tax breaks for businesses that provide on-site daycare for their workers. Furthermore, Democrats are strong advocates for universal prekindergarten, and both federal and state Democratic leaders have proposed or supported legislation to subsidize local schools that adopt pre-K. Since his election in 2008, President Barack Obama has also supported efforts to increase financial support for community groups focused on fatherhood, urged businesses to offer opportunities for fathers to spend time with their kids at the bowling alley or ballpark, and worked to assist men in the armed services who are overseas to better connect with their children.

To keep families healthy, Democrats have also expressed broad support for a number of initiatives to provide universal access to health care through the Children's Health Insurance Program (CHIP), for families whose incomes are too high for Medicaid. Democrats passed the Affordable Care Act, which mandates that companies provide health care coverage for full-time workers. To provide coverage for those who might not qualify for CHIP or Obamacare, they encouraged states to expand their Medicaid programs. To maintain the health of a poorer woman during pregnancy and the infancy of her children, Democrats created and have sought expansion of the Women, Infants, and Children (WIC) program, which provides nourishing foods during critical phases in early childhood. Once children are in school, Democrats have sought to create and greatly expand the National School Lunch Program (NSLP), which provides meals before, during, and after school to students from low-income families. Under President Obama, the program was expanded so that if a school district has half of its population eligible for NSLP, every student in the district is provided with meals free of charge. To provide poor families with healthy food and nutrition, Democrats created and support funding for the Supplemental Nutrition Assistance Program (SNAP), also known as food stamps.

To keep families active, First Lady Michelle Obama created the Let's Move! program that seeks to educate parents and children about healthier lifestyle choices. She urged the government to adopt new mandates for the school lunch program under the direction of the Department of Agriculture, and her organization partnered with corporations, local governments, and community groups to create new green spaces, bike paths, and community playgrounds to allow children and their parents to be more active. To fight obesity, Democrats initiated new standards for school lunch programs that cut down or eliminate empty calories, fats, salt, and sugar in the food prepared or available in schools.

Over the past three decades, Democrats overall have also undergone a major transformation in their attitudes about family units headed by gay individuals. During the 1990s, Clinton and most other Democrats affirmed traditional values by supporting the Defense of Marriage Act (DOMA), which disallowed federal agencies from recognizing anything but heterosexual marriage. Since Barack Obama took office in 2009, Democrats have adopted more progressive stances such as openly seeking legislation to recognize the rights of same-sex couples to marry and adopt, and for transgendered individuals to have similar rights. Thus, they strongly oppose—and in some cases mock—the "family values" positions of the Republican party. Many Democrats see the policies supported by many Republicans as discriminatory to women, minorities, religious believers outside of Christianity, and LGBT couples (Lopoo and Raissan 2014). "It's time we stop just talking about family values and start pursuing policies that truly value families," stated the official Democratic Party platform of 2012.

The President and Democrats have cut taxes for every working American family, and expanded the Child Tax Credit and Earned Income Tax Credit. We believe that all parents and caregivers—regardless of gender—need more flexibility and support in the workplace. We support passing the Healthy Families Act, broadening the Family and Medical Leave Act, and partnering with states to move toward paid leave. We have invested in expanding and reforming Head Start and grants to states to raise standards and improve instruction in their early learning programs, and we support expanding the Child and Dependent Care Tax Credit. We must protect our most vulnerable children by supporting our foster care system, adoption programs for all caring parents, grandparents, and caregivers, and protecting children from violence and neglect.

We recognize that caring for family members and managing a household is real and valuable work. President Obama's administration has offered men who want to be good fathers extra support. We have bolstered community and faith-based groups focused on fatherhood, partnered with businesses to offer opportunities for fathers to spend time with their kids at the bowling alley or ballpark, and worked to help deployed dads connect with their children. We all have a stake in forging stronger bonds between fathers and their children. (Democratic National Committee 2012)

Republicans on Family Policy

Conservative Republicans often speak about family values, a term coined in the 1970s after conservative Christian organizations such as the American Family Association, Focus on the Family, and the Family Research Council formed and began to support Republican candidates for office. Conservative Christians, a core constituency of the Republicans, use the term when defending the traditional heterosexual, two-parent nuclear family against policies, beliefs, and movements they believe are eroding or destroying it. Family values were at the core of the culture wars, debates over abortion and reproductive rights, the Equal Rights Amendment, LGBT rights, pornography in media and on the Internet, and the rise of never and unmarried women, single-parent households, and entitlement programs that according to many conservatives make families dependent on government largess.

Republicans frame the debate over regulating reproductive rights in terms of family-friendly and pro-life arguments. They believe that allowing teens access to contraceptives, including Plan B (the morning after pill), preempts parental rights and promotes permissive sexuality. They argue that this erodes the moral foundation of society and abrogates the role of the family in promoting moral values. Republicans have been active in maintaining government sanctioned "abstinence only" education that protects children and their families from progressive ideas of sexuality. Likewise, in the name of morality, they have been critical of unregulated abortion. In addition to supporting regulations to severely limit access to abortion services, Republicans have sponsored proposals mandating that wives receive permission from their husbands before seeking an abortion and for teenage girls to also have parental consent before undergoing that procedure.

Many Republicans are also opposed to policies that would erode traditional heterosexual marriage and the two parent family. For example, many Republicans opposed the Equal Rights Amendment (ERA), which was sent to the states for ratification in 1972, because opponents of the ERA such as Phyllis Schlafly told followers it would erode the two-parent family and make men unequal to women. During this time period, conservative Christian groups such as the Southern Baptist Convention affirmed the traditional family and the idea that women were to be subordinate to men in the family setting. Republican Dan Quayle was vice president of the United States when he sparked a firestorm of controversy over his remarks regarding single-parent female-headed households. In remarks after the riot in South Central Los Angeles that year, Quayle suggested that problems in the inner cities were compounded by the breakdown of the traditional family. He blamed social welfare programs that created a culture of dependency by unmarried women who had out of wedlock births, then broadsided the media for promoting this lifestyle in shows such as the situation comedy, *Murphy Brown*. Quayle challenged the notion that families could be healthy without the important role of fathers. Although Quayle was mocked by liberals and their allies in the media, his words were cheered by social conservatives. In fact, the Republican national platform in 2004 echoed these sentiments, "Evidence shows us that children have the best chance at success when raised by a mother and a father who love and respect each other as well as their children. We also know that family breakdown makes America less stable. To create a sturdy foundation for the strength and success of our citizens and our nation, Republicans support policies that promote strong families" (Republican National Committee 2004).

In response to calls for same-sex marriage, many Republicans strongly supported the Defense of Marriage Act (DOMA), which rejected same-sex marriage under federal law. When the Supreme Court struck down DOMA and later affirmed the right of same-sex marriage against state laws prohibiting it, some Republican leaders, such as Ted Cruz and Mike Huckabee, both candidates for the 2016 GOP presidential nomination, immediately called for a constitutional amendment to ban same-sex marriage. Many Republicans have expressed concern that same-sex marriage will lead to the end of marriage and increase in cohabitation, serial monogamy, and other arrangements detrimental to individuals, families, communities, and the nation as a whole.

Many Republicans have also been front and center in promoting laws that allow families the right to have religious belief and practices at the center of their lives. One element of the culture war that erupted in the late 1970s concerned a drive by conservatives for more religion in the public realm. This included calls for prayer and Bible reading in schools and support for nativity scenes in town squares. Republican legislatures have been supportive of laws allowing vouchers for parents who wish to send their children to religiously affiliated private schools. The GOP has also been more likely to support homeschooling as an alternative to public education as a means to allow parents to include religious values in education.

It is likely Republicans will increase their emphasis on these policies in light of Supreme Court decisions validating same-sex marriage. Republicans attempted, unsuccessfully, to create religious freedom exceptions for individuals or businesses that believe LGBT lifestyles conflict with their religious doctrines. In the absence of these protections, it is likely that individuals may face sanctions or legal action for refusing to affirm nontraditional marriage arrangements. Republicans are quick to cite the case of Catholic institutions involved in adoption that refused to offer their services to same-sex couples and who lost financial support from state and federal government.

Republican conceptions of family values have placed them in opposition to many of the policies favored by Democrats. They see policies related to the workplace as another example of an intrusive government that creates dependency. They cite their success in reforming welfare in 1996, saying that they created healthier families by moving them from government assistance to earning their own paycheck. They see the many policies related to the SNAP, WIC, and NSLP as "nanny state" intrusions on personal responsibility, which they see as essential to healthy family environments. "We are the party of independent individuals and the institutions they create—families, schools, congregations, neighborhoods—to advance their ideals and make real their dreams," declared the GOP's 2012 platform. "Foremost among those institutions is the American family. It is the foundation of our society and the first level of self government. Its daily lessons—cooperation, patience, mutual respect, responsibility, self-reliance—are fundamental to the order and progress of our Republic. Government can never replace the family. That is why we insist that public policy, from taxation to education, from healthcare to welfare, be formulated with attention to the needs and strengths of the family" (Republican National Committee 2012).

Further Reading

Clinton, Hillary. 2006. *It Takes a Village,* 10th anniversary edition. New York: Simon and Schuster.

Democratic National Committee. 2012. "2012 Democratic Party Platform," September 3. Online by Gerhard Peters and John T. Woolley, "The American Presidency Project." Accessed June 26, 2014: http://www.presidency.ucsb.edu/ws/?pid=101962.

Lopoo, Leonard M., and Kerri M. Raissan. 2014. "U.S. Social Policy and Family Complexity." *The Annals of the American Academy of Political and Social Science,* July, 654 (1): 213–230.

Republican National Committee. 2004. "2004 Republican Party Platform." Accessed June 21, 2015: http://www.presidency.ucsb.edu/papers_pdf/25850.pdf.

Republican Party Platform. 2012. Accessed June 28, 2015: https://www.gop.com/platform/renewing-american-values/.

Santorum, Rick. 2006. *It Takes a Family: Conservatism and the Common Good.* New York: Intercollegiate Studies.

Turner, Jeffrey Scott. 2002. *Families in America: A Reference Handbook.* Santa Barbara: ABC-CLIO.

Woods, Dorian. 2012. *Family Policy in Transformation: US and UK Policies.* New York: Macmillan.

Gay Marriage

At a Glance

For many decades individuals and groups that supported same-sex marriage were unable to gain the support of either the Republican or the Democratic Party. This changed in the 1990s, when the Democratic Party began a slow movement toward acceptance of same-sex marriage. Support for gay marriage among Democrats continued to grow, albeit incrementally, during the first decade of the 21st century, especially among lawmakers in so-called blue states. But after Democratic President Barack Obama declared his support for same-sex marriage in May 2012, most Democrats quickly fell in line and expressed their support for that position as well. The Republican Party, with few exceptions, has resisted same-sex marriage with far greater vigor. But some Republicans, citing shifts in public opinion and Supreme Court rulings, have begun to suggest that fighting against this practice may be both an exercise in futility and a political burden.

Many Republicans . . .

- Believe that religious and cultural traditions support the idea that marriage should be defined as between one man and one woman.
- Assert that the Constitution gives each state the right to define marriage.
- Support laws denying same-sex couples to marry.
- Oppose judicial decisions by courts that strike down state laws banning same-sex marriage.
- Believe that judges should not interfere with the legislative process.
- Support laws that would allow individuals with religious convictions to opt out of providing services that legitimize gay marriage.

Many Democrats . . .

- Believe that marriage laws allowing only for heterosexual marriage are discriminatory.
- Believe that denying marriage between people of the same sex is unconstitutional.

- Support laws to allow same-sex couples to be married.
- Support judicial decisions that strike down state or federal law barring same-sex marriage.
- Oppose attempts by state officials to use "religious freedom" as a justification for refusing to process same-sex marriage licenses.

Overview

Proponents of a legal right for same-sex marriage have found support in the Democratic Party, which officially endorsed same-sex marriage at their national convention in 2012. Religious right and social conservative groups, who defend a traditional definition of marriage as a contract between one man and one woman, are important constituencies within the Republican Party, which officially endorsed this position at their national convention in 2012.

For much of the 20th century there was little or no public support for same-sex marriage. Nonetheless, advocates challenged existing laws in the courts, hoping to stake a civil rights claim for same-sex marriage. Such challenges were unsuccessful until 1993, when the supreme court of Hawaii struck down a state law defining marriage as an institution intended exclusively for a man and woman. Advocates of conventional marriage responded by pushing for legislation or state constitutional

Men and women protesting with "Boycott Colorado" signs at the Gay Pride parade in New York City, on June 1, 1994. (Photo by Barbara Alper/Getty Images)

amendments to make same-sex marriage unlawful. By 1994, all but five states had passed defense of marriage acts that explicitly defined marriage as a one-man, one-woman arrangement. The state of Colorado went further and passed an amendment that made recognition of gay marriages unlawful. The Supreme Court in *Romer v. Evans* (1996) struck down this amendment on the grounds that Colorado violated the equal protection rights of gay and lesbian couples by singling them out based on their sexual orientation (Knowles 2009).

Fearing that the Court's decision in *Romer* would set a precedent for gay marriage, conservative interest groups convinced the Republican-controlled 104th Congress to introduce the Defense of Marriage Act (DOMA) in 1996. DOMA was unique because it was the first time the federal government defined marriage, historically a prerogative of the states. Under DOMA the federal government defined marriage as between one man and one woman and removed the obligation of states to recognize same-sex marriages performed in another state or territory (Helfman 2013). The bill passed Congress by wide majorities. No Republican voted against the legislation and President Bill Clinton, a Democrat, signed the bill into law on September 20, 1996.

After DOMA became law, however, polls showed a steady growth of support for same-sex marriage, especially among youths aged 18–29 years old. As reported by Michael Muskal in the *Los Angeles Times* on February 26, 2014, support for this increased after 2003 when Massachusetts became the first state to legally recognize same-sex marriage. Republicans responded by suggesting an amendment to the U.S. Constitution to ban same-sex marriage, and numerous statewide ballot initiatives banning gay marriage were enacted in 2004.

On May 9, 2012, Obama became the first U.S. president to declare support for same-sex marriage, and this position was subsequently endorsed by the Democratic Party in its 2012 party platform (Democratic Party 2012). Republicans responded by reiterating their adherence to the traditional definition of marriage, adding this position to the 2012 Republican platform (Republican Party 2012).

In 2013, the Supreme Court struck down DOMA in the case of *U.S. v. Windsor.* In the wake of this decision (decided by a narrow 5–4 majority in which the Court's four most conservative justices all dissented), President Obama immediately ordered the executive branch agencies to recognize same-sex marriages and eight states with strong Democratic majorities enacted same-sex marriage laws. Simultaneously, Federal Circuit Courts across the United States applied the precedent of *Windsor* to strike down legislation or state constitutions banning same-sex marriage. Republicans in the House and Senate attempted to protect the traditional view of marriage by introducing the "State Marriage Defense Act" in February 2014. This bill proposed requiring the federal government to defer to states on the definition of marriage, effectively overruling executive orders made by Obama. Republican legislative majorities in many states passed religious freedom bills granting wedding service providers who had religious objections to same-sex marriage the right to refuse to serve gay clients. Widespread public backlash against these laws, however, led Republican Governor

John Lewis, left, and his husband Stuart Gaffney, plaintiffs in the 2008 Defense of Marriage Act (DOMA) case, hold flags and a sign reading "Love is Supreme" outside City Hall after the U.S. Supreme Court same-sex marriage ruling in San Francisco, California, on June 26, 2015. Same-sex couples have a constitutional right to marry nationwide, the U.S. Supreme Court said in a historic ruling that caps the biggest civil rights transformation in a half-century. (Bloomberg/Getty Images)

of Arizona Jan Brewer to veto such legislation. Some political observers suggested that Brewer's decision was an indication that Republican opposition to same-sex marriage was weakening in the face of shifting public attitudes about the issue.

Republicans on Same-Sex Marriage

Social conservatives, whose movement was energized by the religious rights groups of the 1970s, hold a traditional view of marriage as a heterosexual contract between one man and one woman. They fear that same-sex marriage will further the decline of marriage, which they assert has already been eroded by divorce laws, cultural immorality, and feminism (DeGagne 2013). Key advocates for traditional marriage are the Family Research Council (FRC) founded in 1983, the National Organization for Marriage (NOM) founded in 2007, and the American Principles

Justice Scalia Defends Traditional Marriage

In his dissent in *U.S. v. Windsor*, the 2013 Supreme Court decision that legalized gay marriage, conservative Justice Antonin Scalia denounced the majority ruling as a flagrant exercise in judicial overreach:

> That [majority decision] is jaw-dropping. It is an assertion of judicial supremacy over the people's Representatives in Congress and the Executive. It envisions a Supreme Court standing (or rather enthroned) at the apex of government, empowered to decide all constitutional questions, always and everywhere "primary" in its role . . . Even setting aside traditional moral disapproval of same-sex marriage (or indeed same-sex sex), there are many perfectly valid—indeed, downright boring—justifying rationales for this legislation. Their existence ought to be the end of this case . . . To defend traditional marriage is not to condemn, demean, or humiliate those who would prefer other arrangements, any more than to defend the Constitution of the United States is to condemn, demean, or humiliate other constitutions . . . In sum, that Court which finds it so horrific that Congress irrationally and hatefully robbed same-sex couples of the "personhood and dignity" which state legislatures conferred upon them, will of a certitude be similarly appalled by state legislatures' irrational and hateful failure to acknowledge that "personhood and dignity" in the first place . . . As far as this Court is concerned, no one should be fooled; it is just a matter of listening and waiting for the other shoe. . . . Some will rejoice in today's decision, and some will despair at it; that is the nature of a controversy that matters so much to so many. But the Court has cheated both sides, robbing the winners of an honest victory, and the losers of the peace that comes from a fair defeat. We owed both of them better.

Source

Justice Antonin Scalia's dissent in *U.S. v. Windsor*. 2013. Accessed July 5, 2015: http://www2
.bloomberglaw.com/public/desktop/document/United_States_v_Windsor_No_12307
_2013_BL_168683_US_June_26_2013_C/1.

Project (APP) founded in 2013. Their support comes from conservative evangelicals, protestant fundamentalists, and Roman Catholics who argue that marriage is by definition between a man and a woman and that Judeo-Christian tradition requires this. Social conservatives argue that marriage was constructed to further procreation, which is biologically impossible with same-sex couples. Opposition to the legalization of same-sex marriage is framed around the concept of religious or state freedom to define marriage as that between a man and a woman. Promoting same-sex marriage, they believe, will harm the family, undermine religious doctrines, and undercut the right of states to define marriage. Advocates for a traditional view of marriage and family are most likely to use legislation to restrict the definition of marriage (Nichols and Naylor 2013).

Social conservatives were appalled in the early 1990s by court decisions that struck down traditional definitions of marriage and sodomy laws and then granted civil rights status to sexual orientation. In one such case, *Baehr v. Miike*, the State Circuit Court of Hawaii struck down the state's marriage laws (HRS 572-1) as violating the Equal Protection Clause of the state constitution because it narrowly defined marriage in heterosexual terms. This prompted Hawaii and 32 other states to propose amendments to their constitution or to pass so-called "defense of marriage" acts to defend the traditional concept of marriage as that between one man and one woman.

At the national level, in 1994, Republicans took control of the House and Senate by promoting their economic and socially conservative agenda via the Contract with America. In 1996, they responded to increasing court challenges to bans on gay marriage by advancing the DOMA. This bill was introduced in the House by Bob Barr, a conservative Republican congress member from Georgia's seventh congressional district. It was cosponsored in the U.S. Senate by Bob Dole, who was seeking the GOP nomination for president that year. The bill received strong bipartisan support, easily passing in both the House (by a 342–67 vote) and the Senate (85–14). It became law on September 21, 1996, with Clinton's signature. DOMA offered the first ever federal definition of marriage as that between one man and one woman, and defined spouse as the opposite sex of an individual. The law also stated that states need not recognize same-sex marriage performed in other states or territories.

Although DOMA muted legislative responses to same-sex marriages, challenges to existing laws continued. In 2003, the Supreme Court issued a decision on *Lawrence v. Texas* that banned all remaining sodomy laws, which cleared the way for the legalization of same-sex marriage. That year Massachusetts became the first state to recognize same-sex marriages. In response to these challenges to conventional marriage, social conservatives such as Jerry Falwell of the Moral Majority, Tony Perkins of the Family Research Council, and the U.S. Conference of Catholic Bishops voiced support for an amendment to the U.S. Constitution to define marriage as the union between one man and one woman, thereby nullifying the action of the courts. Many Republicans in Congress denounced gay marriage, and one member, Marilyn Musgrave, from Colorado's fourth district, introduced legislation to amend the Constitution to retain the traditional definition of marriage. Republican President George W. Bush responded by proclaiming Marriage Protection Week and signaled his own support for Musgrave's amendment (Bush 2003).

In 2004, an election year, 13 states put ballot propositions defining marriage as between one man and one woman on their ballots. There is some evidence that in Republican-dominated states these initiatives aided in President Bush's reelection by bringing out more evangelical voters (Campbell 2008). These actions were nullified by the Supreme Court in *U.S. v. Windsor* (2013), which struck down the Defense of Marriage Act in language that suggested attempts to stop same-sex marriage were harmful to gay couples and their children. In a dissent to *Windsor*, Associate Justice Antonin Scalia claimed that the majority opinion "arms well every challenger to a state law restricting marriage to its traditional definition.

Henceforth those challengers will lead with this Court's declaration that there is 'no legitimate purpose' served by such a law, and will claim that the traditional definition has the purpose and effect to 'disparage and to injure' the 'personhood and dignity' of same-sex couples." Scalia's prediction was accurate. In 2015, in the case of *Obergefell v. Hodges*, the U.S. Supreme Court recognized the right of same-sex marriage. The opinion, written by Anthony Kennedy, was opposed by the conservatives on the Supreme Court.

In the aftermath of *Windsor* the Republican position on same-sex marriage rapidly evolved. Efforts to amend the Constitution or pass the state Defense of Marriage Act were not embraced by Republican House Speaker John Boehner. In fact, Boehner openly endorsed the candidacies of two gay Republicans running for seats in the House in 2014. Meanwhile, Republican governors in New Mexico and Arizona determined that fighting for a traditional definition of marriage was not in their political interest. Another sign of the evolution of Republican thinking was the continued presence of Log Cabin Republicans, a caucus of LGBT conservatives within the Republican Party, at the party's national convention. In 2014, after years of exclusion, GOProud, a political action committee founded in 2009 to advocate for GOP recognition of LGBT equal rights, was invited to attend an annual gathering of political action committees that work on conservative issues.

Democrats on Same-Sex Marriage

Prior to 1969, neither party endorsed or recognized lesbian, gay, bisexual, or transgendered (LGBT) rights (Eskridge 1993). In the summer of that year, however, a two-day riot against police harassment broke out at the Stonewall Bar in New York City, which signaled the rise of gay rights activism. Open advocacy for LGBT rights gained momentum in the 1970s when political action was fomented by organizations such as LAMBDA legal, which formed in 1973, National Gay and Lesbian Task Force also founded in 1973, the Gay and Lesbian Advocates and Defenders (GLAD) founded in 1978, and Human Rights Campaign founded in 1980. Human Rights Campaign is the largest and most vocal advocacy group for gay and lesbian rights. Boasting over half a million members, it has become a key contributor to Democratic candidates (Newton 2010).

Although individual Democratic candidates supported gay rights or were themselves openly gay candidates (such as Barney Frank, who was elected to the House of Representatives in 1980 and became one of the party's most prominent congress members over the course of a 32-year career on Capitol Hill), the national Democratic Party was slower in embracing these issues. In 1972, party leaders rejected a gay and lesbian rights plank in the party platform. In 1980, the party endorsed an equal rights statement that included LGBT individuals but this was a tepid endorsement at best.

In the 1990s, Democrats under Bill Clinton had a mixed record on gay rights. Clinton imposed the Don't Ask, Don't Tell policy for gays in the military but failed to end discrimination in the military based on sexual orientation. When DOMA passed the House and Senate with wide majorities President Clinton signed DOMA into law, stating that "I have long opposed government recognition of same-gender marriages and this legislation is consistent to that position" (Clinton 1996).

In the early years of the 21st century, however, growing public acceptance of gay rights and gay marriage began to convince Democrats that expressing support for those causes might no longer be a political detriment, at least in states that were not deeply conservative (Klarman 2013). This reassessment accelerated after President Obama voiced support for same-sex marriage in the spring of 2012. A few months later, the Democratic Party added a statement affirming same-sex marriage in their party platform. On March 7, 2013, former president Clinton, after the Supreme Court took up a challenge to DOMA, wrote an Op-Ed piece that indicated his belief that DOMA was unconstitutional (Clinton 2013).

Advocates for same-sex marriage framed the issue as one of fairness and equality and sought to use the courts to remedy the situation (Nichols and Naylor 2013). They claimed that legislation banning same-sex marriage is a violation

---

Justice Kennedy Affirms the Right of Same-Sex Couples to Marry

In his opinion in *Obergefell v. Hodges*, Justice Kennedy, who had been supportive of gay rights since the 1990s, recognized the Constitutional right of same-sex couples to marry.

The right to marry is a fundamental right inherent in the liberty of the person, and under the Due Process and Equal Protection Clauses of the Fourteenth Amendment couples of the same-sex may not be deprived of that right and that liberty. The Court now holds that same-sex couples may exercise the fundamental right to marry. No longer may this liberty be denied to them. *Baker v. Nelson* must be and now is overruled, and the State laws challenged by Petitioners in these cases are now held invalid to the extent they exclude same-sex couples from civil marriage on the same terms and conditions as opposite-sex couples . . . No union is more profound than marriage, for it embodies the highest ideals of love, fidelity, devotion, sacrifice, and family. In forming a marital union, two people become something greater than once they were. As some of the petitioners in these cases demonstrate, marriage embodies a love that may endure even past death. It would misunderstand these men and women to say they disrespect the idea of marriage. Their plea is that they do respect it, respect it so deeply that they seek to find its fulfillment for themselves. Their hope is not to be condemned to live in loneliness, excluded from one of civilization's oldest institutions. They ask for equal dignity in the eyes of the law. The Constitution grants them that right.

Source

Kennedy, Justice Anthony. 2015. "*Obergefell v. Hodges*." Oyez. Chicago-Kent College of Law at Illinois Tech, n.d. November 6. Accessed December 12, 2015: https://www.oyez.org/cases/2014/14-556.

of the right to marry, which the Supreme Court inferred was granted in the Due Process Clause of the Fourteenth Amendment as cited in the case *Loving v. Virginia* (1967), which struck down as unconstitutional state laws forbidding people of different races to marry. They claim that prohibiting same-sex marriage amounts to sexual discrimination and violates the Equal Protection Clause of the Fourteenth Amendment and state equal rights amendments. They also argue that classifying individuals by sexual orientation ought to trigger a heightened scrutiny of the law that would invalidate such acts because states have no compelling interest to justify treating same-sex couples differently from heterosexual couples (Eskridge 1993).

Two Supreme Court cases proved the right of same-sex marriage, the first, *United States v. Windsor* (2013), struck down the Defense of Marriage Act (DOMA) as a violation of the Fifth Amendment's Equal Protection Clause. In his opinion Anthony Kennedy underscored the argument of fairness and equality. This opinion led to passage of same-sex marriage laws throughout Democrat-controlled states. Republican states, on the other hand, sought to prohibit the right of same-sex marriage by changing their constitution or calling for a new amendment to the Constitution. In 2015, Justice Kennedy wrote the opinion in *Obergefell v. Hodges*, which struck down all attempts to prohibit same-sex marriage as a violation of the equal protection laws of the U.S. Constitution.

Further Reading

Bush, George W. 2003. "Marriage Protection Week." Accessed March 1, 2014: http://georgewbush-whitehouse.archives.gov/news/releases/2003/10/20031003-12.html.

Campbell, David. 2008. "The Religion Card: Gay Marriage and the 2004 Presidential Election," *Public Opinion Quarterly,* 72 (3) Fall: 399–419.

Clinton, William J. 1996. "President Clinton's Statement on Doma." Accessed March 1, 2014: http://www.cs.cmu.edu/afs/cs/user/scotts/ftp/wpaf2mc/clinton.html.

Clinton, William J. 2013. "It's Time to Overturn DOMA," March 7, *Washington Post.* Accessed March 1, 2014: http://www.washingtonpost.com/opinions/bill-clinton-its-time-to-overturn-doma/2013/03/07/fc184408-8747-11e2-98a3-b3db6b9ac586_story.html.

DeGagne, Alexa. 2013. "Queer Bedfellows of Proposition 8 Adopting Social Conservative and Neopolitical Rationalities in California's Same-sex Marriage Fight," *Studies in Social Justice,* 7 (8): 1070–1240.

Democratic Party. 2012. "Party Platform 2012." Accessed February 21, 2014: http://www.presidency.ucsb.edu/ws/?pid=101962.

Eskridge, William N., Jr. 1993. "A History of Same-Sex Marriage." Faculty Scholarship Series. Accessed March 1, 2014: http://digitalcommons.law.yale.edu/fss_papers/1504/.

Helfman, Tara. 2013. "Gay Marriage, the Court and Federalism," *Commentary,* 135 (5) May, 18–20.

Klarman, Michael J. 2013. *From the Closet to the Altar: Courts, Backlash and the Struggle for Same-Sex Marriage.* New York: Oxford University Press.

Knowles, Helen. 2009. *The Tie Goes to Freedom: Justice Anthony M. Kennedy on Liberty.* Lanham, MD: Rowman and Littlefield.

Newton, David E. 2010. *Same-Sex Marriage: A Reference Handbook*. Santa Barbara: ABC-CLIO.

Nichols, Heather Wyatt, and Lorenda Ann Naylor. 2013. "The Policy Landscape of Sexual Orientation," *Journal of Public Management and Social Policy*, 19 (1) Spring, 5–18.

Republican Party. 2012. "2012 Republican Party Platform," August 27. Accessed February 21, 2014: http://www.presidency.ucsb.edu/ws/?pid=101961.

Gun Control

At a Glance

Few if any issues divide Republicans and Democrats as much as gun control policy. Many Democrats have been calling for more gun control and regulation of firearm ownership since the assassinations of the Kennedy brothers and Martin Luther King Jr., and their calls for new gun laws have intensified in recent years in the wake of mass shooting events that have claimed many lives. Many Republicans reject these calls, asserting that many Democratic proposals run afoul of Second Amendment guarantees of private firearm ownership. In addition, they assert that gun violence is often unleashed by criminals who would not obey the law anyway and that the best ways of reducing gun violence are harshly punishing those who use guns while committing crimes and more effectively enforcing gun regulations that already exist.

Many Democrats . . .

- Favor stricter gun control laws.
- Believe that violent crime, suicides, and accidental shootings would all be reduced if there were fewer firearms in circulation.
- Want stronger regulations governing who can own and use a gun.
- Believe the Second Amendment right to keep and bear arms guarantees collective rights to have militias, not an individual right to own a gun.
- Have regulated the purchase of ammunition.
- Want to ban specific types of firearms known as assault rifles.
- Supported the Brady Bill.
- Oppose concealed and open carry laws.

Many Republicans . . .

- Oppose stricter gun control laws.
- Believe that violence is a cultural phenomenon and not the consequence of firearms.

- Believe that the Second Amendment right to keep and bear arms is an individual right designed to gives Americans the means to defend themselves from criminals and government tyranny.
- Are closely aligned with the National Rifle Association.
- Opposed major gun control legislation such as the Clinton-era Brady Bill and assault weapons ban.
- Support concealed carry and open carry laws.

Overview

Gun control is an umbrella term used to refer to regulations that impose restrictions on the sale, distribution, and possession of guns or ammunition. Democrats and Republicans have been debating such legislation since the 1960s, and it remains one of the strongest dividing lines between the parties to this day. In general, Democrats favor stricter gun control laws, although there have historically been notable exceptions to this among lawmakers representing rural and or conservative constituencies. The Republican Party, meanwhile, is largely unified in its stance that most gun control efforts infringe on constitutional rights and

Family members of gun violence victims hold up photos of their slain relatives during the House and Senate Democrats' event at the Capitol, with advocates from Newtown Action Alliance and the Coalition to Stop Gun Violence, in Washington D.C., on December 10, 2015. (Photo By Bill Clark/Getty Images)

are ineffective in reducing crime and violence. To the contrary, many Republicans assert that gun control initiatives have been proven to actually worsen problems with crime and violence.

Gun control and gun right advocates cite the Second Amendment to support their viewpoint on firearms. The Second Amendment states that "a well-regulated militia being necessary to the security of a free state, the right of the people to keep and bear arms shall not be infringed." Each side interprets the meaning of this amendment differently. Proponents of gun rights, represented most visibly by the National Rifle Association (NRA), believe that the amendment protects the right of the individual to own and use arms for protection. They believe that the Founders gave the people the right to protect their homes, property, and liberty, even from the government itself if necessary (Waldman 2014). Proponents of gun control, represented by the Brady Campaign to Prevent Gun Violence and many other gun control advocacy groups, have asserted that the amendment refers only to the right of states, not individuals, to form armed militias for the protection of citizens in those states. In recent years, though, the gun control movement has experienced major legal setbacks at the hands of the conservative majority on the U.S. Supreme Court. After decades of decisions that broadly upheld the government's right to regulate firearms, the Court issued several major decisions in the early 21st century supporting the arguments of the NRA and other gun rights enthusiasts.

For much of the 20th century, the Supreme Court upheld federal laws that placed various restrictions on gun sales and ownership. Congressional regulation of firearms was approved by the Court in *United States v. Miller,* a 1939 case that upheld the National Firearms Act of 1934, prohibiting the possession of sawed-off shotguns. The Court also upheld the 1968 Gun Control Act, which denied the right of felons to own firearms (Lemons 2014). The recognition that the Second Amendment does provide an individual the right to gun ownership was made by the Roberts Court in June 2008. Under the leadership of Chief Justice John Roberts the Supreme Court has become more conservative than previous Courts and has been shaped by appointees of Republican Presidents Reagan and both Bushes. In the 2008 case of *District of Columbia v. Heller,* the Supreme Court's conservative majority struck down a congressional law regulating ownership of guns in the District of Columbia and held that the Second Amendment protected the individual's right to own a firearm unconnected with service to the militia, and that persons are entitled to use a weapon for lawful purposes, which included self-defense within the home. The Court's 5–4 decision did acknowledge that there were limits to this right. The majority decision penned by Justice Antonin Scalia, noted one scholar, "explicitly stated that laws that prohibited certain types of people, such as felons and the mentally unstable, from possessing firearms and that restricted where firearms might be carried, such as in churches, schools, and public buildings, are permissible" (Wilson 2016). Nonetheless, the *Heller* decision was broadly seen as a huge legal victory for the gun rights movement. The NRA and its allies celebrated again two years later, when the Supreme Court decided in *McDonald v.*

City of Chicago—another 5–4 decision—that the Second Amendment guarantee of a personal right to keep and bear arms also applied at the state and local level of government.

Meanwhile, the increased frequency of highly publicized mass shootings at schools, movie theaters, and other public venues have prompted renewed outcries from many Democrats to regulate firearms and from many Republicans to defend the rights of gun ownership. These events have included the deadly rampage at Columbine High School in 1999 that killed 13 people; the school shooting at Virginia Tech in 2007 that took 32 lives; the 2012 shooting at a movie theater in Aurora, Colorado, that left 12 dead and another 70 injured; the tragic attack by a deranged gunman at Sandy Hook Elementary School in Newtown, Connecticut, in December 2012 that killed 27 people, including 20 young children; the racist murder of 9 black church members by a white supremacist on June 17, 2015, and the mass shooting at a community college that left 10 dead and 7 wounded in Roseburg, Oregon, October 1, 2015. Polls have found that these events only briefly influence public opinion toward greater gun control, but they do lead to new political action committees (PACs) that work to raise awareness of the issues of gun control and gun rights.

Democrats on Gun Control

In 1968, after a decade of assassinations that claimed the lives of President John F. Kennedy, his brother Robert Kennedy, and civil rights leaders including Medgar Evers, Malcolm X, and Martin Luther King Jr., Democrats sponsored the Omnibus Crime and Safe Streets Act, which banned the shipment of handguns by individuals across state lines and the sale of handguns outside of a person's home state (Carter 2012). The Gun Control Act of 1968 extended the ban on interstate shipments of handguns and included rifles, shotguns, and ammunition. The law also created new criminal penalties for anyone who used a firearm while committing a federal crime. The law regulated federally licensed gun sellers and banned the possession of guns by convicted felons. In 1972, the Democratic Party platform committed the party to gun control and this remains a bedrock issue for Democrats to this day.

The Democratic Party's 1972 and 1976 platforms called for new gun regulations, including a ban on cheap pistols, nicknamed Saturday Night Specials. In 1994, the platform included planks proclaiming a need for a waiting period to purchase handguns and a ban on assault weapons. Mandatory gun locks, gun owner licensing, and background checks on private sales of guns all were explicitly mentioned in the party's 2000 platform (Carter 2012). Democrats also fought for continuation and renewal of the ban on assault weapons and expanded background checks as noted in the party platform in 2004 and again in 2008 (Democratic Party Platform 2004; Democratic Party Platform 2008).

President Bill Clinton, who served in the White House from 1993 until 2001, played a seminal role in enacting gun control legislation during his two terms in

---

Gun Control Advocate James Brady

James Brady (1940–2014) was a lifelong Republican who, after being shot and left disabled by a failed assassination attempt on President Ronald Reagan, became one of the nation's most prominent gun control advocates.

Brady was born in Centralia, Illinois, and served as a Young College Republican at the University of Illinois before graduating in 1962. He went on to serve Republican Senators Everett Dirksen of Illinois and William Roth of Delaware before joining Ronald Reagan's campaign for president in 1980. After Reagan's election, Brady was named White House Press Secretary.

On March 30, 1980, he was shot by John Hinckley Jr., a mentally ill young man seeking to assassinate Reagan. Brady never fully recovered from his wounds, and he used a wheelchair for the remainder of his life. But working in concert with his wife Sarah, Brady subsequently became a leading and effective spokesman for gun control. The couple joined with the National Council to Control Handguns, founded in 1974, to form the Brady Campaign to Prevent Gun Violence. Since its inception, this organization has been at the forefront of gun control advocacy efforts in the United States.

In stark contrast to the majority of Republicans, James and Sarah Brady campaigned vigorously for passage of the Brady Bill in 1993 and even won the support of former president Ronald Reagan for this law. Brady was honored by Bill Clinton and was seated beside the Democratic president when he signed the act into law.

Brady continued to champion gun control laws until his death on August 3, 2014. The coroner who examined Brady ruled his death a homicide, explaining that his death was directly attributable to the injuries he received 34 years earlier. His wife Sarah died eight months later of pneumonia, on April 3, 2015.

Source

Brady Campaign against Gun Violence. Accessed August 22, 2014: http://www.bradycampaign .org/our-history.

---

office. In 1993, after a surge in gun-related crimes, Clinton and the Democrat-controlled Congress passed the Brady Handgun Violence Prevention Act, which was named after former Republican White House press secretary James Brady. Brady had been seriously wounded during a failed assassination attempt on President Ronald Reagan in 1981.

The Brady Bill's major provisions included a five-business-day waiting period for handgun sales through licensed dealers and a requirement that local law enforcement conduct background checks on handgun buyers. Clinton led the fight for passage of the 1994 assault weapons ban that prohibited the manufacture and sale of 19 specific firearms defined as "assault weapons." The bill also limited the use of gun feeding devices or magazines that held more than ten bullets at a time. Following up on regulating the possession of guns, Clinton urged passage of the Gun-Free Schools Act of 1994. The bill required schools receiving federal funding to expel for one year any student caught with a weapon on school grounds (Carter 2012). In the November 1994 midterms, however, Democrats suffered their worst defeat in decades, losing 54 seats in the House and 8 seats in the U.S. Senate. Political analysts and President Clinton himself blamed some of the poor showing on Democratic support for gun control, which was not politically popular in more conservative and rural parts of the country.

After the Columbine school shooting in 1999, however, Democrats renewed their calls for strengthened gun control laws including mandatory child safety locks, a photo ID to buy a gun, more stringent background checks, and training in gun safety before someone could purchase a gun. Despite the relative popularity of Clinton, his handpicked successor and vice president Al Gore narrowly lost the 2000 election to Republican nominee George W. Bush. Some analysts believed that the Democrat's continued insistence on gun control cost the party electoral votes in Gore's home state of Tennessee, which is a state with a culture favorable to gun rights. The electoral pressure on Democrats to appease gun rights groups such as the National Rifle Association may have muted the Democrats' zeal to make changes in gun laws, but it did not stop them altogether. After gaining control of Congress in 2007, Democrats affirmed their support for gun control by passing the National Instant Check System Improvement amendment in 2007. This measure tightened the law surrounding the instant background check system.

However, since their electoral defeat in 2000, Democrats have been more wary about pushing a gun control agenda. President Barack Obama's administration approved just one gun-related measure: a renewal on a law banning plastic firearms. In 2009, Obama also signed a provision allowing guns to be taken into national parks (albeit as part of much larger omnibus legislation), and signed off on an appropriations bill that included an amendment that allowed guns as checked baggage on Amtrak. He dissuaded Attorney General Eric Holder from pursuing a reinstatement of the Assault Weapons Ban. Still, Obama and Democrats in Congress have strongly urged the passage of new gun control measures in the wake of horrible mass shootings such as the 2012 massacre at Sandy Hook Elementary School in Newtown, Connecticut, that left 20 children dead. But with Republicans in Congress unified against any such measures, the Democrats have been stymied at the federal level.

It has been easier for Democrats in states with a majority of citizens registered as Democrats to enact legislation. Many so-called blue states have enacted tough gun control legislation. Even in these instances, however, some politicians have found their careers imperiled by their votes in favor of new gun regulations. In Colorado, for instance, state lawmakers passed several gun control bills in the wake of the Sandy Hook massacre and the mass shooting at a theater in Aurora, Colorado. But gun rights groups quickly organized recall elections against two Democrats who played important roles in passing the gun control bills, and in September 2013 both Democrats were ousted and replaced by Republicans in a special recall election.

Republicans on Gun Control

The Republican Party is strongly aligned against gun control. Since the 1950s, the Republican Party has vigorously opposed most gun control legislation at the local, state, and national levels. Many Republicans adhere to the belief that the Second Amendment guarantees protection of the rights of individuals to own guns, and that most restrictions on the sale or ownership of firearms undermine the ability of individuals to defend themselves and their families. In general, they also see gun control in terms of an expansive government hindering the liberties of the individual.

The GOP opposition to gun control is supported by the NRA and other anti-gun control lobbying organizations. These groups have developed highly effective political networks and raise large contributions for the Republicans, and gun rights advocates have become an important part of the GOP's base.

In the 2000 presidential election, staunch NRA supporter George W. Bush—who as governor of Texas had signed legislation that legalized concealed handguns and limited the ability of citizens to bring lawsuits against gun manufacturers—secured the Republican Party's nomination and subsequently won the presidency. Many political experts believe that the support that Bush gained from the NRA enabled him to win several states—including Tennessee, the home state of opponent Al Gore—that were critical to his election.

In 2004, during Bush's first term in office, he and the Republican-controlled Congress allowed the Assault Weapons Ban to expire. The following year, Republicans in Congress pushed through the Protection of Lawful Commerce in Arms Act over Democratic opposition. This law forbade individuals or groups from suing gun manufacturers or dealers if their weapons were used for crimes. This legislation effectively shielded the gun industry from any liability for how its products were used.

The states with the least stringent gun laws tend to be in politically conservative regions of the South and West. In most cases, the comparatively light regulatory environment for guns in these states stems from alliances between the GOP and the NRA. Even in these states, however, certain gun ownership restrictions exist, such as minimum age restrictions and laws that restrict felons or people with a history of mental illness from possessing guns.

A more controversial law that exists in some states is the so-called "Stand Your Ground" law that allows citizens to use deadly force against perceived assailants. These laws came under national scrutiny when a white vigilante named George Zimmerman shot and killed a 17-year-old black man, Trayvon Martin in Sanford, Florida. Zimmerman was acquitted in court and his defense used the Stand Your Ground law to persuade jurors that Zimmerman only used deadly force because he was convinced his own life was in jeopardy. Many civil rights activists, Democrats, and even President Barack Obama expressed disappointment or outrage with the outcome of the case, and Stand Your Ground laws have subsequently become another flashpoint of division between Republicans and Democrats.

In addition to defending gun rights at the state level, Republicans have led court challenges to gun control legislation. One was the Gun Free School Zones Act passed by Congress, which forbids, under the Commerce Clause, the carrying of guns in a protected area around a school. In the case of the *United States v. Lopez* in 1995, the Court struck down the law claiming Congress had exceeded its constitutional authority. Republicans were also behind a challenge to the Brady Bill and led to the Supreme Court case of *Printz v. United States* in 1997, which overturned the law's requirement that local law enforcement agencies conduct background checks on potential gun buyers (Winkler 2013).

The Republican Party is not blind to the role that guns play in violence. Rather than restrict everyone's right to own a gun, however, the GOP asserts that the wiser path is to focus on disarming the few people who commit gun violence. Thus, they support harsher penalties for criminals and more forceful prosecution under existing laws. They believe that since criminals operate outside of the law, gun control legislation only impacts the ability of lawful citizens to gain access to weapons. Many Republicans point out that even in areas with strict gun control laws criminals still find ways to acquire guns.

In 2000, Republican Governor Jim Gilmore of Virginia, who also headed the Republican National Committee (RNC) at that time worked closely with the NRA to develop a broad program to increase penalties for the illegal use of firearms. The program, Project Exile, mandated substantial prison sentences for the use of a firearm in violent or drug-related crimes by having all gun crimes prosecuted at the federal level. The law makes criminals subject to a mandatory five-year minimum prison sentence with no parole. Versions of the program, which began in Virginia, later expanded into cities such as Baltimore, Chicago, Miami, and Philadelphia. Project Exile has been portrayed by gun rights advocates as a model for state gun legislation and as a means for the Republicans to counter charges that the party ignores gun control issues. This project also formed the basis for the $550 million Project Safe Neighborhoods, a 2001 initiative by the Bush administration's Justice Department to reduce gun violence (Amends 2013).

While Republicans are largely supportive of gun rights—indeed, in many parts of the country, winning GOP primaries necessitates such a stance—there are exceptions to this rule. After James Brady, President Reagan's press secretary, was shot and seriously wounded along with Reagan and two law enforcement officers in 1981, Brady and his wife Sarah became among the most prominent activists in the gun control movement. They founded the organization now known as the Brady Center to Prevent Gun Violence, which continues to rank as one of the leading gun control organizations in the United States. Moderates within the GOP from politically moderate states or districts have also supported specific gun control legislation, including waiting periods and background checks. At the federal level, this translated into support for the Brady Bill (named after Reagan's press secretary, James Brady, who was wounded in the assassination attempt). Moderates gained clout when Reagan announced his support for the measure and when President

George H. W. Bush announced his resignation from the NRA (Brady 2002). As reported by James Barron in an article in the *New York Times* on August 8, 2014, President Bush was irked by the NRA's campaign against moderate Republicans who supported the Brady Bill, as well as by the incendiary antigovernment rhetoric employed by the organization. After the Newtown massacre the Hill newspaper in a January 15, 2014, report noted that former New York City Mayor Michael Bloomberg, a onetime Republican, created and endowed a new political action committee, Every Town for Gun Safety, with $50 million to defeat candidates opposed to gun control.

Further Reading

Amends, Ross. 2013. "Project Exile: Still the Model for Firearms Crime Reduction Strategies," *The Police Chief*, November, 80: 56–59. Accessed August 22, 2014: http://www.policechiefmagazine.org/magazine/index.cfm?fuseaction=display_arch&article_id=3192&issue_id=112013.

American Presidency Project, "Political Party Platforms of Parties Receiving Electoral Votes: 1840–2012." Accessed June 20, 2014: http://www.presidency.ucsb.edu/platforms.php.

Brady, Sara. 2002. *A Good Fight*. New York: Public Affairs.

Carter, Gregg Lee. 2012. *Guns in American Society: An Encyclopedia of History, Politics, Culture, and the Law*. Santa Barbara: ABC-CLIO.

Democratic Party Platform. 2004. Online by Gerhard Peters and John T. Woolley, "The American Presidency Project." Accessed February 7, 2016: http://www.presidency.ucsb.edu/ws/?pid=29613.

Democratic Party Platform. 2008. Online by Gerhard Peters and John T. Woolley, "The American Presidency Project." Accessed February 7, 2016: http://www.presidency.ucsb.edu/ws/?pid=78283

Giffords, Gabby. 2014. *Enough: Our Fight to Keep America Safe from Gun Violence*. New York: Scribner.

Lemons, Jane Fullerton. 2014. "Gun Control," *CQ Researcher,* June 10. Accessed June 11, 2014: http://0-library.cqpress.com.libra.naz.edu/cqresearcher/.

Waldman, Michael. 2014. *The Second Amendment: A Biography*. New York: Simon and Schuster.

Wilson, Harry. 2016. *Gun Politics in America: Historical and Modern Documents in Context*. Santa Barbara: ABC-CLIO.

Winkler, Adam. 2013. *Gunfight: The Battle over the Right to Bear Arms in America*. New York: W. W. Norton.

Health Care

At a Glance

Health care policy has been a perennial source of division for Democrats and Republicans since the early 20th century, when scientific advances in medicine and technology first began increasing both the effectiveness and the expense of medical care. Since that time, Republicans and Democrats have clashed repeatedly over the implementation, function, and funding of the country's leading health-related entitlement programs, including Medicare and Medicaid. They also differ markedly about the role that government should play in providing health care to citizens, with most Democrats asserting that government has a moral duty to ensure that all Americans have access to adequate health care and many Republicans insisting that free market capitalism offers the best path forward—and that health care is not necessarily a "right" enshrined in the Constitution. These divisions were on vivid display in 2010, when Democratic President Barack Obama and a Democratic-majority Congress were able to pass the Affordable Care Act (ACA)—better known as Obamacare—into law over furious objections from many Republicans. Key aspects of the ACA included regulating insurance companies to compel them to allow people with preexisting conditions to purchase health care insurance, allowing parents to keep their children on their insurance plans until age 26, regulations mandating that people purchase health coverage, expansion of the Medicaid program, and limits on health insurance industry profits. Since the ACA became law, Republicans have repeatedly tried to end the law via legislative bills and legal challenges, but to no avail.

Many Democrats . . .

- Assert that there is a basic right to health and that the government is obligated to protect and ensure this.
- Have been in the forefront of legislation that created federal–state health care partnerships such as Medicaid and Medicare.
- Believe in the need for expanding health care coverage for those who cannot afford it.
- Support mandating health care insurance.

- Favor a single-payer system like that in Canada and the United Kingdom.
- Would like to help pay for health care coverage through higher taxes on corporations and the wealthy.

Many Republicans . . .

- Reject the idea that health is a right that government must guarantee and protect.
- Support private health insurance and prefer market solutions to the problem of people not being covered by health insurance.
- Support the right of states to mandate health care insurance.
- Reject a federal requirement mandating health care insurance.
- Believe that single-payer insurance is akin to socialism.
- Want to rein in the cost of entitlement programs including health care.

Overview

During the early 20th century, health insurance was not a priority for lawmakers because inexpensive medical care was routinely available to all but the poorest sectors of society, who wielded little political power. But these circumstances quickly changed. "American medicine in the post–World War I era was revolutionized by spectacular advances in diagnosis and treatment," noted one history of U.S. health care politics. "As the healing capabilities of the medical profession and its institutions—most notably the hospital—continued to grow, the financial expense involved in obtaining health services escalated. When this problem further intensified during the Great Depression, making health care more accessible and affordable became a top priority of social reformers and New Dealers" (Hillstrom 2012).

The scope and scale of government action in this realm expanded dramatically during the presidency of Democrat Franklin Delano Roosevelt (1933–1945). Roosevelt embraced the ideal that Americans were entitled to both economic and social security (Kronenfeld and Kronenfeld 2004). FDR's signature program was the Social Security Act, which provided pensions to the aged and infirm. After FDR died in office, his successor, President Harry Truman (1945–1953), suggested a national health insurance system to cover Americans who could not afford medical insurance.

A conservative Republican backlash in the 1950s prevented Truman from getting a health care law passed, and, to some extent, the urgency of a national health insurance program abated during the 1950s when employer-provided private insurance expanded to cover millions of Americans. During the 1950s, Blue Cross and Blue Shield plans operated in most states and covered municipal and state workers, as well as school employees. By the early 1960s, after unions had won health insurance coverage as a basic benefit for their members, the majority of full-time employed U.S. citizens had the benefits of private health insurance.

For those who were not covered by private health insurance, the U.S. government stepped in during the 1960s when Democrat President Lyndon Johnson and fellow Democratic lawmakers amended the Social Security Act to create Medicare and Medicaid. Medicare is a government insurance program that pays for hospitalization, doctors' visits, and other medical care for U.S. residents age 65 and over. After Social Security, Medicare is the costliest U.S. domestic spending program. Medicaid is a joint federal–state taxpayer funded program that provides health coverage for people below a set income. The legislation provides that the federal government pay 55 percent of the cost, while the states and local governments pick up the remainder of the cost. Neither program provided prescription drug coverage at their inceptions, since this was not a typical benefit of private insurance in the 1960s either. Medicare and Medicaid were expanded in 1967 to provide for medical equipment in the home, podiatric services, and outpatient physical therapy, and again, in 1972, when the acts were amended to include chiropractic, speech pathology, and family planning services. Under the presidency of Republican George W. Bush, prescription drug coverage was added to Medicare with bipartisan support (Jacobs and Skocpol 2012).

Medicare and Medicaid prompted a great deal of debate when they were enacted. Many conservative Republicans rejected the idea that the U.S. government had any constitutional authority to interfere in health care, and they believed such actions ultimately diminished the efficiency and increased the cost of health care for all Americans. They believed that competition within the private sector for the health

President Lyndon B. Johnson, left, with former President Harry S. Truman at his side, complete the signing of the Medicare Bill at the Truman Library in Independence, Missouri, on July 30, 1965. (AP Photo/File)

care consumer would lift the U.S. health care system to new heights of excellence and efficiency. Many Republicans preferred mechanisms to encourage and expand private insurance coverage, insisting that market competition was the best way to keep medical costs down and medical innovation up. Republican President Ronald Reagan, for example, supported sharp decreases in funding for Medicare and Medicaid. The Deficit Reduction Act of 1984, the Graham Rudman Act of 1985, and the Consolidated Budget Reconciliation Act of 1985 cut payments to doctors and hospitals for patients who had Medicare or Medicaid, which led to a drop in the number of health care providers enlisted in these programs.

Economic recession and retrenchment in the 1980s however led to a decline of health care plans offered by employers. The cost of health care increased, in part, some argued, due to the large number of uninsured who used emergency room care and county hospitals for their medical needs. It was estimated that by the early 1990s as many as 15 percent of the U.S. population was without health insurance and that medical costs were consuming an ever-greater share of the nation's overall economic activity.

Health insurance became a defining issue for Democrats in the 1992 presidential election, with multiple candidates promising to reduce the cost of health care and expand it to cover the uninsured. Bill Clinton, a Democrat who served two terms in the White House from 1993 to 2001, spent his first two years in office in a failed attempt to develop and steer a comprehensive health care bill through Congress. The Clinton health care plan not only failed to pass Congress -where Republicans almost unanimously rejected it as a government "takeover" of health care—but the policy defeat may have contributed to his historical rebuke by the electorate in the 1994 midterms. In that election, the Democratic Party lost 54 seats in the House and 8 seats in the Senate, and, for the first time since before the New Deal, Republicans would enjoy a majority in Congress that lasted longer than one term.

As the numbers of the uninsured and the cost of health care insurance premiums climbed in the 1990s both parties offered new prescriptions for health care reform. Many Democrats would continue to argue for new government regulations and programs to rein in costs and expand coverage to uninsured Americans who, because of preexisting conditions or financial hardship, could not secure insurance. Republicans, in general, also recognized that the cost of health care was draining the U.S. economy and that the rising cost of health care insurance was hurting employers who provided coverage, and consumers who saw their employee contributions inexorably increasing. Many Republicans also recognized the economic inefficiency of having the uninsured use county hospital emergency rooms for their preventive, acute, and chronic medical care. But many conservatives continued to claim that the free market should remain central to any health care system.

Democrats on Health Care

Lyndon Johnson enacted the first significant health care reform since the New Deal with passage of the amendments to Social Security that created Medicaid and

Medicare, which provided health care coverage for individuals who were elderly or indigent in 1965. "Medicare [had been] a proposal of the Democratic Party platforms for decades," recalled Lawrence O'Brien, one of Johnson's top advisors on health care policies. "There had been advocacy on the part of Democratic presidents; Harry Truman was the first. It clearly was a commitment made by the party . . . So, with a two-to-one [Democratic] margin in the House . . . you go for a [legislative] program that was so broad in its elements that it spoke to every Democratic Party position leading with Medicare" (O'Brien 1986).

But despite Medicare and Medicaid, and even with most middle-class workers and union members receiving health insurance as part of their compensation, millions of Americans employed in the retail industry and agriculture remained without coverage. The number of Americans without health insurance increased during the economic dislocation of the 1970s, when the United States began a shift from a manufacturing-based economy to a service and information technology economy. Insurance coverage was not an option for employees in the service and retail industry and many Americans lost insurance coverage when they lost their jobs. Other individuals who found new jobs found that, due to preexisting conditions, they could not purchase or could not afford health insurance. Cuts to funding in the 1980s to both Medicare and Medicaid exacerbated the situation and made health care costs and health care gaps headline news in the early 1990s.

In his acceptance speech in 1992, Bill Clinton promised to "take on healthcare profiteers and make health care affordable for every family." President Clinton created a commission, the National Health Care Task Force, headed by First Lady Hillary Clinton, to study and recommend health care reform legislation. The task force alienated the health insurance industry by keeping them outside of their deliberations, and the sheer size of the task force's proposed Health Security Act made it easy for opponents to paint it as too complex to work. Meanwhile, "delivery of the plan to Congress was delayed time and again through the summer of 1993 by a succession of political brushfires," including controversies over the NAFTA trade agreement, whether to allow gays to serve in the U.S. military, and budget battles. "These delays and distractions gave opponents of the Health Security Act an opening, and they were swift to take advantage. Stakeholders in the existing system, including pharmaceutical manufacturers, hospitals, and insurance companies, launched battalions of lobbyists and negative advertisements against the White House's reform efforts" (Hillstrom 2012).

A series of carefully tailored television and radio ads convinced those who already had health insurance that any government run health care system would cost them more money and reduce or ration their care. Despite having a Democratic majority in the House and Senate, opposition mounted from conservative Democrats and Republicans in Congress, and, in the end, the Clinton health reform plan collapsed.

Democrats subsequently abandoned a comprehensive solution, instead focusing on specific issues such as creating mental health coverage in employee insurance and allowing workers who lost their jobs to keep existing medical coverage for 12 months. To assist children of the working poor whose parents were not eligible for Medicaid but who could not afford health insurance, Congress passed a joint federal state program the Children's Health Insurance Program, or CHIP.

Health care reform remained an unresolved promise for Democrats through the 2008 election. Barack Obama campaigned on the need for reform by addressing still escalating economic costs of health care, which he described as a "threat to our economy," and by asserting that access to health care was a "right for every American." In 2009, the debate between Democrats and Republicans focused on fixing the existing health care system not creating a new one. Rather than follow the Canadian model, which is single-payer government-run national health program, debates were about how to best control the cost of private insurance while maximizing the number of people who had health insurance and spreading the cost and risk to healthy uninsured populations. In lieu of a single-payer system many Democrats sought to expand some public insurance, like Medicare, and require an individual mandate that would lead to everyone enrolling in some form of health insurance. They were opposed by Republicans who wanted to incentivize ways to have the private sector expand coverage. Many Republicans opposed any increase in government spending on entitlements and any attempt to regulate the industry.

As a result, the Patient Protection and Affordable Care Act (PPACA), also known as the Affordable Care Act or Obamacare, passed along almost exclusively partisan lines. In November 2009, House Democrats (and one lone Republican) voted 220–215 to approve the Affordable Health Care for America Act (HR 3962). The Senate passed its own version along straight party lines on December 24, 2009. President Obama unveiled a proposal to reconcile the House and Senate bills, placing pressure on the House to pass health care reform legislation. The House and Senate Democrats were able to pass legislation without one Republican vote. On March 23, 2010, Obama signed the Patient Protection and Affordable Care Act into law. Obama followed up this act on March 24, 2010, by signing an executive order withholding federal funds for abortion services, which was consistent with the so-called Hyde Amendment and a promise he had made to antiabortion Democrats.

Obamacare, as it has come to be called by both detractors and supporters, created an individual mandate requiring every American to have medical coverage either through private insurance or public health care or face a fine, made it illegal for insurance companies to deny people insurance for preexisting medical conditions, regulated health care so requiring certain kinds of medical care be included in all insurance packages such as reproductive services for women, regulated the amount of profits insurance companies could reap, and expanded Medicaid to cover the millions of working poor who could not afford insurance. The bill was challenged by Republicans who condemned the law as an unconstitutional invasion of state and individual rights. The case made it all the way to the Supreme Court, which ruled in a 5–4 decision that the federal government did have a constitutional right to regulate health care and that through its power to tax it could mandate individual coverage.

Obamacare has also received criticism from the left. Some progressive Democrats would like to dispense with third-party insurance plans altogether (a third-party insurance plan occurs when the insurance industry regulates the conduct between the individual and their medical care providers, acting as third party in what medical care is covered). These critics would like the United States to follow a national health care system similar to those of Canada or the United Kingdom, which are single-payer systems. A single-payer system allows the individual to choose their physician and health care program, which is paid for by the government. The first state to enact such legislation was Vermont, which is dominated by the Democratic Party. Vermont enacted a single-payer system in 2011 and will gradually end employee provided private insurance. Some progressive Democrats still hold out hope that America might someday move toward a true single-payer health care system.

Still, mainstream Democrats generally see the Affordable Care Act as a triumph, and by 2012 the party as a whole had moved toward a position in which it recognized the importance of defending it from GOP attacks. "We believe accessible, affordable, high quality health care is part of the American promise, that Americans should have the security that comes with good health care, and that no one should go broke because they get sick," asserted the 2012 Democratic Party platform.

> Over the determined opposition of Republicans, we enacted landmark reforms that are already helping millions of Americans, and more benefits will come soon. As a result of our efforts, today, young Americans entering the workforce can stay on their parents' plans. Insurers can no longer refuse to cover kids with pre-existing medical conditions. Insurance companies will no longer be able to arbitrarily cap and cancel coverage, or charge women more simply because of their gender. People with private insurance are getting preventive services like cancer screenings, annual well-woman visits, and FDA-approved contraception with no out-of-pocket costs . . . Small businesses are receiving tax credits to help them cover their workers, and businesses and families are receiving rebates from insurers who overcharged them. Soon, working families will finally have the security of knowing they won't lose health care or be forced into bankruptcy if a family member gets sick or loses their job. And soon, insurance companies will no longer be able to deny coverage based on pre-existing conditions. Medicaid will cover more working families. Those who don't get insurance at work will be able to shop in new exchanges and will be eligible for new tax credits. As a result, all Americans will have access to health care." (Democratic National Committee 2012)

Republicans on Health Care

Conservative Republicans have always rejected the idea that health care is a fundamental right or that government should have a significant role in regulating the health care industry. They argue that under the Constitution health and safety issues were always the provenance of the states, and certain rights not strictly given to the federal government or the states were reserved for the people. In their opposition to government control they have often found strong allies in the American Medical Association (AMA) a professional trade organization for physicians, and America's Health Insurance Plans, a trade organization for insurers.

When Lyndon Johnson enacted Medicare and Medicaid, the conservative backlash was fierce. Republican opponents of these programs joined with the AMA, which rejected the law because it allowed the government to set rates for treatments from doctors and hospitals (thus reducing their profits) but would also determine treatments available to patients (thus reducing the autonomy of health care professionals). Johnson was able to turn aside their objections—and those of many Republicans and conservative southern Democrats—due to a landslide presidential election in 1964 that gave him huge Democratic majorities in both the House and Senate.

Health care reform faded into the background for Republicans during the late 1970s and under presidents Ronald Reagan, who served from 1981 to 1989, and George H. W. Bush who served from 1989 to 1993. The election of Bill Clinton and his subsequent campaign to pass major new health care reforms reenergized conservatives, however. Republican lawmakers allied with conservative talk radio hosts such as Rush Limbaugh, leaders of think tanks such as Bill Kristol, and the health care industry in working to kill rather than amend the Clinton health care plan. Republicans hammered at the health care plan before the midterm elections of 1994 with such success that they derailed the legislation and made historic gains in both the House and the Senate. This victory was so complete that health care reform remained dormant as a big political issue until 2008.

Many Republicans opposed but could not stop the Democratic majority in the House and Senate from enacting Obamacare. Instead they focused on appeals to voters to repeal the law. The health care act was a central point in Republicans significant gains in the House and Senate in the 2010 midterms. Fueled by conservative and Libertarian voters who created the Tea Party, Republicans won back control of the House with a gain of 63 seats and picked up another 6 seats in the U.S. Senate (Sabato 2011). Failing in their efforts to defund or repeal the health care plan, many Republicans and their industry allies challenged the law in Court (Blackman and Barnett 2013). The lawsuit was brought against the U.S. Department of Health and Human Services by 26 states, the National Federation of Independent Business, and two individuals. Many conservatives were dismayed when in June 2014 Republican appointed Chief Justice John Roberts sided with the liberal wing of the Supreme Court, which consists of Democrat appointees to the Court, to give them a 5–4 majority that found the Affordable Care Act constitutional. The court's majority ruling stated that the law's penalty for people who ignore the mandate to purchase health insurance was constitutional under Congress's constitutional power to levy taxes, but that the insurance mandate would not be a constitutional exercise of Congress's power under the Commerce Clause because those powers are still reserved to the states. In response, the aggrieved conservative members of the Supreme Court wrote strongly worded dissents (ProCon.org 2011).

Republican opposition to the health care reform act did not end with the Court's decision. Republican legislators in 36 states rejected the idea of managing their own health care markets and instead demanded that the executive branch run the newly mandated health care exchanges. This created a political and logistical headache for the Obama White House in 2013 (Clemmit 2014). In the 2014 midterms many Republican candidates continued to draw attention to the problems with the White House enrollment and rollout as part of their election campaigns.

Republican opposition to the Affordable Care Act has been near-absolute ever since its passage, despite the fact that many of their most dire warnings have not been borne out. But some Republicans have actually expressed openness to increased government regulation of the health care industry in other contexts

Republican Senator Ted Cruz Filibusters against Obamacare

On September 24, 2013, Republican Senator Ted Cruz of Texas made a failed attempt to halt a bill that included funding for the Affordable Care Act through a filibuster of the legislation. Following is an excerpt from his Senate floor speech, which ran for 21 hours:

Madam President, I rise today in opposition to ObamaCare. I rise today in an effort to speak for 26 million Texans and for 300 million Americans. All across this country Americans are suffering because of ObamaCare. ObamaCare isn't working. Yet fundamentally there are politicians in this body who are not listening to the people. They are not listening to the concerns of their constituents; they are not listening to the jobs lost or the people forced into part-time work, to the people losing their health insurance, to the people who are struggling.

A great many Texans, a great many Americans feel they don't have a voice. I hope to play some very small part in helping provide that voice for them. I intend to speak in opposition to ObamaCare, I intend to speak in support of defunding ObamaCare, until I am no longer able to stand, to do everything I can to help Americans stand together and recognize this grand experiment 3 1/2 years ago is, quite simply, not working . . . We just had a 6-week recess during August where a substantial percentage of Members of Congress chose not to hold townhalls during the 6 weeks we had to be back in our home States, not even to give their constituents a chance to say their views, because it is very easy when those of us who are in elected office have been here for a long time to believe Washington knows better; to believe that all the solutions are found in Washington, DC, and the rest of the country is better—as they say of small children—seen but not heard. We need millions of people to get an answer. Millions of people are asking for accountability, for responsibility, for truth from their elected officials, truth about how ObamaCare is failing the men and women of America.

Source

Cruz, Ted. 2013. "Filibuster against Healthcare," September 24, *Congressional Record*, 113th Congress, page 6701.

and settings. Republican President Richard Nixon floated the idea of mandatory and national health insurance coverage in the early 1970s, largely as a means of cost containment, but his idea was opposed not only by conservative Republicans but also progressive Democrats, such as Senator Edward Kennedy, who wanted a single-payer system (Starr 1984). Governor Mitt Romney of Massachusetts had signed into law a mandatory health care act in 2006. The law mandated that nearly every resident of Massachusetts obtain a minimum level of insurance coverage, provided free health care insurance for residents earning less than 150 percent of the federal poverty level (FPL), and mandated that employers with more than 10 "full-time" employees provide health care insurance. The Massachusetts law was cited by President Obama and many other health care experts as a template for his Affordable Care Act passed by Congress in 2010. After Mitt Romney received the 2012 Republican nomination for president he repudiated his work in Massachusetts in opposition to Obamacare. Romney claimed that it was within a state's right to reform health care but not the federal government's.

Further Reading

Blackman, Josh, and Randy Barnett. 2013. *Unprecedented: The Constitutional Challenge to Obamacare.* New York: Public Affairs.

Clemmit, Marcia. 2014. "Health Care," *CQ Researcher,* April 17. Accessed September 20, 2014: http://0-library.cqpress.com.libra.naz.edu/cqresearcher/.

Democratic National Committee. 2012. "2012 Democratic Party Platform," September 3. Online by Gerhard Peters and John T. Woolley, "The American Presidency Project." Accessed December 21, 2014: http://www.presidency.ucsb.edu/ws/?pid=101962.

Emanuel, Ezekiel. 2014. *Reinventing American Health Care: How the Affordable Care Act Will Improve our Terribly Complex, Blatantly Unjust, Outrageously Expensive, Grossly Inefficient, Error Prone System.* New York: Public Affairs.

Gillette, Internet Copy, LBJ Library Austin Texas. Accessed February 7, 2016: http://www.lbjlib.utexas.edu/johnson/archives.hom/oralhistory.hom/OBrienL/OBRIEN11.PDF.

Hillstrom, Kevin. 2012. *U.S. Health Policy and Politics: A Documentary History.* Washington, D.C.: CQ Press.

Jacobs, Lawrence, and Theda Skocpol. 2012. *Health Care Reform and American Politics: What Everyone Needs to Know.* New York: Oxford University Press.

Kronenfeld, Jennie Jacobs, and Michael R. Kronenfeld. 2004. *Healthcare Reform in America: A Reference Handbook.* Santa Barbara: ABC-CLIO.

O'Brien, Lawrence F. 1986. Transcript, Lawrence F. O'Brien Oral History Interview XI, July 24, by Michael L.

ProCon.org. 2011. "History of the Passage of the March 2010 Health Care Reforms Laws." Accessed February 7, 2016: http://healthcarereform.procon.org/view.resource.php?resourceID=003712.

Sabato, Larry J. 2011. *Pendulum Swing.* New York: Pearson.

Starr, Paul. 1984. *The Social Transformation of American Medicine: The Rise of Sovereign Profession and Making of a Vast Industry.* New York: Basic Books.

HIV/AIDS

At a Glance

Dealing with human immunodeficiency virus (HIV) and acquired immune deficiency syndrome (AIDS) has been an issue dividing Democratic and Republican leaders in Congress and at the state level since the disease was initially identified. The debate centers on how to stop the disease from spreading into healthy populations and how to treat those who already have the disease.

Many Democrats . . .

- Believe HIV and AIDS are illnesses that should be a top priority of federally funded research.
- See the Republican response to AIDS as uncaring.
- Support federal and state policies that provide or subsidize expensive HIV/AIDS drugs.
- Believe the United States should lead the global AIDS fight.
- Believe that the United States should provide free needles to drug users as a means to cut down on the spread of HIV/AIDS.

Many Republicans . . .

- Believe HIV and AIDS should be eliminated through philanthropic and federal research funds.
- Express concern that the Democrat-sponsored HIV/AIDS policy may encourage immoral or even criminal behavior.
- Reject expensive government programs including state and federal HIV/AIDS subsidies.
- Support the global fight against HIV/AIDS.
- Oppose providing clean and free needles to drug users.

Overview

Both Democrats and Republicans see the health crisis created by the rise of HIV and AIDS as a serious one that requires government attention to fund research

Scientists Dr. Kamel Khalili, left, and Rafal Kaminski prepare DNA cells in bacteria as part of the HIV elimination process at Temple University Hospital in Philadelphia, Pennsylvania, on July 31, 2014. Researchers have developed a way to eliminate HIV from cells in the laboratory, but have not set up a time frame for clinical trials. (Photo by William Thomas Cain/ Getty Images)

of the disease, provide better treatment of the illness, and educate the public on prevention. Over the years, however, the parties have often disagreed on the best approaches to reach these goals and the priority given to fight HIV/AIDS domestically and internationally. Many Republicans have been reluctant to support policies they believed might unintentionally promote a gay lifestyle, risky sexual behavior, and drug abuse. Generally, Democratic lawmakers made funding to combat AIDS a higher priority than many Republicans and had fewer qualms about promoting an alternate lifestyle.

The response of elected officials and policy makers to the AIDS crisis in the 1980s was widely criticized by gay rights advocates, historians, and policy experts. In 1981, physicians across the United States noticed the rise of a mysterious viral disease that affected gay men, destroying their natural defenses against infections, and leading to rare types of pneumonia and cancer. Initially medical personnel called this ailment "GRID" for gay-related immune deficiency. After gay rights activists complained that the name stigmatized the LGBT community, and health care officials noted those afflicted included intravenous drug users, heterosexuals who received AIDS-infected blood transfusions, and heterosexuals who had sexual contact with these persons, the Centers for Disease Control renamed the disease AIDS, or acquired immune deficiency syndrome.

Conservative politicians were initially reluctant to address the new health risk, and President Ronald Reagan did not make a major speech on AIDS until 1985.

The development of AIDS occurred at the same time that the Religious Right conservative political movement was rising. Fundamentalist Christian organizations such as the Moral Majority and the Christian Coalition became an important part of the Republican base. These religious conservatives were dedicated to opposing the expansion and acceptance of gay rights. Some members of this coalition believed that AIDS was God's punishment for a homosexual lifestyle. Another coalition within the conservative movement was the "New Right," whose ideas were drawn from economists who called for reducing the size of the federal government in order to allow for more individual initiative. This led conservatives to call for a cut in spending on federal social programs, devolution of federal power back to the states, and a reduction of personal and corporate income taxes.

Conservatives helped put Ronald Reagan in the White House twice, which may explain his administration's initially tepid response to AIDS prevention, research, and treatment. It was only during his second term that officials in the Reagan administration, most notably U.S. Surgeon General Everett Koop, took decisive action to promote research and treatment for AIDS.

During the 1980s, many Republicans and Democrats battled over funding for AIDS prevention and education programs. Fearing that "safe sex" programs would encourage promiscuity and homosexual behavior, conservatives in Congress and the White House sponsored AIDS prevention programs that emphasized abstinence and moral behavior. Public health officials wanted the administration to sponsor large-scale HIV testing, but efforts to fund this were stymied by debates between Republicans and Democrats over whether such testing would be anonymous so as to protect individuals who tested positive for HIV from reprisals, such as losing one's apartment or being fired.

Conservative resistance to funding AIDS research faded in the 1990s. The decade began with Reagan's successor and former vice president, President George H. W. Bush, signing into law the Ryan White CARE Act, also known as the Comprehensive AIDS Resources Emergency Act, which appropriated over $2.6 billion to combat the disease. Compromise legislation in the 1990s provided laws protecting HIV-positive individuals from discrimination, and federal courts struck down restrictions on the dissemination of AIDS educational materials. The decade of the 1990s also saw great strides in the development of treatments for those afflicted with HIV/AIDS. A series of new and expensive treatments for AIDS was developed after 1987 when the FDA approved the use of azidothymidine, or AZT. In 1995, researchers discovered that protease inhibitors were more effective than AZT alone. In 1996, medical caregivers added nonnucleoside reverse transcriptase inhibitors to the mix to create an "AIDS cocktail" that proved to reduce the HIV virus, sometimes to almost untraceable amounts AIDS deaths peaked in early 1990 when about 51,000 people were dying annually. The death rate dropped dramatically after 1996 when new treatments were offered, but the debate continued over how to assist patients who could not afford treatment and how to stop the spread of infections.

Democrats on HIV/AIDS Policy

Liberals, civil rights activists, and gay advocates all expressed great anger with the Reagan administration and the Religious Right during the AIDS epidemic of the 1980s (Shilts 2007). They formed organizations such as AIDS Action to pressure elected officials to take action and to publicly castigate those who neglected this vital health issue. The Democratic Party had already shown greater sympathy and support for laws protecting the civil rights of the LGBT community and was a natural ally with these groups. Some groups, such as the AIDS Coalition to Unleash Power (ACT UP), took their cue from civil rights groups that used nonviolent direct action to confront power. ACT UP used public demonstrations, including one in March 1987 that drew 500,000 attendees in New York City. Organizer Larry Kramer denounced President Reagan for his lack of action on the disease by declaring, "AIDS is our Holocaust and Reagan is our Hitler" (Patterson 2005).

Congressional Democrats allied with these groups played important roles in challenging the Reagan administration's response to HIV/AIDS. Representative Ted Weiss of New York, who chaired the Subcommittee on Human Resources and Intergovernmental Relations, launched an investigation of the U.S. Public Health Service (PHS) response to AIDS. The Weiss report highlighted the lack of AIDS funding in the Reagan administration and decried delays in research into AIDS-related drugs. In the U.S. Senate, Edward Kennedy (D-Mass.) consistently fought Jesse Helms's (R-N.C.) efforts to block funding for HIV/AIDS education. These widely publicized adversarial political battles between Democratic members of Congress and the Reagan administration continued throughout Reagan's two-term presidency and into that of successor George H. W. Bush (Harden 2012).

Representative Barney Frank, who had openly declared his gay sexual orientation in 1987, played a critical role in connecting the Clinton White House to mainstream LGBT movements. Bill Clinton, who served as president from 1993 to 2001, reached out to the LGBT community during his presidential campaign and promised to support lesbian and gay rights. Clinton told members of the LGBT community, "I have a vision of America, and you're part of it" (Clendinen and Nagourney 1999). Clinton called for a Manhattan Project on AIDS, a concomitant increase in funding for AIDS research, and the appointment of an AIDS czar. Clinton also promised to appoint lesbians and gays in crucial positions in the federal government, to overturn the ban on lesbians and gays in the military, to issue an executive order banning discrimination on the basis of sexual orientation in all federal agencies, and to support a gay civil rights bill. Clinton asked Roberta Achtenberg, a California lesbian, and Bob Hattoy, a gay man with AIDS, to speak at the 1992 Democratic National Convention and later hired them to work in his administration.

President Clinton Speaks Out on the AIDS Crisis

On May 18, 1997, Democratic President Bill Clinton delivered a commencement address at Morgan State University in which he described the development of an effective AIDS vaccine as both a public health and moral imperative:

> Today, let us look within and step up to the challenge of our time, a challenge with consequences far more immediate for the life and death of millions around the world. AIDS will soon overtake tuberculosis and malaria as the leading infectious killer in the world. More than 29 million people have been infected, 3 million in the last year alone, 95 percent of them in the poorest parts of our globe . . . This year's budget contains increased funding of a third over 2 years ago to search for this vaccine. In the first 4 years, we have increased funding for AIDS research, prevention, and care by 50 percent, but it is not enough. So let us today set a new national goal for science in the age of biology. Today let us commit ourselves to developing an AIDS vaccine within the next decade. There are no guarantees. It will take energy and focus and demand great effort from our greatest minds . . . Today I'm pleased to announce the National Institutes of Health will establish a new AIDS vaccine research center dedicated to this crusade. And next month, at the summit of the industrialized nations in Denver, I will enlist other nations to join us in a worldwide effort to find a vaccine to stop one of the world's greatest killers. We will challenge America's pharmaceutical industry, which leads the world in innovative research and development to work with us and to make the successful development of an AIDS vaccine part of its basic mission.

Source

Clinton, William J. 1997. "Commencement Address at Morgan State University in Baltimore, Maryland," May 18. Online by Gerhard Peters and John T. Woolley, "The American Presidency Project." Accessed June 22, 2015: http://www.presidency.ucsb.edu/ws/?pid=54156.

Opposition from conservative Democrats, Republicans, and the Christian right kept many of Clinton's promises to the LGBT community from being fulfilled but he had success in providing government support to combat AIDS. Clinton established the White House Office of National AIDS Policy to provide federal oversight of the national response to AIDS. In 1999, Clinton established the LIFE (Leadership and Investment in Fighting an Epidemic) initiative to address the AIDS epidemic overseas. Conservative opposition to supporting AIDS research and treatment domestically declined after the Clinton years, as policy debates shifted to how much money to spend in the United States and overseas and whether to incorporate safe-sex or abstinence-only educational materials into AIDS educational curricula. Democrats advocated for more money and to include "safe sex" materials in HIV/AIDS education (Smith 2013).

After President Barack Obama took office in 2009, he removed the ban on individuals with HIV/AIDS from entering the United States and committed tens of millions of dollars to open HIV medical clinics in the United States and to supplement state programs that provided access to expensive drugs to fight the illness. In a speech on World AIDS Day in 2011, Obama announced new funding for HIV/AIDS and noted to a receptive audience that "this fight is not over—not for the 1.2 million Americans who are living with HIV right now, not for the Americans who are infected every day." Obama acknowledged that, while the rate of HIV is declining in the United States, it is still disproportionately found in African American and Hispanic populations, and he called for new tactics to battle the disease within these communities. Under pressure from members of his own party and from members of the LGBT community for not expanding the global fight against AIDS, Obama rescinded restrictions on abstinence-only educational materials and announced new funding of nearly $50 billion to support treatment for nearly six million people with HIV/AIDS across the globe (Mantel 2012).

Democratic lawmakers have also responded at the state level by opening up treatment facilities, creating programs in their states to subsidize expensive and lifesaving drugs, and supporting needle exchange programs. During the recession that began in 2008, however, many of these programs were targeted by conservative lawmakers for spending cuts.

Republicans on HIV/AIDS Policy

The dominance of the conservative wing of the Republican Party began in the 1980s with the election of Ronald Reagan. During the 1980s, the GOP was resistant to dealing with the brewing HIV/AIDS health care crisis, in part because of conservative hostility toward gays and lesbians. Reagan went so far as to endorse a bill from Senator Roger Jepsen (R-Iowa) called the Family Protection Act that proposed to bar the dispersal of federal funds to "any organization that suggests that homosexuality can be an acceptable alternative lifestyle," prohibit the federally funded Legal Services Corporation from engaging in litigation to defend gay and lesbian rights, and amend the Civil Rights Act to make clear that the law did not apply to discrimination based on sexual discrimination.

Although Reagan never endorsed the ideas of the Reverend Jerry Falwell of the Moral Majority, who suggested AIDS was "divine retribution for sodomy," such sentiment permeated conservative discussion of AIDS policy and left many Republicans in Washington unenthusiastic about funding research or treatment for the illness. Further proof of this came when a Reagan official told a Senate panel in 1986 that the care of and funding for people with AIDS were the responsibilities of state and local governments. Republicans, in general, addressed the HIV/AIDS crisis in a meaningful way in 1987, but even after the GOP embraced spending on HIV/AIDS research, treatment, and education, members of Congress were quick to impose policy guidelines to ensure that spending did not promote homosexual behavior. In fact, at one point during this this period, Orrin Hatch, a Republican senator from Utah, called Democrats the party of homosexuals. Senator Jesse Helms, a Republican from North Carolina, successfully proposed the Helms

Ronald Reagan Provides His Perspective on the Federal Role in Combating AIDS

Ronald Reagan was president when AIDS was identified. Liberals excoriated Reagan for lack of urgency in addressing the public health crisis. In this speech on AIDS delivered at the American Foundation for AIDS Research on May 31, 1987, Reagan shows the conservative view on the disease. His words make a distinction between "innocent victims" and those whose immoral behavior led to illness. He also calls for imposing restrictions on immigrants who test positive for HIV/AIDS.

I hope that AIDS education or any aspect of sex education will not be value-neutral. A dean of St. Paul's Cathedral in London once said: "The aim of education is the knowledge not of facts, but of values." Well, that's not too far off. Education is knowing how to adapt, to grow, to understand ourselves and the world around us. And values are how we guide ourselves through the decisions of life. How we behave sexually is one of those decisions. As Surgeon General Koop has pointed out, if children are taught their own worth, we can expect them to treat themselves and others with greater respect. And wherever you have self-respect and mutual respect, you don't have drug abuse and sexual promiscuity, which of course are the two major causes of AIDS . . . Now, we know there will be those who will go right ahead. So, yes, after there is a moral base, then you can discuss preventives and other scientific measures . . . It's time we knew exactly what we were facing, and that's why I support some routine testing. I've asked the Department of Health and Human Services to determine as soon as possible the extent to which the AIDS virus has penetrated our society and to predict its future dimensions. I've also asked HHS to add the AIDS virus to the list of contagious diseases for which immigrants and aliens seeking permanent residence in the United States can be denied entry.

Source

Reagan, Ronald. 1987. Remarks at the American Foundation for AIDS Research Dinner. May 31. Ronald Reagan Presidential Library Web site. Accessed December 1, 2015: http://www.reagan.utexas.edu/archives/speeches/1987/053187a.htm.

amendment to AIDS funding. This legislation prohibited the Centers for Disease Control from spending federal money on programs that would "promote, encourage or condone homosexual activities." Helms also thwarted funding for programs that would have provided clean needles for intravenous drug users. From 1987 on, the Helms amendment appeared in every major appropriations bill.

Republican hostility toward members of the gay community diminished somewhat during the presidency of George H. W. Bush (1989–1993), and, as a result, funding for AIDS increased. Bush himself called for an end to discrimination against those who were HIV positive or had AIDS. Bush also signed into law the Ryan White Comprehensive AIDS Resources Emergency (CARE) Act, which funded medical care for America's most severely afflicted in urban centers. Republicans in the 1990s, however, remained concerned that conservative Christians would withdraw support from the party and resisted policies that would have recognized gay rights. Thus, Republicans fully supported the Defense of Marriage Act in 1996, the same year that Bob Dole, the unsuccessful GOP candidate for president, was forced by conservatives within his own party to return a campaign donation from Log Cabin Republicans, a group comprised of gay and lesbian Republicans.

By the end of the 1990s, evangelicals like Franklin Graham were pressing for the need to fight AIDS across the globe. Evangelicals supported George W. Bush's two successful bids for the White House and helped shape his HIV/AIDS policy, which was dramatically different than that of his Republican predecessors. Their support was largely responsible for Bush's 2003 President's Emergency Plan for AIDS Relief (PEPFAR), a five-year, $15 billion commitment to fight AIDS globally. "We have confronted, and will continue to confront, HIV/AIDS in our own country. And to meet a severe and urgent crisis abroad, tonight I propose the Emergency Plan for AIDS Relief . . . I ask the Congress to commit $15 billion over the next five years, including nearly $10 billion in new money, to turn the tide against AIDS in the most afflicted nations of Africa and the Caribbean" (Bush 2003). However, Bush and fellow Republicans also continued to support abstinence-only HIV/AIDS prevention programs. In 2004, the Republican Party platform endorsed the "ABC" approach to prevention that encourages abstinence, and being faithful to one lifetime partner, along with other behavioral changes intended to eliminate or reduce exposure risk.

Some Republican legislators, officials, and voters have also shown increased support for needle exchange programs. Though evidence suggests that needle exchanges are an effective tool in helping stop the spread of HIV/AIDS, this policy has been anathema to many Republicans who express concern that these policies encourage drug abuse. "As Republicans, we don't want to look like we are facilitating drug use," said Representative Tom Cole (R-Okla.) in 2015. Cole's perspective is a particularly important one because that year he served as chairman of the appropriations subcommittee that distributes health funding. Cole was quoted in Carle Hulse's May 16, 2015, article in the *New York Times* "We want to get you help, but we want to do other things." However, when Indiana Governor Mike Pence was faced with a rise of hepatitis C and HIV in his state in 2015 due to the sharing of dirty needles by drug users, he passed emergency legislation to allow the state to provide fresh needles to address the public health menace. This thinking has the potential to spread to Congress, where a ban on this practice has been in place since the era of Senator Jesse Helms in the 1980s.

Further Reading

Bush, George. 2003. Transcript of State of the Union. Accessed June 1, 2015. http://www
.cnn.com/2003/ALLPOLITICS/01/28/sotu.transcript.5/.

Clendinen, Dudley, and Nagourney, Adam. 1999. *Out for Good: The Struggle to Build a Gay
Rights Movement in America.* New York: Simon & Schuster.

Harden, Victoria. 2012. *AIDS at 30: A History*. Washington, D.C.: Potomac Books.

Mantel, Barbara. 2012. "Conquering AIDS," *CQ Global Researcher*, September 18.

Patterson, James. 2005. *Restless Giant: The United States from Watergate to Bush v. Gore*. New York: Oxford University Press.

Shilts, Randy. 2007. *And the Band Played On: Politics, People, and the AIDS Epidemic,* 20th anniversary edition. New York: St. Martin's.

Smith, Raymond A. 2013. *Global HIV/AIDS Politics, Policy, and Activism,* in three volumes. Santa Barbara: Praeger.

Illegal Drugs

At a Glance

Over the past five decades, Democrats and Republicans have engaged in an often-acrimonious debate over the most effective government policies for reducing the spread of illicit drugs and treating those addicted to them. Many Republicans have favored punishment as a means of deterrence to the spread of narcotics and incarceration for drug users. Many Democrats have been more likely to see drug abuse and addiction as medical, not criminal, issues and have supported programs of therapy and treatment for users. Both parties, though, have historically favored harsher penalties for drug traffickers than for users.

Many Democrats . . .

- Have, after years of support for the so-called War on Drugs, begun to express reservations about its impact on American society.
- Suggest that drug abuse should be treated as a health issue as well as an issue of law enforcement.
- Believe vulnerability to drug addiction can be exacerbated by physiological factors like brain chemistry.
- Would like to reform U.S. statutes requiring mandatory minimum sentences for nonviolent drug offenders.
- Want to increase spending for treatment of addiction.
- Want more federal money for drug prevention programs at the community level.

Many Republicans . . .

- Support the War on Drugs but suggest reforms to address issues like escalating prison populations.
- Suggest that illegal drugs should be treated primarily as a criminal matter, not an issue of health care.
- Believe that addiction is at the root due to moral failing, not brain chemistry.

- Question expenditures of tax dollars for drug treatment facilities and drug addiction programs.
- Want more money for law enforcement of drug laws.

Overview

How should society combat illegal drugs? Is drug addiction caused by moral failings, social environment, physiological characteristics—or some combination of the three? Is drug addiction an illness that needs to be treated as such? And what about recreational users of illegal drugs, some of whom view marijuana as the rough equivalent of a glass or two of wine?

For sellers and users of illegal drugs, federal policy for many years was harsh and unforgiving and treated users and dealers as criminals. This stance was a bipartisan one, as lawmakers rushed to address rising crime rates and spiraling drug use and inoculate themselves politically from charges that they were "soft on crime." In 1971, Republicans and Democrats joined together to forge the "War on Drugs," legislation

Mariann Avery, of Tarzana, California, spent 15 months going through the drug court program before graduating with seventeen other men and women that made up the latest class of graduates from drug court, a diversion court that enables successful participants to earn reduced sentences for their crimes. At right is judge Michael Tynan, who runs the court. (Photo by Rick Loomis/Getty Images)

that led to harsh sentencing for illicit drug users, stronger punishments for drug dealers, and an attempt to curb addiction through incarceration. Under Republican Presidents Richard Nixon, Ronald Reagan, George H. W. Bush, and George W. Bush, the federal government increased the size and scope of federal drug control agencies, established mandatory sentencing for drug offenders, and initiated mandatory drug testing for persons receiving federal money. The 1988 Drug Free Workplace Act required federal contractors and grant recipients to maintain a drug-free workplace. This expanded the scope of drug testing for those in workplaces, college loan recipients, students in schools, and welfare recipients. During the presidency of Bill Clinton, a Democrat, the Welfare Reform Act and other federal government initiatives banned convicted drug users from access to student loans, public housing, and welfare. Many state laws paralleled federal policy, and, in addition, stripped away the right to vote for those convicted of drug felonies.

By the 1990s, prison rates for drug offenses were soaring. But addiction rates had not declined, perhaps because prisoners were just as likely to have access to drugs in prison as outside of prison. In that decade some Democrats called for a reassessment of government policy toward drugs. President Clinton's perspective, for example, appeared to undergo considerable change by the end of his second term. Back in 1996, Clinton had been so concerned about political attacks charging him with lax drug policies that he rejected a U.S. Sentencing Commission recommendation to bring severe sentences for crack cocaine (most popular in poor minority communities) in line with more modest sentencing guidelines for the sale or possession of powder cocaine (more often associated with affluent and white users). Clinton also rejected another recommendation to end the federal ban on funding for syringe access programs. As his time in the Oval Office drew to a close, however, Clinton indicated that America needed to closely scrutinize its illegal drug policies. In a December 29, 2000, *Rolling Stone* interview with Jann Wenner, for example, President Clinton suggested "a re-examination of our entire policy on imprisonment" that included treatment options for users.

After Republican George W. Bush replaced Clinton in 2001, some Democrats representing minority and urban constituencies called for sentencing reform and treatment rather than prison for drug abusers and new funding for alternate therapies to treat addiction. They complained that the social cost of the drug laws was taking a disproportionate toll on poor families and minority neighborhoods in the form of disrupted families, untreated addictions, and laws that barred ex-felons from working, voting, and housing.

Meanwhile, new forms of drug abuse arose after 2000. Experts noted that overly prescribed painkillers in the opiate class, such as Vicodin and OxyContin, created a new class of addicts who, once they were unable to get prescription medication, turned to the cheaper source of heroin. Heroin and methamphetamine (meth) use soared during the first decade of the 21st century as well, taking a heavy toll on small towns and big cities across the United States. Concomitant with this epidemic was a surge in HIV and Hepatitis C cases from heroin users sharing unclean syringes.

By 2010, with nearly half the 2.4 million prisoners in the United States in jail for nonviolent and drug offenses, and a rising epidemic of heroin abuse, some Republicans began to join with Democrats in seeking new policy solutions. These Republicans argued that legislation to end automatic jail time, end the ban on federal benefits for ex-convicts, and provide more funding for addiction treatment, would, in the long run, be a cost savings for states and the federal government. Many Republicans pointed out that the cost for housing the over 2 million imprisoned is estimated at over $80 billion a year.

As a result of all these factors, Democrats and Republicans have found drug policy reform to be a rare area of bipartisan agreement in recent years. Sentencing reform for drug offenses is being spearheaded by the Coalition for Public Safety, which boasts support from conservatives ranging from the Koch brothers to the FreedomWorks Tea Party organization. Meanwhile, the American Civil Liberties Union (ACLU) is leading a campaign of its own to end mandatory sentencing related to drug crimes, with funding from such organizations as George Soros's Open Society and the Center for American Progress.

Experts also indicate that the zeal for drug sentencing reform has been at its strongest at the state level. According to a 2010 Pew Research Center analysis of bills passed by state legislatures, 40 states passed laws easing prosecution for drug-related offenses. Pew reported that of these states, 27 moved only in the direction of easing, while the remaining 13 "eased some laws and toughened others—often as part of a broader rethink of their drug policies."

Particularly dramatic evidence of this shift in attitude was evident in November 2014, when voters in California voted on a proposal to reduce criminal classification of possession of so-called hard drugs like cocaine, meth, and heroin from a felony to a misdemeanor. This proposal, known as Proposition 47, passed with the support of 59 percent of California voters. According to some estimates, the new classification could impact as many as 24,000 drug convictions annually in the state. Supporters of the proposal say that the change will save state taxpayers hundreds of millions of dollars in incarceration costs every year. And according to *Rolling Stone,* "Prop 47 captures those savings and steers them into community programs" for drug abuse prevention and treatment (Dickinson 2015).

Democrats on Illegal Drugs

Democratic policy on drug-related crimes has gradually moved away from punitive action against those convicted of drug crimes and has moved toward compassion for those seeking rehabilitation from drug addiction. Many Democrats supported the War on Drugs during the 1970s and 1980s, and they continued to take a tough stance on drug crime right through the 1990s under President Bill Clinton. For example, one of Clinton's signature pieces of legislation during his presidency was the Welfare Reform Act of 1996, which included a ban on felons with drug convictions from receiving welfare or food stamps, unless a state otherwise chose to waive these restrictions. Significantly, these bans did not apply to convictions for any other crimes. In addition, under Clinton, the U.S. Department of Housing and Urban Development placed a lifetime public housing ban on those convicted of making methamphetamine in subsidized housing. It also imposed a three-year ban from public housing on those evicted from public housing for drug-related activity (Provine 2007).

The Democratic national platform in 2000 called for drug testing for prisoners to provide treatment for addicts and also to break up drug rings inside the prison system: "Drug and alcohol abuse is implicated in the crimes of 80 percent of the criminals behind bars. We should make prisoners a simple deal: get clean to get out, stay clean to stay out. We should impose strict supervision of those who have just been released on parole. In return, we should help them make it in the workplace." On the same platform, they called for drug prevention programs in schools and stronger laws to fight drug cartels that were bringing drugs across the U.S. border and dealing them on American streets. "We should open more drug courts to speed justice for drug-related crimes; double the number of drug hot-spots where we aggressively target our enforcement efforts; expand drug treatment for at-risk youth; make sure that all of our school zones are drug-free; and provide drug treatment upon demand" (Democratic Party 2000).

After the 2004 election, Democrats showed less enthusiasm for the policies they had helped enact in the 1990s, although one could still find plenty of party members who maintained a staunch zero-tolerance stance, especially in more conservative parts of the country. Nonetheless, Democrats took the lead in advocating treatment options over prison sentences and government-funded therapeutic programs for those struggling with addiction. Democratic supporters have urged more government funding for community organizations to create prevention programs and to provide clean syringes for intravenous drug users (Hari 2015). Democrats cited research studies that showed addiction was a neuropsychological phenomenon and not a deviant behavior. For example, in 2012, Gil Kerlikowske, Barack Obama's director of national drug control policy, gave an address to Europeans involved in battling drug abuse. He indicated that the Obama administration was increasingly moving toward a drug policy strategy that treated drug abuse as a public health issue as well as a law enforcement issue. Emphasizing that medical research increasingly indicated that drug abuse disorders are chronic diseases of the brain that can be effectively prevented and treated, he said that criminal justice reforms were necessary to stop the revolving door of drug use, criminal behavior, jail, release, and re-arrest. "It's very clear we can't arrest our way out of this problem," he said. "The availability of quality treatment and the engagement of the public health sector and primary care physicians in drug issues is very critical . . . The scientists . . . have all recognized addiction as a disease, and it doesn't take a huge amount of reading of research papers to understand and accept the scientific evidence" (Kelland 2012).

Since 1996, two dozen states headed by Democrats have lifted restrictions on those convicted of drug crimes from receiving the Supplemental Nutrition

Assistance Program (SNAP). A number of states enacted new legislation to repeal the harsh drug sentencing enacted in the 1970s. Erin Durkin in a January 20, 2015, article in the *New York Daily News* noted that after the election of Democrat Andrew Cuomo as the New York governor, the state repealed their drug laws and provided more options for treatment. In Vermont, which saw a dramatic rise in heroin abuse, Democratic Governor Pete Shulmin reshaped public policy by developing more rigorous addiction prevention programs in schools and offering those arrested for heroin use rehabilitation rather than imprisonment. Shulmin labeled the situation in Vermont a public health crisis that the state needed to meet by "providing treatment and support rather than simply doling out punishment" (Eidelson 2014). Congressional Democrats have cited the example of Vermont and other states as a model for federal legislation and have called for a federal drug court system similar to those at the state level. Senator Claire McCaskill of Missouri, citing the success of drug courts in that state, has taken a prominent leadership role in proposing legislation to reform U.S. drug laws (Fisher 2006).

Part of this shift within the Democratic Party as a whole has been traced to long-standing and persistent racial disparities in drug sentencing. The Democratic platform in 2012 called for ending "racial disparities in sentencing for drug crimes." President Obama, working with Attorney General Eric Holder, crafted the Fair Sentencing Act aimed at eliminating these racial disparities (Democratic Party 2012). Obama also ceremonially commuted the sentences of 22 federal drug offenders who had been imprisoned for what he called "an outdated sentencing regime." One policy outcome of this has been a bipartisan attempt to pass the Smarter Sentencing Act in the Senate. This bill would eliminate mandatory sentencing, give judges more discretion when sentencing drug offenders, and reduce sentences for low-level drug offenders. The legislation enjoyed bipartisan support and was sponsored by Senator Richard J. Durbin, Democrat from Illinois, and Senator Mike Lee, Republican from Utah. Cosponsors included liberal Democrats Cory Booker of New Jersey and Patrick J. Leahy of Vermont, along with conservative Republicans Ted Cruz of Texas and Rand Paul of Kentucky.

This recent bipartisan shift in sentiment about federal drug policies is reflective of changes in public opinion on the issue. A 2014 Pew poll found that two out of three Americans believe that "the government should focus more on treating people who use illegal drugs, compared with 26% saying prosecution should be the focus. More than six-in-ten (63%) now say that state moves away from mandatory prison sentences for non-violent drug offenders is a good thing, versus 32% who called it a bad thing." The Pew poll found that these sentiments commanded even higher support from Democrats and independents (Pew 2014).

The evolution of the Democratic view on dealing with drug crimes from the 1990s through the present may best be seen in former first lady Hillary Clinton. While President Bill Clinton signed legislation creating mandatory sentencing and long sentencing for drug offenders, Hillary Clinton in her 2016 campaign for the White House called for federal laws to allow for "nonviolent offenders who stay clean to stay out of prison" and the development of specialized drug courts for treatment and education programs for prevention (Brennan Center 2015).

Republicans on Drug Crime Policy

Harsh sentences for drug users and pushers, mandatory minimum sentences for those caught with drugs, and punishment for all drug offenders were the main features of the Republican War on Drugs policy from the 1970s until after the 2010 midterm elections. Since that time, some Republicans, concerned about the escalating cost of imprisoning millions of Americans and the high rate of recidivism, or repeat offenses, have suggested alternative policies. Some have even made common cause with Democrats. The debate within the Republican Party mirrors recent surveys that show an even split between Republicans on this issue. Only about 51 percent of Republicans favor government policies that focus on treatment over incarceration. The split has a significant generational component, as older Republicans tend to reject this idea (Pew 2014).

Many scholars trace the War on Drugs to laws passed in New York state under Republican Governor Nelson Rockefeller. The Rockefeller Drug Laws were the most stringent in the nation and were advocated as an important tool for dealing with crime that rose across the United States from the late 1960s through the early 1990s. Ronald Reagan, who was president from 1981 to 1989, used his office to ensure that there was zero tolerance for drug abuse. First Lady Nancy Reagan's signature program was her antidrug campaign, "Just Say No to Drugs" policy implemented in the mid-1980s. In the 1990s, congressional Republicans were important supporters of crime and welfare bills that stripped those convicted of drug use from access to public housing, food stamps, welfare, and, at the state level, restricted their right to vote, sometimes for life. Republicans drew a rhetorical picture of drug abuse as part of a sinister plot by Columbian drug lords who were ruining America. Many Republicans verbally attacked Democrats who suggested alternate sentencing in the 1990s. In their 2000 party platform, the GOP said that "the entire nation has suffered from the administration's virtual surrender in the war against drugs . . . [while] Drug kingpins have turned entire neighborhoods into wastelands and ruined uncounted lives with their poison." They also raised the image of vulnerable children targeted by drug pushers (Republican Party 2000).

In 2004, Republicans conceded some funding for drug prevention and treatment, but they maintained the law needed to "ensure that jail time is used as an effective deterrent to drug use and support the continued funding of grants to assist schools in drug testing. At the same time, we should make drug treatment available to people willing to take the courageous step of admitting they have a problem and working hard to overcome it" (Republican Party 2004). When President Barack Obama, who took office in 2009, sought to eliminate mandatory minimum sentences for those convicted of drug crimes, many Republicans objected. Senate

Judiciary Committee Chairman Charles E. Grassley (R-Iowa) spoke for many in his party when he disparaged the idea as "lenient" and "dangerous."

Republicans remain more likely than Democrats to oppose providing social services to convicted drug users. For example, in Texas, even though the food stamp program is open to anyone convicted of using or selling drugs, those who violate their probation or parole are ineligible for benefits for two years. If they are convicted of another felony, drug-related or otherwise, they are barred for life. In Pennsylvania, Republicans sponsored a bill to deny food stamps and welfare benefits to anyone who served more than 10 years for a drug offense. Republicans in a dozen states have proposed drug testing for welfare recipients and vowed to take away benefits from anyone caught using illicit drugs. An AP story on August 5, 2015, described Ohio's measures to use drug testing to save taxpayer money and to punish lawbreakers, even though some studies indicate that these drug testing programs actually cost states more than they saved. Following the economic recession of 2008 and state budget shortfalls that accompanied the economic meltdown, members of the GOP proposed budget cuts for drug rehabilitation programs and drug education programs as a means of balancing budgets. After the recession was over, Republican leaders were still more apt to respond to drug crimes with a call for more law enforcement to deter and punish criminals, rather than call for more investment in social services.

There are a few notable exceptions. Chris Christie, the sometimes iconoclastic Republican Governor of New Jersey, was quoted by Claude Brodessor-Atkinson in a September 14, 2014, story for NJ.com: "The war on drugs has been a failure . . . well-intentioned, but a failure." Christie called for legislation making drug and alcohol treatment "more available for everybody" because it was "part of government's job." Senate Republicans who are affiliated with the Tea Party movement, Rand Paul of Kentucky, Mike Lee of Utah, and Ted Cruz of Texas, have sought to end excessive and expensive incarceration by joining with Democrats to give federal judges more leeway in deciding sentencing for those convicted of drug offenses (Carney 2015).

Further Reading

Brennan Center. 2015. Center for Justice Essays, April 28.

Carney, Eliza Newlin. 2015. "Left Meets Right in Prison Politics," *CQ Weekly*, April 13, 20–23. Accessed July 20, 2015: http://0-library.cqpress.com.libra.naz.edu/cqweekly /weeklyreport114-000004660482.

Democratic Party. 2000. "Platform of 2000," by Gerhard Peters and John T. Woolley, "The American Presidency Project." Accessed August 7, 2015: http://www.presidency.ucsb .edu/ws/?pid=29612.

Democratic Party. 2012. "Platform of 2012," by Gerhard Peters and John T. Woolley, "The American Presidency Project." Accessed August 7, 2015: http://www.presidency.ucsb .edu/ws/?pid=101962.

Dickinson, Tim. 2015. "The War on Drugs Is Burning Out," *Rolling Stone*, January 8.

Eidelson, Josh. 2014. "Vermont Quits War on Drugs to Treat Heroin Abuse as Health Issue," *Bloomberg Businessweek*, August 22. Accessed August 7, 2015: http://www.bloomberg .com/news/articles/2014-08-22/vermont-quits-war-on-drugs-to-treat-heroin-abuse -as-health-issue.

Fisher, Gary L. 2006. *Rethinking Our War on Drugs*. Santa Barbara: Praeger.

Hari, Johann. 2015. *Chasing the Scream: The First and Last Days of the War on Drugs*. New York: Bloomsbury.

Kelland, Kate. 2012. "U.S. Says Drug Abuse Needs Treatment, Not Just Jail," *Chicago Tribune*, May 22. Accessed December 1, 2015: http://articles.chicagotribune.com/2012-05-22/news /sns-rt-us-usa-drugs-treatmentbre84l183-20120522_1_drug-abuse-drug-enforcement -experts-drug-courts.

Pew Research Center. 2014. "America's New Drug Policy Landscape." Accessed August 7, 2015: http://www.people-press.org/2014/04/02/section-1-perceptions-of-drug-abuse -views-of-drug-policies.

Provine, Doris Marie. 2007. *Unequal under Law: Race in the War on Drugs*. Chicago: University of Chicago Press.

Republican Party. 2000. "Republican Platform of 2000," by Gerhard Peters and John T. Woolley, "The American Presidency Project." Accessed June 12, 2014: http://www .presidency.ucsb.edu/ws/?pid=25849.

Republican Party. 2004. "Republican Party Platform of 2004," by Gerhard Peters and John T. Woolley, "The American Presidency Project." Accessed August 5, 2015: http://www .presidency.ucsb.edu/ws/?pid=25850.

Swartz, James. 2012. *Substance Abuse in America: A Documentary and Reference Guide*. Santa Barbara: Greenwood.

Immigration

At a Glance

Overall, Democrats and Republicans agree that American immigration policies in the 21st century are flawed—perhaps even broken. Both parties agree that the current presence of millions of unauthorized immigrants in the United States presents challenges that need to be addressed by legislation. However, the two parties are deeply divided over how to fix the system and the nature of legislation needed to address these issues. Many Democrats believe that to stem the flow of unauthorized immigrants, laws should be enacted that target corporations that attract, hire, and exploit undocumented aliens. In addition, Democrats generally believe that these undocumented immigrants should be presented with a realistic pathway to citizenship. Many Republicans, meanwhile, insist that before any action on amnesty can be considered, laws need to be enacted and enforced to better secure the American border with Mexico. Republicans also generally oppose allowing undocumented immigrants—or "illegal immigrants," as they are more likely to call them—to stay in the United States. As a result, they frequently express support for various proposals to deport them en masse.

Many Republicans . . .

- Believe that the existing immigration policy is broken.
- See unauthorized immigrants as criminals or illegal immigrants.
- Believe that immigration reform begins with protecting America's borders.
- Believe a "path to citizenship" is merely amnesty, which they oppose.
- Believe that amnesty will only encourage more illegal immigration.
- Favor denying illegal immigrants social services and educational benefits created for U.S. citizens.
- Favor deportation for illegal immigrants.
- Would use state power to enforce immigration if allowed.
- Would approve of a limited guest worker program to assist farmers and businesses.
- Oppose unilateral executive action on immigration.

Many Democrats . . .

- Believe that the existing immigration policy is broken.
- See unauthorized entrants into the United States as victims of the broken system.
- Want to reform the system in ways that recognize the reasons why unauthorized immigrants come to America.
- Would like to create a "path to citizenship" for those already in the United States.
- Support the U.S. Dream Act, which provides benefits and educational assistance to immigrants who came to the United States as children.
- Believe that undocumented workers are often exploited by corporations.
- Assert that the great majority of undocumented immigrants are hard workers who contribute their fair share of taxes to the government.
- Suggest that animosity toward undocumented immigrants is sometimes motivated by racial or ethnic hatred and prejudice.
- Have been involved in creating sanctuary cities and attempting to protect unauthorized immigrants from being deported.
- Are amenable to guest worker programs but would like to ensure workers are not exploited.
- Favor President Obama's decision to use his executive authority to defer deportation of many undocumented immigrants.
- Emphasize that U.S. history underscores that America has always been a nation of immigrants.

Overview

Since the 1980s, the issue of unauthorized immigration—usually referred to as illegal immigration in conservative circles—has divided policy makers and politicians in the Republican and Democratic Parties. Although over a million people a year legally immigrate to the United States following the passage of the Hart-Cellar Act of 1965, hundreds of thousands of people without proper documentation enter the United States every year with the intent to permanently remain (Barkan 2013). As of 2014, an estimated 11.3 million unauthorized immigrants lived in the United States (Pew Research Center 2015).

To a large extent legal immigrants coming to the United States are from Latin America and are of Hispanic origin. The unauthorized entrants are of the same background. In fact, about 52 percent of the people living and working illegally in the United States as of 2014 were from Mexico (Pew Research Center 2015). Many of these unauthorized residents have family members legally residing in the United States, which complicates enforcement of the law and deportation of unauthorized immigrants. Due to these migratory patterns, the percentage of Hispanics in the United States has surpassed African Americans as the largest minority in the United States, with around 13 percent or more of the U.S. population having Hispanic origins.

In general, the position of the Democratic Party is that these immigrants are a net benefit to U.S. society. They argue that the unauthorized migrants who hold jobs contribute to the Social Security and Medicaid system, pay income taxes, and provide valuable services in many sectors of the labor pool—including areas in which American citizens are often reluctant to work. In addition, these alien residents have a strong work ethic and are motivated by the American dream. Many Democrats say that the vast majority of them are also peaceful, law abiding, contributing members of their communities. These attitudes have made Hispanics an important constituency within the Democratic Party. Many Latino organizations advocate for laws and policies to allow the unauthorized immigrants to take steps to become full citizens, and they frequently work with Democratic lawmakers on these efforts.

In general, the Republican Party, on the other hand, has little tolerance for unauthorized immigration. Many Republicans argue that illegal immigrants have shown a disregard for U.S. law by crossing into the United States without proper documentation or by overstaying their visas. They point out that it is not fair to the million or so legal immigrants that annually come to the United States, most of whom have had to wait for substantial periods of time to enter the United States, for American legislators to in effect reward undocumented immigrants by giving them a path to citizenship or access to social services. Many Republicans also believe illegal immigrants are a social and economic burden to law-abiding, tax-paying Americans. As a result, Republicans frequently argue for tougher enforcement of immigration laws, oppose amnesty for illegal immigrants, and favor deportation of people residing in the United States illegally.

GOP opposition is particularly strong in the so-called sun belt, the line of states running from California to Texas then to Florida. Within the sun belt, local and state governments have struggled since the 1970s with economic and social issues created by the additional residents in their communities. After Texas denied the children of unauthorized immigrants access to public education, the state was sued by proimmigration rights groups. The Supreme Court ruled in 1982 that denying these children the right to an education violated the Equal Protection Clause of the Fourteenth Amendment. This decision, combined with data from the 1980 Census showing that there were anywhere from 2 to 4 million unauthorized immigrants in the United States, led to congressional action (Warren and Passel 1987). Congress began serious debate over immigration in 1982 but it took another four years for Democrats and Republicans to agree to the Immigration Reform and Control Act (IRCA) of 1986.

This law took a moderate approach to the issue, with provisions that pleased Republicans and Democrats alike. The law provided immigrants who had entered the United States illegally prior to January 1, 1982, with a path to citizenship, which pleased Democrats. The law also increased enforcement along U.S. borders, which pleased Republicans who wanted a hard line on immigration. As a means to deter unauthorized immigration to the United States in the future, the law also provided penalties and fines to U.S. employers who hired illegal immigrants (Cooper and O'Neil 2005). Since then, enforcement of U.S. immigration laws has fallen heavily on the private sector, which is required by law to verify the eligibility for employment from new hires. However, this process is underfunded and has done little to slow the influx of unauthorized immigration.

In light of the failure of federal reforms, states led by conservative governors and lawmakers tried to address the social and economic issues associated with unauthorized immigration. Many enacted tough anti-immigration policies including attempts to halt bilingual education and measures meant to stop unauthorized immigrants from receiving state benefits. In 1994, for example, California voters were convinced by Republican Governor Pete Wilson to approve Proposition 187, a ballot measure that withheld health care, education, and welfare benefits to illegal immigrants. The measure was widely supported by Republicans and Independents but was rejected two to one by Democrats. Federal courts struck down the measure. The issue has remained highly controversial ever since, as both the administrations of George W. Bush and Barack Obama struggled to enact compromise reform legislation.

Republicans on Immigration

Many members of the Republican Party prioritize, by wide margins, the idea of denying illegal immigrants social services and securing U.S. borders against illegal immigration over devising any amnesty policy for those who entered the United States improperly (Motel 2014). When George W. Bush entered the White House in 2001, he challenged this widespread position within his party. Bush had courted Hispanic voters during his campaign and signaled support for a compromise solution to illegal immigration. Furthermore, the Bush family has strong ties to Mexico through both business and marriage. It was in Mexico that George H. W. Bush, president from 1989–1993, began to amass his fortune through oil speculation in his oil exploration company, Zapata Oil. Jeb Bush, son of one president, brother to another, married a naturalized U.S. citizen, Columba Gallo, who had been born in Mexico. Jeb's son, George Peabody Bush, is fluent in Spanish and spoke at the Republican National Convention in favor of comprehensive immigration reform. In a symbolic move, President George W. Bush made his first official state visit to Mexico in February 2001.

In August 2001, the Development Relief and Education of Alien Minors (DREAM) Act was introduced but not passed in the Senate. The bill would have given a path to citizenship to children who were brought into the United States and who completed high school and went on to do military service or two years of college. However, after the terrorist attacks on September 11, 2001, immigrant reform was subsumed by greater concerns about border safety, and comprehensive reform was set aside as a policy issue during Bush's first term. In 2002, Bush signed the bipartisan Enhanced Border Security and Visa Entry Reform Act, which provided more resources and personnel to Border Patrol and the Immigration and Naturalization Service (Jenks 2002). Bush followed this up in 2004 with a proposal to create a temporary guest worker program that would allow unauthorized aliens in the United States to sign up, thereby granting them temporary legal status to remain in the United States. The suggestion was unpopular with both Democrat and Republican lawmakers who took no action on this proposal (U.S. Immigration and Naturalization Service).

Republicans who controlled the House of Representatives from 2001 to 2007 insisted instead on securing the border before reforming the status of unauthorized immigrants. To that end, they passed the Border Protection, Anti-Terrorism and Illegal Immigration Control Act of 2005. The bill would have tightened border security, penalized both illegal immigrants and those who hired them, and criminalized the action of assisting illegal immigrants. The bill failed to muster the necessary support in the Senate, which attempted to pass its own legislation instead. The bipartisan Comprehensive Immigration Reform Act of 2006 set out to reform the status of undocumented immigrants. However, the Republican minority in the Senate launched a filibuster that effectively killed the legislation. Perhaps hoping to win Republican support, the Senate and House agreed to the Secure Fence Act in October 2006, which further enhanced border security and included a provision to build a 700-mile fence along the U.S.–Mexican border (White House Fact Sheet 2006). Efforts to address the unauthorized immigrants already living in the United States foundered, however, as many Republicans and Democrats continued to clash over policy prescriptions.

Frustrated with federal inaction in stopping the continued flow of unauthorized immigrants into the United States—from 3.5 million in 1990 to 12.2 million in 2007—local and state officials and residents living along the U.S.–Mexican border increasingly responded to the policy vacuum with laws and programs of their own. This in turn sparked yet another debate—this one about the role states may play in shaping immigration policy, which is the constitutional responsibility of the federal government. In 2004, an Arizona-based citizens group that called itself the Minutemen to invoke the citizen soldiers who protected Americans from the British in the era before the Revolutionary War, recruited civilian volunteers to patrol the U.S.–Mexican border. In 2007, the Democratic governor of Arizona, Janet Napolitano, signed into law legislation passed by the Republican legislative majority that suspended or revoked the licenses of businesses in Arizona that hired unauthorized immigrants. The law was challenged by business groups that argued that the federal government had exclusive authority in this area. In 2011, though, the Supreme Court upheld Arizona's right to sanction businesses, stating that the federal immigration law did not bar such action. In 2010, Napolitano's successor in office, Jan Brewer, a Republican, signed the toughest state legislation on immigration to date. The law made it a state crime to be in the United States illegally and compelled immigrants to carry paperwork demonstrating their legal status. Police were given broad discretion to detain and question individuals who they "reasonably suspected" of being unauthorized. The law was challenged in federal court and most of the provisions were struck down as interfering with the federal government's constitutional authority to regulate immigration.

In 2012, Republicans drafted an official platform that sought to condemn illegal immigration while simultaneously extolling America's heritage as a nation of immigrants:

> The greatest asset of the American economy is the American worker. Just as immigrant labor helped build our country in the past, today's legal immigrants are making vital contributions in every aspect of our national life. Their industry and commitment to American values strengthens our economy, enriches our culture, and enables us to better understand and more effectively compete with the rest of the world. Illegal immigration undermines those benefits and affects U.S. workers. In an age of terrorism, drug cartels, human trafficking, and criminal gangs, the presence of millions of unidentified persons in this country poses grave risks to the safety and the sovereignty of the United States. Our highest priority, therefore, is to secure the rule of law both at our borders and at ports of entry.
>
> We recognize that for most of those seeking entry into this country, the lack of respect for the rule of law in their homelands has meant economic exploitation and political oppression by corrupt elites. In this country, the rule of law guarantees equal treatment to every individual, including more than one million immigrants to whom we grant permanent residence every year. That is why we oppose any form of amnesty for those who, by intentionally violating the law, disadvantage those who have obeyed it. Granting amnesty only rewards and encourages more law breaking. (Republican National Committee 2012)

Despite their party's criticism of unauthorized immigration, however, some Republicans have supported reform measures. After Republican presidential nominee Mitt Romney was defeated by Barack Obama in 2012, Republican Party Chairman Reince Priebus created the Growth and Opportunity Project, which reported on the need for the GOP to enact immigration reform. The report took a swipe at the failed 2012 Republican nominee Mitt Romney for his disparaging remark that illegal immigrants should self-deport (Republican National Committee 2013). In the Senate, Arizona Senator John McCain and South Carolina Senator Lindsey Graham announced a need for immigration reform and in the House, Speaker John Boehner said he supported immigration reform, which he claimed would help the U.S. economy. Since then, however, prominent Republicans have been reluctant to discuss any programs of immigration "reform" that do not lead with the prosecution of illegal immigrants and new border security measures. This stance is widely seen as a response to deep anger with illegal immigration in the GOP base of white conservative voters.

Democrats on Immigration

Many Democrats have supported immigration reform since the presidency of Lyndon Johnson However, efforts to address unauthorized immigration in any kind of comprehensive fashion remained unresolved throughout the administration of President Bill Clinton. In 1996, Clinton did sign the Illegal Immigrant Reform and Immigrant Responsibility Act, a bipartisan bill that allowed over 300,000 Central Americans who were in the United States a legal path to citizenship, but it also tightened up the rules for those seeking asylum. The law did little to stem the 600,000 or more undocumented immigrants who came into the United States annually.

During his successful campaign for the presidency, Democratic candidate Barack Obama echoed other members of his party in calling for a path to citizenship for unauthorized immigrants and sanctioning businesses for hiring undocumented workers. But he also noted that as a U.S. senator, he had voted for legislation that authorized the building of a 700-mile fence along the U.S.–Mexico border. Obama garnered support from Hispanic voters when he advocated for states to issue driver's licenses to undocumented residents; used a campaign slogan that echoed the words of Cesar Chavez, the Hispanic leader who led the United Farm Workers in the 1970s whose rallying cry was "Yes it is possible," or "Si se puede"; and then promised to seek comprehensive immigration reform in his first year in office. In his first election in 2008, Obama won 65 percent of the Latino vote.

During his first term in office, however, Obama's stated goal of finding common ground with Republicans on the subject of immigration reform remained out of reach. Many analysts assert that the GOP adopted such an uncompromising hard-line position on the issue that meaningful immigration reform became an impossibility. This inability to bridge the partisan gap occurred despite the fact that the Obama administration adopted a policy of strong enforcement of immigration laws. In fact, the United States deported more than two million unauthorized immigrants from 2009 to 2013.

In the run up to his reelection bid in 2012, Obama issued the Deferred Action for Childhood Arrivals (DACA) policy, sometimes called the DREAMers Act because DACA was modeled on the DREAM Act first suggested in 2001. The executive order stopped the Department of Homeland Security from deporting unauthorized immigrants who came to the United States as children and granted them a two-year waiver that was renewable for those who finished high school, military service, and some college. By the fall of 2014, upward of 800,000 individuals became eligible for work permits and social security cards under the president's authorization. Obama's executive action on immigration, combined with the unpopularity of GOP candidate Mitt Romney with Hispanics, gave the president an even higher percentage of the Hispanic vote in his reelection bid. Overall, there were more Hispanic voters in the 2012 election than voted in 2008 and 71 percent of these voted for Obama (Schwab 2013).

Immigrants fill out forms for Deferred Action for Childhood Arrivals (DACA), at a workshop in New York City on February 18, 2015. The immigrant advocacy group Make the Road New York holds weekly workshops to help immigrants get legal status under DACA to work in the United States. (Photo by John Moore/Getty Images)

Electoral politics aside, DACA also inspired states with large Hispanic populations and Democratic majorities to enact statewide legislation to assist the newly authorized immigrants. In 2013, at least seven states passed legislation allowing unauthorized immigrants to get driver's licenses and some states such as California, Illinois, and Maryland launched programs to assist DACA eligible residents by granting in-state tuition and scholarships (Pew Charitable Trust 2014). In October 2013, California, which had 20 years earlier voted for a proposition restricting entitlements to unauthorized immigrants, enacted a law prohibiting local police departments from alerting federal immigration authorities when undocumented immigrants are arrested for minor crimes, such as traffic violations, and were eligible for release from custody. Connecticut and the District of Columbia enacted similar laws, and several other states with Democratic majorities are considering such actions. Meanwhile, states with strong Republican majorities such as Arizona have denied undocumented immigrants benefits and been outspoken against DACA.

Obama's reelection in 2012 did not lead to comprehensive immigration reform. Sharp divisions continued between the House, which remained in the control of Republicans, and the Democrat-controlled Senate and the Obama White House. In November 2014, after it was clear that there would not be a comprehensive immigration reform bill, Obama took additional executive action to expand DACA and to defer deportations.

Barack Obama Speaks Out on Immigration Reform

On November 20, 2014, Democratic President Barack Obama delivered a special address to the nation on the subject of immigration, and about his support for a so-called path to citizenship for undocumented immigrants. Below are excerpts from those remarks:

Millions of us, myself included, go back generations in this country, with ancestors who put in the painstaking work to become citizens. So we don't like the notion that anyone might get a free pass to American citizenship.

I know some worry immigration will change the very fabric of who we are, or take our jobs, or stick it to middle-class families at a time when they already feel like they've gotten the raw deal for over a decade. I hear these concerns. But that's not what these steps would do. Our history and the facts show that immigrants are a net plus for our economy and our society. And I believe it's important that all of us have this debate without impugning each other's character.

Because for all the back and forth of Washington, we have to remember that this debate is about something bigger. It's about who we are as a country, and who we want to be for future generations.

Are we a nation that tolerates the hypocrisy of a system where workers who pick our fruit and make our beds never have a chance to get right with the law? Or are we a nation that gives them a chance to make amends, take responsibility, and give their kids a better future?

Are we a nation that accepts the cruelty of ripping children from their parents' arms? Or are we a nation that values families, and works together to keep them together?

Are we a nation that educates the world's best and brightest in our universities, only to send them home to create businesses in countries that compete against us? Or are we a nation that encourages them to stay and create jobs here, create businesses here, create industries right here in America? . . .

My fellow Americans, we are and always will be a nation of immigrants. We were strangers once, too. And whether our forebears were strangers who crossed the Atlantic, or the Pacific, or the Rio Grande, we are here only because this country welcomed them in, and taught them that to be an American is about something more than what we look like, or what our last names are, or how we worship. What makes us Americans is our shared commitment to an ideal—that all of us are created equal, and all of us have the chance to make of our lives what we will.

That's the country our parents and grandparents and generations before them built for us. That's the tradition we must uphold. That's the legacy we must leave for those who are yet to come.

Source

Obama, Barack. 2014. "Remarks by the President in Address to the Nation on Immigration," November 20. Accessed September 21, 2015: http://www.whitehouse.gov/the-press-office /2014/11/20/remarks-president-address-nation-immigration.

Further Reading

Barkan, Elliot Robert, ed. 2013. *Immigrants in American History: Arrival, Adaptation, and Integration.* Santa Barbara: ABC-CLIO.

Cooper, Betsy, and Kevin O'Neil. 2005. "Lessons from the Immigration Reform and Control Act of 1986," *Policy Briefing 3,* Migration Policy Institute, August. Accessed August 2, 2014: http://www.migrationpolicy.org/research/lessons-immigration-reform -and-control-act-1986.

Jenks, Rosemary. "Enhanced Border Security Visa Reform Act of 2002," Center for Immigration Studies. Accessed August 2, 2014: http://cis.org/EnhancedBorderSecurityVisaReformAct 2002-HR3525.

Motel, Seth. 2014. "On Immigration, Republicans Favor Path to Legal Status, but Differ Over Citizenship," Pew Research Center, January 28. Accessed August 2, 2014: http://www .pewresearch.org/fact-tank/2014/01/28/on-immigration-republicans-favor-path-to -legal-status-but-differ-over-citizenship/.

Pew Charitable Trusts. 2014. "Five Things We Learned about DACA." Accessed August 29, 2014: http://www.pewtrusts.org/en/about/news-room/news/2014/08/19/five-things-we -learned-about-daca.

Pew Research Center. 2015. "5 Facts about Illegal Immigration in the U.S.," July 24. Accessed September 21, 2015: http://www.pewresearch.org/fact-tank/2015/07/24/5 -facts-about-illegal-immigration-in-the-u-s/.

Republican National Committee. 2012. "GOP Platform: The Rule of Law, Legal Immigration." In *Reforming Government to Serve the People.* Accessed December 1, 2015: https:// www.gop.com/platform/reforming-government/.

Republican National Committee. 2013. *Growth and Opportunity Project.* Accessed August 2, 2014: https://goproject.gop.com/RNC_Growth_Opportunity_Book_2013.pdf.

Schwab, William A. 2013. *Right to DREAM: Immigration Reform and America's Future.* Little Rock: University of Arkansas Press.

U.S. Immigration and Naturalization Service. "Guest Worker Program," U.S. Immigration and Naturalization Service. Accessed August 2, 2014 http://www.usimmigrationsupport .org/guestworkerprogram.html.

Warren, Robert, and Jeffrey S. Passel. 1987. "A Count of the Uncountable: Estimates of Undocumented Aliens Counted in the 1980 United States Census," *Demography,* August.

White House Fact Sheet. 2006. "The Secure Fence Act of 2006." Accessed August 2, 2014: http://georgewbush-whitehouse.archives.gov/news/releases/2006/10/20061026-1 .html.

LGBT Rights

At a Glance

The lesbian, gay, bisexual, and transgender (LGBT) communities have fought against discrimination for decades. Their allies in the fight for inclusion into mainstream American society have been the many Democrats who see them as victims of social and political prejudice. Many Republicans have been more resistant to the idea that sexual orientation be included within the penumbra of civil rights and reject the idea that it should be a protected class.

Many Democrats . . .

- Believe that the LGBT community has historically suffered from systemic discrimination.
- Propose laws protecting LGBT individuals from discrimination in employment and housing.
- Support same-sex marriage.
- Want to allow LGBT individuals to serve in the military.
- Want insurance companies to include gender reassignment surgery coverage as standard coverage.
- Feel that some religious freedom laws passed by Republican legislatures are discriminatory against people who may be lesbian, gay, bisexual, or transgender.

Many Republicans . . .

- Believe that current laws adequately protect everyone, including members of the LGBT community.
- Oppose news laws protecting LGBT people from discrimination in employment and housing.
- Oppose state laws supporting same-sex marriage.
- Support religious freedom laws.
- Are concerned that gender quality laws might lead to frivolous lawsuits.

Overview

Many members of the Democratic Party are likely to support and demand that members of the LGBT community receive equal rights and acceptance in society. Many Republicans would prefer to balance the rights of individuals who may be lesbian, gay, bisexual, or transgender against traditional definitions of marriage, family, and sexuality. The term "transgender" refers to individuals who express their gender differently from traditional heterosexual norms; it can include transvestites, and transsexuals who opt for hormone treatment or sex reassignment surgery.

The LGBT movement in American society and politics often posit that in many ways their efforts mirror the civil rights struggle of other groups such as African Americans, women, and Latinos. LGBT members had few civil rights in the late 1960s, and their behavior was often considered criminal or deviant and their sexual orientation labeled as a form of mental illness. In 1969, however, an uprising against police harassment and police brutality led by gay men and transvestites outside of Stonewall, a gay nightclub in New York City, sparked a broader movement to bring LGBT from the shadows and to provide space for them to publicly declare their sexual identity, known as "coming out" as gay, and to gain the acceptance and approval of U.S. society.

Gay activists embraced classic civil rights tactics such as marches, demonstrations, and protests to gain media and public attention. They formed groups such as ACT UP and Human Rights Campaign to press for social and legal recognition of LGBT rights. To secure laws protecting members of the LGBT community from discrimination in housing, the workplace, and employment, LGBT individuals ran for office or formed political action committees to support gay-friendly candidates, most often under the umbrella of the Democratic Party.

Conservative Christians, fearing that LGBT rights did not align with their religious beliefs and posed a threat to the nation's moral foundations, organized to fight this movement. In the late 1970s, Anita Bryant, a former Miss USA and spokesperson for Florida orange growers, successfully led an effort to overturn an antigay discrimination law in Florida, which sparked the overturning of laws in a variety of states and localities.

By the 1980s, the conflict between pro- and antigay rights activists formed one of the many battlefields in the culture wars between conservatives and liberals. This conflict sharpened after the rise of acquired immunodeficiency syndrome (AIDS), which was labeled by some religious conservatives as "the gay plague" because of the high percentage of young gay men with the illness. Conservatives were pleased by the 1986 Supreme Court decision in *Bowers v. Hardwick* that ruled against gay individuals and in favor of the right of states to criminalize homosexual sodomy.

As the death toll from AIDS climbed, many Democrats in Congress joined with moderate Republicans to urge federal funding for research on AIDS, but conservative Republicans allied with conservative Democrats battled the effort to fund AIDS research. Senator Jesse Helms of North Carolina, one of the most ardent conservatives of the 1980s, argued that such federal expenditures amounted to promoting "homosexuality." Conservatives lost this battle, but they were more successful in blocking congressional legislation that sought to protect gays from discrimination or hate crimes. Failing to win support at the national level, pro-LGBT rights groups shifted their efforts to state and local ordinances to protect people from civil rights violations based on their sexual orientation. These efforts succeeded in cities, counties, and states with large Democratic majorities even in the face of mobilized opposition by conservative groups.

Although the 1980s saw victories for both advocates and opponents of LGBT rights, by the end of the 1990s public support had begun to swing more decisively in favor of LGBT rights. With support from Republican president George H. W. Bush, Democratic lawmakers enacted a hate crimes policy that included sexual orientation as a protected class. Bush also signed into law the Americans with Disabilities Act (ADA), which protected persons with HIV/AIDS from discrimination. Throughout this decade more Democrats who advocated for LGBT civil rights were elected to Congress, supported by LGBT activists who donated more than $3.2 million to the Democratic Party.

Support from the gay community also helped lift Bill Clinton to the White House. Clinton called for an end to discrimination against gays and lesbians in the military but opposition from Republicans and members of the military stymied his efforts. In the end, the Clinton administration instituted its controversial "Don't Ask, Don't Tell" policies for military service. Under this policy, the U.S. military stopped asking applicants and active service members whether they were homosexual. In return, individuals who did not disclose their gay orientation could stay in the military. However, anyone who did reveal that they were gay would be forced to leave the military.

But while public opinion in the 1990s was mixed about whether gays should be allowed to serve in the military, LGBT efforts to solicit support for gay marriage enjoyed much less success. Conservative Republicans, many of whom were elected to Congress in 1994, successfully fashioned the 1996 Defense of Marriage Act (DOMA) to block efforts by activists seeking to enact same-sex marriage. This measure was signed into law by Clinton.

Opponents of gay rights found support for limiting or removing antigay discrimination laws in those states with large Republican majorities. In Colorado, citizens passed an amendment to the state constitution prohibiting the recognition of protections for individuals based on their sexual orientation but this was struck down as unconstitutional by the Supreme Court in 1996. The Court also reversed its decision on *Bowers* in the 2003 case of *Lawrence v. Texas,* and now claimed the right of privacy trumped state laws against homosexual sodomy. Outside of Washington, legislation protecting LGBT civil rights was spreading in Democratic states such as Connecticut, Hawaii, Massachusetts, Minnesota, and New Jersey all providing legal protection against discrimination by 1993. By 2010, nearly 300 localities had laws banning discrimination on the basis of sexual orientation. In addition, 20 states had enacted similar anti-LGBT discrimination laws, and all but 17 had adopted hate crime laws protecting LGBT individuals from violence. Overall, by 2010 national trends showed greater support for civil and social rights for members of the LGBT community, especially from traditional Democrats, such as people who lived in urban areas, people who have higher levels of education, and people who identified as liberal and heterosexual women.

Democrats on LGBT Rights

The Democratic Party began embracing the LGBT movement in the 1970s. President Jimmy Carter made a signature move in the history of civil rights in 1977, when his special assistant, Midge Costanza, met with representatives from the National Gay Task Force (NGTF) to hear their grievances about discriminatory federal policies. The meeting led to more high-level meetings and Carter enacted new policies at the Bureau of Prisons and the Public Health Service to assist and protect the rights of people who were LGBT. The meeting initiated further policy discussions that ultimately led the Democratic Party to incorporate gay rights within the Democratic Party (Mattingly and Boyd 2013).

During the 1980s, openly gay candidates became comfortable running for office as Democrats in some parts of the country. In 1983, Democratic congress member Gerry Studds of Massachusetts publicly proclaimed his sexual identity and became the first openly gay member of Congress. He was followed by Barney Frank, another Massachusetts Democrat, who revealed his sexual orientation in 1987. Both men used their political platform to advocate for more equitable treatment for the LGBT community. This was especially important during the Reagan years when gay advocates castigated the Reagan administration for not paying enough attention to the AIDS crisis (Endean 2006).

Studies by political scientist Donald Haider-Markel find that the presence of LGBT legislators increases the likelihood of laws prohibiting discrimination on the basis of sexual orientation (Haider-Markel 2010). LGBT legislators played a leading role in promoting and advocating for bills that advance LGBT civil rights and educating other policy makers on the issue (Reynolds 2013). By 2015, 20 Democratic leaning states, which also had higher than average LGBT representation in their state legislatures, enacted bans on discrimination based on sexual orientation and gender identity.

LGBT Democrats and civil rights organizations such as the American Civil Liberties Union (ACLU) and Human Rights Campaign put pressure on state and national party leaders to pass legislation banning discrimination against individuals based on sexual orientation and to include a plank recognizing gay rights in the party platform. Responding to what had become an important constituency in the Democratic Party, the Democrats in 1992 included for the first time in their program an openly gay official, Bob Hattoy, who said, "AIDS knows no class or gender, race or religion, or sexual orientation, AIDS does not discriminate, but George Bush's White House does" (Human Rights Campaign 2007).

In the 1990s, President Clinton took an incremental step to end discrimination in the military based on sexual orientation. Clinton instituted the Don't Ask, Don't Tell policy, a practice whereby the government no longer asked candidates for military service if they were homosexual, but it required members of the gay community to keep their sexual orientation secret or face court martial and dismissal from the service. This policy remained in effect until 2010, when it was repealed by Democratic members of Congress over the objections of many Republicans. Clinton also disappointed members of the LGBT community by supporting DOMA, which defined marriage as a heterosexual institution.

During this same period, however, many Democrats remained hesitant to embrace same-sex marriage. In 2008, leaders within the Democratic National

Obama's Evolution on Same-Sex Marriage

During his Senate career and his first campaign for the presidency in 2008, Democratic President Barack Obama stated that he thought marriage should be reserved for unions between men and women—although he opposed proposals to pass a constitutional amendment to that effect as unnecessarily divisive.

After reaching the Oval Office, however, Obama's stance on gay marriage began to change—or "evolve," as he put it. In 2010, Obama made news when he said that "I have been to this point unwilling to sign on to same-sex marriage primarily because of my understandings of the traditional definitions of marriage. But I also think you're right that attitudes evolve, including mine. And I think that it is an issue that I wrestle with and think about because I have a whole host of friends who are in gay partnerships."

The final dramatic step in Obama's change of heart on the subject came in May 2012, when he told ABC News that "over the course of several years as I have talked to friends and family and neighbors, when I think about members of my own staff who are in incredibly committed monogamous relationships, same-sex relationships, who are raising kids together, when I think about those soldiers or airmen or Marines or sailors who are out there fighting on my behalf and yet feel constrained, even now that 'don't ask, don't tell' is gone, because they are not able to commit themselves in a marriage, at a certain point I've just concluded that for me personally, it is important for me to go ahead and affirm that I think same-sex couples should be able to get married."

In the days following Obama's announcement, many political observers openly speculated that it might be damaging to the Democrats' election prospects later that year. Instead, public opinion polls showed a jump in support for gay marriage, especially among traditional Democratic constituencies.

Source

Memoli, Michael A., and Kathleen Hennessey. 2012. "Obama Declares Support for Same-Sex Marriage," *Los Angeles Times*, May 9. Accessed May 19, 2014: http://articles.latimes.com/2012/may/09/news/la-pn-obama-abc-gay-marriage-position-20120509.

Committee still refused to mention same-sex marriage during televised coverage of the convention during prime time. This changed dramatically in 2012, however. President Obama publicly expressed his support for gay marriage, and public opinion polls showed strong majority support for gay marriage for the first time (Taylor and Haider-Markel 2014).

Later that year, the Democratic Party embraced same-sex marriage and acknowledged gay rights in its 2012 party platform: "The core of the Democratic Party is the principle that no one should face discrimination on the basis of race, ethnicity, national origin, language, religion, gender, sexual orientation, gender identity, or disability status" (Democratic Party 2012). Furthermore, the line-up of speakers at the convention showcased well-known members of the party who were also members of the LGBT community that articulated the party's support for civil rights and social justice.

President Obama, first elected in 2008, played a pivotal role in these developments. He fulfilled his campaign promise and ended discrimination based on sexual and gender orientation in the military, opening it up to all members of the LGBT community. With Congress in Republican hands since 2010, Obama signed an executive order barring federal contractors from hiring or firing employees based on their sexual orientation or gender identity. Obama also called for new laws that would give workers in the private sector who feel they were denied employment or fired due to sexual or gender orientation greater rights to sue their employer, although such legislation was shelved in the Republican-controlled House. In 2015, Obama further demonstrated his commitment to LGBT rights by appointing Randy Berry, an openly gay State Department official, as the International Envoy on LGBT rights whose job was to defend and extend the human rights of all LGBT people worldwide.

States whose party enrollment favors Democrats are at the forefront of legislation protecting LGBT rights. More recently, states have acted to protect those in the transgender community. Until recently, transgender individuals did not have the same legal protections afforded to gays, lesbians, and bisexuals. New York Governor Andrew Cuomo, first elected in 2010, led the successful effort to pass a same-sex marriage law in 2011. Cuomo also signed orders making it easier for transgender New Yorkers to change their gender on their birth certificates and demanded that health insurance companies cover gender reassignment surgery for New Yorkers. Cuomo and Democrats in the state legislature passed the Gender Equality Non-Discrimination Act, or GENDA, banning discrimination based on gender identity or expression in employment, housing, and other services, and increased penalties for hate crime against transgender individuals. The bill had been passed eight times by Democrats, but was never brought to a vote in the state senate, which is controlled by Republicans.

Republicans on LGBT Rights

Republican opposition to LGBT rights grew sharply in the 1980s due to the influence of conservative Christian political activists within the party. Many Republicans believe there is a gay agenda led by LGBT activists to undermine traditional religious beliefs, redefine marriage and the family, and promote immoral sexual behavior. In the 1980s, conservative Christians such as Jerry Falwell, who founded an organization called the Moral Majority, argued that AIDS was a gay plague, "a definite form of judgment by God on society" ("Falwell Campaigns against Gays, AIDS" 1983). Under pressure from this important group within the party, conservative Republican lawmakers voted against funding for research on AIDS. Supreme Court justices appointed by Republicans who were ideological moderate or conservative found no compelling right to deny states the power to enforce laws criminalizing homosexual sodomy in the 1986 decision in *Bowers v. Hardwick* (Ball and Bronski 2011). Republicans were unwilling to support new civil rights legislation covering sexual orientation but they ultimately supported fighting AIDS. President Ronald Reagan was often pilloried by gay activists for not supporting funding for AIDS research in the early 1980s, but he increased AIDS research funding during his second term. Reagan established a presidential commission to study the disease.

As LGBT activists were working with moderates and liberals in cities and states to enact laws banning discrimination based on sexual orientation, conservative Republicans worked to repeal or block such legislation and enjoyed great success when voters were asked to choose between enacting laws to protect sexual orientation or to reject new laws. However, conservatives were less successful when such issues were brought before the courts. For example, in 1992, Colorado conservatives passed a state referendum, Amendment 2, banning local governments from passing ordinances protecting gays from discrimination. Claiming this was a violation of their rights to protect against discrimination, LGBT rights advocates challenged the law in court. In the 1996 case, *Romer v. Evans,* the Supreme Court, in a 6–3 decision, declared that singling out sexual orientation was a violation of the equal protection guaranteed in the Fourteenth Amendment and effectively ended the repeal efforts of conservatives. The *Romer v. Evans* decision worried conservatives, who urged Congress to protect traditional marriage by enacting DOMA in 1996. This served to block federal recognition of same-sex marriage until the 2013 case of *United States v. Windsor,* which struck down DOMA, claiming it violated the equal protection rights of same-sex couples. Within two years of this decision, a dozen states had recognized the right of same-sex marriage through legislation or court decision.

As they failed to stop the advance of the LGBT rights movement at the national level, Christian conservatives hoped to enact state laws protecting their right to refuse business services to same-sex couples based on their religious convictions. Laws were considered or enacted in a number of Republican or Republican-leaning states such as Arkansas, Georgia, Indiana, and Oklahoma. Meanwhile, Democratic governors in New York and Connecticut banned official travel to states that had passed such laws. Lawmakers were forced to abandon these bills or modify them to indicate they were not intended to discriminate against the LGBT community. Conservative Christians were dismayed by this backtracking.

Ted Cruz Introduces "The Restoration of Marriage" Amendment

Republican Ted Cruz of Texas was first elected to the U.S. Senate in 2010 with strong backing from the Tea Party, a bloc of conservative voters within the GOP who oppose any compromise with Barack Obama and his fellow Democrats. Since joining the Senate, Cruz has regularly voiced his opposition to gay marriage and other aspects of LGBT rights. In 2015 he provided clear evidence of this stance with his introduction of a proposed "Restoration of Marriage" amendment to the U.S. Constitution. This amendment would legally define marriage as the union of one man and one woman and prevent federal courts from striking down state bans on gay marriage. Here is the full text of the proposed amendment:

> The United States and each State, territory, and possession thereof shall have the power to define marriage as limited to the union of one man and one woman. Nothing in this Constitution shall be construed to require that marriage or the legal incidents thereof be conferred upon any union other than the union of one man and one woman or to require that a State recognize a marriage that was licensed in another State. No decision or order of any court to the contrary, including any decision or order issued before the date of ratification, shall have any force or effect.

Source

Cruz, Ted. 2015. "Sen. Cruz: The People Should Decide the Issue of Marriage, Not the Courts," April 24. Accessed December 1, 2015: http://www.cruz.senate.gov/?p=press_release&id=2303.

Russell Moore, spokesman for the Southern Baptist Convention, the largest organization of Protestants in the United States, said, "We do not ask the government to bless our doctrinal convictions or to impose them on others. We simply ask the government not to set itself up as lord of our conscience" (Eckholm 2015).

Within the ranks of the Republican Party, a move to eschew the antigay rhetoric was led by the Log Cabin Republicans who were openly gay, socially moderate, and economically conservative members of the GOP. They influenced the party in the 2012 Republican National Convention, which, rather than condemn homosexuality, simply remained silent on the issue of LGBT rights, a signal that after three decades, the GOP was pivoting its policy on LGBT rights.

Since then, Republicans have not completely abandoned their resistance to LGBT rights. Mindful of public support for gay marriage and other LGBT rights, however, they are increasingly couching their opposition in economic terms as well as under the guise of religious liberty. When Republican leaders in the House refused to allow a vote on the Employment Non-Discriminatory Act, which had been passed by Senate Democrats, they claimed their actions were motivated by a desire to stop frivolous lawsuits and affect the religious liberty of some employers. Republican leaders in Utah have attempted to find balance between conservative religious believers and LGBT rights by passing an antidiscrimination law to protect LGBT individuals but allowing for reasonable accommodation for religious organizations.

Further Reading

Ball, Carlos, and Michael Bronski. 2011. *From the Closet to the Courtroom: Five LGBT Rights Lawsuits That Have Changed Our Nation.* Boston: Beacon Press.

Democratic Party. 2012. "Party Platform," Gerhard Peters and John T. Woolley, "The American Presidency Project." Accessed July 10, 2015: http://www.presidency.ucsb.edu/ws/?pid=101962.

Eckholm, Erik. 2015. "Eroding Freedom in the Name of Freedom," *New York Times,* March 30. Accessed July 10, 2015: http://www.nytimes.com/2015/03/31/us/politics/religious-protection-laws-once-called-shields-are-now-seen-as-cudgels.html.

Endean, Steve. 2006. *Bringing Lesbian and Gay Rights into the Mainstream: Twenty Years of Progress.* New York: Harrington Park.

"Falwell Campaigns against Gays, AIDS," 1983. *Boca Raton News,* July 6, 4B.

Haider-Markel, Donald P. 2010. *Out and Running: Gay and Lesbian Candidates, Elections, and Policy Representation.* Washington, D.C.: Georgetown University Press.

Human Rights Campaign. 2007. "Bob Hattoy at 1992 Democratic National Convention," Accessed March 7, 2015: https://www.youtube.com/watch?v=RUashmbh1zQ.

Mattingly, Doreen J., and Ashley Boyd. 2013. "Bringing Gay and Lesbian Activism to the White House: Midge Costanza and the National Gay Task Force Meeting," *Journal of Lesbian Studies,* 17 (3–4): 365–379.

Reynolds, Andrew. 2013. "Representation and Rights: The Impact of LGBT Legislators in Comparative Perspective," *American Political Science Review,* May, 1–16. Accessed July 12, 2015: http://reynolds.web.unc.edu/files/2011/10/APSRLGBTReynolds.pdf.

Taylor, Jami Kathleen, and Donald P. Haider-Markel. 2014. *Transgender Rights and Politics: Groups, Issue Framing, and Policy Adoption.* Ann Arbor: University of Michigan Press.

Marijuana Legalization

At a Glance

Is marijuana a dangerous gateway drug to more addictive drugs? Should it be classified with alcohol and be decriminalized? Is the alleged medicinal value of marijuana overblown, or is "medical marijuana" a potentially valuable tool in treating chronic pain and other health issues? Should users or dealers be punished or left alone? These and other questions have been part of the debate between Democrats and Republicans since the 1970s. Generally speaking, Republicans believe that marijuana is unhealthy, that it can act as a "gateway drug," leading to the abuse of much harder drugs, and that the sale, possession, and use of marijuana should remain illegal. Democrats, on the other hand, are more likely to believe that the health risk of using marijuana is minimal—and in some cases can be beneficial—that it is no more likely to inspire someone to use harder drugs than alcohol, and that people convicted of marijuana-related offenses are a key contributor to the country's overcrowded prison system. They are thus more likely to be supportive of efforts to legalize medical marijuana or even marijuana for recreational use.

Neither party is monolithic in its stance upon this issue, however. Some Republicans, especially those with libertarian leanings or those concerned with penal reform, have expressed support for legalization of marijuana in at least some cases. Meanwhile, some Democrats remain opposed to legalization, whether because of personal conviction or concern that such a position might leave them vulnerable to "soft on crime" charges.

Many Democrats . . .

- Reject the idea that marijuana is especially dangerous to a person's health.
- Reject the idea that use of marijuana would increase the likelihood that someone would try more addictive drugs such as heroin.
- Have tolerance for allowing marijuana for recreational use.
- Believe that individual recreational use of marijuana should be legalized.
- Support the use of medical marijuana.
- Want to revisit harsh drug laws.

Many Republicans . . .

- Believe that smoking marijuana is a health risk.
- Believe that smoking marijuana will be a gateway to stronger drugs.
- Support keeping marijuana illegal.
- Are skeptical of the health claims about medical marijuana.
- Believe legalization of marijuana will lead to more crime.
- Are open to rethinking mandatory drug sentencing.

———————————

Overview

Marijuana, known variously as cannabis, ganja, grass, pot, reefer, or weed, has been available since colonial times. A strain of cannabis plant known as hemp, in fact, was an early cash crop of the American colonists. It was used to make canvas sails, cloth, rope, paper, and other materials. By the mid-19th century, hemp was the country's third-largest crop, behind only cotton and tobacco (Johnson 2014).

Government regulation of marijuana did not begin until the 20th century when state governments during the Progressive Era (1890–1920) banned and criminalized the use of cannabis. California took the lead in 1913, and it was soon followed by several other states. This turn toward criminalization stemmed from three factors. First, hemp fell out of commercial favor as cotton became the primary material for clothing, blankets, and similar goods. In addition, a movement to outlaw *any* mind-altering substances, including alcohol, was picking up steam at this time. This movement would ultimately result in the Prohibition Era (1920–1933), when alcohol production, sales, and consumption became illegal in the United States. Finally, marijuana's popularity with Mexican immigrants was noticed by whites in states like California and Texas. "[Whites] viewed the immigrants as intellectually and morally inferior—and as potential threats to their jobs," noted one historian. "Laws that outlawed cannabis . . . became a way for whites to show the immigrants that they were not welcome" (Hillstrom 2014).

The federal government began regulating the drug in the 1930s at the insistence of Harry Anslinger, who directed the Federal Bureau of Narcotics from 1930 until 1970. Anslinger was convinced that marijuana posed a deadly threat to the American people. "It is a drug," he declared, "that causes insanity, criminality, and death—the most violence-causing drug in the history of mankind" (Gerber 2004). The first federal act regulating marijuana was the Marihuana Tax Act of 1937, which imposed a $1 tax on anyone who bought, sold, grew, possessed, and prescribed the drug. However, failure to pay the fee led to five year's imprisonment and a $2,000 fine. A mandatory minimum sentence of two years for selling marijuana was added by Congress in 1952 and 1956. For the next two decades, legislation increasing the punishment and regulating the use of marijuana was passed by Congress through the Controlled Substance Act of 1970, which ended mandatory sentences but also placed marijuana on schedule 1, the same class as heroin and LSD.

The National Organization for the Reform of Marijuana Laws

The National Organization for the Reform of Marijuana Laws (NORML) is the oldest, largest and best-known organization that advocates for legalization of marijuana for medical or recreational purposes. NORML was founded in 1970 with a grant from the Playboy Foundation by Keith Shoup, a Washington D.C. public-interest attorney. Since its founding, NORML has been a voice in the public policy debate for Americans who oppose marijuana prohibition. A nonprofit public-interest advocacy group, NORML says that it represents the interests of more than 10 million Americans who smoke marijuana responsibly. The organization is headquartered in Washington D.C. and has chapters in every state. With a budget in the millions of dollars, the organization lobbies to change both state and national laws to end the prohibition on marijuana. NORML also has a political action committee that seeks to assist and to endorse candidates who support their goal of supporting the decriminalization of marijuana.

Source

National Organization for the Reform of Marijuana Laws. "About NORML." Accessed September 23, 2015: www.norml.org/about.

Opposition to criminalizing marijuana developed around the same time Congress passed the Controlled Substance Act of 1970. Unexpectedly, advocates of legalization received support for their position from the National Commission on Marijuana and Drug Abuse, a task force appointed by Richard Nixon who served as president from 1969 to 1974. The commission issued a report in 1972 that suggested marijuana be decriminalized and not punished by either criminal or civil law. Nixon ignored the report and continued to prosecute a war on drugs.

One of the most significant proponents for changing laws governing the use of marijuana has been NORML, which lobbies state and federal officials to end the prohibition on marijuana. The efforts of this organization, which was founded in 1970, began to pay visible dividends in the late 1970s and early 1980s, when a number of states passed bills approving limited use of marijuana for medicinal purposes or research into its possible medical application. An even bigger triumph came in 1996, when California voters passed Proposition 215, which legalized medical marijuana. Several other states followed suit with bills or referendums that legalized medical marijuana, despite continued federal prohibitions against marijuana use of any kind. In these states, marijuana is being prescribed to treat nausea and vomiting associated with cancer chemotherapy in patients who have failed to respond adequately to conventional antiemetic treatments, the treatment of anorexia associated with weight loss in patients with AIDS, and a range of diseases such as Tourette's syndrome and multiple sclerosis (Aggarwal et al. 2009).

Advocates of decriminalization of marijuana have even managed to change perceptions of marijuana use for recreational purposes. In 2012, Washington formally

Senator Kirsten Gillibrand (D-N.Y.) speaks alongside Senator Cory Booker (D-N.J.), right, during a news conference at the Drug Policy Alliance in New York, on March 15, 2015. The senators met with New York and New Jersey families to announce the endorsement by the Epilepsy Foundation of their newly introduced Compassionate Access, Research Expansion and Respect States Act (CARERS). The bipartisan bill will allow patients in states that have legalized medical marijuana to access the treatment without fear of federal prosecution. (AP Photo/John Minchillo)

legalized marijuana, and Colorado followed suit two years later. These developments are deeply upsetting to opponents, who continue to see marijuana as having long-term and dangerous health effects that far outweigh the medical benefits that proponents claim. Opponents claim that one marijuana cigarette is equivalent to four cigarettes of tobacco, which makes inhaling the smoke from marijuana four times more likely to cause lung disease (Hillstrom 2014). Opponents also believe that marijuana is a gateway drug to stronger and even more serious substances such as speed or heroin. This is the position taken by organizations such as the Drug Free America Foundation and Smart Approaches to Marijuana (SAM).

Pro-legalization efforts are divisive. A 2013 Gallup poll found 58 percent of Americans supported legalization of marijuana. This figure represents the strong support of legalization by younger Americans. The support of younger Americans is often cited as a key factor in the sharp rise in the number of states holding referendums on legalizing marijuana.

Democrats on Marijuana

Public support for legalizing marijuana has grown since 1970 and is popular among voters aged 18–29, Democrats, and Libertarians. It is clear that the issue of legalizing or allowing medical marijuana shows a split between elected Democrats and rank-and-file members of the party. Democrats in public office may fear that they will be portrayed by Republican opponents as soft on crime if they come out in favor of relaxing penalties for marijuana or outright legalization, and they have sometimes been reluctant to embrace the issue.

The first highly visible elected Democrat official to advocate for changing marijuana laws was President Jimmy Carter, who suggested to Congress in 1977 that the country should decriminalize the possession of less than an ounce of marijuana. Carter told Congress that "penalties against possession of a drug should not be more damaging to an individual than the use of the drug itself" (Carter 1977). After Carter's defeat in 1980, no sitting president, Democrat or Republican, embraced tolerance for marijuana, even though when running for the office candidates were often forced to admit using it. Bill Clinton reluctantly confessed that he tried marijuana but also infamously claimed that "he did not inhale" (Patterson 2005). After the conservative Republican victories in Congress and in statehouses across the United States in 1994, Clinton was careful to oppose medical marijuana and threatened to use his executive power to revoke a physician's federal license to prescribe medicine if they even suggested that patients try medical marijuana (Martin and Rashidian 2014). President Barack Obama alluded to his days of smoking pot while a teen in Hawaii in the 1970s, but made it clear that while he would support medical marijuana, his administration opposed legalization. Officially federal policy has remained antimarijuana from that time to the present, although President Obama restrained the Department of Justice from enforcing federal statutes in states that have allowed recreational and medicinal use of marijuana or decriminalized that activity. Under the Obama administration, the U.S. Department of Veterans Affairs released a Veterans Health Administration (VHA) directive in 2010 stating that veterans who participated in legal state medical marijuana programs would no longer be disqualified from "substance abuse programs, pain control programs, or other clinical programs."

After Jimmy Carter, the most visible elected national Democrat to speak out in favor of medical use of marijuana and decriminalization was Massachusetts Representative Barney Frank. Frank sponsored a number of unsuccessful bills in the House to authorize the use of marijuana for medicinal purposes (Newton 2013). States where registered Democrats outnumber registered Republicans are sometimes called blue states. These are states in which the Democrats dominate public office from the Statehouse to the congressional delegation. Blue states were the first to initiate legislation to decriminalize possession of an ounce or less of marijuana. They were also the first states to embrace the use of medical marijuana. For example, California decriminalized marijuana in 1996. The first states to embrace legalizing marijuana for recreational use were the blue states of Washington and Colorado, where Democratic voters and legislators played a key role in ensuring passage of laws ending cannabis prohibition (Martin and Rashidian 2014).

Democratic governors have by and large avoided any formal endorsements of marijuana legalization although Governor Andrew M. Cuomo of New York has expressed support for legalizing marijuana for medical purposes. In New Hampshire, however, Democratic Governor Maggie Hassan invoked her state's struggle with heroin abuse in arguing against weakening marijuana laws. "Legalizing marijuana won't help us address our substance use challenge," she said in her 2014 state of the state address. "Experience and data suggests it will do just the opposite." Nonetheless, many Democratic-leaning states have in recent years introduced laws or referendums that would allow for recreational use of marijuana. Resistance to recreational marijuana will likely fade as policy experts track what is happening in Colorado, which began the regulated sale of marijuana for recreational use on January 1, 2014. Indications are that state and local taxes on marijuana may bring in over $100 million in revenue, and this new revenue stream may be attractive when states are setting budgets.

Republicans on Marijuana

Republicans have been the most vocal opponents of marijuana use. Republicans invoke both law-and-order and public-health arguments in opposing decriminalization, whether for medical or recreational purposes. Many Republicans believe marijuana is a gateway drug to the use of more addictive psychotropic drugs and cite reports showing the detrimental health effects of smoking marijuana (Ball 2014).

Republicans have been associated with the War on Drugs since Richard Nixon declared drugs "public enemy number one" in 1971. Nixon oversaw the creation of the Drug Enforcement Agency (DEA) in 1973. New York Governor Nelson Rockefeller, a Republican, led the nation by imposing the harshest mandatory drug laws in the country in 1973 with mandatory minimum sentences of 15 years to life for possession of four ounces of narcotics—similar to what someone would receive who was convicted of second-degree murder (Madison 2009).

After defeating incumbent Jimmy Carter in the 1980 presidential election, Ronald Reagan, a Republican, dismissed the idea of decriminalization and continued the so-called War on Drugs. In fact, First Lady Nancy Reagan made "Just Say No" to marijuana and other drugs a centerpiece of her activities during her years in the White House. President Reagan even persuaded the Democrat-controlled Congress to pass the Anti-Drug Abuse Act of 1986, which continued to classify marijuana with stronger drugs. The legislation also added more mandatory minimum sentences for drug offenses—a move that has been widely cited as a major factor in escalating racial disparities in America's prison population.

Reagan's successor in office, George H. W. Bush, created the Office of National Drug Control Policy (ONDCP) and appointed a national "drug czar" to fight drugs. Bush's War on Drugs was unveiled on September 5, 1989, in a nationally televised speech from the oval office that featured the president holding a bag of crack cocaine

Nelson Rockefeller and the War on Drugs

Nelson Rockefeller (1908–1979) was the economically conservative, socially liberal governor of New York from 1959–1973. He was the grandson of John D. Rockefeller, the founder of Standard Oil. Nelson earned his BA in Economics in 1930 from Dartmouth College then went on to work for Chase Bank, which was largely owned by the Rockefeller family. In 1938 he was named president of the newly constructed Rockefeller Center in New York City. From 1940 through the 1950s he served presidents Roosevelt, Truman and Eisenhower in various appointed positions before running and winning the 1958 gubernatorial race in New York.

In January 1973, after a rash of heroin overdoses in New York City, and with a new fear of drug abuse spreading through in popular culture as seen in films such as *Panic in Needle Park*, the governor announced a new initiative to penalize drug users and pushers. He called for mandatory sentencing from 15 years to life for those selling and abusing drugs, including marijuana. The Rockefeller Drug Laws were quickly adopted and these, the most draconian in the nation, were soon modeled by other states. In New York the number of inmates climbed from 300,000 in the 1970s to over 2.3 million two decades later, largely due to those receiving mandatory sentencing under the new drug laws.

Source

Mann, Brian. 2013. "The Drug Laws That Changed How We Punish." NPR.com, February 15. Accessed December 1, 2015: http://www.npr.org/2013/02/14/171822608/the-drug-laws-that -changed-how-we-punish.

that had been bought in Lafayette Park across the street from the White House. Not surprisingly, given this emphasis on drug interdiction, calls to decriminalize marijuana found little traction with the Bush White House or Republicans on Capitol Hill.

Many Republicans continued the War on Drugs under Bush's son George W. Bush, who served two terms in the White House from 2001 to 2009. Bush used the Drug Enforcement Agency (DEA) to raid medical marijuana clinics in California. Bush took the War on Drugs overseas and attempted to eradicate drugs, including marijuana, before they could be shipped to the United States. Bush also sought to intervene and stop drug abuse among youths by funding treatment programs and drug testing in schools along with antidrug education programs.

Republicans tried to stop the use of medical marijuana in Washington, D.C. Republican Bob Barr, a member of the House from Georgia, amended bills meant to fund operations in the district to exclude the use of medical cannabis, and these so-called Barr amendments were not removed until 2007. Republicans elsewhere have opposed changing laws. Former drug czar William Bennett wrote a scathing rebuke to those who would legalize the drug and labeled pot a "public health menace" (Bennett and White 2014). Not all Republicans oppose medical marijuana. Republican Governor Rick Scott of Florida signed a medical marijuana law in June

2014. Florida is also one of the states proposing a constitutional amendment to broaden the use of medical marijuana, which would, opponents of the measure claim, lead to a de facto legalization of marijuana.

One prominent Republican who consistently voiced support for medical marijuana legalization was congress member Ron Paul, a member of the House of Representatives in the 1970s and again from 1997 until 2013. A Libertarian by nature, Paul supported measures to decriminalize cannabis and for adopting it for medical reasons, although he never supported legalization. For many years, Paul stood alone among Republican's in the House but there is some evidence that the GOP opposition to legalizing marijuana is not as strong as it once was. In 2012, the Republican party platform dropped the "War on Drugs" language that had been part of the GOP platform since the 1970s. At a 2014 meeting of the Conservative Political Action Conference, an annual meeting that draws libertarian-thinking Republicans who are often in their 20s, attendees ridiculed a speaker at a panel intended to condemn the use legalized pot (Ball 2014). U.S. Senator Rand Paul, son of Ron Paul, who was an aspirant for the 2016 Republican presidential nomination, expressed support for legalizing marijuana, decriminalization, and medical marijuana although he has not formerly endorsed these positions as a presidential candidate. Dana Rohrabacher, a libertarian-leaning Republican from California introduced a bill into the House of Representatives, called the Respect State Marijuana Laws Act, which would allow each state to decide its own marijuana laws without federal interference (Hillstrom 2014). Rohrabacher was also the first Republican member of Congress to endorse legalization. Rohrabacher said he would support legalization if the ballot measure as planned came to a vote in California in 2016.

Further Reading

Aggarwal, Sunil K., Gregory T. Carter, Mark D. Sullivan, Craig ZumBrunnen, Richard Morrill, and Jonathan D. Mayer. 2009. "Medicinal Use of Cannabis in the United States: Historical Perspectives, Current Trends, and Future Directions," *Journal of Opioid Management,* May/June: 153–168.

Ball, Molly. 2014. "The Republican Party's Pot Dilemma," *The Atlantic,* March 7.

Bennett, William A., and Robert A. White. 2014. "Legal Pot Is a Public Health Menace," *Wall Street Journal,* August 14.

Carter, Jimmy. 1977. "Drug Abuse Remarks on Transmitting a Message to the Congress." August 2. Accessed December 12, 2014: http://www.presidency.ucsb.edu/ws/?pid=7907.

Gerber, Rudolph Joseph. 2004. *Legalizing Marijuana: Drug Policy Reform and Prohibition Politics.* Westport, CT: Greenwood.

Hillstrom, Kevin. 2014. *Medical Marijuana.* Farmington Hills, MI: Lucent.

Johnson, Michelle. 2014. "Legalizing Marijuana," *CQ Researcher.* March 25.

Lee, Martin A. 2012. *Smoke Signals: A Social History of Marijuana—Medical, Recreational, and Scientific.* New York: Scribner.

Madison, Gray. 2009. "A Brief History of New York's Rockefeller Drug Laws." April 2. Accessed July 30, 2014: http://content.time.com/time/nation/article/0,8599,1888864,00 .html.

Martin, Alyson, and Nushin Rashidian. 2014. *A New Leaf: The End of Cannabis Prohibition.* New York: Free Press.

Newton, David E. 2013. *Marijuana: A Reference Handbook.* Santa Barbara: ABC-CLIO.

Patterson, James T. 2005. *Restless Giant: The United States from Watergate to Bush v. Gore.* New York: Oxford University Press.

Mental Health Policy

At a Glance

Republicans and Democrats express concern for the mentally ill but disagree about the best method of treatment for persons suffering from mental disorders. Democrats, in general, have been more sympathetic to the rights of the individual suffering from a mental malady. They champion individuals who have been in the past stigmatized for the illness and want to provide more services for these people. Republicans, in general, are more protective of the rights of the community and would like to see lawmakers give the courts greater discretion in placing individuals with mental illness in institutions that will ensure their treatment and compliance in taking medication.

Many Democrats . . .

- Believe that people with mental illness should be treated the same as those with a physical illness.
- Support laws and court action that protect the rights of the mentally ill.
- Would like more funding for community mental health centers.
- Would like an expansion of federal programs like Medicare to pay for mental health hospitalizations.
- Support legislative reforms that would provide access to affordable therapies for people suffering from mental ailments.
- Would like to see more government intervention in schools, community centers, etc., to prevent the mentally ill from being hospitalized or incarcerated.
- Would like to reform the way prisoners with mental illnesses receive treatment.

Many Republicans . . .

- Believe that people with mental illness should be treated the same as those with a physical illness.
- Support laws and court actions that empower families and governments to require the mentally ill to receive treatment.

- Would like to see more efficient and less expensive government programs dealing with the mental health system.
- Have not been supportive of mandating that insurance companies provide mental health coverage in all policies.
- Oppose expanding government programs to pay for long-term mental health treatment.
- Would like more voluntary intervention in schools, community centers, etc., to prevent the mentally ill from being hospitalized or incarcerated.

Overview

Mental health policy has been more amorphous than other policy areas largely due to a lack of consensus within as much as between the political parties. Many Democrats have seen mental health issues through the lens of civil liberties and disability rights. They would like to see all illnesses treated equally. They have called for third-party private insurance to cover treatment for mental illnesses and have sought to create more expansive government programs to deal with mental health problems in local communities and prisons. Many Republicans see mental health issues through the lens of community rights and individual responsibility. They have called for stronger involuntary commitment laws to protect individuals who are a danger to themselves or others and who are refusing medical treatment. They have objected to increasing the role of the federal government in health care, including mental illness, and are concerned about policies that place the expense and burden for care of the mentally ill on insurance companies and the government.

During the civil rights struggle in the 1960s and 1970s, federal laws along with state and federal court cases demanded that people with mental illness be housed in the "least restrictive environments." This movement coincided with the rise of psychopharmacology, which provided new drug treatments for schizophrenia, depression, and anxiety disorders. The inclusion of psychiatric services in the legislation creating Medicaid and Medicare in 1965 provided for federal assistance and funding for individuals with mental illness who were in nursing homes but not state mental hospitals, which furthered a decline of patients in state mental wards. Since the 1970s, states have closed over 100 state psychiatric hospitals and deinstitutionalized tens of thousands of former patients from these facilities. To compensate for these closures many have turned to community-based outpatient programs that rely heavily on drug therapy and the patient's compliance. In 1999, two women sued the state of Georgia under the Americans with Disabilities Act, claiming that they were being segregated from the community due to their illnesses. The case reached all the way to the Supreme Court, which ruled in *Olmstead v. L.C.* (1999) that mentally ill people be housed in the "most integrated" settings in the community.

Under these guidelines there were fewer restrictions and civil commitments for the mentally ill. Critics charge that deinstitutionalizing the patient population created a new set of social problems, such as the thousands of mentally ill homeless people living on city streets across the United States, a common feature of U.S. society after patients were released into society in the 1980s (Fuller 2013). "Deinstitutionalization is the name given to the policy of moving severely mentally ill people out of large state institutions and then closing part or all of those institutions; it has been a major contributing factor to the mental illness crisis," wrote psychiatrist Edwin Torrey Fuller, a strong critic of the deinstitutionalization trend. "[It] helped create the mental illness crisis by discharging people from public psychiatric hospitals without ensuring that they received the medication and rehabilitation services necessary for them to live successfully in the community. Deinstitutionalization further exacerbated the situation because, once the public psychiatric beds had been closed, they were not available for people who later became mentally ill, and this situation continues up to the present . . . Deinstitutionalization was based on the principle that severe mental illness should be treated in the least restrictive setting . . . For a substantial minority, however, deinstitutionalization has been a psychiatric Titanic . . . The 'least restrictive setting' frequently turns out to be a cardboard box, a jail cell, or a terror-filled existence plagued by both real and imaginary enemies" (Fuller 1997).

Budget cuts in the 1980s led to further decline in the number of community mental health centers. It also meant that services across the nation were limited. Meanwhile, health insurance coverage was uneven across the United States, and many individuals were denied or unable to get treatment. Thus, for many people, the drug treatments necessary for their health were too expensive and not covered by insurance programs. Thus, some experts came to the conclusion that the civil rights movement, intended to liberate patients from state institutions, did not benefit the chronically mentally ill who now lacked the structure and medications to treat their illness.

In some cases, random acts of violence and murder, including mass shootings, have been committed by individuals with untreated mental illness. This in turn sparked 45 states to pass laws requiring involuntary treatment for mental illness. However, these laws have rarely been enforced, and while the number of mentally ill patients in state hospitals fell from 500,000 in the 1950s to less than 40,000 today, the number of untreated mentally ill in prisons has risen accordingly. By the year 2000, one in five prisoners in Michigan were also mentally ill. Due to state budget cuts, Michigan closed 75 percent of its state psychiatric hospitals between 1987 and 2003, and Michigan's prisons and jails replaced the now closed mental hospitals (Glazer 2015).

Advocates for the mentally ill also raise issues of access to quality care, affordability of psychiatric medications, and insurance coverage for individuals who have preexisting conditions such as schizophrenia. Insurance companies were reluctant to provide coverage for some patients with mental disorders due to the costs associated with their treatment and medication. Without federal action, a dozen states offered their own version of insurance mandates, and, even after the Affordable Care Act was passed in 2010, these issues were only partially resolved and remain the fodder for future debate between the political parties.

Democrats on Mental Health Policy

Democratic initiatives to assist those suffering from mental illness came to fruition under President Jimmy Carter who sought to create a more uniform national mental health policy. After he was elected in 1976, Carter created a special commission to study mental health policy, which led to his legislative solution, the Mental Health Systems Act. To provide better coverage for those suffering from mental illness, President Jimmy Carter proposed the act in 1979, which, after lengthy debate and amendments suggested by various health care interests, was enacted into law in 1980.

President Carter Speaks Out on the Need to Reform U.S. Mental Health Care Policies

President Carter and First Lady Rosalynn Carter made mental health care a signature policy during their time in the White House. After creating a commission to study the issue, President Carter offered legislation to improve the care of the nation's neglected mentally ill. Carter's message to Congress on May 15, 1979, contains key ideas showcasing the Democrat Party view on this issue.

I am today submitting to Congress the Mental Health Systems Act. This proposed legislation establishes a new partnership between the federal government and the states in the planning and provision of mental health services. It seeks to assure that the chronically mentally ill no longer face the cruel alternative of unnecessary institutionalization or inadequate care in the community. It provides local communities with more flexible federal support for mental health services and places a new emphasis on the prevention of mental illness. I am deeply committed to reducing the tragic toll which mental illness exacts from our citizens and our country. Less than one month after entering office I signed an Executive Order creating the President's Commission on Mental Health with Rosalynn Carter as Honorary Chairperson I directed the Commission to undertake an intensive study of the mental health needs of our nation and to recommend appropriate ways of meeting these needs.

- According to the most recent estimates, between ten and fifteen percent of the population—20–32 million Americans—need some form of mental health services at any one time.
- Substantial numbers of Americans do not have access to mental health care of high quality and at reasonable cost. For many, this is because of where they live; for others, it is because of who they are—their race, age, or sex; for still others, it is because of their particular disability or economic circumstance.

- There are approximately 1.5 million chronically mentally disabled adults in mental hospitals, nursing homes and other residential facilities. Many of these individuals could lead better lives in less restrictive settings if mental health and supporting services were available in their communities. The problem is that for them—and for the hundreds of thousands of patients who have been returned to their communities from large institutions over the past few years—such support services are seldom readily available. As a result, evidence indicates that half the people released from large state mental hospitals are readmitted within a year of discharge.
- There is insufficient emphasis at federal, state, and local levels on prevention and early detection of mental disorders. Infants and children would especially benefit from expanded prevention efforts, since early intervention with problems in physical, emotional and cognitive development can prevent more serious mental and emotional problems in the future.
- Conflicting policy objectives in various Federal health and mental health programs and between federal and state programs often lead to confusion, fragmentation of services, and a lack of continuity of care for those with mental and emotional problems.

I am convinced that these actions and the passage of the Mental Health Systems Act will reduce the number of Americans robbed of vital and satisfying lives by mental illness. I ask the Congress to join with me in developing a new system of mental health care designed to deal more effectively with our nation's unmet mental health needs.

Source

Carter, Jimmy. 1979. "Mental Health Systems Legislation, Message to the Congress." May 15, Online by Gerhard Peters and John T. Woolley, "The American Presidency Project." Accessed July 14, 2015: http://www.presidency.ucsb.edu/ws/?pid=32339.

Before any of the provisions of the bill could take effect, newly elected president Ronald Reagan rendered the legislation moot. President Reagan, reflecting the Republican agenda, sought to restore power to the states and eliminated many of the costly programs associated with the law. Instead, he substituted block grants to the states but this did not enhance existing policy and left a patchwork of state laws and what some believed were underfunded health services for the mentally ill. After failing to pass a health care reform act in 1994, President Bill Clinton, a Democrat, secured passage of the Mental Health Parity Act of 1996, which did not mandate that insurance companies provide full coverage for those suffering from mental illness. It provided regulation of some of the existing benefits for mental illness but also provided exceptions for small businesses. The failure to enact health care reform at the federal level under President Clinton led some Democrats, including Howard Dean, Governor of Vermont to propose health care reform at the state level of government. Governor Dean signed a comprehensive state parity measure that mandated insurance providers to cover mental and physical ailments equally, "I've said many times that illness of the brain should be treated just like illness of any other organ," Dean said. "This bill begins to end the stigma in our society around mental illness and substance abuse" (Tovino 2011). To close the gap in mental health coverage across the nation, congressional Democrats in 2008 passed the Mental Health Parity and Addiction Equity Act. The bill was amended to the Troubled Asset Relief Program (TARP) legislation and was signed by Republican President George W. Bush. This legislation required health insurance companies to provide parity in covering mental health services but the Bush White House refused to define exactly what parity meant, and thereby delayed action. Full insurance coverage and the end of the right of insurance companies to deny coverage for those with preexisting mental illness was mandated by President Obama in the Patient Protection Affordable Care Act of 2010 (Barry et al. 2010).

As Obama's second term in office came to an end, Republicans and Democrats were debating, at both the state and national level, what to do about the large number of incarcerated mentally ill. Despite the over 300 mental health courts established to deal with this issue, over 16 percent of all prisoners are mentally ill, and, in some prisons, such as Riker's Island in New York City, that number is closer to 40 percent. Rather than put such patients into hospitals or coerce them into becoming medically compliant through involuntary means, as some Republicans have suggested, many Democrats wish to preserve the civil liberties of the mentally ill. Democrats generally have criticized efforts by Republicans to pass laws to expand the control that families and states have over the treatment of mentally ill individuals. They prefer to support the mentally ill through community treatment programs aimed at reaching people with mental disorders before things get out of control. Democrats have called for more federal and state funding for such programs as ACT, the Assertive Community Treatment program, which brings a team of professionals, psychiatrists, social workers, nurses, and substance abuse counselors to work with mentally ill patients. The team ensures that the individuals suffering mental illness are compliant with their medicine and works to keep them from being institutionalized in a hospital or prison. Symbolic of Democratic efforts was a bill, "The Strengthening Mental Health in Our Communities Act," which emphasized increased mental health funding for various groups such as schools, veterans outreach programs, and community organizations. The Democratic bill created a new agency, the White House Office for Mental Health Policy, and expanded Medicare to cover long hospital stays for mental health care.

Republicans on Mental Health Policy

Republican policy on mental health has been tied into their philosophy of reducing the size and cost of the federal government in this policy area. For example, after the election of Ronald Reagan in 1980, Republicans were able to work with conservative Democrats to end the Mental Health Systems Act that was passed in 1980. Reagan ended the move for more government programs by offering states uncategorized block grants to use for their own mental health policies while cutting planned budget increases for mental health care by a third. Republicans in Congress were successful in resisting Democratic aims to mandate mental health parity in group insurance plans from the 1980s to 2008. In 2008, congressional Democrats included a provision mandating parity in the Troubled Asset Relief Program (TARP) during the financial meltdown that beset the nation in that year. President Bush signed the document but refused to define the terms of parity, which thwarted the Democratic plan. Many Republicans refused to endorse or vote for President Obama's 2010 Affordable Care Act, which imposed new regulations on insurance companies to provide full benefits for mental health.

Republicans have fewer concerns about the civil rights of those with mental illness. As defenders of the Second Amendment, Republicans are fully supportive of state and federal laws that deny those with serious mental illness from legally acquiring firearms. After mass shootings, Democrats are more likely to call for banning certain guns or ammunition, whereas Republicans are more likely to call for tightening gun ownership laws for individuals with mental illness. For example, after the murder of 36 children and adults at Sandy Hook Elementary School in December 2012, Republican House member Tim Murphy introduced a bill to require that all states have involuntary outpatient commitment laws that would strengthen the ability of a family and state officials to commit individuals who are a danger to themselves or others. Murphy introduced the "Helping Families in Mental Health Crisis Act," which he claimed would "prevent the Newtowns, Tucsons, Auroras, Pittsburghs, and Columbines" (Murphy 2013). Many congressional Democrats rejected this on the grounds that it did not protect the civil rights of the mentally ill and pushed their own legislation to fund more programs and agencies to deal with mental illness. Despite Democratic opposition, some Republicans in Congress have introduce similar legislation annually (Brown 2014).

After the economic recession that began in 2008, nearly every state in the United States cut their budget for mental health services (Parks, Radke, and Haupt 2014). The result, according to mental health advocates, was the rise of imprisonment for those with mental illness (Ford 2015). Many Republicans are concerned about the cost of housing so many mentally ill individuals in prison and have aligned with Democrats to reform the system. They would like to see more efficient and effective programs for intervening before individuals have to be incarcerated. These include mental health courts to divert people from jail to treatment programs, programs for those leaving prison to adjust to society and prevent recidivism, and moving the culture within prisons from punishment to treatment. Republicans and Democrats differ on whether these programs should be funded by the federal or state government or should be voluntary programs.

Further Reading

Barry, Colleen, Haiden A. Huskamp, and Howard H. Goldman. 2010. "A Political History of Federal Mental Health and Addiction Insurance Parity," *The Milbank Quarterly*, 88 (3), 404–433.

Brown, Elizabeth Nolan. 2014. "House Democrats Push Tepid Mental Health Policy Bill to Compete with Popular Republican-Led Efforts," *Reason*, May 14. Accessed July 7, 2015: http://reason.com/blog/2014/05/09/democrats-and-republicans-mental-health.

Ford, Matt. 2015. "America's Largest Mental Hospital Is a Jail," *The Atlantic*, June 8. Accessed August 12, 2015: http://www.theatlantic.com/politics/archive/2015/06/americas-largest-mental-hospital-is-a-jail/395012/.

Fuller, Edwin Torrey. 1997. *Out of the Shadows: Confronting America's Mental Illness Crisis.* New York: John Wiley.

Fuller, Edwin Torrey. 2013. *American Psychosis: How the Federal Government Destroyed the Mental Illness Treatment System.* New York: Oxford University Press.

Glazer, Sarah. 2015. "Prisoners and Mental Illness," *CQ Researcher,* 25: March 13, 241–264.

Murphy, Tim. 2013. "Murphy Introduces the Helping Families in Mental Health Crisis Act," December 12, 2013. Accessed July 20, 2015: http://murphy.house.gov/latest-news/murphy-introduces-the-helping-families-in-mental-health-crisis-act/.

Parks, Joe, Alan Q. Radke, and Meighan B. Haupt. 2014. *The Vital Role of State Psychiatric Hospitals.* Alexandria, VA: National Association of State Mental Health Program Directors, July. Accessed July 8, 2015: http://www.nasmhpd.org/sites/default/files/The%20Vital%20Role%20of%20State%20Psychiatric%20HospitalsTechnical%20Report_July_2014.pdf.

Tovino, Stacey A. 2011. "Reforming State Mental Health Parity." *Houston Journal of Health, Law and Policy*, Volume 11.

Minimum Wage

At a Glance

Many Republicans are skeptical that hiking the minimum wage assists lower income workers. They believe that it only leads to higher inflation and lost jobs, as business owners choose to absorb higher payroll costs by raising prices for customers or cutting their workforce. Many Democrats, on the other hand, are much more likely to believe that a higher minimum wage boosts the economy by putting more money in people's pockets, diminishes income inequality by raising the floor on compensation, and helps strengthen families by reducing the need for parents to work two or more jobs to make ends meet.

Many Democrats . . .

- Support minimum wage hikes.
- Assert that current minimum wage levels in many parts of the country are not high enough to keep people out of poverty.
- Frame raising the minimum wage as a "family values" issue because it reduces the need for some parents to work multiple jobs, thus giving them more time with their children.
- Believe that raising the minimum wage diminishes the wage gap between rich and poor.
- Support fair and living wages.
- Urge greater pay equity.
- Contend that higher wages reduce employee turnover, which can reduce employment and training costs for businesses.

Many Republicans . . .

- Oppose raising the minimum wage.
- Believe that raising the minimum wage leads to more layoffs.
- Believe that a higher minimum wage will raise the cost of goods and services.

- Believe that raising the minimum wage hurts the economy more than it helps.
- Oppose allowing cities to set a higher minimum wage than the state government.

———————————

Overview

A minimum wage is the lowest amount an employer can legally pay its workers per hour of labor. As such the minimum wage debate has historically pitted progressives and labor groups, who have been more likely to support the legitimacy of government intervention to address social problems, against conservative business interests, who prefer to allow the free market to resolve economic and social issues. This division remains a stark one today, as Democrats and Republicans at all levels of government—local, state, and federal—do battle over proposed minimum wage hikes.

Many Republicans continue to argue that rather than providing the working poor with a stable living wage, proposed and recently enacted minimum wage increases instead force employers to reduce the number of workers they hire or cut the hours for full-time and part-time employees. Thus, unskilled workers find that their overall earnings are reduced. Minimum wage, they claim, hurts all Americans because it causes price inflation as businesses pass on the cost of the minimum wage to their customers.

Many Democrats counter by framing their efforts to provide "a living wage" for the working poor not only as sound public policy, but as a moral issue. Indeed, supporters of minimum wage increases typically do not accept GOP claims that a higher minimum wage requires trade-offs that are injurious to the overall economy. To the contrary, they claim a higher minimum wage helps the American economy. Since the U.S. economy is driven by consumer spending, a higher minimum wage stimulates consumption and puts more money into the economy by allowing low-paid workers to spend more. Furthermore, a livable wage draws people into the workforce from social welfare programs, thus saving the nation billions in government programs. It is also a social good in that it might encourage people to join the workforce, rather than seek other illegal means of earning money by becoming a drug dealer or a prostitute.

The first federal minimum wage was signed into law by Democratic President Franklin D. Roosevelt in 1938 as part of the Fair Labor Standards Act. Since then, the federal minimum wage has been increased 22 times. But advocates of a higher minimum wage point out that minimum wage levels have not kept pace with the cost of living, and that GOP opposition in Congress has made increases difficult to achieve in recent decades. In 2007, however, a bipartisan Fair Minimum Wage Act was passed by Congress and signed into law by Republican President George W. Bush. This Democrat-led legislation, which received broad support from Republicans after tax cuts for small businesses were included in the bill, provided a significant boost to the federal minimum wage, which had remained at $5.15 an hour since the mid-1990s. The 2007 legislation provided for a three-step increase in the minimum wage, culminating at $7.25 an hour in July 2009.

Since that time, Democratic President Barack Obama and his fellow Democrats have repeatedly called for another federal minimum wage increase, but their efforts have been thwarted by Republicans.

In the absence of federal action some state governments opted to increase their state wages above the federal minimum wage. As of mid-2015, 29 states and the District of Columbia have raised their rates above the federal level. Some states have even passed laws tying the wage to the consumer price index, which requires an annual increase. As expected, those states with highest minimum wage rates are found in Democratic-leaning states clustered in the Northeast, in the Great Lakes region, and in the West. Meanwhile, Republican-leaning states have set their rates to the federal minimum and five conservative states in the South—Alabama,

Fast Food Forward

Fast Food Forward is a leading organization in the "living wage" movement. This group was founded in New York City by restaurant workers with the support of community organizers such as New York Communities for Change, formerly an office of ACORN, and financed by the Service Employees International Union (SEIU), the second-largest union in the United States. The group caught national attention when they led a one-day walkout of food service workers in New York City on November 29, 2012. Within a year the movement, which supports a $15 an hour wage and unionization rights for fast-food workers, had spread to 60 cities across the United States. The organization has the support of labor unions and leading Democrats such as Barack Obama, who acknowledged their fight for higher wages on Labor Day 2014.

The SEIU's interest in this movement is clear; it hopes to recruit the nearly 13 million food service workers in the country to its banner. SEIU first began organizing service industry workers in the 1990s at a time when union membership was falling. At that time SEIU successfully organized health care workers and custodial staff, but they were stymied in their efforts to unionize fast-food workers. In addressing the demand for a $15 an hour wage, Mary Kay Henry, the president of SEIU, said "This fight for fifteen is growing way beyond fast food. It's getting to be what the eight-hour day was in the twentieth century."

Sources

Finnegan, William. 2014. "Dignity: Fast Food Workers and a New Form of Labor Activism," *The New Yorker*, September 15. Accessed December 1, 2015: http://www.newyorker.com /magazine/2014/09/15/dignity-4.

Weissmann, Jordan. 2014. "The Fast-Food Strikes Have Been a Stunning Success for Organized Labor." Slate.com. September 7. Accessed December 1, 2015: http://www.slate.com /blogs/moneybox/2014/09/07/the_fast_food_strikes_a_stunning_success_for_organized _labor.html.

Louisiana, Mississippi, South Carolina, and Tennessee—have no state minimum wage at all. Employers in these states, however, are still required to abide by the federal minimum wage.

Many of the states that have raised their minimum wage have done so at least partly in response to the so-called "living wage" movement. Living wage laws require any business providing a service to a city or county, or businesses receiving a city or county subsidy, to pay wages high enough to keep a family of four above the federal poverty line without having to rely on charity or having the employee work two jobs. Calls for a living wage intensified in the 1990s in response to stagnant wages that were not keeping pace with cost-of-living increases. This dynamic remained in place in the early 2000s as well, so living wage campaigns remained an important part of many antipoverty initiatives and movements. As of 2015, more than 120 cities and counties have imposed their own separate minimum wage systems.

Since 2010, polls have consistently shown that nearly two-thirds of Americans say the minimum wage should be increased. This explains why, despite opposition by Republican leaders and business interests, minimum wage hikes put on state-wide ballots usually pass with high voter approval. Furthermore these ballot initiatives have, in the past, been successful in increasing the turnout of low-income and young voters on whom many Democrats count for winning elections. Therefore it is widely expected that the minimum wage will not only be a topic of debate between the Republican and Democrat presidential nominees in 2016, but that it will be a major ballot issue across the United States that year.

Democrats on the Minimum Wage

Supported by labor unions such as the Service Employees International Union (SEIU) and liberal think tanks such as Fast Food Forward, the Democratic Party is in the forefront of the battle to raise the minimum wage. This position is consistent with the party's historical stance on the issue. Democratic President Franklin D. Roosevelt and fellow New Deal Democrats were responsible for passing the first federal minimum wage law in 1938 in order to counter the devastating effects of the Depression on wages. And since the presidency of Roosevelt's successor Harry Truman, Democrats, in general, have sought an increase in every administration—Republican or Democrat.

Truman faced opposition from both Republicans and Southern Democrats and secured legislation to raise the rate from 40 cents to 75 cents an hour but as a concession this was only given to workers already covered (employees not covered included people employed by very small businesses, some agricultural workers, workers with disabilities, and waiters and waitresses who receive tips). Fearing the Democrats would raise the wage even higher, President Eisenhower, who served during the 1950s, agreed to have the federal minimum wage raised to $1 an hour but limited it to those already protected by a minimum wage. During the 1960s,

Democratic presidents John F. Kennedy and Lyndon B. Johnson used Democratic majorities in Congress not only to increase the minimum wage but also to extend it to include hundreds of thousands of new workers not previously covered.

When Republicans won control the House of Representatives in 1994, Democrats found themselves unable to move the issue forward. Their ability to make any headway on a federal minimum wage increase was constrained even more when Republicans secured the White House and both houses of Congress in the 2000 elections. After Democrats gained control of the House and Senate in 2006, however, they added a provision to raise the minimum wage into an appropriations bill that was aimed at lowering taxes and funding the War on Terror. President George W. Bush signed the bill, which raised the wage to $7.25 in 2009.

In the aftermath of the Great Recession of 2008 progressives, labor unions, and groups representing low-income wage earners pressed Democrats in Congress to raise the federal minimum wage but a shift in control of Congress in 2010 made this unlikely. Following President Obama's reelection in 2012 some Democratic lawmakers saw a potential to use his popularity to raise the minimum wage. In 2013, congressional Democrats introduced legislation to raise the federal minimum to $10.10 an hour, to be phased in over a little more than two years. "Income inequality is one of the greatest threats to America's long-term economic vitality, yet we are widening that inequality with wages that subject people to live in poverty," said cosponsor George Miller in 2013 (Mantel 2014). The proposed legislation would raise the minimum wage to $10.10 an hour in three increments of 95 cents each over the course of two years and three months after that the minimum wage would be tied to inflation and adjusted annually. The bill also sought to increase the minimum wage for tipped workers whose base pay had not risen from $2.13 an hour for 23 years. When Republicans in the House managed to derail the proposed increase, President Obama used his executive power to raise the federal minimum wage for contract employees. In his 2014 State of the Union Address, he declared "I will issue an Executive Order requiring federal contractors to pay their federally-funded employees a fair wage of at least $10.10 an hour—because if you cook our troops' meals or wash their dishes, you shouldn't have to live in poverty" (Obama 2014).

When the Republican-controlled Congress did not act in 2014, an already detectable shift in the minimum wage battle to individual states accelerated. In 2015, over half of all the states had a minimum wage in place higher than the one set by the federal government. Most of these states are generally regarded as "blue"—i.e., Democratic majority—states. In addition, in states that have resisted increases in the minimum wage, some cities with progressive leaders have taken to raising the local minimum wage. Baltimore was the first to mandate a separate minimum wage for workers in that city in 1994 and the most recent cities to follow suit have been Seattle, Washington, and San Francisco, California. Both of these cities, which are led by Democrats, have raised their minimum wage to $15.00 an hour.

Republicans on the Minimum Wage

Republicans have historically resisted attempts to raise the federal minimum wage, a stance that has been applauded by business groups ranging from the National Chamber of Commerce to the National Restaurant Association (NRA). Many Republicans assert that raising the minimum wage hinders economic growth and ultimately hurts low-income wage earners because it forces fast-food outlets, retailers, and other employers to cut jobs for the poorest, lowest-skilled workers. Republicans note that only 2 percent of all those employed earn the minimum wage and that overall only 7 percent of those who are employed are beneath the poverty level (Mantel 2014).

Republican hostility to federal minimum wage increases dates back more than a half century. Republican President Dwight Eisenhower agreed to raise the minimum wage in the 1950s when the economy was growing rapidly. President Richard Nixon, who served from 1969 to 1974, stifled congressional attempts to raise the minimum wage until the Watergate scandal eroded the president's ability to deal with Congress. Taking advantage of Richard Nixon's drop in public approval, Democrats in Congress successfully introduced a minimum wage bill that raised

Protesters stand outside a McDonald's restaurant as they ask the hamburger chain to raise its wages to $15 an hour in Miramar, Florida, on April 2, 2015. The protesters, some of whom work for McDonald's, held the event a day after McDonald's announced a pay increase of at least $1 an hour more than the minimum wage set by local law for some of its workforce. (Photo by Joe Raedle/Getty Images)

The National Restaurant Association and the Minimum Wage

The National Restaurant Association is the world's largest food service trade associations. Founded in 1919 the NRA represents nearly 500,000 restaurants with millions of employees. They advocate for "food service industry interests with local, state, and national policymakers." Which means that the NRA has opposed paid-sick-leave laws, the Affordable Care Act, worker-safety regulations, regulation of food marketing aimed at children, requirements to include nutritional information in restaurants, and attempts by public-health officials to limit sugar, sodium, and trans fats in food.

The National Restaurant Association opposed a $10.10 minimum wage hike, citing a Congressional Budget Office (CBO) report that suggested between 500,000 and one million workers might lose their jobs due to workforce cutbacks by small businesses seeking to avoid increases in their overall employee expenses. The organization has criticized calls to increase the hourly wage of tip workers on the same grounds. The NRA has also been highly critical of union attempts to organize fast-food workers, describing it as a cynical effort to boost organized labor's power at the expense of workers.

Sources

National Restaurant Association. "About Us." Accessed December 1, 2015: http://www.restaurant
    .org/About-Us.
National Restaurant Association. 2014. "10 Reasons That Sen. Harkin's & Rep. Miller's
    $10.10 Legislation Won't Work." Accessed December 1, 2015: http://www.restaurant.org
    /Downloads/PDFs/News-Research/10-Reasons-Against-10-10-August-2014.pdf.

the hourly rate to $2.30 and extended it to cover an additional 6 million workers. The bill passed the Senate 71–19 and 345–50 in the House, largely due to Republican members of Congress who were worried about reelection in the 1974 midterms.

Ronald Reagan was more successful in thwarting Democratic attempts to increase the minimum wage during his two terms in office. Reagan claimed that the minimum wage had "caused more misery and unemployment than anything since the Great Depression" (Time 1980). Reagan and his Republican allies in Congress kept House Democrats from bringing a minimum wage bill to the floor for a vote, while a Senate bill was killed by a Republican filibuster. Reagan's successor, George H. W. Bush, vetoed a Democrat-sponsored bill that would have raised the wage to $4.55, but then negotiated with Republicans to raise the minimum wage incrementally to $4.25 by 1991.

The Republican victories in the midterm election of 1994 gave them control of the House and Senate and for a decade they kept the federal minimum wage from rising. Republican losses in the 2006 midterms ceded control of the House and Senate to Democrats who seized on their chance to increase the wage despite the presence of Republican George W. Bush in the White House. When congressional

Democrats included a minimum wage hike in an appropriations bill that also contained tax cuts for small business and funding for U.S. military action in Iraq and Afghanistan, Bush signed the bill and the minimum wage went up in three stages over two years—to $7.25 an hour in 2009. Since then, the GOP has managed to block efforts by Democrats to further lift the federal minimum wage. But some Republican leaders have begun to question their party's intransigence on the issue, expressing fears that it will alienate working-class voters. Even Mitt Romney, the GOP's presidential nominee in 2012, came out in support of raising the minimum wage in 2014.

Meanwhile, Republicans are losing the battle at holding back increases in the minimum wage in many states and cities led by Democrats. After some cities under Democratic mayors set local wages higher than the state minimum, Republican lawmakers and their small business supporters enacted legislation banning city-enacted minimum wages. Republican-controlled state houses enacted bans in Arizona, Florida, Louisiana, Missouri, Oregon, South Carolina, Oklahoma, and Utah. However, over 120 counties and cities have been able to boost wages locally in the face of Republican opposition. And in the 2014 midterm elections, voters in Republican-leaning states such as Alaska, Arkansas, Nebraska, and South Dakota voted to increase their state's minimum wage.

Further Reading

CNN. 2014. "Minimum Wage State by State." Accessed November 8, 2014: http://money .cnn.com/interactive/pf/state-minimum-wage.

Mantel, Barbara. 2014. "Minimum Wage," *CQ Researcher,* 24 (4), January 24: 73–96.

Obama, Barack. 2014. "President Barack Obama's State of the Union Address, January 28. 2014." Accessed November 8, 2014: http://www.whitehouse.gov/the-press-office/2014 /01/28/president-barack-obamas-state-union-address.

Raise the Minimum Wage. "Minimum Wage Questions and Answers." Accessed September 24, 2015: http://www.raisetheminimumwage.com/pages/qanda.

Time. 1980. "Nation: They've Got a Little List." September 1. Accessed November 8, 2014: http://content.time.com/time/magazine/article/0,9171,922113,00.html.

Waltman, Jerrald. 2000. *The Politics of the Minimum Wage.* Urbana: University of Illinois Press.

Net Neutrality

At a Glance

Democrats and Republicans are debating whether to regulate the Internet. Many Democrats, drawing on the belief in the legitimacy of business regulation espoused by their progressive forebears, believe that Internet Service Providers (ISPs) such as Comcast, Verizon, and AT&T are monopolies whose practices need to be monitored and subject to governmental limitations for the greater public good. Many Republicans, who are much more favorably disposed to free market philosophies that see regulations and restrictions on business activity as burdensome drags on economic growth and vitality, believe that ISPs should have greater flexibility to offer different content delivery packages at different prices. However, GOP perspectives on this issue are mixed, as members of the general public who identify themselves as Republicans have shown greater support for net neutrality than many GOP lawmakers in Washington.

Many Democrats . . .

- Are concerned that access to the Internet is increasingly influenced by a relatively small number of companies.
- See net neutrality as vital to ensuring that the benefits of the Internet are equally available to all, regardless of economic or social status.
- Believe that without net neutrality, monopolies will decide what you can and cannot access online.
- Have encouraged the FCC to declare that the Internet is a public utility.

Many Republicans . . .

- Believe that the success of the Internet stems in part from the free market nature of its creation to this point.
- Do not want the FCC to have the power to regulate the practices of ISPs.
- Believe that excessive government regulation of the Internet will stall the expansion and innovation this technology has already displayed.
- See net neutrality requirements as an illegitimate government incursion into the telecommunications industry.

Overview

Net neutrality is the common term used to refer to a system in which Internet Service Providers (ISPs), which consist of phone and cable companies, treat all Internet traffic equally. The concept of net neutrality, then, covers several different issues. It calls for equal access to all legal Internet content and applications, opposes giving ISPs the option of charging content providers extra fees for the privilege of delivering their content at a faster rate, and opposes giving ISPs the option of artificially slowing down the transmission speeds of content from competitors or other content sources in disfavor with the ISPs. Net neutrality regulations, summarized *USA Today,* "aim to ensure that all the Internet content you want to access—be it streaming video, audio or other material—will be treated equally by ISPs. Another goal: to give start-ups and entrepreneurs access to broadband networks without undue influence from the ISPs" (Snider, Yu, and Brown 2015).

Some companies such as Google, public interest groups such as Demand Progress, and members of the Democratic Party want the Federal Communications Commission (FCC) to create rules to prevent ISPs from giving special treatment and higher speed downloads to some Web sites while slowing down data from other Web sites. For example, Comcast is both a cable company and an ISP provider. As Larry Downes wrote in a story for the *Washington Post* on November 11, 2014, theoretically a company that wants customers to subscribe to its cable services could decide to slow the content of Internet traffic from business rival Netflix, which sells access to streaming television and movies.

Those who oppose these rules claim that government regulation is tantamount to stifling free speech and property rights. Advocates for free trade, antiregulatory conservatives, public interest groups such as American Commitment, several large Internet Service Providers, and many lawmakers with the Republican Party characterize net neutrality rules as violations of ISPs' rights to conduct business as they see fit over the wires and cable lines they built and own. According to these parties, regulating ISPs to force them to treat all Internet traffic equally is another example of government overreach and a violation of the Fifth Amendment protection against government "takings" of private property "for public use, without just compensation." They reject claims by supporters of net neutrality that such regulations are necessary to keep cable and phone companies from throttling certain traffic of interest to their Internet customers. Critics of net neutrality assert that if Comcast tried to protect its cable services by slowing down the download speeds for Netflix, the likely result would be mass desertions from Comcast in favor of another ISP offering more satisfactory service (Clemmit 2012). In other words, the free market system would ensure that slowdown of Internet traffic or throttling of the Internet would not happen.

The debate over net neutrality resembles prior debates between Democrats and Republicans over government regulation of business. Republicans, in general, prefer to allow market forces to dictate the direction of the Internet, while Democrats, in general, are mistrustful and concerned that, unregulated, the Internet will favor the rich and powerful. The debate first began in the 1990s and continues to this day.

The Internet was first created in the 1960s when engineers at a government funded think tank created a communications network capable of surviving a nuclear war. In 1969, seven research university computers constituted the entire network, but by the 1990s millions of Americans were connected together through their personal computers (PCs). It was in that decade that Congress first debated the new telecommunications bill in 1996. This debate did not include discussion of cable television or telephone companies since, at that time, people were not using the Internet in place of these institutions. The result of congressional debate was the Telecommunications Act of 1996, which focused on cable TV and landline phone service. The law established different regulatory structures for the various modes of information transfer, with cable companies operating under a completely different set of rules than telephone companies. Lawmakers did not foresee that Internet data would flow through television cables, phone wires, fiber-optic cables, and wireless transmitters, most of which were placed under separate and very different systems of regulation. In 1996, Congress designated cable TV broadband, also known as "high-speed" Internet service, as a loosely regulated "information service" business rather than the more tightly regulated "telecommunications carrier business," such as a phone company. Under law, phone companies must provide access to their phone lines to anyone who seeks it, including competing businesses. Because of this, dial-up Internet service traveling over regular phone lines was offered by many independent ISPs, all of whom the phone companies had to accommodate. However, cable broadband Internet is less regulated and under law they could deny some companies access to their service (Clemmit 2012).

By the turn of the 21st century, government officials at all levels were urging the creation of broadband access to the Internet for consumers, businesses, and educational institutions. With commerce, entertainment, and social interactions all increasingly taking place via the Web, some officials wanted to require that all ISPs abide by a principle of "net neutrality," treating data from all Web sites the same. In 2005, the Supreme Court rejected this idea because it violated the 1996 law. Once again in 2010 the FCC tried to impose regulation, but the agency was sued by a consortium of opponents including phone and cable companies. The Supreme Court once again revisited the issue. It agreed that net neutrality was "essential for preserving environment that encourages new investment in the network, new online services and content" but once again cited the 1996 telecommunications act and struck down the regulations as outside the reach of the FCC.

In 2013, the FCC then adopted an "Open Internet Order," proposing to maintain net neutrality through three rules. Network operators must publicly disclose methods for managing network traffic, may not block legal applications or Web sites except as required for network management, and may not practice "unreasonable discrimination" among Web sites. These provisions by the FCC acknowledged that ISPs might need to slow some data to avoid network congestion. Before doing so,

Barack Obama on Net Neutrality

On November 10, 2014, President Obama explicitly urged the Federal Communications Commission (FCC) to institute strong new measures to ensure so-called net neutrality on the Internet. Excerpts from his remarks are below.

> An open Internet is essential to the American economy, and increasingly to our very way of life. By lowering the cost of launching a new idea, igniting new political movements, and bringing communities closer together, it has been one of the most significant democratizing influences the world has ever known. "Net neutrality" has been built into the fabric of the Internet since its creation, but it is also a principle that we cannot take for granted. We cannot allow Internet service providers (ISPs) to restrict the best access or to pick winners and losers in the online marketplace for services and ideas. That is why today, I am asking the Federal Communications Commission (FCC) to answer the call of almost 4 million public comments, and implement the strongest possible rules to protect net neutrality. The Internet has been one of the greatest gifts our economy—and our society—has ever known. The FCC was chartered to promote competition, innovation, and investment in our networks. In service of that mission, there is no higher calling than protecting an open, accessible, and free Internet. I thank the Commissioners for having served this cause with distinction and integrity, and I respectfully ask them to adopt the policies I have outlined here, to preserve this technology's promise for today, and future generations to come.

On February 26, 2015, the FCC met Obama's wishes by approving and implementing a comprehensive net neutrality rule. Obama praised the decision, saying that "it will protect innovation and create a level playing field for the next generation of entrepreneurs."

Source

Obama, Barack. 2014. "The President's Message on Net Neutrality." November 10. Accessed December 1, 2015: https://www.whitehouse.gov/net-neutrality.

however, they had to disclose the methods used to manage traffic and to ensure that they were not blocking others. ISPs and their allies again took the FCC to court, but this time the court system ruled in favor of the FCC. In January 2014, the U.S. Court of Appeals for the District of Columbia Circuit affirmed the commission's authority to regulate broadband Internet access service and upheld the commission's judgment that Internet openness encourages broadband investment and that its absence could ultimately inhibit broadband deployment. The court upheld the transparency rule, but vacated the no-blocking and no-unreasonable-discrimination rules. The court also invited the FCC to act to preserve a free and open Internet.

In February 2015, under considerable urging from Democratic President Barack Obama, the FCC voted 3–2 to regulate the Internet by declaring it a public utility and reclassifying high-speed Internet service as a telecommunications service instead of an information service. All three Democrats voted for the policy, while

Apple co-founder Steve Wozniak, right, applauds after the Federal Communications Commission voted to approve Net Neutrality during a hearing at the FCC headquarters in Washington, D.C., on February 26, 2015. The FCC voted to approve regulating Internet service like a public utility, prohibiting companies from paying for faster lanes on the Internet. (Photo by Mark Wilson/Getty Images)

both Republicans on the committee were opposed. According to the *New York Times,* Republican commissioner Ajit Pai condemned the new rules as "government meddling in a vibrant, competitive market" that would "deter investment, undermine innovation and ultimately harm consumers." But the Democratic majority said that the changes were vital to ensuring the Internet's role as a "core of free expression and democratic principles." "It's simply too important to be left without rules or a referee on the field," said FCC Chairman Tom Wheeler, a Democratic appointee. "The Internet has replaced the function of the telephone and the post office . . . These are a 21st-century set of rules for a 21st-century industry." Wheeler's views were echoed by a wide assortment of public interest groups and leading Internet companies. Michael Beckerman, president of the Internet Association, which includes Google, Facebook, and smaller online companies, called the FCC's move to make broadband a public utility "a welcome step in our effort to create strong, enforceable net neutrality rules" (Ruiz 2015).

Democrats on Net Neutrality

Many Democrats say that they are determined to keep the Internet open and equally accessible to everyone, regardless of their socioeconomic circumstances.

They see the potential for the Internet to promote democracy and to level the educational playing field for K-12 students in failing schools. President Obama has made access to broadband a key element of his education, technology, and economic proposals. Democrats are concerned that unless the federal government imposes and maintains net neutrality conditions, broadband cable TV and phone companies such as Comcast, AT&T, and Verizon, which provide high-speed Internet services, will use their position to undercut rivals such as Amazon prime and Netflix by forcing them to pay for faster streaming on the Internet. They might also interfere with smaller competitors by throttling their access to customers by establishing Internet "fast lanes" for corporations with the money to pay extra fees for the fastest transmission speeds. Democratic concerns about this issue have risen as the number of ISPs has declined due to mergers. The sheer size and financial power of these conglomerates has led many Internet advocates and Democrats to conclude that without government action, the free flow and free speech now available on the Internet will be lost. Furthermore, the lack of competition for providing broadband limits access. Nearly 5 percent of the U.S. population, or 15 million people, lack access to any wireless broadband provider. In many parts of the country only two providers are available, and in others the offered speeds of alternatives vary greatly, leaving users without high-speed alternatives.

The Democrats' concern with this issue was sharpened after a federal court decision in 2008 that ruled that cable giant Comcast selectively blocked some users' peer-to-peer file sharing in order to enhance their own business. Following the court's decision, Representative Edward Markey (D-MA), introduced legislation to establish net neutrality as national policy. This legislation failed to come up for a vote.

Barack Obama, however, made the goal of net neutrality part of his campaign for the presidency in 2008. After assuming the presidency in 2009, Obama expressed optimism that the Federal Communications Commission (FCC) would impose new regulations on the Internet to preserve open and equal access. In 2010, the FCC tried to impose regulation but this was struck down by the Supreme Court. The FCC then adopted an "Open Internet Order," proposing to maintain net neutrality but once again the concept was voided by a federal court that ruled in January 2014 that unless the FCC declared the Internet a public utility it could not impose strict regulation.

Undeterred, Democratic officials and lawmakers joined with activists in continuing to push for policies that would strengthen net neutrality policies. The February 2015 vote by the FCC to place broadband under Title II regulation and make high-speed Internet a public utility was praised by Obama, who responded to the decision by sending out a tweet: "The @FCC just voted to keep the internet open & free. That's the power of millions making their voices heard. Thank you! #NetNeutrality -bo." This decision to regulate the Internet so that all Web content is treated the same was also welcomed by rank-and-file Democrats. A 2014 survey by the University of Delaware's Center for Political Communication, for example, found that 81 percent of self-described Democrats supported net neutrality principles (Center for Political Communication 2014).

Republicans on Net Neutrality

Republican lawmakers and some of the nation's most influential conservative think tanks have been generally critical of Internet regulation and see it as unnecessary government interference in the free market. As one Republican critic stated, "If access to Facebook is important to you, and an ISP provides poor (or no) connectivity to Facebook, you can fire your ISP. That is how markets work" (Clemmitt 2012). Republicans are also quick to point out that there is little evidence to support the idea that ISPs have historically adopted policies damaging to their competitors. Larry Downes, an antiregulatory authority on the Internet, asserted in a November 11, 2014, editorial in the *Washington Post* that the FCC has only found four cases in the past 10 years of what it believed to be nonneutral behavior. All four were quickly resolved. Another technology expert, Richard Bennett of the conservative American Enterprise Institute, said:

> The business practices of network industries need the same sort of anti-trust scrutiny that every industry faces, but they do not need precautionary prescriptions that throw the baby out with the bath water. Twenty years of experience with the commercial Internet has proved that fast-lane services like CDNs are beneficial, so we should be looking for ways to grow the Internet economy by creating more services like them. Network neutrality is simply a bad idea that has run its course. (Bennett 2014)

Finally, they express fear that such government interference might discourage future investments in broadband networks because, according to then Republican senator Jim Demint, "It would give government control over them and limit the ability of Internet network retailers, such as cable, wireless, satellite and telephone companies to provide the highest quality and lowest price services to their customers" (Moyers on America 2006).

After a federal court ruled against Comcast in 2008, Congress was sharply divided on the issue of Internet regulation, with Democrats like Ed Markey of Massachusetts offering new legislation to regulate it, and Republicans like John McCain offering a Senate bill to ban the FCC from issuing any rules governing the Internet. A similar Republican-sponsored bill protecting the Internet was offered in the House. In the end, neither side was able to get a bill to a floor vote. Since that time partisan divisions in Washington have spilled into public view. Democratic policy makers who sought government oversight of the Internet seemed to score a victory in 2015 when the FCC approved net neutrality rules.

The Republican response was immediate and negative. Then House Speaker John Boehner said Republicans would fight the plan, which he called a misguided scheme to regulate the Internet. Ted Cruz, a Texas senator who was elected in 2012 with support from the conservative antigovernment and antitax Tea Party, tweeted that this was "Obamacare for the Internet; the Internet should not operate at the speed of government" (Alman 2014). According to Aaron Kessler in a *New York Times* story published on January 21, 2015, the Republican chairman of the House subcommittee that oversees the Internet, Greg Walden, called the expected FCC plan the "nuclear option." To stop the agency, some Republicans in Congress proposed a bill that would have given the FCC limited authority to enact net neutrality that would bar Internet providers from blocking online content, slowing down traffic, or offering any pay-for-priority deals. It also would have prohibited the Federal Communications Commission from reclassifying the Internet as a public utility. The bill was not enacted after facing stiff opposition from many Democrats and a veto threat from President Obama.

In February 2015, the FCC along straight partisan lines voted 3–2 to reclassify the Internet as a public utility and impose new net neutrality regulations. ISPs responded with a dire prediction "the FCC has abandoned over 15 years of successful bipartisan policy that, by nearly everyone's acknowledgement, has worked exceedingly well. The result? Years of legal uncertainty that will chill investment and innovation in the most successful sector of our economy while likely raising new taxes and fees on middle class families" (Welch 2015). The ISPs looked to Republicans whose opposition to the regulation could take a number of directions. Some of the ways that Republicans have suggested that they will battle over net neutrality include lawsuits in court. To date, ISPs have won every time they sued the FCC over regulation. Another approach would be to enact legislation to strip the FCC of the power to regulate the Internet (Welch 2015). But other Republican officials and congress members offered more measured responses to the new FCC rules—perhaps because of public opinion polls that indicate widespread support for net neutrality even among Republican voters. A 2014 University of Delaware poll, for instance, found that 85 percent of Republican respondents opposed "allowing Internet service providers to charge some Web sites or streaming video services extra for faster speeds" (Center for Political Communication 2014).

Further Reading

Alman, Ashley. 2014. "Ted Cruz Lashes Out against Net Neutrality, Calls It 'Obamacare for the Internet.'" Huffington Post, November 10. Accessed January 24 2015: http://www .huffingtonpost.com/2014/11/10/ted-cruz-net-neutrality_n_6133584.html.

Bennett, Richard. 2014. "Net Neutrality Is a Bad Idea That's Run Its Course." Real Clear Markets Web site. May 21. Accessed December 1, 2015: http://www.realclearmarkets.com /articles/2014/05/21/net_neutrality_is_a_bad_idea_thats_run_its_course_101068.html.

Center for Political Communication. 2014. "National Survey Shows Public Overwhelmingly Opposes Internet 'fast lanes.'" Accessed January 17, 2015: http://www.udel.edu /cpc/research/fall2014/UD-CPCNatAgenda2014PR_2014NetNeutrality.pdf.

Clemmitt, Marcia. 2012. "Internet Regulation," *CQ Researcher*, April 13, Volume 22. Accessed January 17, 2015: http://0-library.cqpress.com.libra.naz.edu/cqresearcher/.

FCC.gov. "Open Internet." Accessed January 24, 2015: http://www.fcc.gov/openinternet.

Moyers on America. 2006. "The Internet@Risk." Accessed January 17, 2015: http://www
.pbs.org/moyers/moyersonamerica/net/documents.html#debate.

Ruiz, Rebecca. 2015. "Reaction to Regulation: 1934 vs. Today," *New York Times*, March 5.
Accessed March 6, 2015: http://bits.blogs.nytimes.com/2015/03/05/reaction-to-regulation
-1934-vs-today/?_r=0.

Snider, Mike, Roger Yu, and Emily Brown. 2015. "What Is Net Neutrality and What Does
It Mean for Me?" USA TODAY, February 27. Accessed February 28, 2015: http://www
.usatoday.com/story/tech/2015/02/24/net-neutrality-what-is-it-guide/23237737/.

Welch, Chris. 2015. "Reactions to the FCC's Historic Net Neutrality Vote." NWB Magazine, February 26, 2015. Accessed February 27, 2015: http://www.nwbmagazine
.com/?p=17454.

Obesity and Public Health

At a Glance

Many Democrats believe that in order to improve public health and wellness, the government has a legitimate role to play in regulating the food industry and guiding consumers toward making informed food choices. To many Republicans, however, such actions seem like another manifestation of "nanny-state" thinking.

Many Democrats . . .

- See obesity as a serious disease caused by the mass marketing of low-quality foods, limited consumer knowledge, and a lack of sustainable healthy food options for the urban poor and children.
- Believe that childhood obesity is the result of marketing by corporations of readily available fatty foods and sugary drinks to the young and less educated.
- See the promotion of healthy lifestyle choices through government regulation and taxation as legitimate.
- Support federal funding for bike paths, school playground equipment, and other resources for active living.
- Favor regulating school lunches by requiring more fruits and vegetables and reducing consumption of salty and fatty foods.
- Have tried to persuade corporations to voluntarily reduce unhealthy food options in their menus or food products.

Many Republicans . . .

- Believe that obesity and other health problems associated with poor dietary and lifestyle choices are primarily the result of individual choices made by consumers.
- Reject many proposals to restrict salt, sugar, and other ingredients in processed foods.
- Support waivers for schools that seek to opt out of the regulation of the school lunch program.

———————

Overview

When it comes to the issue of diet and nutrition, the major debate between Democrats and Republicans concerns the best methods for tackling obesity—and especially childhood obesity—in the United States. Obesity is a condition wherein a person has an excessive amount of body fat as measured by the body mass index (BMI). According to U.S. officials at the Centers for Disease Control and Prevention (CDC), more than one-third of American adults—about 78.6 million people—are obese, while about 17 percent of American children and teens—approximately 12.7 million total—are obese. In 2013, the American Medical Association (AMA) moved to officially designate obesity as a disease. This decision was criticized in some quarters, as some critics asserted that obesity is better understood as a key *risk factor* for disease rather than a disease itself. However it is classified, though, obesity is widely recognized as one of the most challenging health issues in contemporary American society (Stern and Kazaks 2009).

Health concerns about diet and weight have a long history in the United States. As far back as the 19th century, healthy foods and better diets were promoted by health crusaders such as Sylvester Graham, inventor of the Graham cracker (Lobel 2014). Averages and standards for height and weight were constructed by the insurance industry in the 1940s. The first chart was constructed by Louis Dublin of Metropolitan Life, who used charts to show the relationship between height, weight, and longevity. Dublin found a strong correlation between life expectancy and body weight, with heavier individuals experiencing comparatively shorter life spans. These charts, although made for internal and commercial purposes, were quickly adopted by health care workers as the standard for healthy living. Health care practitioners also adopted the BMI to discern whether an individual was carrying excessive weight. An individual's BMI is calculated by taking their weight and dividing it by the square of his or her height (kg/m^2). The "normal" BMI range is between 18.5 and 24.9, "overweight" is 25–29.9, and "obese" is 30 and above. With this measurement in hand, health practitioners were able to statistically track obesity as a distinct category and what they found alarmed them.

Obesity first emerged as a major public health issue in the 1980s, when experts from commerce and business, mass media, and the U.S. health care industry began to sound the alarm about the relationship between health and body weight—and about rising rates of obesity in the general population. The seriousness of the issue was underscored in 1985, when the National Institutes of Health declared obesity a disease. As discussion of the dangers of obesity became more widespread, U.S. policy makers began to discuss new government initiatives to reduce the public health risks associated with being morbidly overweight.

The CDC began collecting data on obesity in 1994. Obesity rates steadily climbed throughout the 1990s, and the disease was declared a public health crisis. In 2001, the surgeon general of the United States issued a special report on the nation's growing problem with obesity, and the following year the CDC called for

Kelly Brownell on the Causes of Obesity in America

Named by *Time* magazine in 2006 as one of the hundred most influential people in America, Kelly Brownell (1951–) is currently the dean of the Sanford School of Public Policy at Duke University. Brownell was founder and director of the Rudd Center for Food Policy and Obesity at Yale and began his academic career at the University of Pennsylvania. Brownell is an expert on eating disorders, obesity, and body image.

Brownell first came to public prominence in 1994, when he wrote a guest Op-Ed in the *New York Times* urging the passage of a "fat tax" or "twinkie tax" on high-fat foods with little nutritional value as a way to address America's "toxic food environment." He asserted that a tax on unhealthy foods, similar to those imposed on products in the cigarette industry, would help reduce consumption of foods that may lead people to obesity. He also suggested subsidizing the sale of healthier foods to make them more accessible to lower-income Americans and called for new measures to rein in deceptive food industry marketing.

Since then, Brownell has written 15 books and 350 articles about the history and causes of obesity. Brownell continues to believe that the mass marketing, structure of the food industry and their influence over lawmakers and government agencies is a leading factor in the current obesity crisis confronting the United States. To educate the public he has worked with organizations such as The Center for Science in the Public Interest, a consumer advocacy organization dedicated to promoting a healthier lifestyle by advocating for nutrition, health and food safety. Brownell also supports efforts to improve labeling and limit salt, fat, and sugar in processed foods. Over the years he has regularly advised the White House, members of Congress, and national and international organizations on obesity and food industry issues.

Sources

Biography of Kelly Brownell, Sanford School of Public Policy Web site. n.d. Accessed September 3, 2015: http://fds.duke.edu/db/Sanford/kelly.brownell.

Brownell, Kelly D. 1994. "Get Slim with Higher Taxes," *New York Times,* December 15.

more government efforts to increase healthy activity and encourage healthy eating. In 2005, the Institute of Medicine (IOM) at the National Academy of Sciences urged the U.S. government to take new steps to treat and prevent the disease. The CDC reported an "epidemic" of 72 million obese people in the United States in 2005–2006. As the concerns about obesity mounted, researchers were able to identify key aspects of the disease. They found that obesity tends to be highest in the southeastern states, and 1 out of 10 deaths is attributed to obesity. Studies also indicated that obesity-related health conditions accounted for an estimated 10 percent of annual medical spending in the United States—nearly $147 billion in 2008 (Johnson 2014).

Democrats and Republicans have both acknowledged the crisis and health risks associated with obesity. Generally speaking, however, the parties have different opinions on the underlying causes of obesity and have therefore approached the issue with different policy prescriptions. For Democrats, in general, obesity is the result of systemic social problems such as an unhealthy consumer reliance on the fast-food industry, the ready availability of sodas that contain sugar, marketing campaigns that advertise fatty and sugary foods to children, and a dearth of healthy food options in many communities, especially in urban areas. Republicans, in general, share some of these concerns, but they are more likely to believe that obesity is rooted in the poor choices individuals make. Thus, while Democrats have attempted to regulate the marketing and sale of certain kinds or quantities of food, Republicans have rejected this as government intrusion and overreach into the personal lives and freedom of people to make their own choices. Republicans and Democrats alike agree that more education and information for consumers is beneficial.

Democrats on Obesity and Public Health

Many Democrats see obesity as a serious disease caused by the ill effects of industrialization, mass marketing of low-quality foods, and lack of sustainable healthy food options for the urban poor and children. They believe that childhood obesity is the result of marketing by corporations of readily available fatty foods and sugary drinks to the young and less educated. Exacerbating obesity is a lack of grocery stores and farmers' markets that would provide fresh fruit and healthy options in urban America, which is sometimes called a food desert by some Democrats. City officials and school administrators have also been criticized for failing to provide sufficient opportunity and incentives for physical activity for citizens and students.

Democrats have approached the problem of obesity in the same manner as they did in their successful campaign against tobacco use. They seek to regulate the food industry, reduce the availability of sugary and fatty options in school lunch programs funded by the federal government, and restrict marketing of unhealthy foods to children. To date, Democrats have shown less support for more controversial ideas such as taxing junk food to reduce consumption, another idea drawn from the antitobacco playbook (Brownell 2004).

Democrats first began to seek policy solutions to this problem when George W. Bush was president from 2001 to 2009. Many of their ideas were rejected by the Bush White House and Republicans in the House and Senate. After Democrat Barack Obama was elected to the White House in 2008, though, the issue of obesity—and specifically childhood obesity—became the signature issue of First Lady Michelle Obama (Obama 2009). The First Lady initially launched a program called Let's Move in February 2010. Let's Move was a comprehensive approach to childhood obesity that sought to encourage healthy eating and an active lifestyle, thus establishing habits that would hopefully endure through adolescence and adulthood. The program was supported by President Obama, who also signed a presidential memorandum creating the Task Force on Childhood Obesity requiring all federal agencies to examine their program and policies and to encourage their support of the Let's Move initiative.

The White House Task Force on Childhood Obesity subsequently released a report billed as the campaign's action plan. It made 70 specific recommendations, including ones urging food companies to create voluntary standards for marketing food to children. Much like tobacco, junk food was seen as being marketed to children who then developed lifelong habits that were inimical to their long-term health. The report also indicated that if voluntary standards were not developed the government might move to regulate nutrition labels.

In 2009, the Democrat-controlled Congress ordered four federal agencies—the Federal Trade Commission, the Food and Drug Administration, the Centers for Disease Control and Prevention, and the Department of Agriculture—to form what became known as the Interagency Working Group to create new voluntary marketing guidelines for companies that produce and market foods for children (Huber 2012).

The Healthy, Hunger-Free Kids Act, a bipartisan school lunch reform bill, was signed into law in December 2010. This law gave the Department of Agriculture (USDA) the power to regulate all foods sold in school cafeterias, vending machines, and school-run stores. The USDA quickly established new guidelines limiting the amount of sugar and fat in school breakfasts and lunches and setting new calorie restrictions and nutritional requirements. Under these rules, which were implemented in 2012, all school meals had to include fruits, vegetables, dairy products, proteins, and products rich in whole grains. The rules also banned trans fats—the artificial fat that was linked to heart disease, strokes, and diabetes—and limited sweetened high-fat desserts to only two a week. Starting with the 2014–2015 school year, snack foods sold on school grounds had to comply with USDA rules limiting calories, sodium, sugar, and fat content. Snacks were also required to contain at least 50 percent whole grain or a fruit, vegetable, dairy, or protein as a first ingredient. Other changes included removing: full-sugar sodas and junk food from school vending machines, replacing whole milk with low-fat milk and mandating that every child be required to have at least one serving of fruits or vegetables at each meal (Johnson 2014).

Outside of the school lunch program, other antiobesity measures were implemented by the Obama administration. One of the provisions in the Affordable Care Act, President Obama's signature health care reform program, required that chain restaurants with 20 or more locations provide nutritional information on all standard menu items. Michelle Obama's Let's Move program also created a nonprofit, nonpartisan group, Partnership for a Healthier America led by Larry Soler to work with private groups to encourage voluntary measures by corporate America and state and local governments to implement recommendations (Partnership for a Healthier America 2010). Related to this, the Federal Trade Commission (FTC), which is responsible for protecting consumers against anticompetitive, deceptive, or unfair trade practices, put pressure on food companies and advertisers to curtail their marketing of unhealthy foods to children. To avoid regulation, some companies began voluntary efforts to change the nutritional content of products and how they are marketed to children. For example, the Coca-Cola Company,

First Lady Michelle Obama helps students from five District of Columbia schools make a meal using the summer crop from the White House Kitchen Garden in the State Dining Room at the White House on June 12, 2014, in Washington, D.C. The students, who helped plant the garden earlier in the year, were joined by visiting school nutrition directors from Orlando, Dallas, and West Virginia, where they have seen success in their new school lunch programs thanks to the standards put in place by the Healthy, Hunger-Free Kids Act. (Photo by Chip Somodevilla/ Getty Images)

Dr. Pepper, Snapple Group, and PepsiCo all announced plans to voluntarily post beverage calorie counts on their vending machines and to add more low-calorie and no-calorie drink choices.

Republicans on Obesity and Public Health

Many Republicans agree that obesity is a health care crisis but they tend to support policies to educate or inform the public so that individuals can make better lifestyle choices. Democratic proposals to impose new antiobesity regulations on the food industry have generally received a cool reception from Republicans, who criticize such proposals as examples of regulatory overreach.

The foundations for this stance date back to 1994, when Republicans won a majority in both the House and the Senate. Newt Gingrich was the leader of the conservative Republicans who engineered the GOP's resounding election victory. One of the party's key campaign assets was the so-called Contract with America, a series of pledges to the American people. Many of these promises focused on

---

Mayor Bloomberg's War on Sugar

One of the most highly publicized efforts to reduce Americans' consumption of unhealthy foods implicated in high obesity rates was spearheaded by a politician who has identified himself as a Democrat, a Republican, and an Independent at various times in his career.

Prior to his entrance into political life, Wall Street executive Michael Bloomberg was a registered Democrat. When he decided to run for mayor of New York City in 2001, he changed his party affiliation to Republican. He identified as a Republican for the next five years, but in 2007 he became an independent, and he maintained that status until he retired from office in 2013.

Mayor Bloomberg gained nationwide notoriety in 2012 when he convinced the New York City Board of Health to ban the sale of many sugary drinks larger than 16 ounces within New York City, a metropolis with over 10 million people. When the ban was struck down by a judge just hours before it was scheduled to take effect, a heated legal battle ensued. Ultimately, Bloomberg's proposed law, which he consistently framed as a tool to help reduce childhood obesity and improve public health, was rejected as "arbitrary and capricious" by the New York Supreme Court in 2014.

Sources

Hellmich, Nancy. 2012. "Health Advocates Go Sour on Sugar." *USA Today,* June 8. Accessed December 1, 2015: http://usatoday30.usatoday.com/news/health/story/2012-06-08/sugar-wars-bloomberg/55470574/1.

Tomasky, Michael. 2012. "Mayor Bloomberg Is Right to Declare a War on Sugar." *The Daily Beast,* June 2. Accessed December 1, 2015: http://www.thedailybeast.com/articles/2012/06/02/michael-tomasky-mayor-bloomberg-is-right-to-declare-a-war-on-sugar.html.

---

deregulating industry and getting government out of the personal lives of Americans. Behind the scenes Gingrich received more campaign money for himself and his political action committee from the restaurant industry than any other member of Congress. The meatpacking industry, which is tied to the fast-food industry, has also been a generous campaign benefactor of conservative Republican candidates for political office (Schlosser 2012). Considering the GOP support of the food industry, it is not surprising that the Republican candidate for president Mitt Romney received over half a million dollars from this industry in his 2012 bid for the presidency, according to Tim Murphy in a story written for *Mother Jones,* July 13, 2012 (Murphy 2012).

Many Republicans have also worked to shield the fast-food and beverage industries from health-related lawsuits. The administration of President George W. Bush offered praise for such legislation, stating that "food manufacturers and sellers should not be held liable for injury due to a person's consumption of legal, unadulterated food and a person's weight gain or obesity" (Hulse 2004). In addition, the GOP attempted to thwart FTC regulations on marketing of foods to children, and they have modified demands for changes in food processing and school lunch programs.

Although generally opposed to government programs, many Republicans supported First Lady Michelle Obama's campaign against childhood obesity and her advocacy for voluntary regulation and reforms within the school lunch program. There was bipartisan support for "The Healthy, Hunger-Free Kids Act of 2010," which provided $4.5 billion in new resources to the National School Lunch and Breakfast programs. The legislation also created a new program within the existing Women, Infants, and Children (WIC) program, a new Child and Adult Care Food Program (CACFP), a Summer Food Service Program, and an Afterschool Meal Program, as well as funding for the Supplemental Nutrition Assistance Program Education or SNAP-Ed (NSLP 2016).

Criticisms of the USDA regulations governing the school lunch program, however, spurred increased opposition from the GOP. Complaints by parents, children, and school administrators led to a series of nationwide print and broadcast news stories that highlighted alleged flaws in the outcomes of the new rules. According to an article written by Stephanie Armour for the Wall Street Journal on August 1, 2014, an unanticipated result was the end of the popular in-school bake sale, since the baked goods sold at these fundraisers were disallowed as having too much fat and sugar for consumption within schools. Republicans suggested that the program be modified to relax the limits on portion sizes for whole grains and meat.

The issue became even more contentious in 2014 when the Republican-led House Appropriations Committee passed a new agricultural budget, largely along party lines, that included a provision allowing schools to opt out of the new nutritional guidelines. Democratic legislators called the new provision a poison pill that would undermine the antiobesity campaign. Republicans countered, though, by complaining that the entire antiobesity campaign was turning into another example of the liberal "Nanny State," which is to say a government that makes too many "for your own good" laws governing the behavior of its citizens. Republicans were not the only ones who objected to the USDA guidelines that included a reduction of both potatoes and frozen foods in school lunches. A bipartisan group of farm-state senators with powerful agriculture industry constituencies also tried to block these new initiatives.

Republicans also expressed unhappiness when the FTC sought to mandate that foods marketed to children and youths contain at least one of a list of healthy ingredients suggested by the FTC. These foods were also to reduce the amount of sodium and sugar consumed by adolescents. House Republicans, with support from food-industry groups and other stakeholders in this food fight, resisted these guidelines. Republicans claimed that these suggestions, drawn from President Obama's Working Group on Food Marketed to Children, amounted to de facto government mandates and overregulation.

Further Reading

Armour, Stephanie. 2014. "Put Down the Cupcake: New Ban Hits School Bake Sales," *Wall Street Journal*, August 1. Accessed: February 8, 2016: http://www.wsj.com/articles/schools-plan-to-lighten-up-on-bake-sales-1406923280.

Brownell, Kelly. 2004. *Food Fight: The Inside Story of the Food Industry, America's Obesity Crisis, and What We Can Do about It.* New York: McGraw Hill.

Huber, Bridget. 2012. "Michelle's Move," *The Nation*, October 29: 11–12.

Hulse, Carl. 2004. "Vote in House Offers a Shield on Obesity Suits," *New York Times*, March 11: 1.

Johnson, Michelle. 2014. "Obesity," *CQ Researcher*, May 13. Accessed July 28, 2014: http://0-library.cqpress.com.libra.naz.edu/cqresearcher/.

Lobel, Cindy. 2014. "Sylvester Graham and Antebellum Diet Reform," Gilder Lehman Institute. Accessed July 28: http://www.gilderlehrman.org/history-by-era/first-age-reform/essays/sylvester-graham-and-antebellum-diet-reform.

Murphy, Tim. 2012. "Why Fast Food Loves Mitt Romney," Mother Jones, July 13, 2012. Accessed July 28, 2014: http://www.motherjones.com/mojo/2012/07/why-fast-food-loves-mitt-romney.

NSLP. 2016. "National School Lunch Program." Accessed February 8, 2016: http://www.fns.usda.gov/sites/default/files/NSLPFactSheet.pdf.

Obama, Michelle. 2009. *Michelle Obama in Her Own Words: The Views and Values of America's First Lady,* edited by Lisa Rogan. New York: Public Affairs.

Partnership for a Healthier America. 2010. Accessed July 28, 2014: http://ahealthieramerica.org/about/about-the-partnership/.

Schlosser, Eric. 2012. *Fast Food Nation: The Dark Side of the All American Meal.* Reprint, New York: Mariner Books.

Stern, Judith, and Alexandra Kazaks. 2009. *Obesity: A Reference Handbook.* Santa Barbara: ABC-CLIO.

Policing

At a Glance

Democrat and Republican lawmakers at every level of government are debating police tactics and conduct in light of falling crime rates and high-profile incidents in which unarmed citizens as young as 12 have been killed by police. In light of the latter incidents, many Democrats—especially those representing urban communities with high minority populations—have called for a variety of law enforcement reforms and reviews of police procedures. Republicans have generally been less supportive of such calls and have been more likely to treat charges of police brutality or misconduct as suspect. Both parties agree that investigation of civilian deaths at the hands of law enforcement personnel would best be performed by an independent agency.

Many Democrats . . .

- Assert that overzealous police practices unfairly target minorities and the poor.
- Believe that police practices would be enhanced if more people of color were represented in law enforcement.
- Believe that African Americans and other minorities are not treated fairly in the criminal justice system or by police.
- Promote civilian review boards to scrutinize police actions and practice.
- Criticize the practice of giving surplus military hardware to local law enforcement.
- Were appalled at the grand jury decisions in the Michael Brown and Eric Garner cases in 2014.

Many Republicans . . .

- Hold that police are not sufficiently supported by elected officials when carrying out their duties.
- Support the broken window theory, which holds that cracking down on vandalism and other minor offenses checks the growth of crime in communities.

- Assert that targeting certain neighborhoods not only stops the spread of crime but protects minorities and the poor from being preyed upon.
- Do not believe that the police treat people of color unfairly.
- Support the placement of surplus military equipment into the hands of local law enforcement.
- Believe that the grand juries in the highly publicized cases of Michael Brown and Eric Garner of 2014, in which young unarmed black men died in encounters with white police officers, were right not to bring charges against either officer.

Overview

The issue of policing has become intertwined with other social policies that separate Republicans and Democrats, as each party has strong and contrasting views on the best way to maintain strong police departments that provide public safety to all members of their communities. Political conservatives, most of whom are affiliated with the Republican Party, tend to give police the benefit of the doubt when it comes to accusations of police abuse. They believe that police work is both essential and dangerous and that police are best trained to deal with issues of crime and control. They are thus more likely to dismiss accusations of police abuse as exaggerated or as the result of the actions of a few individuals, and not as evidence of systemic racism or antipathy toward the poor. Liberals, who are much more likely to reside within the Democratic Party, believe that given the vast powers that police agencies have they must be placed under greater scrutiny. They are more likely to see police abuse as a significant issue—and as part of a systemic problem in which marginalized groups are treated unfairly by American institutions. They would like to increase the participation of community groups in overseeing police and create more pluralistic police forces, which they see as all too often white and male.

Prior to the 1960s, public concern about policing concentrated on issues of corruption, but since that time attention has turned to police brutality, coercive interrogation, unlawful searches, and questions about planted evidence. The American Civil Liberties Union has promoted the establishment of civilian review boards, and it frequently works with communities to file complaints against the police for racial profiling and excessive force.

During the 1950s and 1960s, a series of laws and court actions restricting and regulating the conduct of police were handed down. They included new rules for detaining, searching, and interrogating suspects. From the 1970s through the early 1990s, however, violent crime rates steadily rose across the United States. Congress and Democratic President Bill Clinton responded to this alarming trend with the Violent Crime Control and Law Enforcement Act of 1994 (Gallup 2010). Embodied in this legislation was the concept of community policing and problem-oriented policing, which both Democrat and Republican leaders at the city, state, and national level embraced as the solution to crime (Greene 2000).

This emphasis on community policing stemmed in large part from the work of two social scientists, James Q. Wilson and George L. Kelling. In the early 1980s, they advanced a "broken window" theory of policing that held that stopping and prosecuting small "nuisance" crimes like littering and vandalism had the capacity to create a law-abiding, orderly community atmosphere that would make it more difficult for serious crimes like robbery, rape, and murder to take root. "At the community level, disorder and crime are usually inextricably linked, in a kind of developmental sequence," they wrote. "Social psychologists and police officers tend to agree that if a window in a building is broken and is left unrepaired; all the rest of the windows will soon be broken. This is as true in nice neighborhoods as in rundown ones. Window breaking does not necessarily occur on a large-scale because some areas are inhabited by determined window breakers whereas others are populated by window lovers; rather, one unrepaired broken window is a signal that no one cares, and so breaking more windows costs nothing. (It has always been fun.) We suggest that "untended" behavior also leads to the breakdown of community controls. A stable neighborhood of families who care for their homes, mind each other's children, and confidently frown on unwanted intruders can change, in a few years or even a few months, to an inhospitable and frightening jungle. A piece of property is abandoned, weeds grow up, and a window is smashed. Adults stop scolding rowdy children; the children, emboldened, become more rowdy. Families move out, unattached adults move in. Teenagers gather in front of the corner store. The merchant asks them to move; they refuse. Fights occur. Litter accumulates. People start drinking in front of the grocery; in time, an inebriate slumps to the sidewalk and is allowed to sleep it off. Pedestrians are approached by panhandlers . . . Though citizens can do a great deal, the police are plainly the key to order maintenance . . . we must return to our long-abandoned view that the police ought to protect communities as well as individuals" (Wilson and Kelling 1982).

From the 1990s forward, aggressive policing and prosecutions have been abetted by so-called tough-on-crime legislation. The concept of community policing meant different things to Democrats, who saw in it a bridge between the police and communities of color, than to Republicans, who imagined it as a means of capturing low-level criminals before they could graduate to more violent crime. Community policing has become the standard since the 1990s and has been cited as a factor in the reduction of the overall crime rate in the United States, but some critics point to improvements in the economy and tougher gun laws as factors in reducing crime as well. Critics also point out that the zero tolerance approach on crime has led to greater friction between poorer communities and police (U.S. Department of Justice 2013).

Long-standing complaints from civil rights advocates about police brutality and excessive force in black communities came to the fore in the summer of 2014, after Michael Brown, an unarmed 18-year-old African American man, was

People gather during a service marking the anniversary of Michael Brown's death in Ferguson, Missouri, on August 9, 2015. Brown was shot and killed by a Ferguson police officer on August 9, 2014, which sparked months of violent protests in Ferguson and drew nationwide focus on police treatment of black suspects. (Photo by Scott Olson/Getty Images)

shot and killed by a white policeman in the city of Ferguson, Missouri, a suburb of St. Louis. Ferguson's population is over 60 percent black, but its police force only has three black officers. The controversial shooting occurred under heavily disputed circumstances, sparked several days and nights of widespread civil unrest throughout Ferguson. After the grand jury rejected an indictment of the white police officer who killed Brown, hundreds of angry protesters took to the streets of Ferguson chanting: "Hands up, don't shoot!" After looting broke out, local law enforcement responded with tear gas, rubber bullets, and road blocks. President Obama said that "Ferguson laid bare a problem that is not unique to St. Louis or that area, and is not unique to our time, and that is a simmering distrust that exists between too many police departments and too many communities of color."

The Brown shooting also triggered renewed scrutiny of other deadly encounters between white policemen and unarmed black suspects. Earlier that summer, for example, a black man named Eric Garner was put in a chokehold by white police officers in Staten Island and died as a result of injuries sustained by the restraining maneuver. In Cleveland, Ohio, meanwhile, 12-year-old Tamir Rice was shot by a rookie police officer in a playground while holding an airsoft pellet gun.

President Obama Comments on "Distrust" between Police and Minority Communities

When an unarmed black teenager named Michael Brown was shot and killed in Ferguson, Missouri, on August 9, 2014, by a white police officer, the incident sparked sometimes violent protests by members of Ferguson's black community. Many participants in the protests said that the Brown shooting symbolized the abusive treatment that their entire community had been subjected to for years by Ferguson's mostly white police force. When it was announced on November 24, 2014, that a grand jury had decided not to indict the white officer who shot Brown, a fresh wave of protests ensued. A few hours after he learned about the grand jury's decision, President Obama gave an address to the nation on the events in Ferguson, excerpted here:

> The fact is, in too many parts of this country, a deep distrust exists between law enforcement and communities of color. Some of this is the result of the legacy of racial discrimination in this country. And this is tragic, because nobody needs good policing more than poor communities with higher crime rates. The good news is we know there are things we can do to help. And I've instructed Attorney General Holder to work with cities across the country to help build better relations between communities and law enforcement. That means working with law enforcement officials to make sure their ranks are representative of the communities they serve. We know that makes a difference. It means working to train officials so that law enforcement conducts itself in a way that is fair to everybody. It means enlisting the community actively on what should be everybody's goal, and that is to prevent crime . . . So those should be the lessons that we draw from these tragic events. We need to recognize that this is not just an issue for Ferguson; this is an issue for America. We have made enormous progress in race relations over the course of the past several decades. I've witnessed that in my own life. And to deny that progress I think is to deny America's capacity for change. But what is also true is that there are still problems and communities of color aren't just making these problems up. Separating that from this particular decision, there are issues in which the law too often feels as if it is being applied in discriminatory fashion. I don't think that's the norm. I don't think that's true for the majority of communities or the vast majority of law enforcement officials. But these are real issues. And we have to lift them up and not deny them or try to tamp them down. What we need to do is to understand them and figure out how do we make more progress. And that can be done.

Source

President Obama Delivers a Statement on the Ferguson Grand Jury's Decision, November 24, 2014. Accessed December 10, 2014: http://www.whitehouse.gov/blog/2014/11/24/president-obama-delivers-statement-ferguson-grand-jurys-decision.

Despite the racial and political tensions created by the incidents in Ferguson, Cleveland, and New York City, Republicans and Democrats agree on two ways to improve policing and to better hold individual law enforcement agents accountable for their actions. Polls show bipartisan support for requiring patrol officers to have a small camera on their person to record their daily activities, and for an outside agency to investigate police when they are involved in shooting unarmed suspects (Blake 2014).

Democrats on Policing

For many years, the Democratic Party has grappled with GOP accusations that it is too soft on crime, and therefore too soft on criminals. But many Democrats contend that such claims, which they say are groundless, will not prevent them from protecting the rights of minorities when they are the victims of overzealous and sometimes racist police tactics. In the 1960s, Supreme Court justices appointed by Democratic presidents were the majority in key cases protecting or expanding the rights of those arrested or detained by police, including stipulations that suspects be read their rights and that police searches be limited to the specifics of warrants. When a more conservative and pro–law-and-order perspective became apparent in the American public in the 1980s and 1990s, though, Democrats became increasingly defensive about these positions.

In the 1990s, President Bill Clinton, who served two terms in the White House from 1993 to 2001, sought to both reduce crime and neutralize charges that Democrats were out of touch on law-and-order issues by signing anticrime bills that featured heavy criminal penalties and used federal funds to assist local law enforcement and provide more police. The party's 1996 platform declared that "today's Democratic Party believes the first responsibility of government is law and order." Clinton and the national party supported the death sentence for violent crimes, urged community policing, which included neighborhood watch programs, and educational programs in schools, such as the DARE program, to raise awareness of drugs. Clinton repeatedly pointed to his efforts to put 100,000 more police on the streets to stop crime before it happened and arrest perpetrators before they could go on to commit other crimes (Democratic Party 1996). Clinton and other Democrats subscribed to James Q. Wilson's theory of "broken windows" crime detection and prevention but viewed this as a means of building community relations with the police, as well as crime fighting technique (Wilson 1978).

As a result of these efforts, community policing and targeting of high-crime areas became the norm across the United States. But minorities—who are an important and growing constituency of the Democratic Party—frequently charged that people of color continued to be unfairly targeted for police scrutiny. One 2014 poll found that only 1 in 10 African Americans believed that blacks and other minorities received equal treatment with whites in the U.S. criminal justice system, and only 2 in 10 expressed confidence that the police treat whites and blacks equally, whether or not they have committed a crime. According to the same poll, 70 percent of Democrats agreed that minorities are not treated equally in the criminal justice system, and over half think the police treat blacks unequally. These poll results were consistent with the results of other polls taken around the same time period (Balz and Clement 2014).

In the wake of Michael Brown's death in Ferguson, Obama directed Attorney General Eric Holder to conduct an investigation of the case. Holder subsequently criticized overzealous police practices and launched investigations of more than 20 police departments for potential civil rights violations for actions against African American citizens. He has also criticized the aggressive prosecution of young black men and called for alternatives to prison for juvenile offenders.

Other Democrats have intensified their calls for new standards of police interactions with the public and increased oversight of their operations and conduct, even as they simultaneously emphasize their appreciation for the hard and dangerous nature of police work, in general, and the professional manner in which most officers conduct themselves. For example, some Democrats have condemned the so-called militarization of the police in many American communities. Some Republicans joined Democrats in supporting a bill that would rein in the practice of giving surplus military equipment to police departments. The Republican leadership in the House of Representatives opposed the measure, however, and stopped the bill from coming to a floor vote.

Political observers believe that long-standing partisan tensions and jockeying for political advantage may make it difficult for the two parties to come together on passing any meaningful new police standards. In May 2015, for example, a House Judiciary Committee hearing on police and community relations quickly degenerated into "partisan mudslinging" as "Democrats on the panel, many of them African-Americans, spent their time seeking guidance from policing experts about what Congress should do to help and sharing personal stories of being stopped by the police. Republicans, meanwhile, lectured witnesses about the need for the public and Congress to respect local officers—or pointed the finger back at protesters critical of police" (Bade 2015).

Republicans on Policing

Republicans generally support John Q. Wilson's broken windows theory of policing and see it primarily as a means of reducing crime rather than building community relations. Wilson, a political scientist, theorized that when police aggressively enforce laws against minor crimes and misdemeanors they tamp down the growth of more violent crimes (McCabe 2008). Since the presidency of Richard Nixon, who served in the White House from 1969 to 1974, Republicans have characterized themselves as dedicated to waging an "unrelenting war on crime." (Republican Party 1972). Republicans have subsequently made crime control a campaign issue in election after election, and in the process frequently deride their Democratic opponents as soft on criminals. Historically, much of the GOP rhetoric has been aimed at building support for mandatory sentencing, and longer prison terms. But while these "tough on crime" policies and rhetoric resonated with many Americans, they were criticized by many Democratic lawmakers, as well as liberals and minority activists, for too often appealing to white racism (Hurwitz and Peffley 2005).

Rudy Giuliani, a former federal prosecutor, was elected mayor of New York City in 1993 in part because of his promises to reduce crime in the city. He worked across party lines to support the tough-on-crime stance of President Bill Clinton and hired William Bratton as police commissioner. Bratton was a proponent of the broken windows theory of policing and implemented computerized targeting of high crime areas. The crime rate fell dramatically in New York City during the Giuliani years and he became a national symbol of the Republican Party's no nonsense anticrime platform, and eventually ran for his party's nomination for president.

As crime rates fell nationwide in the 1990s and 2000s, however, Republicans began to devote greater attention to other law enforcement issues, including overcrowded courts and prisons and frayed relations between law enforcement and the minority community. As a result there was a move by some Republicans to work with Democrats in developing new methods to rehabilitate or intercede in communities before young people became involved in crime. In light of the outrage that was provoked by the controversial deaths of a number of unarmed black youths and men at the hands of white officers in 2014, some Democrats and Republicans have both agreed that investigations into police conduct should be led by outside agencies or special prosecutors.

Republicans are still more likely than Democrats to view use of police force as justified, however. According to one poll, a majority of Americans believed the grand jury was wrong not to charge the officer involved in the choking of Garner, but only 35 percent of Republicans agreed with this sentiment (Blake 2014). Meanwhile two out of every three Republicans say minorities and whites are treated equally in the criminal justice system, and more than four out of five white Republicans say they are confident that police treat blacks and whites equally. Nor is the idea of an outside agency accepted by all Republicans. As Zusha Elinson reported in the *Wall Street Journal,* January 12, 2015, "just because people don't like the outcome of two different cases doesn't mean we should change the whole system," said William Fitzpatrick the president elect of the National District Attorney's Association.

Attempts to reform police departments that have been criticized for civil rights violations and other misconduct have been tried in cities such as Seattle, Washington. Seattle was sued by the Justice Department under Eric Holder and began to limit police tactics in dealing with citizens in high-crime areas. A subsequent rise in violent crime in Seattle sparked severe criticism from Republicans who claimed that the higher crime rates were a direct result of the new policies.

Further Reading

Bade, Rachael. 2015. "House Hearing on Police Turns Ugly," *Politico*, May 19. Accessed February 7, 2016: http://www.politico.com/story/2015/05/racial-epithets-mudslinging -house-hearing-police-reform-ghetto-118108.

Balz, Dan, and Scott Clement. 2014. "On Racial Issues, America Is Divided Both Black and White and Red and Blue," *The Washington Post,* December 27. Accessed January 2, 2014:http://www.washingtonpost.com/politics/on-racial-issues-america-is-divided-both -black-and-white-and-red-and-blue/2014/12/26/3d2964c8-8d12-11e4-a085 -34e9b9f09a58_story.html.

Blake, Aaron, 2014. "Republicans and Democrats Have Vastly Different Views on Race and Police. But They Agree on Solutions," *The Washington Post*, December 29. Accessed January 2, 2015: http://www.washingtonpost.com/blogs/the-fix/wp/2014/12/29/republicans -and-democrats-have-vastly-different-views-on-race-and-police-but-they-agree-on -solutions/.

Democratic Party. 1996. "Democratic Party Platform of 1996," August 26. Accessed December 31, 2014: http://www.presidency.ucsb.edu/ws/?pid=29611.

Elinson, Zusha. 2015. "Police Reviews in Deaths Scrutinized," Wall Street Journal, January 11. Accessed February 8, 2016: http://www.wsj.com/articles/police-reviews-in-deaths -scrutinized-1421016273.

Gallup. 2010. "Nearly 4 in 10 Americans Still Fear Walking Alone at Night," November 5. Accessed December 1, 2014: http://www.gallup.com/poll/144272/nearly-americans -fear-walking-alone-night.aspx.

Greene, Jack R. 2000. "Community Policing in America: Changing the Nature, Structure, and Function of the Police," *Criminal Justice*. Accessed December 1, 2014: https:// ncjrs.gov/criminal_justice2000/vol_3/03g.pdf.

Hurwitz, John, and Mark Peffley. 2005. "Playing the Race Card in the Post-Willie Horton Era: Impact of Racialized Code Words on Support for Punitive Criminal Policy," *Public Opinion Quarterly*, 69 (1), Spring: 99–112.

McCabe, James E. 2008. "What Works in Policing?" *Police Quarterly*, 11 (3), September: 289–314.

Republican Party. 1972. "Republican Party Platform of 1972," August 21. Accessed December 10, 2014: http://www.presidency.ucsb.edu/ws/?pid=25842.

Steverson, Leonard A. 2008. *Policing in America: A Reference Handbook*, 2nd edition. Santa Barbara: ABC-CLIO.

U.S. Department of Justice. 2013. "Crime in the United States, 2013." Accessed December 30, 2014: http://www.fbi.gov/about-us/cjis/ucr/crime-in-the-u.s/2013/crime-in-the-u.s.-2013 /cius-home.

Wilson, James Q. 1978. *Varieties of Police Behavior.* Cambridge: Harvard University Press.

Wilson, James Q., and George L. Kelling. 1982. "Broken Windows," *Atlantic Monthly*, 249 (3), March: 29–38.

Poverty and Income Inequality

At a Glance

What causes poverty and why is it more prevalent within America's Hispanic and African American communities? Republicans and Democrats will answer these questions very differently, which sets their policies on poverty and income inequality at odds with one another. Many Democrats believe that poverty is often a reflection of underlying racial or sexist worldviews that are perpetuated in the economic and social structures that deny lower income African Americans, Hispanics, and women the opportunity to earn their way out of poverty. Republicans are much more likely to believe that poverty is a reflection of individual capabilities and lifestyle choices. Democrats are thus more supportive of Federal or State programs and policies to help impoverished Americans and reduce income inequality between the nation's richest and poorest citizens. Republicans, by contrast, believe that social programs too often hinder individual initiative and perpetuate poverty, and they reject "redistributionist" economic policies.

Many Democrats . . .

- Believe that poverty and income inequality are often due to racism, sexism, corporate profiteering.
- Express concern that America's political system is increasingly rigged in favor of the wealthiest Americans and corporate interests.
- Support welfare and other programs of the social safety net as necessary to protect people from the worst effects of poverty.
- Support redistribution of wealth through the tax code.
- Decry the huge and growing gap in income between the top 1 percent of earners and the other 99 percent.
- Believe that stagnant wages are a growing problem for middle-class as well as working-class and poor families.
- Agree with Republicans that government assistance should be a "hand up not a hand out."

Many Republicans . . .

- Believe that poverty and income inequality are primarily reflections of personal choices and capabilities, rather than structural problems with American capitalism.
- Emphasize that dropping out of school, having children out of wedlock, and becoming addicted to drugs are crucial factors in poverty and income inequality.
- Fear that government social welfare programs only make people more dependent on government.
- Support cuts in funding for government antipoverty programs.
- Believe that most people have high incomes because they earn their pay.
- Oppose attempts to redistribute wealth through tax policy.
- Support tax cut proposals that give the great majority of savings to wealthier Americans.

Overview

Democrats and Republicans generally acknowledge that income inequality—the divide between America's wealthiest and poorest citizens—has grown over the past few decades. They disagree, however, on the causes of this trend, as well as policy prescriptions to combat it. Indeed, some Republicans see income inequality as a natural outgrowth of free market capitalism that doesn't necessarily require government intervention to address.

Democrats believe that poverty and the unequal distribution of income are caused by underlying systemic issues such as racism, sexism, unregulated profiteering by corporations, and problems with the tax code. To combat poverty and bridge the wide gap between rich and poor, they favor government programs that assist people with food stamps, housing allowances, and cash payments through direct government assistance and the earned income tax credit, as well as economic policies ranging from a boost to the federal minimum wage to a more progressive tax code that requires rich Americans to pay higher taxes.

Republicans believe that poverty and income inequality are often due to individual choices such as individuals dropping out of school, having children out of wedlock, or not undergoing treatment for drug addiction. Republicans are convinced that government programs make people dependent upon government and weaken their ability to care for themselves which stifles the move from welfare to work. Republicans have attempted to cut funding for government welfare programs while demanding that recipients demonstrate a desire to become independent from government assistance by seeking employment, returning to school, or getting treatment for their addictions.

The New Deal policies and programs of Democratic President Franklin D. Roosevelt—and especially Social Security—marked the first major federal efforts to address poverty in the United States. But while Social Security dramatically reduced the number of elderly Americans living in poverty, the poverty rate in America was still 22.4 percent in the late 1950s. This amounted to nearly 40 million impoverished people across the country (National Poverty Center, n.d.). In 1964, Democratic President Lyndon B. Johnson declared a "War on Poverty," and ever since that time Democrats and Republicans alike have pushed liberal and conservative philosophies, plans, and programs to reduce poverty and hunger in America.

Economic growth and expansion of the social safety net have both worked to reduce the percentage of Americans living in poverty over the past 50 years, although Republican and Democratic lawmakers and activists differ on which of those two drivers have had the greatest impact. The poverty rate declined throughout the 1960s and early 1970s, reaching a low of 11.1 percent (22.9 million Americans) in 1973. By 1983, however, the poverty rate had risen again, to 15.2 percent (35.3 million people), and it was still at that approximate level a decade later. In 1993, however, America experienced a broad economic expansion that helped drop the poverty rate to 11.3 percent by 2000. At that point, however, the poverty rate began creeping up again, and in 2007 a severe economic recession exacerbated

Lauren Scott shares a moment with her 18-month-old daughter Za'Niyah, in Clayton County, Georgia, on November 29, 2015. They both stay at a homeless shelter where 64,000 people live in poverty but only 137 receive the benefits. She has applied for welfare but the system in place makes it quite difficult to obtain. (Photo by Michael S. Williamson/Getty Images)

this trend. By 2010, the national poverty rate had risen to 15.1 percent, its highest level since 1993. Since that time, the poverty rate has held steady or declined slightly. In 2014, the poverty rate stood at 14.8 percent, with 46.7 million Americans living in poverty. That year, 20 percent of children lived in households with incomes below the poverty level which is $23,707 for a single parent with three dependents under 18 (U.S. Census Bureau n.d.).

Meanwhile the income gap between the top 1 percent of earners and the rest of earners has grown steadily since 1979. Income inequality was exacerbated by the Great Recession that began in 2008. From 2009 to 2012, the top 1 percent of wage earners saw their income grow faster than the incomes of the bottom 99 percent in every state except West Virginia. In 39 states, the majority of income gains after the 2008 recession were experienced by the top 1 percent (Price and Sommeiller 2015). The United States ranks third among all the advanced economies in the size of the income inequality, and it is calculated that the top 1 percent of all Americans control nearly a quarter of all the country's income, the highest share since 1928.

After the Great Recession of 2008, many progressive Democrats including Massachusetts Senator Elizabeth Warren, complained that Democrats were being too complacent about the rising income gap and the increase in poverty and suggested more regulation and taxes on wealthy earners to redistribute some of the wealth to those in poverty or close to the poverty line. Most Republicans remain adamantly opposed to such proposals. They continue to assert that the best way to address poverty is to make people less reliant on government assistance, reduce taxes across the board, and let free market principles "lift all boats."

Democrats on Poverty and Income Inequality

Public concern about poverty rose in the 1950s and gained the attention of Presidents John F. Kennedy and Lyndon Johnson, his successor. Inspired by accounts of poverty such as Michael Harrington's *The Other America: Poverty in the United States,* Kennedy signaled his desire to change the dynamics of American welfare by giving "a hand, not a handout" to the poor. Even then, however, poverty loomed as a partisan issue. To the consternation of many Republicans, liberal Democrats proposed an array of government programs and social policy to address poverty. Senator Paul Douglas of Illinois, a liberal Democrat, repeatedly brought up the issues of poverty and income inequality. He offered a series of proposals that were not enacted but brought the issue to national attention. Prominent Democrats outside of Congress also raised the issue of poverty. New York's Governor Averell Harriman, asked the state legislature for funds to study the causes of poverty and to enact programs to assist families in raising their incomes. Adlai E. Stevenson, the Democratic presidential nominee in 1956, recounted his party's efforts to assist the impoverished and declared that, if elected, "We can abolish poverty" (Brauer 1982).

When Lyndon Johnson launched his War on Poverty in his 1964 State of the Union message, though, he acknowledged that it could not be won only by taking action in Washington. His program, he said, necessitated a "cooperative approach" that included "better schools, and better health, and better homes, and better training, and better job opportunities to help more Americans, especially young Americans, escape from squalor and misery and unemployment rolls where other citizens help to carry them" (Johnson 1964).

Nearly 30 years later, pressure from conservatives, combined with a public disenchantment with existing antipoverty programs, led newly elected Democratic President Bill Clinton to promise that he would "end welfare as we know it." After vetoing a Republican bill that he found to be too discriminatory and punitive, Clinton worked with Congress to fashion the Personal Responsibility and Work Opportunity Reconciliation Act, which reflected many of the Republican criticisms of welfare. Clinton trumpeted his handiwork as welfare rolls declined in the late 1990s and the middle class grew. This trend was reversed by a recession that struck the United States in 2000, when poverty and income inequality grew.

Historically, the antipoverty efforts of the Democrats have attracted large numbers of working-class and low-income whites, Latinos, and African Americans to their party. The burdens of poverty and income inequality fall heaviest on African Americans and Latinos, who make up 29 percent of the U.S. population but account for 41 percent of the population living in America's high-poverty and high-inequality counties. Although these groups show higher concentrations of poverty and income inequality, the issue is really a national one. Study after study shows that the gap in economic fortunes has widened along all class, age, race, and ethnicity lines. Median wealth did not change between 2010 and 2013. Median earnings for full-time U.S. workers aged 18 to 34 have fallen nearly 10 percent since 2000.

The public mood and Democratic agenda was reshaped with the election of Barack Obama in 2008 who took office during the greatest economic crisis since the Great Depression. Armed with Democratic majorities·in both houses of Congress during his first two years in the Oval Office, Obama included a wide range of antipoverty measures in his nearly $1 trillion economic stimulus package in 2009, from unemployment checks for those unable to find jobs to infrastructure projects that required large numbers of workers. In 2010, the Affordable Care Act addressed the health security of America's impoverished by expanding Medicaid and requiring business owners to supply health care to workers who worked 30 hours or more per week. This was followed by the rise of a progressive movement called Occupy Wall Street (OWS) in 2010.

The Occupy movement called for new regulations on corporate wealth and changes in the existing economic system to assist the 99 percent of workers who, the activists claimed, were being mistreated and marginalized by the top 1 percent of wage earners. The OWS movement began on Constitution Day, September 17, 2011, in Manhattan's Financial District and spread to over 100 cities in the United States. The group declared that it intended to fight back "against the corrosive power of major banks and multinational corporations over the democratic process . . . [and]

against the richest 1% of people that are writing the rules of an unfair global economy that is foreclosing on our future" (della Porta and Mattoni 2014). The rhetoric used by OWS was echoed at the Democratic National Convention in 2012. One speaker in particular aroused the convention. Elizabeth Warren, a progressive Massachusetts Democrat who worked in the Obama administration and went on to win the election to the U.S. Senate in 2012, called for a return of traditional Democratic programs to address poverty and income inequality. Similar sentiments have been expressed by a wide range of other progressive Democrats as well, including Cory Booker, the former mayor of Newark, New Jersey, who in 2013 won a special election for the U.S. Senate to become the first African American senator to serve New Jersey. "Fifty years after the War on Poverty began, we can greatly advance our common cause if we recommit to policies that have been successful and update our approach, based on the evidence of what works and what doesn't," wrote Booker. He continued:

> There are many sound ideas, ranging from addressing the educational needs of our children to stimulating more investment and entrepreneurship in pockets of urban poverty . . . In a global, knowledge-based economy, the genius of our children is our nation's greatest asset. Universal pre-K is a must: Based just on cost-benefit analysis, the evidence is overwhelming. We know that every dollar spent on high-quality early education returns roughly $7—through reduced spending on social services, as well as higher earning and productivity for participants as adults (Booker 2014).

In 2015, President Obama in his State of the Union Address and later in his budget proposal suggested raising taxes on the very wealthiest Americans to fund new programs to reach the poor, free two-year college education to assist people in obtaining the skills they need to move out of poverty or to increase their income, and expansion of the earned income tax credit to redistribute money from the wealthy to the poor. The credit indirectly transfers money from those who pay taxes to those who pay no taxes.

Republicans on Poverty and Income Inequality

In the 1950s, when some liberals and Democrats were pointing to the issue of poverty in America and questioning how so wealthy a nation could have so many impoverished citizens, many conservatives and Republicans were instead celebrating the decade's heady economic growth, which they attributed to American ingenuity and the benefits of the free enterprise system. They believed poverty or low wages were more likely the result of an individual making poor life choices. Thus, the Eisenhower administration expanded some social programs such as Social Security but resisted special assistance to the poor. Campaigning for president in 1960, the Republican candidate and vice president of the United States, Richard Nixon, castigated his Democratic opponent's assertion that 17 million people went to bed hungry every night. Elected president in 1968, Nixon attacked the Democrat's antipoverty program, telling Congress: "The present welfare system has failed us—it has fostered family breakup, has provided very little help in many States and has even deepened dependency by all-too-often making it more attractive to go on welfare than to go to work" (Nixon 1969). This became an article of faith among many Republicans, including iconic leaders like Ronald Reagan. Indeed, from the 1970s forward, Reagan and other Republicans argued with increasing conviction that most federal social welfare policies fostered dependency on government without alleviating poverty in any meaningful or long-lasting way. They pointed to works such as Charles Murray's *Losing Ground: American Social Policy, 1950–1980* (1984) to provide support for their contention that the Kennedy–Johnson era created a culture of dependence on government programs while also increasing poverty.

This was certainly the perspective of Reagan, who served as president from 1981 to 1989. The Reagan administration repeatedly tried to cut welfare spending and to reduce or eliminate some antipoverty programs. In 1988, Reagan persuaded Congress to pass the Family Support Act, which required recipients of Aid to Family of Dependent Children (AFDC) to complete 20 hours of work or job training.

When Republicans took control of Congress in 1995 they offered a bill to end welfare dependency and stem the rising tide of poverty. Although vetoed by Clinton, Republicans prevailed in the Personal Responsibility and Work Opportunity Act, which mandated that recipients undergo training for work, ended automatic increases to states and replaced these with block grants, and cut lifetime eligibility to all welfare recipients (O'Connor 2004). During the two-terms of President George W. Bush, who served from 2001 to 2009, the minimum wage stayed the same, the welfare reform act remained in place, and poverty rose while real income declined. Bush reflected Republican policy by placing an emphasis on individual initiative, on the use of faith-based organizations to assist people who were in poverty, and urging low-income earners to use their Section 8 housing vouchers for down payments on new homes (Brownstein 2009). In their 2012 platform, Republicans trumpeted their accomplishments. "We took the belief of most Americans—that welfare should be a hand up, not a hand out—and made it law. Work requirements, though modest, were at the heart of this success" (Republican Party 2012).

After the Great Recession in 2008, President Obama and his fellow Democrats expanded programs to assist the poor and to keep people from falling into poverty. Impelled by progressives in their own Party, they also shone a spotlight on income inequality in America. Many Democrats called for higher taxes on the rich and economic assistance to poor, working-class, and middle-class Americans to reduce the size of this divide. Republicans labeled these proposals as unvarnished class warfare and emphasized that government programs had failed to keep people from entering poverty after the Great Society. They believe that poverty is correlated with the rise in children born out of wedlock, which has risen to 40 percent of all children born. Studies by conservative groups such as the Heritage Foundation show that children born to middle-class married couples are less likely to fall into poverty, while children born out of wedlock have high rates of being born into and then staying in poverty (Katel 2011). Many Republicans believe that the solution to poverty will be to enact tax reforms that will help businesses create jobs, require mandatory drug testing for welfare recipients accompanied by free or low-cost drug treatment for addicts, and include regulations that make the welfare-to-work transition more seamless. They blame persistent poverty on misguided Democratic policies and insist that America should chart a new course in reducing poverty and inequality. Prominent GOP lawmaker Paul Ryan (R-Wis.) spoke for much of his party in a 2014 *Wall Street Journal* Op-Ed in which he declared that

> for years, politicians have pointed to the money they've spent or the programs they've created. But despite trillions of dollars in spending, 47 million Americans still live in poverty today. And the reason is simple: Poverty isn't just a form of deprivation; it's a form of isolation. Crime, drugs and broken families are dragging down millions of Americans. On every measure from education levels to marriage rates, poor families are drifting further away from the middle class. And Washington is deepening the divide. Over the past 50 years, the federal government has created different programs to fix different problems, so there's little or no coordination among them. And because these programs are means-tested—meaning that families become ineligible for them as they earn more—poor families effectively face very high marginal tax rates, in some cases over 80%. So the government actually discourages them from getting ahead.
>
> Poverty isn't a rare disease from which the rest of us are immune. It's the worst strain of a widespread scourge: economic insecurity. That's why concern for the poor isn't a policy niche; it goes to the heart of the American experiment. What the poor really need is to be reintegrated into our communities. But Washington is walling them up in a massive quarantine . . . For 50 years, we've been going in the wrong direction, and liberals want to march on. Some in Washington insist that you're concerned for the poor only if you're committed to a path that has failed the poor. But the question isn't whether we should do more or less of the same. It is which new direction will work best (Ryan 2014).

Further Reading

Booker, Cory. 2014. "Building on the Success of the War on Poverty," *The Wall Street Journal*, January 24, 2014. Accessed October 28, 2015: http://www.wsj.com/news/articles/SB1 0001424052702303448204579338671653433800.

Brauer, Carl M. 1982. "Kennedy, Johnson and the War on Poverty," *The Journal of American History,* 69 (1), June: 98–119.

Brownstein, Ronald. 2009. "Closing the Book on the Bush Legacy: The Final Words on Bushonomics and Poverty," *The Atlantic,* September 11. Accessed October 31, 2015: http://www.theatlantic.com/politics/archive/2009/09/closing-the-book-on-the-bush -legacy/26402/.

della Porta, Donatella, and Alice Mattoni. 2014. *Spreading Protest: Social Movements in Times of Crisis.* Colchester, UK: ECPR Press.

Harrington, Michael. 1997. *The Other America: Poverty in the United States.* New York: Touchstone.

Johnson, Lyndon B. 1964. "Annual Message to the Congress on the State of the Union," January 8. Accessed January 28, 2015: http://www.presidency.ucsb.edu/ws/?pid=26787.

Katel, Peter. 2011. "Child Poverty," *CQ Researcher*, 21 (38), October 28: 901–928.

Murray, Charles. 1984. *Losing Ground: American Social Policy, 1950–1980*. New York: Basic Books.

National Poverty Center. n.d. "Poverty in the United States: Frequently Asked Questions." National Poverty Center, University of Michigan. Accessed October 2, 2015: http://www.npc.umich.edu/poverty/#3.

Nixon, Richard. 1969. "Special Message to the Congress on Reform of the Nation's Welfare System," August 11. Accessed January 28, 2015: http://www.presidency.ucsb.edu/ws/?pid=2194.

O'Connor, Brendan. 2004. *A Political History of the American Welfare System: When Ideas Have Consequences*. Lanham, MD: Rowman and Littlefield.

Price, Mark, and Estelle Sommeiller. 2015. "How Unequal Is Your State?" Economic Policy Institute, January 28, 2015. Accessed January 28, 2015: http://www.epi.org/publication/how-unequal-is-your-state-the-ratio-between-the-average-incomes-of-the-top-1-percent-and-the-bottom-99-percent-in-each-state/.

Quadagno, Jill. 2004. *The Color of Welfare: How Racism Undermined the War on Poverty*. New York: Oxford University Press.

Reese, Ellen. 2013. *They Say Cutback, We Say Fight Back! Welfare Activism in an Era of Retrenchment*. New York: Russell Sage Foundation.

Republican Party. 2012. "2012 Republican Party Platform," August 27. Accessed June 26, 2014: http://www.presidency.ucsb.edu/ws/?pid=101961.

Ryan, Paul. 2014. "A New Direction in the War on Poverty," *The Wall Street Journal*, January 24, 2014. Accessed October 29, 2015: http://www.wsj.com/articles/SB10001424052702304632204579337000386366182.

U.S. Census Bureau. n.d. "How the Census Bureau Measures Poverty." Accessed December 10, 2014: https://www.census.gov/hhes/www/poverty/about/overview/measure.html.

Prisons and Sentencing

At a Glance

Democrats and Republicans have come to agreement on some aspects of the criminal justice system. In the 1990s there was broad bipartisan support for tough sentencing, including so-called three-strikes laws and mandatory minimum sentences. Since that time, crime rates have fallen steadily, even as the nation's prison population has continued to grow. These divergent trends have prompted many Democrats—as well as some Republicans—to support legislation aimed at reducing the prison population, such as through the development of alternate sentencing for nonviolent offenders and the use of job-training and drug rehabilitation programs within prison populations.

Many Democrats . . .

- Believe that the composition of the population in the American penal system reflects racial and economic disparities in American society.
- Believe that prisons create hardened career criminals.
- Want to create new sentencing guidelines to address the disparate treatment of black and white offenders.
- Want to reform mandatory sentencing guidelines.
- Support alternative sentencing for nonviolent criminals.
- Support granting greater latitude to judges to sentence offenders.
- Support programs inside of prison to assist in offenders' transition to society.

Many Republicans . . .

- Believe that the American penal system needs reformation.
- Believe that the threat of prison can be a deterrent to crime.
- Support mandatory sentencing.
- Oppose paroling offenders from overcrowded prisons.
- Support prosecutors who use tough sentencing guidelines to induce criminal defendants to cooperate with police in ongoing.
- Express concern about the budgetary impact of America's crowded correctional institutions; in some cases, these concerns have prompted support for sentencing reforms.

———————————

Overview

In many respects, modern sentencing and prison policies continue to reflect rates of violent crime from a half-century ago. During the 1960s and 1970s, the incidence of numerous type of crime—including violent crimes—increased dramatically. The murder rate, for example, went from 4.9 per 100,000 people in 1964 to 9.3 by 1994 (Disaster Center n.d.). This prompted a variety of "tough on crime" measures during the 1980s, including mandating longer prison sentences for a wide range of offenses. Republicans were particularly vocal in supporting these measures, but they also often received support from Democrats. In 1994, Democratic President Bill Clinton, asserting that "gangs and drugs have taken over our streets and undermined our schools," signed into law the bipartisan Violent Crime Control and Law Enforcement Act (Johnson 2014). On the state level, meanwhile, many legislatures passed habitual offender laws, also known as the three-strike laws, which are statutes that mandate imposition of harsher sentences for habitual offenders who were previously convicted of two prior serious criminal offenses and who then commit a third.

Since 1995 the crime rate has fallen. The reason for the decline is at the heart of debate between Democrats and Republicans. Democrats, in general, see the falling crime rate as a result of economic growth and the expenditure of federal dollars on curbing crime. Some Democrats also champion the idea that the reduction of lead-based paint has been responsible, and some point to the aging population, which historically commits fewer crimes. Republicans, in general, have acknowledged that some of the above factors could play a role, but they also have been vocal supporters of heavy sentences for a range of crimes, including those related to illegal drugs. In their 2012 party platform, for example, the GOP asserted that "criminals behind bars cannot harm the general public" (Republican Party 2012).

As the number of people in jail increased, prison construction underwent a corresponding boom (Rafter and Stanley 1999). From 1980 to 2014, Texas alone built over 120 new prisons, while California added 83 and Florida 84. By 2014 the total number of jails and prisons in the United States was 5,000, which is larger than the number of degree-granting colleges and universities in the United States. Some of these prisons were built and run by private companies as state governments outsourced these tasks (Price and Morris 2012).

In recent years, however, lawmakers and voters on both sides of the aisle have voiced growing uneasiness with America's surging prison population. In 1990 the overall prison population was only 1.1 million but this figure grew by nearly 4 percent a year peaking at 2.3 million in 2010. Federal prison populations have seen particularly heavy increases—with corresponding budget implications. As Politico noted in 2015, the inmate population in federal correctional facilities "has ballooned to 219,000—40 percent over capacity—from 24,000 before the tough-on-crime mentality that dominated the 1980s. And the price tag for running the prisons has grown from $970 million to $6.7 billion over the past 30 years, taking up about a quarter of the Justice Department's budget" (Bade 2015). Today the U.S. prison population is higher than that of any other country. In the United States, more men than women are in prison. African Americans are disproportionately represented in the prison population and make up over 40 percent of all people incarcerated (Glazer 2014).

With more than 1.5 million Americans in federal, state, and county prisons and jails at the close of 2013, the majority of them for violating drug laws, overcrowding has become a high-profile issue, even with the explosion of prison construction. Some judges ruled that keeping prisoners in overcrowded conditions violated a prisoner's Eighth Amendment protection from cruel and unusual punishment and forced states to parole prisoners early. In addition, local and state authorities are grappling with the cost of caring for prisoners. Each prisoner costs tens of

President Barack Obama, alongside Charles Samuels, right, Bureau of Prisons Director, and Ronald Warlick, a correctional officer, tours a cell block at the El Reno Federal Correctional Institution in El Reno, Oklahoma, on July 16, 2015. Obama is the first sitting U.S. president to visit a federal prison, in a push to reform one of the most expensive and crowded prison systems in the world. (Photo by Saul Loeb/AFP/Getty Images)

thousands of dollars per year to incarcerate and it is estimated that the amount of money spent on prisons has risen six times faster than that spent on higher education (Glazer 2014).

The policies that led to the high prison population, such as mandatory long sentences, were largely the result of bipartisan legislation. Some civil rights and prison reform organizations, however, have condemned this state of affairs. They cite a weak correlation between longer incarceration and lower crime rates and are quick to point out racial disparities in sentencing. A spokesman for the progressive Vera Institute of Justice, for example, stated that "if you're a black baby born today, you have a 1 in 3 chance of spending some time in prison or jail. If you're Latino, it's a 1 in 6 chance. And if you're white, it's 1 in 17" (Johnson 2014). They attempt to provide alternates to jail time and there is growing bipartisan support for alternative sentencing, providing judges with more discretion when sentencing offenders, and for providing services for inmates to prepare them for restoration to society and reduce recidivism. "America's overreliance on incarceration is exacting excessive costs on individuals and communities, as well as on the national economy," wrote former Clinton administration treasury secretary Robert Rubin and Nicholas Turner of the Vera Project for Justice in a 2014 Op-Ed. "Sentences are too long, and parole and probation policies too inflexible. There is too little rehabilitation in prison and inadequate support for life after prison. Crime itself has a terrible human cost and a serious economic cost. But appropriate punishment for those who are a risk to public safety shouldn't obscure the vast deficiencies in the criminal-justice system that imposes a significant drag on the economy" (Rubin and Turner 2014).

Democrats on Prisons and Sentencing

Until the 1970s much of U.S. public policy was predicated on the belief that criminals could be rehabilitated. Many Democrats believed that crime was the result of social problems such as unemployment, poverty, and injustice. During the 1960s, Democratic President Lyndon Johnson argued that his antipoverty Great Society programs would diminish the crime rate. Instead, crime rates rose in the decades of the 1970s and 1980s, leaving Democrats vulnerable to GOP charges that they were soft on crime, overly concerned with criminals, and negligent when it came to victims of crime. To reverse this image, Democratic President Bill Clinton ardently supported anticrime legislation during his two terms in office in the 1990s. He signed into law several pieces of legislation including a crime bill in 1994 that provided states with more funds to build prisons if they included "truth-in-sentencing" laws that required that certain types of violent convicts spend 85 percent of their sentence behind bars. The changing Democratic position was reinforced by strong language in the party's platform in the 1990s through 2012. Nonetheless, some Democrats—especially those representing minority districts—also continued to emphasize their support for community policing, alternative sentencing, and programs to reintroduce parolees back into society (Glazer 2014).

For many years, calls to reform the criminal justice system were ignored. However, the problem of overcrowding, declining crime rates, and increasing racial disparities led members of both political parties to consider revisions to existing laws (Alexander 2012).

President Obama's Attorney General Eric Holder was a vocal and controversial advocate for prison reform. Holder once told the Congressional Black Caucus that mandatory sentencing left "an unmistakable destabilizing effect on particular communities—largely poor and of color" (Glazer 2014). Holder pointed out that African Americans make up nearly 82 percent of defendants sentenced in federal court for dealing crack. According to a study by the U.S. Sentencing Commission, in 2013 about 83 percent of crack offenders were African American, 10 percent were Hispanic, and only 5.8 percent were white. Holder used his office to redirect federal prosecutors from bringing maximum charges on nonviolent drug offenders and sought to have mandatory sentencing laws changed by Congress. Holder also pressured public schools to change their policies regarding juvenile offenders to keep young people from going from school to prison. To back up these demands he even threatened to sue schools that did not (Millhiser and Flatow 2014).

To deal with the transition from prison to civilian life the Vera Institute sponsored a pilot program offering college classes and reentry support such as financial literacy training, legal services, employment counseling, and workshops on family reintegration to inmates. The results inspired some Democrats to take action on the state and local level. Governor Andrew Cuomo noted that it cost New York state over $60,000 dollars a year to care for inmates and proposed providing up to $5,000 in state money for college classes in prison to cut down on recidivism. Strong criticism from statewide Republicans led the governor to back off of his plan. Bill de Blasio, the progressive mayor of New York City, has instituted mandatory training for new corrections officers to deal with mentally ill inmates and has expanded substance abuse treatment for city inmates. In addition, officials in New York City planned to increase support for people who left prison by providing services to aid them in gaining access to Medicaid and placement in supportive housing. Some Democrats have also spoken out in support of Drug Treatment Courts, which mandate and supervise drug rehabilitation programs rather than prison for illegal drug offenders. The goal of these special courts is to put selected individuals into treatment programs rather than prison. There are thousands of such courts and they have allowed offenders to avoid jail time.

Republicans on Prisons and Sentencing

Many Republicans crafted a "tough on crime" stance during the era when crimes rates were rising in the 1970s, and they have cultivated that image ever since with support for the death penalty, mandatory minimum sentences, prison construction, three-strikes measures, and so on. Some Republicans in the 1980s and 1990s, for example, pushed for action on the state and federal level to require mandatory sentencing and harsher sentences and to make prisons less comfortable for criminals. In 1994, they worked with Democrats such as Bill Clinton to support an omnibus crime bill that created stringent, mandatory, and longer sentences for people convicted of violent and drug crimes. They rejected attempts to include programs aimed at drawing young people from the streets and into community centers, such as the Midnight Basketball program. They were also successful in ending federal grants for prisoners who wanted to take college courses while incarcerated.

In the decade of the 1990s there was bipartisan support for longer imprisonment. After 1995 crime rates declined but the GOP continued to promote a tough-on-crime party platform. They called for no-frills prisons to make the threat of jail time a deterrent to crime; they called for increased penalties for various offenses; and they called for passage of a constitutional amendment to protect victim's rights. In the early 2000s, as federal judges mandated the early release of prisoners to relieve overcrowding, many Republicans responded by calling for a congressional bill to end this practice. "Liberals do not understand this simple axiom: criminals behind bars cannot harm the general public," summarized the 2012 GOP platform. "To that end, we support mandatory prison sentencing for gang crimes, violent or sexual offenses against children, repeat drug dealers, rape, robbery and murder" (Republican Party 2012).

Conservative Republicans remain mostly supportive of the harsh mandatory sentencing requirements that have sprouted up across the country since the 1990s, and they warn that reducing these sentences would only encourage more crime. Senator Charles E. Grassley, the chairman of the Senate Judiciary Committee, rejected legislation in 2014 that called for across the board reduction in sentencing (Eckholm 2015). Republicans in New York were outraged when Governor Andrew Cuomo, a Democrat, suggested spending state money to give a college education to prisoners. Republicans were generally incensed that middle-class, law-abiding, and rule-following tax payers who worked hard to get a college education would have to use loans, while criminals who did not pay taxes and who has been socially irresponsible would receive a college education for free. "It should be 'do the crime, do the time,' not 'do the crime, earn a degree,'" said George Mazar, a state senator from western New York.

Despite the "lock them up and throw away the key" rhetoric of the national GOP, some Republicans have questioned the wisdom of the longer sentencing. Concerns about the cost of long-term incarceration led GOP governors in Southern states to seek cost reductions by creating alternatives to jail time for nonviolent offenders. In Washington, meanwhile, even deeply conservative GOP congress members have suggested cautious support for reforms to the existing prison system, which they see as both costly to taxpayers and a failure in terms of rehabilitation. "More than 90 percent of people who go to a federal prison are going to come back out," said House Oversight Committee Chairman Jason Chaffetz (R-Utah) in July 2015.

Republican Opposition to Sentencing "Reforms"

Although some conservatives have expressed support for sentencing reforms, many Republicans are skeptical and express concern that some reforms might go too far. These fears can be seen in the following 2014 speech from Republican Senator Charles Grassley in opposition to a proposed Smarter Sentencing Act.

I rise again today to express my strong opposition to this bill and argue against taking up the Senate's time to consider it. Mr. President, this country has experienced a tremendous drop in crime over the past 30 years. We have achieved hard-won gains in reducing victimization.

More effective police tactics played a significant role. Congress assisted with funds for law enforcement and mandatory sentencing guidelines to make dangerous offenders serve longer sentences. But after the Supreme Court applied novel constitutional theory, those mandatory guidelines were made advisory only. Federal judges then used their discretion to sentence defendants more leniently than the guidelines had called for. Today, the only tool Congress has to make sure that federal judges do not abuse their discretion in sentencing too leniently is mandatory minimum sentences. This bill would cut a wide range of mandatory minimum sentences by half or more. Those sentences include people convicted of manufacture, sale, possession with intent to distribute, and importation of a wide range of drugs, including heroin, cocaine, PCP, LSD, ecstasy, and methamphetamine.

When supporters of this bill discuss how it increases discretion for judges and keeps current maximum sentences, what they really mean is that judges will gain discretion only to be more lenient. The bill does not increase discretion for judges to be more punitive. When supporters of this bill say that the bill only applies to nonviolent offenders, don't be misled into thinking it applies to people in federal prison for simple possession of marijuana. Importing cocaine is violent. The whole operation turns on violence. Dealing heroin also involves violence or the threat of violence. And the offense for which the offender is sentenced may have been violent. The defendant's codefendant might have used a gun. And while the bill does not apply to a drug crime for which the defendant used violence, it does apply to criminals where the defendant has a history of committing violent crime . . . Current mandatory minimum sentences play a vital role in reducing crime. They do more than keep serious offenders in jail so that they cannot prey upon innocent citizens. They also induce lower-level drug offenders to avoid receiving mandatory minimum sentences by implicating higher-ups. As FBI Director Comey recently stated, "I know from my experience . . . that the mandatory minimums are an important tool in developing cooperators."

Source

Grassley, Chuck. 2014. "Grassley Floor Statement on the Smarter Sentencing Act, Part II." May 13. Accessed November 12, 2015: http://www.grassley.senate.gov/news/news-releases/grassley-floor-statement-smarter-sentencing-act-part-ii.

"We have a duty and an obligation to make some determinations as to how we structure that: Are we sending the right people to prison? Are we doing the right things once they're there and what are we doing as a nation to reduce the rate of recidivism?" (Bade 2015).

One of the most influential of the conservative prison reform voices to emerge in recent years is a group called Right on Crime. This organization is supported by a cross-section of influential Republicans, from noted antitax crusader Grover Norquist to former Reagan administration attorney general Ed Meese and former house speaker Newt Gingrich. The group "urges reduced costs of incarceration by reducing both numbers and length of prison sentences. It also seeks more programs in prison that are proven to reduce re-offense, like drug treatment. And it calls for smaller criminal codes, because 'criminal law should be reserved for conduct that is either blameworthy or threatens public safety, not wielded to grow government and undermine economic freedom'" (Hurst 2014).

As a result of this reexamination of prison and sentencing laws, in late 2015 the Senate Judiciary Committee crafted a bill that would reduce automatic sentencing, end the three-strikes rule for repeat offenders, and limit the application of mandatory sentencing for nonviolent offenders. A similar bill was crafted in the House by Republican congress member Bob Goodlatte of Virginia. Whether the bills will pass in either chamber remains unclear as of this writing, but it will be a bellwether of the changing attitudes of the Republican leadership to prison policy (Le Tourneau 2015).

Further Reading

Alexander, Michelle. 2012. *The New Jim Crow: Mass Incarceration in the Age of Colorblindness.* New York: The New Press.

Bade, Rachael. 2015. "Criminal Justice Reform Gains Bipartisan Momentum," Politico, July 15. Accessed October 5, 2015: http://www.politico.com/story/2015/07/criminal-justice -reform-gains-bipartisan-momentum-120125.

Disaster Center. n.d. United States Crime Rates 1960–2014. Accessed October 15, 2015: http://www.disastercenter.com/crime/uscrime.htm.

Eckholm, Erik. 2015. "In a Safer Age, U.S. Rethinks Its 'Tough on Crime' System," *The New York Times*, January 13. Accessed January 19, 2015: http://www.nytimes.com/2015/01 /14/us/with-crime-down-us-faces-legacy-of-a-violent-age-.html?_r=0.

Glazer, Sarah. 2014. "Sentencing Reform. Are Mandatory Sentences Too Harsh?" *CQ Researcher,* 24 (2), January 10: 25–48.

Hurst II, A. J. 2014. "Federal Sentencing and Prison Reform Now Bipartisan Issues," The Hill: Crime [blog], August 13. Accessed October 5, 2015: http://thehill.com/blogs /pundits-blog/crime/214998-federal-sentencing-and-prison-reform-now-bipartisan -issues.

Johnson, Carrie. 2014. "20 Years Later, Parts of Major Crime Bill Viewed as Terrible Mistake," NPR. Accessed January 18, 2015: http://www.npr.org/2014/09/12/347736999/20-years -later-major-crime-bill-viewed-as-terrible-mistake%20accessed%20December%201.

Le Tourneau, Nancy. 2015. "Momentum for Criminal Justice Reform Continues to Build," The Washington Monthly, October 14. Accessed November 5, 2015: http://www .washingtonmonthly.com/political-animal-a/2015_10/momentum_for_criminal _justice058105.php.

Millhiser, Ian, and Nicole Flatow. 2014. "Eric Holder's Historic and Little-Noticed Civil Rights Legacy," Think Progress, October 1. Accessed January 18, 2015: http://thinkprogress .org/justice/2014/09/25/3572134/holder-civil-rights/.

Price, Byron Eugene, and John Charles Morris, eds. 2012. Prison Privatization: The Many Facets of a Controversial Industry. Santa Barbara: Praeger.

Rafter, Nicole Hahn, and Debra L. Stanley. 1999. Prisons in America: A Reference Handbook. Santa Barbara: ABC-CLIO.

Republican Party. 2012. "2012 Republican Party Platform," August 27. Accessed January 18, 2015: http://www.presidency.ucsb.edu/ws/?pid=101961.

Rubin, Robert, and Nicholas Turner. 2014. "The Steep Cost of America's High Incarceration Rate," Wall Street Journal, December 25. Accessed December 2, 2015: http://www.wsj .com/articles/robertrubinandnicholasturnerthesteepcostofamericashighincarcerationrate 1419543410.

Privacy Rights

At a Glance

Republicans and Democrats both embrace the right to privacy but differ over when that right should be constrained by the need for safety and security. Many Republicans, except for libertarian leaning Republicans, have been more willing to accept the invasion of privacy by the government in the War on Terror. Many Democrats have rejected the idea that government agencies need access to the personal data of millions of Americans who are not suspected of any crime.

Many Democrats . . .

- Fear that civil rights have been compromised by government laws aimed at identifying terrorists and criminals and stopping activities by such individuals.
- Have called for reforms to government surveillance programs.
- Support great transparency by U.S. government agencies charged with intelligence gathering.

Many Republicans . . .

- Fear that safety and security will be lost if the government is not allowed broad surveillance powers.
- Would like to retain government surveillance programs.
- Express concerns, despite their support for robust national security and surveillance programs, that government scrutiny of private citizens is sometimes overzealous and doesn't respect constitutional rights.
- Support oversight of U.S. government agencies charged with intelligence gathering.

Overview

Privacy rights protect individuals from government intrusion into their personal affairs. These rights, while not specifically addressed in the U.S. Constitution, were recognized by the U.S. Supreme Court in the 1960s. In the case of *Griswold v. Connecticut,* Justice William O. Douglas's majority opinion asserted that Americans have a constitutional right to privacy founded on elements of the First, Third, Fourth, Fifth, and Ninth Amendments. This idea has become universalized for all U.S. citizens and remains the ground for conflict between Republicans and Democrats on hot button topics such as abortion rights and the right to die. The right to privacy is often invoked in debates surrounding how much power to grant U.S. intelligence and security agencies in the War on Terror. Some people have expressed fear that the U.S. government has become the Big Brother of George Orwell's novel *1984.* But unlike many issues in which Democrats and Republicans form unified blocs of opposition, the issue of privacy rights has sparked the creation of unusual alliances across parties and divisions within parties. For example, liberal lawmakers and conservative Tea Party members who agree on virtually nothing else have sometimes found themselves on the same side of debates about proposed policies and laws with implications for personal privacy. Meanwhile, Republicans and Democrats alike frequently disagree within their own respective caucuses about whether certain crime-fighting and antiterrorism measures violate basic privacy rights.

These unusual alliances and divisions have proliferated since the beginning of the so-called War on Terror—a national security campaign that began in the wake of the infamous September 11, 2001, terrorist attacks on the World Trade Center, the Pentagon, and the attempted attack on the White House. After that tragedy, Congress passed and President George W. Bush signed legislation creating the Department of Homeland Security (DHS), a new cabinet department meant to consolidate and enhance U.S. intelligence operations. In addition to the new agency, Congress passed additional antiterror legislation that provided the U.S. government with broad powers to investigate suspected terrorists. The key legislation authorizing this new power was the USA Patriot Act of 2001, which granted the government unprecedented authority to secretly search a suspected terrorist's home; to monitor Internet activity, phone conversations, banking information, and book purchases; and to open mail. The law required the government to show cause for this action but did not allow a judge to refuse a request for these secret search warrants. Furthermore, the law made it illegal for telecommunications or financial institutions to disclose to the public the very existence of the warrants. Some Americans—both Republicans and Democrats—saw this as a threat to the right of privacy, and others—both Republicans and Democrats—as a justified means of protecting Americans from the horrors of terrorism.

To be sure, though, support or opposition was dictated at least somewhat by party affiliation. When the Bush administration's warrantless eavesdropping was revealed to the public by the *New York Times* in 2005, for example, conservative Republicans were more likely to argue that law-abiding citizens had nothing to fear from the enhanced surveillance powers of the federal government, and that warrantless wiretapping and other surveillance measures carried out by the National

The Foreign Intelligence Surveillance Act

The Foreign Intelligence Surveillance Act (FISA) of 1978 is one of the major legal foundations for intelligence-gathering and surveillance activities of American intelligence agencies. But in the 21st century, debates intensified over reauthorizing, reforming, and remaking FISA to meet modern surveillance challenges and perennial civil liberties concerns. In 2012 the FISA Amendments Act was renewed for another five years, despite expressions of concern that government surveillance under FISA authority had become so widespread and intrusive that they posed a danger to constitutional rights to privacy. Despite such expressions of concern—from liberal Democrats and Tea Party Republicans alike—the law passed Congress with bipartisan support and was signed into law by President Barack Obama on December 31, 2012.

Security Agency (NSA), Central Intelligence Agency (CIA), and Federal Bureau of Investigation (FBI) were necessary to ensure the disruption and defeat of terrorists at home and abroad. During that same time, progressive Democrats and civil rights advocates were the chief source of complaints that these programs and laws eroded civil liberties and were being abused by government agencies.

But when Democrat Barack Obama became president in 2009 and maintained many Bush-era surveillance programs and activities, a noticeable shift took place in the positions of many members of the two parties. "At the time of the 2005 NSA warrantless eavesdropping controversy, liberals and Democrats overwhelmingly viewed the [NSA] agency's surveillance program as menacing," wrote Glenn Greenwald. "Part of this, of course, was typical partisan hackery: George W. Bush was president and Democrats saw an opportunity to inflict political harm on him and his party. But a significant part of their fear was genuine: because they considered Bush malicious and dangerous, they perceived that state surveillance under his control was therefore threatening and that they in particular were endangered as political opponents. Accordingly, Republicans had a more benign or supportive view of the NSA's actions." But when whistleblower Edward Snowden revealed other NSA surveillance activities in 2013, "Democrats and progressives had converted to the leading NSA defenders. Ample polling data reflected this shift" (Greenwald 2014, 194–195).

Similarly, Republicans became much more uncomfortable with government surveillance when it was a Democrat rather than a Republican in charge. Similar polling data from the *Washington Post* revealed that conservatives were far more concerned than liberals about NSA spying. When asked, "How concerned are you, if at all, about the collection and use of your personal information by the National Security Agency?" 48 percent of conservatives were "very concerned," compared to only 26 percent of liberals. As law professor Orin Kerr noted, this represented a fundamental change: "It's an interesting reversal from 2006, when the President was a Republican instead of a Democrat. Back then, a Pew poll found 75% of

Republicans approved of NSA surveillance but only 37% of Democrats approved" (Greenwald 2014).

As noted above, party positions on privacy rights in an age of growing techno-logical surveillance were shaken up considerably by Snowden's 2013 revelations of sweeping NSA electronic surveillance of U.S. citizens. Snowden revealed how an NSA program called PRISM was scouring e-mails, Facebook posts, and instant messages to gather information. The agency also collected phone records from U.S. phone service providers that included numbers dialed from and to and the date and duration of the phone calls. The NSA claims all its operations are legal under the Patriot Act but this did little to assuage fears of privacy rights advocates and ordinary American citizens uncomfortable with the apparent extent of domestic surveillance being undertaken by government agencies under the auspices of vari-ous laws.

As a result, a comprehensive slate of surveillance reforms known as the USA Freedom Act passed with broad bipartisan support in both the House and the Senate in the summer of 2015. This law, which was crafted to better protect the privacy of Americans, increase transparency of the government's surveillance oper-ations, and end the NSA's bulk collection of U.S. call data, was signed into law by President Obama.

Meanwhile, privacy rights advocates have attempted to pass legislation in states to protect citizens from law enforcement agencies. They have had some success in states with Democratic legislative majorities, such as Minnesota, where a dozen or more proposals have been offered "This is the most pervasive push I've seen on this issue," said John Lesch who was elected to office on the Democratic-Farmer-Labor ticket and served as chair of the Minnesota House Civil Law Committee. Advocates were also heartened when the U.S. Supreme Court ruled unanimously in *Riley v. California* that police must obtain a warrant in most cases to search cell phones and smart phones (McCutcheon 2014).

Democrats on Privacy Rights

Democrats advocate policies to confront the threat of terrorism. But they have also repeatedly expressed concerns that this not disrupt the American value on privacy and that, as their 2012 platform stated, all such "practices must always be in line with our Constitution, preserve our people's privacy and civil liberties" (Demo-crat Party 2012). This statement reflects concern from rank-and-file members of the Democratic Party who typically side with privacy rights advocates such as the American Civil Liberties Union (ACLU) on many issues of civil rights and liberties.

The Democratic concern over government surveillance and its impact on per-sonal privacy began in the 1970s when Democratic Senator Frank Church of Idaho chaired a series of congressional investigations into misconduct by the FBI and the CIA. Revelations that these agencies were unlawfully spying on Americans and sometimes provoking them to criminal activity led to new legislation to make these agencies more accountable, including the Foreign Intelligence Surveillance Act of 1978, which mandates that intelligence agencies must gain judicial authorization for electronic surveillance and physical search of persons engaged in espionage or international terrorism against the United States.

Following the terrorist strike on the United States on September 11, 2001, there was a public clamor for greater safety and security. The Bush administration responded by sending Congress the Patriot Act, which granted the U.S. government broad powers to spy on potential terrorists. Democratic leaders, including then senate majority leader Tom Daschle and Senate Judiciary Committee Chair Patrick Leahy, wanted more time to discuss the bill and the implications of its various provisions for civil rights. After an anthrax attack on the U.S. Senate, however, Democrats bowed to mounting political pressure. In the end, only 62 House Democrats and one Democratic senator voted against the bill.

In the aftermath of the legislation and in light of apparent violations of civil rights, however, a number of congressional Democrats argued for amending the Patriot Act to require security agencies to show greater restraint and transparency and provide more information to Congress about their activities. In 2005 when the Patriot Act was up for renewal this cohort of progressive Democrats formed a coalition with libertarian-leaning Republicans to urge for the amendments listed above. Their attempts to amend the law were foiled by Republicans as well as by some Democrats who were stung by their party's loss in the 2004 presidential election and feared that amending the Patriot Act would make the party look weak on terror and lead to an electoral backlash in the 2006 midterms.

Many Democrats were appalled at revelations by Edward Snowden in 2013 of the backdoor practices used by the NSA to gain access to American citizens' personal information. Many Democrats were surprised and angered to learn of the existence of a massive government database created by the NSA to house the records of e-mails and phone calls of millions of Americans, which were then searched for signs of terrorism. Rush Holt, a congressional Democrat from New Jersey, spoke for many in his party when he declared that "it's time to stop treating Americans as suspects first and citizens second." Senator Elizabeth Warren (D-Mass.) urged Congress to "go further to protect the right to privacy, to end the NSA's dragnet surveillance of ordinary Americans, to make the intelligence community more transparent and accountable" (Congressional Record 2014).

There is disagreement within the Democratic Party, however, over the surveillance practices of the NSA and other agencies. President Barack Obama, who took office in 2009, has defended many of the surveillance laws and practices used by the NSA (even though he criticized the Patriot Act for privacy violations in 2003, when he was an Illinois state senator). In 2010, Obama specifically requested that Congress reauthorize key provisions of the Patriot Act that were due to expire in 2010. These included the roving wiretap that allows the government to request an open-ended search warrant. In early 2014, Obama defended the agency in a speech aimed at dissuading fellow Democrats from voting for new restrictions on the agency. In this speech Obama acknowledged the privacy concerns voiced by critics of the U.S. intelligence community, but explained how his administration was providing oversight and imposing new controls to safeguard the privacy rights of U.S. citizens. Obama sought to balance privacy against the need for security. "We cannot unilaterally disarm our intelligence agencies . . . a number of countries, including some who have loudly criticized the NSA, privately acknowledge that America has special responsibilities as the world's only superpower; that our intelligence capabilities are critical to meeting these responsibilities; and that they themselves have relied on the information we obtain to protect their own people" (White House 2014).

Republicans on Privacy Rights

Members of the Republican Party are concerned that government actions not violate the right to privacy, but for many years they have been the more vocal of the two parties in advocating for surveillance of private e-mails, telephone records, and social media as a tool in combating terrorism. Within the GOP, however, significant tensions on this issue are evident. Libertarian-leaning Republicans and members of the Tea Party have been the most zealous about the right to privacy and have continually warned of abuse by spy agencies.

Since the Cold War, the majority of elected Republicans have argued that innocent Americans had nothing to fear from government surveillance. They have supported passage of a variety of legislation to increase government powers for purposes of the national defense and security, ranging from the Cold War–era McCarran Internal Security Act to the Patriot Act.

Many Republicans point to the role that increased surveillance powers played in disrupting terror cells in the United States and in assisting in the prosecution of would-be terrorists. President George Bush signed the Patriot Act into law on October 6, 2001. Bush noted that surveillance was an essential tool for pursuing and stopping terrorists. "This new law that I sign today will allow surveillance of all communications used by terrorists, including e-mails, the Internet, and cell phones." The Patriot Act was supported by nearly every Republican in Congress and polls at that time indicated the majority of Republican or Republican-leaning voters also supported the enhanced surveillance powers of America's intelligence agencies.

For example, when elements of the Patriot Act were set to expire in 2006, the Bush administration and Republicans in Congress supported the renewal and polls found that while many Democrats objected to the reauthorization, the majority of Republicans agreed with Bush who claimed "that law enforcement officials needed to have the same tools against terrorists that are already used against drug dealers and other criminals, while safeguarding the civil liberties of the American people" (Bush 2006).

Support for the Patriot Act did not significantly diminish within the GOP until Edward Snowden released his information about NSA surveillance activities in 2013. In the wake of Snowden's revelations, some polls showed that upward of 70 percent of Republicans polled had lost confidence in the government's ability to protect their privacy (Pew Research Center 2015). Even before this, libertarian leaning Republicans argued against the Patriot Act. In 2001, three Republicans in the House voted against the measure. Congress member Ron Paul, one of the opponents of the bill in 2001, argued throughout the War on Terror that the Patriot Act had gutted the Fourth Amendment guarantee against unwarranted searches and seizures. The Patriot Act, Paul exclaimed, ushered in "the era of warrantless wiretapping, monitoring of our Internet behavior, watering down of probable cause, and much more" (Paul 2014).

Even former proponents of the Patriot Act now believe that American's right to privacy has been lost to the bill. James Sensenbrenner, a Republican congress member from Wisconsin, supported the legislation in 2001 but after the leaks by Edward Snowden in 2013, Sensenbrenner became a vocal critic of the law. Sensenbrenner claimed that the original purpose of the bill had been warped by the wholesale collection of domestic phone records, data dragnets, and warrants issued to public libraries that went beyond the specific targets of terrorism investigations. "The time has come to stop it, and the way we stop it is to approve this amendment," he declared (Weisman 2013).

Further Reading

Bush, George W. 2006. "President Applauds Senate for Voting to Renew Patriot Act," The White House, March 2. Accessed July 10, 2015: http://georgewbush-whitehouse .archives.gov/news/releases/2006/03/20060302-18.html.

Congressional Record. 2014. "Department of Defense Appropriations Act of 2015," *Congressional Record*, June 23, 160 (98): E1048. Accessed July 12, 2015: https://www .congress.gov/congressional-record/2014/6/23/extensions-of-remarks-section/article /E1048-2.

Democratic Party. 2012. Democratic National Platform 2012, "Moving Forward America." Accessed July 11, 2015: http://www.democrats.org/democratic-national-platform.

Greenwald, Glenn. 2014. *No Place to Hide: Edward Snowden, the NSA, and the U.S. Surveillance State*. New York: Metropolitan Books.

McCutcheon, Chuck. 2014. "Privacy," *CQ Researcher*, July 14. Accessed July 10, 2015: http://0-library.cqpress.com.libra.naz.edu/.

Orwell, George. 1983. *1984*. New York: NAL.

Paul, Ron. 2014. "Defeat of USA FREEDOM Act is a Victory for Freedom," The Ron Paul Institute for Peace and Prosperity, November 23. Accessed July 10, 2015: http:// www.ronpaulinstitute.org/archives/featured-articles/2014/november/23/defeat-of -usa-freedom-act-is-a-victory-for-freedom/.

Pew Research Center. 2015. "Americans Privacy Strategies Post Snowden," March 16, 2015. Accessed July 11, 2015: http://www.pewinternet.org/files/2015/03/PI_Americans PrivacyStrategies_0316151.pdf.

Weisman, Jonathan. 2013. "Momentum Builds against N.S.A. Surveillance," *New York Times*, July 29. Accessed July 11, 2015: http://www.nytimes.com/2013/07/29/us/politics/momentum-builds-against-nsa-surveillance.html.

White House. 2014. "Remarks by the President on Review of Signals Intelligence," January 17. Accessed July 12, 2015: https://www.whitehouse.gov/the-press-office/2014/01/17/remarks-president-review-signals-intelligence.

Racial Profiling

At a Glance

Can you apply criminal profiling to law enforcement without prejudice? Some Democrats have expressed concerns that racial and ethnic profiling is inherently discriminatory, and that in some cases the practice has been used as a means of social control over America's poor, black, Latino, and Muslim populations. They are more likely than their GOP counterparts to oppose profiling on civil rights grounds and to question its efficacy as a law enforcement and public safety tool. Generally speaking, Republicans believe that good policing needs to rely on data that includes profiling, and they reject arguments that police blindly target minorities.

Many Democrats . . .

- Believe that police abuse their powers when using racial profiling.
- Support civil rights activists who believe that poor people and minorities are unfairly scrutinized by police.
- Publicize studies that show profiling is ineffective at deterring crime.
- Support legislation barring federal law enforcement from using racial profiling.
- Agree with Republicans that exceptions for profiling be granted to federal antiterrorist agencies.
- Support language condemning racial and religious profiling in their party platform.
- Believe community policing would be improved if police departments were more sensitive to diversity.

Many Republicans . . .

- Believe that criminal profiling is an effective means of identifying those who commit crimes.
- Believe that the disproportionate amount of minorities detained in motor stops and police encounters is due to the high crime rate in urban districts where minorities often live.

- Support stop-and-frisk initiatives to thwart criminal activity.
- Reject the idea that community police tactics are used as a cover for racial profiling.

Overview

Racial and ethnic profiling occurs when law enforcement officials treat individuals as suspicious based on a set of characteristics such as race, class, or ethnicity, which police believe to be associated with crime, rather than any credible evidence or information linking a specific person to a specific crime (NAACP 2014). Racial profiling is prohibited under the Fourteenth Amendment and banned by the federal government. Racial profiling is distinctive from criminal profiling, which correlates behavioral patterns with crime. Profiling is a controversial issue and divides criminal justice officials and civil rights advocates who feel that the poor and minorities are unfairly targeted and harassed by police officials as a result of the practice.

Advocates of profiling claim that it makes sense for police and national security personnel to take such characteristics as race, ethnicity, and gender into consideration when making discretionary decisions in the course of their duties (Bumgarner 2014). Political conservatives argue that academic studies and self-reporting from law enforcement agencies indicating that African Americans and Hispanics are disproportionately subjected to traffic stops and stop-and-frisk actions by police are not a reflection of racial bias by police but the result of these citizens living in high crime districts within cities.

Critics of profiling claim that the practice does not reduce crime. Civil liberties groups such as the American Civil Liberties Union (ACLU) and the National Association for the Advancement of Colored People (NAACP), as well as many elected Democrats, have called on police departments to eliminate racial and ethnic profiling. African Americans have complained that they are too often stopped by police for "driving while black" rather than for any driving violations. Hispanics and Muslims also complained about racial profiling. Hispanics feel singled out by immigration authorities and Muslims by antiterrorist agents (Jost 2013).

Profiling is sometimes associated with the "broken windows" theory of community policing. This theory, popularized by the political scientist James Q. Wilson in the 1980s, hypothesized that if law enforcement was used to reduce petty crimes in a community it would also thwart the rise of serious crimes (Withrow 2010). This theory lay behind the decision of Michael Bloomberg, the mayor of New York City from 2002 to 2013, to institute a "stop and frisk" practice in high crimes areas of the city, whereby officers stopped and frisked pedestrians in hopes of intercepting and seizing weapons or other contraband. The practice was halted with the election of progressive Democrat Bill De Blasio to succeed Bloomberg. De Blasio responded to civil rights activists who used data collected by the city to show that 53 percent of those stopped were African American and 34 percent were Hispanic. A federal judge ruled that the city had to change the practice since it constituted a "policy of indirect racial profiling." The issue of racial profiling assumed new prominence as a political issue in 2014 after several highly publicized cases in which unarmed African Americans were killed in encounters with white police officers.

Democrats on Racial Profiling

The majority of Democrats agree with civil liberty groups that profiling is racist and an unwarranted violation of the Fourth Amendment protection against

---

The End Racial Profiling Act

In 1999, President Clinton condemned the use of racial profiling as a law enforcement tool, echoing the sentiments of many of his Democratic colleagues. In 2001, Democratic lawmakers in Washington introduced a bill called the End Racial Profiling Act (excerpted below). Versions of the End Racial Profiling Act have been introduced in many subsequent Congresses, but as of 2015 supporters have not been able to secure enough support from Republicans for passage.

> End Racial Profiling Act of 2001—Prohibits any law enforcement agency or agent from engaging in racial profiling. Authorizes the United States, or an individual injured by racial profiling, to bring a civil action for declaratory or injunctive relief to enforce this prohibition. Specifies that proof that the routine investigatory activities of law enforcement agents in a jurisdiction have had a disparate impact on racial or ethnic minorities shall constitute prima facie evidence of a violation. Authorizes the court to allow a prevailing plaintiff, other than the United States, reasonable attorneys' fees as part of the costs, including expert fees. Requires Federal law enforcement agencies to:
>
> (1) maintain adequate policies and procedures designed to eliminate racial profiling; and
> (2) cease existing practices that encourage racial profiling
>
> Directs that any application by a State or governmental unit for funding under a covered program include a certification that such unit and any agency to which it is redistributing program funds:
>
> (1) maintains adequate policies and procedures designed to eliminate racial profiling; and
> (2) has ceased existing practices that encourage racial profiling.
>
> Authorizes the Attorney General to make grants to States, law enforcement agencies and other governmental units, Indian tribal governments, or other public and private entities to develop and implement best practice devices and systems to ensure the racially neutral administration of justice. Directs the Attorney General to submit to Congress a report on racial profiling by Federal, State, and local law enforcement agencies.

Source

Govtracks United States. Accessed January 8, 2015: https://www.govtrack.us/congress/bills /107/s989#summary/libraryofcongress.

unreasonable searches and seizures and the Fourteenth Amendment mandate of equal protection under the law. In the 1990s, African Americans, noting that they were subjected to traffic stops more than white drivers, popularized the phrase "driving while black" to explain the cause of their detention by police. In 1999, Democratic President Bill Clinton issued an order requiring the Department of Justice (DOJ) to collect data on racial profiling, which he called a "morally indefensible, deeply corrosive practice . . . Racial profiling is, in fact, the opposite of good police work, where actions are based on hard facts, not stereotypes. It is wrong; it is destructive; and it must stop" (Clinton 1999). The data collected demonstrated a disproportionate number of traffic stops aimed at Hispanic and black motorists. During Clinton's presidency the DOJ investigated numerous complaints of racial profiling and ordered several of these police departments to alter the way they targeted and treated suspects (Weitzer and Tuch 2002).

In 2001, Russell Feingold, a liberal Democratic senator from Wisconsin, introduced the End Racial Profiling Act (ERPA). The bill was believed by some to be on track for passage but after the September 11, 2001, terrorist attacks, legal authorities and elected officials became leery of any legislation that might conceivably limit the ability of federal, state, and local law enforcement officials to detect and thwart potential terrorist or criminal action before it occurred. As a result, no action was taken on ERPA (NAACP 2014). The Democrats responded to this setback by adding a plank to their party platform "Racial and religious profiling is wrong and we will work to stamp it out" (Democratic Party 2004). After the election of Barack Obama to the White House in November 2008, Ben Cardin a Democratic senator from Maryland, reintroduced a similar bill. It failed but Cardin tried again in 2012 and 2013. The bill has strong support from the NAACP and the ACLU and a version of the bill has been offered in the House by Michigan Democrat John Conyers in every Congress since 2011 (Shurford 2012).

In 2009, Henry Louis Gates Jr., a well-known academic, was arrested outside of his own home in Cambridge, Massachusetts, by a white police officer who suspected the black intellectual and Harvard University professor of attempted breaking and entering. President Obama, a Harvard graduate, saw this as an act of racial profiling and used it as a platform to address the issue. "Separate and apart from this incident is that there's a long history in this country of African-Americans and Latinos being stopped by law enforcement disproportionately" (Smith 2009). The case lead to a national discussion on profiling and contributed to Attorney General Eric Holder's directive ordering the DOJ to prepare new guidelines dealing with the issue of racial profiling. After the death of Trayvon Martin, an African American teenager shot by the white vigilante George Zimmerman, President Obama held an unscheduled press briefing on July 19, 2013, in which he asserted that African Americans are too often subjected to groundless scrutiny from law enforcement while engaged in innocent activities like walking, shopping, or driving. Obama suggested that state and local governments enhance training for police officers to instill more sensitivity within them of their own racial biases and to collect data on police actions to determine if patterns of racial profiling existed in their operations (Obama 2013).

Attorney General Holder issued a new set of guidelines in 2014 for local law enforcement. The new guidelines call for action to end all incidents of profiling with limited exceptions for national security but not all civil rights groups were pleased. The ACLU in particular criticized the new guidelines as inadequate (ACLU 2014).

Democrats have also allied with civil rights advocates who criticize the practice of "stop and frisk," a strategy that many police departments used across the United States as part of their community policing strategy. The idea behind this is to interdict most contraband before it can be sold or to confiscate weapons and arrest individuals before they can commit a crime. Cops see this as a deterrent against crime, since potential lawbreakers would know they might be stopped and frisked and would, the theory goes, avoid breaking the law. In most cases, though, the individuals subject to this procedure were people of color and the poor. Civil rights advocates were able to persuade a federal judge in New York to end the practice in Manhattan, but the practice continued in Newark, New Jersey, Philadelphia, and Chicago (Bergner 2014).

Republicans on Racial Profiling

Republicans, in general, have been known as the law-and-order party since the presidency of Richard Nixon, who served from 1969 to 1974. In his 1970 State of the Union address Nixon declared a War on Crime and accused liberal justices of caring more about the criminal than the victim. He satirized his predecessor in the White House, Lyndon Johnson, who served from 1963 to 1969, for declaring War on Poverty. "If there is one area where the word 'war' is appropriate it is in the fight against crime. We must declare and win the war against the criminal elements which increasingly threaten our cities, our homes, and our lives" (Nixon 1970).

Unable to get many of his anticrime initiatives through Congress, Nixon sought to change the ideological direction of the Supreme Court by nominating more politically conservative justices. In tone and action, the Supreme Court did change after one of Nixon's nominees, William H. Rehnquist, was elevated in 1986 to be chief justice of the Supreme Court by President Ronald Reagan. During Reagan's presidency, which lasted from 1981 to 1989, Rehnquist wrote the Court's decision in the 1988 case *United States v. Sokolow*, which upheld the right of police to use objectively constructed profiles to identify possible criminals. Under Rehnquist, the Court unanimously approved the right of police to use suspected traffic violations as a means of stopping motorists and searching for evidence of other crimes. This eventually led to charges by civil rights advocates that the police were stopping motorists for driving while black.

Republicans generally have also advocated the use of community policing using political scientist James Q. Wilson's "broken window" model of zero tolerance for minor crimes to improve the overall sense of community and acts as a deterrent to major crimes (Bergner 2014). Community policing has become the standard since the 1990s, and many Republicans believe that its implementation has played a key role in the overall decline of the crime rate in the United States. Democrats, however, have criticized some community policing policies as exacerbating friction between poorer communities and police (U.S. Department of Justice 2013). With one of the largest police forces in the nation, New York City has an influential role in shaping how communities across the United States respond to crime. Thus, after community policing was implemented in New York City in the 1990s, many cities across the United States followed suit. One aspect of community policing was the creation of the stop-and-frisk program in which police detained people on the street and searched their persons for contraband items. The program was so successful that it continued until 2013 and was widely credited by city officials with reducing overall crime in the city and protecting lives in minority neighborhoods.

Under the administration of Democratic Mayor Bill de Blasio, New York police were told to stop the practice and Republicans responded with an Op-Ed piece in the *Wall Street Journal,* a paper with a track record of supporting and shaping Republican opinion. "The NYPD's critics object, in particular, to the department's long-standing practice of maintaining order in public spaces. This practice, referred to as Broken Windows or quality-of-life or order-maintenance policing, asserts that, in communities contending with high levels of disruption, maintaining order improves the quality of life for residents and reduces crime." The author, Police Commissioner Bratton, cited several academic articles and studies that tied community policing to lower crime rates. Bratton also cited evidence that many African American and Hispanic community members appreciated the better quality of life community policing provided. The practice is also common in cities like Detroit, Philadelphia, Chicago, and Los Angeles. However, with the death of Michael Brown in Ferguson, Missouri, and the rise of the #blacklivesmatter movement, many cities began to scrutinize their policing policies to reflect on whether they constituted racial profiling. This incensed many tough-on-crime Republicans. One scholar even argued that based on statistics, "Police officers have more to fear from the public than the public has to fear from police."

In the aftermath of the September 11, 2001, terrorist attacks, civil rights advocates and some Muslim and Arab-American groups charged that Muslims and people of Arab descent were increasingly becoming victims of racial profiling. The Transportation Safety Administration (TSA), which is responsible for security at U.S. airports, noted that people of varying races and ethnicities have been subjected to special security searches. But many conservative American lawmakers, voters, and pundits defended racial profiling as a legitimate and vital national security tool. One such advocate of racial and ethnic profiling is columnist Charles Krauthammer. "As it happens, the suicide bombers who attacked us on Sept. 11 were . . . al-Qaeda: young, Islamic, Arab and male," he wrote. "That is not a stereotype. That is a fact. And there is no hiding from it, as there is no hiding from

Linda Sarsour, director of the Arab American Association of New York, speaks to a crowd of March 2 Justice supporters in Staten Island, New York, on April 13, 2015. Sarsour is co-chairperson of the 250-mile march from New York to Washington, D.C., to support an end of racial profiling and justice against police brutality. (Photo by Robert Nickelsberg/Getty Images)

the next al-Qaeda suicide bomber. He has to be found and stopped. And you don't find him by strip searching female flight attendants or 80-year-old Irish nuns" (Krauthammer 2002).

Under President George W. Bush, who served in the White House from 2001 to 2009, the DOJ issued its first racial profiling guidance under then attorney general John Ashcroft. The DOJ banned profiling based on race but did not cover religion, ancestry, or other factors and made exceptions for national security and border protection agents (Johnson 2004).

Further Reading

American Civil Liberties Union (ACLU). 2014. "ACLU Response to Revised DOJ Guidance on the Use of Race by Federal Law Enforcement Agencies," December 8. Accessed January 6, 2015: https://www.aclu.org/criminal-law-reform-racial-justice/aclu-response -revised-doj-guidance-use-race-federal-law-enforceme.

Bergner, Daniel. 2014. "Is Stop and Frisk Worth It?" The Atlantic, April edition. Accessed October 31, 2015: http://www.theatlantic.com/magazine/archive/2014/04/is-stop-and -frisk-worth-it/358644/.

Bumgarner, Jeff. 2014. Profiling and Criminal Justice in America: A Reference Handbook. Santa Barbara: ABC-CLIO.

Clinton, William J. 1999. "Opening Remarks at a Roundtable Discussion on Increasing Trust Between Communities and Law Enforcement Officers," June 9. Accessed January 6, 2015: http://www.presidency.ucsb.edu/ws/?pid=57700.

Democratic Party. 2004. "Democratic Party Platform of 2004," July 26. Accessed January 11, 2015: http://www.presidency.ucsb.edu/ws/?pid=29613.

Johnson, Kevin R. 2004. "Racial Profiling after September 11: The Department of Justice's 2003 Guidelines," *Immigration and Nationality Law Review*, 85.

Jost, Kenneth. 2013. "Racial Profiling," *CQ Researcher* 23 (42), November 22: 1005–1028. Accessed January 6, 2015: http://0-library.cqpress.com.libra.naz.edu/cqresearcher /cqresrre2013112200.

Krauthammer, Charles. 2002. "The Case for Profiling," *Time,* March 10. Accessed January 8, 2015: http://content.time.com/time/magazine/article/0,9171,216319,00.html.

NAACP. 2014. *Born Suspect: Stop-and-Frisk Abuses & the Continued Fight to End Racial Profiling in America.* Baltimore: NAACP, 19.

Nixon, Richard. 1970. "Annual Message to the Congress on the State of the Union," January 22. Accessed January 8, 2015: http://www.presidency.ucsb.edu/ws/?pid=2921.

Obama, Barack. 2013. "Transcript: President Obama Addresses Race, Profiling and Florida Law," CNN, July 19. Accessed January 6, 2015: http://www.cnn.com/2013/07/19 /politics/obama-zimmerman-verdict/.

Shurford, Reginald T. 2012. "The End Racial Profiling Act: Giving Us a Way to Fight Back," ACLU, April 20. Accessed January 8, 2015: https://www.aclu.org/blog/racial-justice /end-racial-profiling-act-giving-us-way-fight-back.

Smith, Ben. 2009. "Obama: Cambridge Police Acted 'Stupidly,'" Politico, June 22. Accessed January 9, 2015: http://www.politico.com/blogs/bensmith/0709/Obama_Cambridge _police_acted_stupidly.html.

U.S. Department of Justice. 2013. "Crime in the United States, 2013," Federal Bureau of Investigation. Accessed December 30, 2014: http://www.fbi.gov/about-us/cjis/ucr /crime-in-the-u.s/2013/crime-in-the-u.s.-2013/cius-home.

Weitzer, Ronald, and Steven Tuch. 2002. "Perceptions of Racial Profiling: Race, Class, and Personal Experience," *Criminology,* 40 (20), May: 435–456.

Withrow, Brian. 2010. *The Racial Profiling Controversy: What Every Police Leader Should Know.* New York: Looseleaf Law Publications.

Religious Freedom

At a Glance

The Constitution guarantees the free exercise of religion in the First Amendment, but determining how this should be implemented in government policy has been a dividing point for Democrats and Republicans since the 1960s. Many Democrats believe that the free exercise of religion means an individual's private right to worship as they want should not be infringed. They reject an expansive reading of this right that would allow religious convictions to enter into public life, for example, in schools, government agencies, or laws that would allow individuals or companies to discriminate against other people. Many Republicans embrace an expansive reading of this and some would still like to see the reinstatement of school prayer as well as religious exemptions for people who do not want to provide services for a lifestyle they deem sinful.

Many Democrats . . .

- Believe in the free exercise of religion as long as it does not discriminate against others.
- Support the right of minority religions to openly practice their faith.
- Believe that there should be a strict wall dividing church and state.
- Are opposed to religious groups and houses of worship imposing their beliefs on the public.
- Reject mandatory or officially sanctioned prayer and Bible reading in public schools.
- Believe that most religious freedom laws are a means to discriminate against the LGBT community.

Many Republicans . . .

- Believe in the free exercise of religion and argue that it should not be regulated by the government.
- Support the right of everyone including Christians to openly advocate and practice their faith in public.

- Believe that Supreme Court decisions that ended school prayer and Bible reading undercut religious freedom and hurt public morality.
- Believe that it is acceptable to have nativity scenes and the 10 commandments displayed on government property.
- Worry that liberal social policies may force people to choose between abandoning the principles of their religion and facing legal action for violating government imposed regulations.

Overview

Any question of religious freedom in the United States leads directly back to the First Amendment of the Constitution. The First Amendment contains the Establishment Clause, which forbids the U.S. government from establishing a state-sponsored religion, and the Free Exercise Clause, which forbids the United States from interfering with a person's right to worship as they please. Debate over how to protect Americans from government interference in their religious worship is thus as old as the nation itself.

In the 20th century the question of religious freedom became a hotly contested political issue and led to a number of Supreme Court cases that struck down practices deemed to be governmental promotion of religion, such as Bible reading and prayer in public schools, or the placement of nativity scenes on government property. The Supreme Court also raised questions of public funding for religious schools and enacted new measures to ensure that any financial assistance be used only to promote secular or nonreligious aims. The Supreme Court also tempered the absolute right of a person to exercise their religion if such practices interfere with public policies, such as requiring vaccinations, attending public schools, or receiving treatment for various ailments in established medical facilities.

Supreme Court decisions that cited the Establishment Clause to eliminate government sanctioned religious activity outraged conservative Christians who wanted to maintain the status quo of reading scripture and observing public prayer in public schools, as well using religious symbols in their town squares for Christmas or other religious holidays. They organized and began voting for candidates who supported the restoration of prayer in schools, the display of nativity scenes, and antiabortion legislation. Responding to the rise of the religious right, many liberal progressives and people who reject religion formed their own organizations to oppose government sanctioned religious practices and overwhelmingly supported Democrats for public office. These voters want to keep churches and other centers of worship from influencing public policy, believing such actions violate their rights and erase the "separation of church and state," a phrase commonly used by individuals and organizations associated with this position.

Debates about religious practices, or the free exercise of religious faith, further intensified in the 1990s after a Supreme Court ruling that the government no longer had to show a "compelling state interest" to justify laws restricting religious practices but could restrict religious practices as long as the law was not aimed at religious groups alone. In the 1990s, there was a sharp rise in first generation Americans, many of whom had non-Western belief systems. Worried that the new ruling might undercut cultural diversity and the right to worship as they pleased, Democrats and Republicans worked together to pass the Religious Freedom Restoration Act in 1993. Signing the law, President Clinton claimed that it held the government "to a very high level of proof before it interferes with someone's free exercise of religion" (Steinfels 1993). Over the next 20 years, 20 states enacted similar laws to protect individuals from state interference.

The religious freedom laws protected individuals from the undue burden of government interference, but what of corporations? The answer to this question came about after the Affordable Care Act was passed in 2010 by President Obama and Democrats in Congress. Obamacare generated a host of legal challenges, including several suits aimed at the mandate requiring employers to offer all female employees free contraception in their health care plans. Some employers felt this violated their religious freedom because their faith rejected the use of contraception and abortion. The Supreme Court in *Burwell v. Hobby Lobby* in 2014 cited the Religious Freedom Restoration Act in its decision to allow privately held corporations, such as Hobby Lobby, to be removed from the mandate to provide contraceptives to employees (Burwell 2013). Many women's rights groups and Democrats argued that the decision in the Hobby Lobby case extended the original law too far and allowed for discrimination against women. They also suggested that the decision might allow some businesses to discriminate against same-sex couples who sought wedding services such as florists, catering, etc.

After Indiana passed a religious freedom law in March 2015, social liberals attacked it as a transparently homophobic bill. As journalist Jonathan Cohn wrote in a story for the Huffington Post, April 1, 2015, "There's no real mystery about the purpose of the 'Religious Freedom Restoration Act,' which Republican Governor Mike Pence signed last week. The goal is to give business owners a stronger legal defense if they refuse to serve lesbian, gay, bisexual and transgender customers and want to cite their faith as justification for their actions." The negative reaction to the new law, including announcements of boycotts of the state from high-profile organizations and criticism from business and civic leaders within the state, led Indiana, which had no laws protecting the rights of same-sex couples, to amend the bill to protect against discrimination. Several other states that had been considering religious freedom laws, such as Georgia, withdrew their bills from consideration after witnessing the public backlash experienced by Indiana. Nonetheless, numerous states have established religious freedom laws in the past 20 years.

Democrats on Religious Freedom

Democrats support religious freedom but are more likely to see it as flourishing when the government maintains a strict divide between church and state. Although many Democrats practice some form of religion, research has shown that voters with Democratic leanings are less likely to describe themselves as religious or attend a house of worship or religious institution than voters who self-identify as Republican or leaning Republican (Pew Research Center for Religion and Public Life 2012).

In the 1990s, though, Democratic President Bill Clinton signed the Religious Freedom Restoration Act of 1993, which many observers have cited as a model for state-level religious freedom laws that have been criticized by liberals as discriminatory. The 1993 law actually passed with broad bipartisan support—it sailed through the House without objection and was passed in the Senate by a 97–3 vote—and Clinton argued that the bill would protect people's right to worship without government interference. The law effectively protected the rights of religious minorities including Muslims, Sikhs, and Native Americans by allowing them to practice their religious faith without government intrusion. From 1993 to 2013, 19 states passed laws with at least some similarities to this federal law, though none became as divisive as Indiana's 2015 law.

In light of the 2013 Supreme Court decision recognizing the right of same-sex marriage that was followed by the 2014 Hobby Lobby decision that allowed corporations the same free exercise rights as individuals, many Democrats have expressed heightened concern that the Freedom of Religion laws would allow Christians to legally discriminate against gays and lesbians simply by stating that the LGBT lifestyle offended some religious sensibilities. The laws were criticized by an array of elected Democrats and also by former secretary of state Hillary Clinton, who had been first lady during Bill Clinton's presidency. Clinton attacked the laws in Arkansas and Indiana, claiming that rather than allowing religious liberty they allowed religious bigotry.

Other Democrats castigated these laws as well, describing them as bigoted, intolerant, and dismissive of the rights of non-Christians. One such critic was Elliot Mincberg, who was an Obama appointee to the Department of Housing and Urban Development from 2010 to 2014. Mincberg noted that the number of states introducing laws modeled on the Religious Freedom Restoration Act in 2015 alone nearly matched the number of states that had passed RFRA-style laws from a two-decade span of time between 1993 and 2013. "Why the huge uptick now?" he asked. "I think it's a combination of the perceived dangers to the far right from the move towards LGBT marriage equality and the perceived opportunity created just last year by the Supreme Court's 5–4 rewriting of RFRA in *Burwell v. Hobby Lobby* . . . For far-right activists and legislators concerned about marriage equality and other LGBT rights, Hobby Lobby provided the perfect opportunity: Pass state RFRA laws and effectively grant a religious exemption claim from LGBT anti-discrimination laws and local ordinances" (Mincberg 2015).

But although many Democrats have been quick to condemn so-called religious liberty laws as thinly veiled efforts to provide legal cover for discriminatory treatment of LGBT individuals, reporter David Weigel of *Bloomberg News* speculated that the Democrats could pay a political price for their position. "Democrats are settling in as the party that opposes religious liberty laws," he wrote. "Most of the party's potential presidential candidates have taken that stance . . . [But] all of the critics are on the wrong side of public polling. According to a March [2015] edition of the Marist poll, 54 percent of Americans agreed with "allowing First Amendment religious liberty protection or exemptions for faith based organizations and individuals even when it conflicts with government laws" (Weigel 2015).

Tensions within the Democratic Party are more likely to surface over issues of religion due to the nature of the Democratic coalition of voters. Catholics remain the second largest segment of Democratic-leaning voters after the "nones," voters who are uninterested in religion. Catholic voters are more likely to want religion recognized in public and are also against social policies such as abortion. Thus, some Catholics were displeased by Supreme Court decisions in the 1960s such as *Engel v. Vitale,* which ended the practice of public prayer in schools, and *Murray v. Curlett*, which ended the practice of Bible reading in the classroom. The influence of these voters may explain why President Bill Clinton initially seemed to support a constitutional amendment to restore prayer or a moment of silence to public education. His early comments about the amendment sparked controversy within his party as organizations that are affiliated with liberal and progressive issues, such as People for the American Way and the American Civil Liberties Union (ACLU) were skeptical of religious interference in the political process and pressured Clinton and other elected officials to maintain secularism in public policy. The ACLU urged Democrats to oppose the Republican-sponsored proposal to amend the Constitution to allow for school prayer and disparaged Clinton for comments showing support for the amendment. Within a week, Clinton withdrew his support, stating, "I think that that is inherently coercive in a nation with the amount of religious diversity we have in this country" (Wines 1994).

Some Catholics were also unhappy with the 1973 Supreme Court decision of *Roe v. Wade*, which legalized abortion, which is condemned by Catholic doctrine. Thus, freedom of religion issues surfaced within the Democratic Party when they fashioned the Affordable Care Act in 2010. A debate erupted within the party between House Democrats, led by Bart Stupak of Michigan, who wanted the bill to include a statement saying federal funds would not be used to pay for an abortion or any of the costs associated with this procedure. Pro-choice Democrats balked at this, and the issue was only resolved when President Barack Obama offered to issue an executive order banning the use of federal funds for abortion after the bill became law. He did so immediately after the law was passed by signing Executive Order 13535.

Democrats have traditionally been very supportive of the right of religious minorities to worship as they please. For example, in the aftermath of the September 11,

2001, attacks, Democrats were critical of police agencies that have used the religion of individuals as a pretext for profiling. President Barack Obama has reached out to the Muslim community in the United States and abroad to show respect for practitioners of that faith. However, Democrats were divided when members of the Muslim faith wanted to build a mosque two blocks from the site where the Twin Towers fell on September 11. Some Democrats, such as President Obama and New York City congress member Jerrold Nadler, supported the effort. Other Democrats disagreed and wanted the mosque to relocate elsewhere or have the zoning board of New York City reject the application. Representative John Hall, a Democrat whose district was outside of New York City, was quoted in a story for the online publication Daily Caller on August 19, 2010, "I think honoring those killed on September 11 and showing sensitivity to their families, it would be best if the center were built at a different location." Despite protests and street clashes the project went on with the support of the Democrat-led New York City government and opened to the public in 2011.

Republicans on Religious Freedom

The Republican Party generally is less concerned with First Amendment issues surrounding the Establishment Clause but is deeply concerned that individuals within society are not able to freely exercise their religious beliefs and practices. This concern stems from Supreme Court decisions made in the 1960s, which created a clear demarcation between church and state. Many Republicans wanted to keep religion, especially Christianity, in the public eye to promote not only their religious convictions but also public morals and to honor the United States, which many believed was founded as a Christian nation.

In the 1970s, many conservative Christians sought to influence public policy by creating organizations, such as the Moral Majority, to shape public policy and support political parties in hopes of reversing the Supreme Court decisions. Although in 1976 evangelicals supported a Democratic governor for president, they found Carter's support for religion too weak and his government policies too liberal. Since 1980, self-identified conservative Christians have overwhelmingly voted Republican in local, state, and national elections. These voters believe that churches and other houses of worship should have their say in social and other political matters (Pew Research Center on Religion in Public Life 2014). This belief was enshrined in the GOP platform in 2012: "We assert every citizen's right to apply religious values to public policy and the right of faith-based organizations to participate fully in public programs without renouncing their beliefs, removing religious symbols, or submitting to government-imposed hiring practices" (Republican Party 2012).

The rise of the religious right in the 1970s and 1980s coincided with the shift within the Republican Party away from moderate positions that were socially liberal and fiscally conservative, to positions that embraced traditional family and social values. Once conservatives dominated the party, the party platform began to call for a restoration of prayer in schools. Newt Gingrich, Speaker of the House, 1995–1999, solidified the conservative domination of the Republican Party by leading the GOP to majority rule in both the House and the Senate. Immediately after that election Gingrich offered an amendment to the Constitution that would have restored prayer to public schools. Although the amendment was rejected, the call for a return to voluntary student-led prayer continues to the present.

Republicans applauded, in 2007, when the Bush administration issued a legal memorandum that detailed a very broad interpretation of the Religious Freedom Restoration Act. According to the Bush administration's reading of the law, faith-based organizations received sweeping exemptions from most U.S. discrimination laws. Since that time, Republican efforts to give religious belief—and particularly Christian teachings—a more prominent place in American public life have continued. In 2012, for example, the Republican Party platform called for "the public display of the Ten Commandments as a reflection of our history and of our country's Judeo-Christian heritage." The platform also affirmed "the right of students to engage in prayer at public school events in public schools and to have equal access to public schools and other public facilities to accommodate religious freedom in the public square." Efforts by Republicans to restore what they see as the legitimate right of people of faith to pray in schools also led to legislation in Southern

Hobby Lobby supporters react to the U.S. Supreme Court decision in Washington, D.C., on June 30, 2014. The high court ruled in a 5-4 decision in favor of Hobby Lobby saying that some private companies can be exempted on religious grounds, from health care reform's requirement that employer-sponsored health insurance policies cover contraception. (Photo by Mark Wilson/Getty Images)

states. For example, in 2014, Republican legislators in South Carolina passed a law requiring a moment of silence and private prayer at the start of the school day.

According to the GOP platform in 2012, Republicans "oppose government discrimination against businesses due to religious views." As a practical matter, this is a statement of support for the right of businesses to opt out of social policies that conflict with their religious beliefs, such as the Hobby Lobby Corporation, which sued the federal government over a health care mandate requiring them to pay for contraception and chemical abortion aids in their employee health care plan. The company successfully argued to the Supreme Court that this mandate amounted to the company assenting to the belief that abortion is not murder. Citing the 1993 Freedom of Religion law passed by Congress and signed by Bill Clinton, the Supreme Court in a 5–4 narrowly written ruling, sided with Hobby Lobby. In the wake of Hobby Lobby ruling in 2014, Republicans in Indiana, Arkansas, and Georgia urged passage of religious freedom laws to protect businesses and individuals from state interference. Progressives saw this as a means to discriminate against same-sex couples and mounted an effective social media campaign. They elicited disparaging remarks from Democratic leaders about Republican prejudice, and large corporations such as Apple and Walmart pressured lawmakers to rescind the measures. Republican leaders abandoned the law in Georgia and rewrote the Indiana and Arkansas legislation to address accusations that they would provide legal cover for discrimination against members of the LGBT community.

The Republican Party is not entirely monolithic when it comes to issues of social conservatism and religion, however. Economic conservatives are not as tied to the dogma of social conservatives, and this cleavage was seen when Indiana passed the religious freedom law. Republicans between the ages of 18–29 who support same-sex marriage allied with economic conservatives to pressure Indiana officials to revise the law. In a press release, the U.S. Chamber of Commerce—typically closely aligned with the Republican Party on economic issues—urged changes in the law. Former Florida governor Jeb Bush, when he was still a contender for his party's nomination for the White House in 2016, also called for revision of the law. Other Republican lawmakers expressed similar sentiments. For example, Senator Mark Kirk of Illinois stated in 2015 that "married same-sex couples deserve equal treatment under the law." Meanwhile, social conservatives in the GOP, such as Senator Ted Cruz of Texas and other potential candidates for the 2016 GOP presidential nomination, announced their support for the law as originally passed.

Further Reading

Burwell v. Hobby Lobby Stores. 2013. The Oyez Project at IIT Chicago-Kent College of Law. Accessed April 2, 2015: http://www.oyez.org/cases/2010-2019/2013/2013_13_354.

Mincberg, Elliot. 2015. "Hobby Lobby Comes Home to Roost as States Consider 'Religious Freedom' Legislation," Huffington Post, March 31. http://www.huffingtonpost.com /elliot-mincberg/hobby-lobby-comes-home-to_b_6980412.html.

Pew Research Center for Religion and Public Life. 2012. "'Nones' on the Rise," October 9. Accessed July 7, 2015: http://www.pewforum.org/2012/10/09/nones-on-the-rise/.

Pew Research Center on Religion in Public Life. 2014. "Religion in Public Life," September 22. Accessed July 6, 2015: http://www.pewforum.org/2014/09/22/section-1-religion-in -public-life.

Republican Party. 2012. "We the People: The Restoration of Constitutional Government." Accessed July 6, 2015: https://www.gop.com/platform/we-the-people/.

Steinfels, Peter. 1993. "Clinton Signs Law Protecting Religious Practices," *New York Times*, November 17. Accessed July 7, 2015: http://www.nytimes.com/1993/11/17/us/clinton -signs-law-protecting-religious-practices.html.

Weigel, David. 2015. "Democrats Turn against Religious Freedom Laws. Voters Don't Agree with Them." Bloomberg News, April 1, 2015. http://www.bloomberg.com/politics /articles/2015-04-01/democrats-turn-against-religious-freedom-laws-voters-don-t -agree-with-them-.

Wines, Michael. 1994. "Clinton Backs Off on School Prayer Proposal," *New York Times,* November 23. Accessed July 7, 2015: http://www.nytimes.com/1994/11/23/us/clinton -backs-off-on-school-prayer-proposal.html.

Reparations

At a Glance

Should modern-day Americans be held accountable for past discrimination, oppression, and murder against generations of African Americans? This is the key question raised in the debate over reparations for the descendants of enslaved African Americans. Reparations are financial payments to individuals who have suffered a wrong. For example, more than 80,000 Japanese Americans received reparations totaling $1.6 billion from the U.S. government for their internment during World War II.

Some scholars and liberal civil rights activists, including men and women closely allied with the Democratic Party, have proposed that similar restitution be offered to African Americans today in recognition of the enslavement and oppression experienced by their ancestors. As scholar Alfred L. Brophy wrote, "The moral claim [for reparations] persists because the brutality and stolen labor of slavery, and the grim years of Jim Crow segregation that followed, have left a legacy of lost wealth and opportunity. Such legacy continues to burden African-Americans today" (Brophy 2014). Conservative Republicans have opposed the idea of reparations payments for African Americans. They claim that it penalizes a generation of individuals who had nothing to do with the crimes of the past, while forcing them to make payments to individuals who have not been directly wronged by slavery.

Many Democrats . . .

- Believe that African Americans today continue to suffer vestigial damage from the institution of slavery.
- Believe that African Americans should receive financial reparation for this long-term damage.
- Have supported apologies for slavery in the House and Senate and many state governments.
- Support proposals to create a federal commission to study slavery and reparations.

Many Republicans . . .

- Believe that while slavery was horrific, its scars have faded and do not hinder today's African American community.
- Believe that talk of reparations merely stokes the feeling of victimization among African Americans, which erodes their capacity to take steps to succeed in U.S. society.
- Are concerned that a formal apology to African Americans by state and federal legislatures would lay the basis for a legal claim for reparations.
- Reject proposals to establish a commission to study reparations.
- Believe that it would be unjust and racist to hold the white population responsible for actions that occurred hundreds of years in the past.

Overview

Should living African Americans be compensated for the transatlantic slave trade, slavery, sexual slavery, genocide, disfranchisement, and the multiple forms of discrimination and oppression their ancestors experienced even after the end of slavery? Liberal academics and civil rights activists have suggested that the lasting scar of American slavery has contributed for endemic social and economic problems faced by a plurality of African Americans in the United States. They would like a formal apology from the U.S. government and some form of economic payment for the suffering of generations of black Americans. As precedent, they point to the apology and small restitution offered Japanese Americans by the United States in the wake of their suffering at the hands of the American government during World War II.

Conservatives, some of whom are Republican, have rejected this call. Slavery, they argue, was a horrific institution but one that occurred generations ago. They reject the idea that something that happened two centuries ago is the cause of poverty in the African American community today. Furthermore, they point out that government programs for affirmative action already exist to compensate for any past injustices.

The debate over reparations has its origins in the aftermath of the American Civil War, when many Radical Republicans advocated for a plan to provide the new freedmen with 40 acres and a mule each to assist them in the transition from enslavement to freedom. The plan was quashed by then president Andrew Johnson, who was allied with conservative Republicans and Democrats. The idea was reborn during the Civil Rights era when Audley Moore, a political activist located in Harlem, founded the Reparations Committee of Descendants of United States Slaves. Moore, who was nicknamed "Queen Mother," pioneered grassroots education on reparations and spent the next 30 years educating and enlisting black activists and intellectuals to her cause. Moore influenced many African Americans, including Charles Ogletree Jr., a professor at Harvard Law School.

Ogletree cochaired the Reparations Committee and sought to make corporations involved in the 18th- and 19th-century slave trade pay reparations through court claims (Coates 2014).

Simultaneously, survivors of the Japanese relocation program, which forcibly evacuated thousands of American citizens of Japanese descent living on the West Coast to internment camps during World War II, organized in 1970 to press their claim to reparations for lost property and hardship. They succeeded in 1987 when Congress issued a formal apology and reparations in the form of $20,000 payments to survivors and their families (Henry 2003). In 1993, Congress issued a formal apology for the U.S. conquest of Hawaii and the deprivation of sovereignty to the indigenous peoples. These developments encouraged African American activists to organize the National Coalition of Blacks for Reparations in America or N'COBRA. It also led John Conyers, a U.S. representative from Michigan, to introduce H.R. 40, the Commission to Study Reparation Proposals for African Americans Act, in 1989. The bill's purpose is to create a government study on the impact of slavery and to make recommendations for reparations to the 35 million American descendants of enslaved Africans. Conyers has introduced the bill in every Congress for the past 25 years (Conyers n.d.).

Opponents of the bill believe the entire idea is flawed and doubt the benefits of giving a select group of people money they have not earned. These critics readily acknowledge that slavery was a pernicious institution that had devastating consequences for millions of people, but they see little connection between the wrongs committed against the slaves in the past and the lives of their descendants today.

Democrats on Reparations

Support for reparations is strong among African Americans, who are a key voting constituency within the Democratic Party. Groups such as the National Association for the Advancement of Colored People (NAACP), the Southern Christian Leadership Conference (SCLC), the Rainbow PUSH Coalition, and the Leadership Conference for Civil Rights have all endorsed the idea of reparations. Polls of Africans Americans show the majority strongly favor this idea. Because these civil rights groups and African American voters are important and effective members of the Democratic coalition, the call for reparations is not easy for party leaders to discount. The seriousness of this issue is shown in the intense debate over how the government and private industries, which were historically involved in the slave trade, should appropriately show remorse. Some people maintain that a sincere apology would alleviate tension between the government and the African American community. Many feel that financial restitution is necessary to redress wrongs and make amends. One estimate is that financial restitution to the descendants of slavery might run as high as $10 trillion, with a low estimate of $1.5 trillion. Civil rights organizations have suggested this should be granted in the form of free education and job opportunities for African Americans. Many individuals on the other hand would prefer to see the money given to individual families or to black communities across the United States.

At the national level, few Democrats have publicly supported reparations for descendants of victims of the trans-Atlantic slave trade, and the party made no mention of it in their official 2012 party platform. However, elected Democrats in large northern cities such as Baltimore, Chicago, Cleveland, Dallas, Detroit, and Evanston have all endorsed calls to consider reparations. The Democrat-led state legislature of California also endorsed the study of reparations (Mount Holyoke College n.d.). In 2012, the Green Party, a small progressive party to the left of mainstream Democrats, officially called for reparations in their party platform. "We commit to full and complete reparations to the African American community of this nation for the past four hundred plus years of genocide, slavery, land-loss, destruction of original identity and the stark disparities which haunt the present evidenced in unemployment statistics, substandard and inadequate education, higher levels of mortality including infant and maternal mortality and the practice of mass incarceration" (Green Party 2012).

Some Democratic presidents have issued apologies for enslavement. President Bill Clinton, who served as president from 1993 to 2001, offered a formal apology to the indigenous people of Hawaii for the role the United States played in the overthrow of their government and later annexation by the United States. Later in his presidency, Clinton expressed regret to West African nations for U.S. involvement in the international slave trade (Robinson 2001). America's first African American president, Barack Obama, who took office in 2009, has remained silent on the issue of reparations. The author of a recent biography of Obama suggested that the president is ideologically in favor of the idea but believes the issue politically untenable in the face of stiff opposition from Republicans and many whites in his own party (Remnick 2011).

Advocates for reparations believe this is more evidence of racism in the United States. "It's because it's black folks making the claim," Nkechi Taifa, who helped found N'COBRA, said. "People who talk about reparations are considered left lunatics. But all we are talking about is studying [reparations]. As John Conyers has said, we study everything. We study the water, the air. We can't even study the issue? This bill does not authorize one red cent to anyone" (Coates 2014).

Although financial reparations have not been forthcoming, apologies for slavery have grown since the mid-2000s. In 2008, Representative Steve Cohen, a Democrat representing a black majority district in Tennessee, offered a resolution in Congress apologizing to African Americans for slavery and post–Civil War oppression. The House, under the control of the Democratic Party, passed the resolution by voice vote, which meant that individual votes were not recorded (NPR 2008). According to a report by Krissah Thompson in the *Washington Post* published on June 19, 2009, the Senate also under Democratic control, unanimously passed a similar apology in 2009. Many states with Democratic control of the legislature mirrored the actions of Congress. Beginning in 2007 with Virginia, Alabama, Connecticut,

Florida, North Carolina, and Maryland issued apologies or expressed regret for slavery, but none endorsed reparations. Advocates for reparations have made the case that such acknowledgments are useful for any future movement on the issue and could be the basis of a lawsuit against the United States, individual states, or even private companies that were involved in the slave trade (Davis 2014).

Republicans on Reparations

Conservative Republicans frequently frame reparations as a course of action that would in effect make all whites collectively guilty for crimes committed centuries in the past. David Horowitz, a conservative writer and founder of the eponymously named Horowitz Foundation, claimed that reparations were another "attempt to turn African-Americans into victims. It sends a damaging message to the African-American community." One of the main criticisms of the movement voiced by Horowitz and other conservative thinkers is that it perpetuates the stereotype that African Americans are victims who are incapable of reshaping their own environment and controlling their own destiny. From their perspective, reparations talk is counterproductive because it makes it more difficult for African Americans to take the initiative in improving their own lives (Horowitz 2001). Opponents also claim that this situation is perpetuated by leaders of civil rights organizations who gain political clout by speaking on behalf of these "victims." This idea is echoed by conservative African Americans such as Juan Williams (Williams 2007), a writer and broadcaster for PBS and Fox News, and Walter Williams a conservative economist and pundit (Williams 2011). The conservative position on reparations has been featured on conservative talk radio by hosts such as Rush Limbaugh, Laura Ingraham, Glenn Beck, Sean Hannity, and dozens of other broadcast outlets that attract millions of Republican listeners. Many of these critics have charged that reparations proposals are merely typical liberal redistributionism under another guise.

In addition, conservatives frequently scoff at the very idea of reparations for actions that occurred in the distant past. As Henry Hyde, a leading Republican in the House of Representatives for many years, stated, "The notion of collective guilt for what people did [220 plus] years ago, that this generation should pay a debt for that generation, is an idea whose time has gone. I never owned a slave. I never oppressed anybody. I don't know that I should have to pay for someone who did [own slaves] generations before I was born" (Mount Holyoke College n.d.).

Republicans who oppose financial reparations may also oppose formal apologies for the institution of slavery, fearing that these might be used by pro-reparations groups in lawsuits against the United States or against specific states involved in slavery. Virginia, Maryland, Connecticut, Florida, Maryland, New Jersey, and North Carolina have issued apologies or expressed sincere regret for slavery (Davis 2014). These measures were opposed by many Republicans. When Virginia offered its resolution in 2007, one Republican argued that "our black citizens should get over it . . . are we going to force the Jews to apologize for killing Christ?" (Davis 2014).

As reported by Jeremy Peters in the *New York Times,* January 13, 2008, Richard Merkt, a New Jersey state assemblyman, ridiculed the idea of an apology, stating that "an apology is an admission that you have committed a wrong, and herein lies my problem . . . For not one—not one—of the 215,000 people that I represent in my district is culpable in any way in the sin of slavery. Nor for that matter, my colleagues, are any of the living individuals in any of your home districts." When the U.S. Senate offered a resolution apologizing for slavery, cosponsor Sam Brownback, a Kansas Republican, made sure that the document included a disclaimer about reparations (Becker 2009).

Some Republicans have suggested that the United States has already created reparations in the form of certain entitlement programs. As Brian Beutler reported in the *New Republic* in 2014, Republican U.S. Senate candidate Thom Tillis argued to supporters that "a subset of the Democrat majority has never ceased to propose legislation that is de facto reparations and they will continue to do so as long as they are in the majority. Federal and State governments have redistributed trillions of dollars of wealth over the years by funding programs that are at least in part driven by their belief that we should provide additional reparations."

Further Reading

Becker, Bernie. 2009. "Senate Approves Slavery Apology, with Reparations Disclaimer," *New York Times*, June 18. Accessed January 12, 2015: http://thecaucus.blogs.nytimes .com/2009/06/18/senate-approves-slavery-apology-with-reparations-disclaimer/.

Biondi, Martha. 2003. "The Rise of the Reparations Movement," *Radical History Review*, 87, Fall: 5–18.

Brophy, Alfred L. 2014. "Who Would Pay for Reparations, and Why?" *New York Times*, June 9, 2014. Accessed January 10, 2015: http://www.nytimes.com/roomfordebate/2014/06/08 /are-reparations-due-to-african-americans/who-would-pay-for-reparations-and-why.

Coates, Ta-Nehisi. 2014. "The Case for Reparations," *The Atlantic,* May 21. Accessed January 12, 2015: http://www.theatlantic.com/magazine/archive/2014/06/the-case-for -reparations/361631/.

Conyers, John, Jr. n.d. "Issues: Reparations." Accessed January 12, 2105: http://conyers .house.gov/index.cfm/reparations.

Davis, Angelique M. 2014. "Apologies, Reparations, and the Continuing Legacy of the European Slave Trade in the United States," *Journal of Black Studies,* 45 (4), May: 271–286.

Green Party. 2012. "Party Platform 2012." Accessed January 12, 2015: http://www.gp.org /committees/platform/2012/social-justice.php.

Henry, Charles P. 2003. "The Politics of Racial Reparations," *Journal of Black Studies,* 34 (2), November: 131–152.

Horowitz, David. 2001. "Ten Reasons Why Reparations for Blacks Is a Bad Idea for Blacks— and Racist Too," *Front Page Magazine*, January 3. Accessed January 12, 2015: http:// archive.frontpagemag.com/readArticle.aspx?ARTID=24317.

Mount Holyoke College. n.d. "What Are Reparations?" Accessed January 12, 2015: https:// www.mtholyoke.edu/~kmporter/whatarereparations.htm.

National Public Radio (NPR). 2008. "Congress Apologizes for Slavery, Jim Crow," July 30. Accessed January 12, 2015: http://www.npr.org/templates/story/story.php?storyId= 93059465.

Peters, Jeremy W. 2008. "A Slavery Apology, but Debate Continues," *New York Times*, January 13. Accessed February 9, 2016: http://www.nytimes.com/2008/01/13/nyregion/nyregionspecial2/13slaverynj.html?_r=0.

Remnick, David. 2011. *The Bridge: The Life and Rise of Barack Obama.* New York: Vintage.

Robinson, Randall. 2001. *The Debt: What America Owes to Blacks.* New York: Plume.

Thompson, Krissah. 2009. "Senate Unanimously Approves Resolution Apologizing for Slavery," Washington Post, June 19. Accessed February 8, 2016: http://www.washingtonpost.com/wp-dyn/content/article/2009/06/18/AR2009061803877.html.

Williams, Juan. 2007. *Enough: The Phony Leaders, Dead-End Movements, and Culture of Failure That Are Undermining Black America—and What We Can Do about It.* New York: Broadway Books.

Williams, Walter E. 2011. *Race and Economics: How Much Can Be Blamed on Discrimination?* Stanford: Hoover Institution Press.

Right to Die

At a Glance

Do people have a right to end their own life? Should physicians assist them? Democrats, in general, have said, yes, to both these statements and Republicans have said, no. Many Democrats believe that a person's right to privacy includes the right to die a good death without excessive pain and suffering from a terminal illness. Republicans believe that the sanctity of life demands that individuals be protected from laws that might hasten their death, or encourage them to commit suicide.

Many Democrats . . .

- Support the right of a person who is terminally ill to use physician-assisted suicide (PAS) to end their life.
- Support the value of living wills, providing people a right to choose to refuse artificial life support.
- Want more states to adopt laws allowing physician-assisted suicide.
- Equate the right to die with other privacy issues such as abortion.

Many Republicans . . .

- Do not believe a moral society would allow euthanasia.
- Believe that the right to die is part of a culture of death that includes abortion on demand.
- Reject the right of the terminally ill to PAS.
- Are concerned that people may be coerced into ending their life by relatives or others who see them as a burden.
- Oppose laws and referendums supporting physician-assisted suicide.
- Want to reverse state laws that allow physician-assisted suicide.

Overview

The right to die is a contested right in the United States that was only officially recognized in the 1970s. The right received legal protections after a series of court cases regarding whether patients have a right to remove or refuse life support when they have no medical hope of recovery. It has evolved to include medical participation to end a life through physician-assisted suicide. Since 1994, the states of Oregon, Washington, Montana, Vermont, and New Mexico have all passed laws recognizing the right of a specific subset of terminally ill patients to choose physician-assisted suicide: A dozen or more states are considering the practice as well. In most of these instances, the political battle over PAS is pitting Democrats who support this right against Republicans who oppose it (Dowbiggin 2003).

Civil libertarians, many of whom are Democrats, support living wills and physician-assisted suicide also known as PAS. They believe terminally ill people have the right to end their suffering with a quick, dignified, and compassionate death. They argue that the right to die is protected by the same constitutional safeguards that guarantee such rights as same-sex marriage, procreation, and the refusal

Debbie Ziegler holds a photo of her daughter, Brittany Maynard, as she receives a hug from Ellen Pontac, after a right-to-die measure they supported was approved by the State Assembly in Sacramento, California, on September 9, 2015. Maynard moved to Oregon from California to legally end her life due to brain cancer in 2014 when California enacted the bill to allow terminally ill people to take life-ending medications. (AP Photo/Rich Pedroncelli, File)

or termination of life-saving medical treatment. Nongovernmental organizations such as Compassion and Choices and the American Civil Liberties Union (ACLU) are working to expand the right in other states by legislation or referendums.

Opponents of right-to-die laws include the American Medical Association (AMA) and conservative religious groups, such as the Roman Catholic Church, Orthodox Jews, and evangelical Protestant denominations. They argue that this practice, along with legalized abortion, is contributing to a "culture of death" that demeans all Americans. Many Republicans and others express concern that physician-assisted suicide is a "slippery slope" that begins with voluntary euthanasia and culminates in outright murder. Some critics have even expressed the concern that legalizing euthanasia could lead to the targeting of the poor, the disabled, and other groups judged by authorities to be of lesser value to society.

The modern debate over the right to die can be traced to the 1971 case of Karen Ann Quinlan, a 21-year-old woman who fell into a coma in April 1975 and was placed on a ventilator. Doctors found Quinlan had no brain activity and determined that she was in a persistent vegetative state (PVS) and unlikely to ever recover. Her parents asked that her artificial life support be removed so that she could die in peace rather than remain alive by artificial means. When the hospital refused their request, the Quinlans sued the hospital and won the right to remove life support. This sparked a national debate across the United States and led to new laws allowing the removal of artificial life support for patients in a PVS.

This debate was renewed in 1989, when 25-year-old Nancy Cruzan, who fell into a PVS after a car crash, became the subject of a court debate over whether the right to die was a fundamental right or one that could be controlled by the state. Along partisan lines, the Supreme Court ruled in a 5–4 decision that the right to die was a constitutionally protected liberty. But the majority stipulated that this right could only be exercised when the desire of the comatose patient was already established and thereby upheld a state's interest in preserving life. Testimony from her relatives that Nancy had not wanted to be left on life support led a lower court to order the removal of Cruzan's life support, and she died a short time later (Cruzan 1989). The Court decision in *Cruzan v. Missouri Department of Health* led to a spate of state laws requiring individuals to prepare living wills that contained their written rejection or consent to prolonged care should they become incapacitated.

Removing artificial life support was one means to end of life, but some individuals with terminal illnesses wanted to establish the right to end their life before incapacitation, if they so desired, through physician-assisted suicide. Dr. Jack Kevorkian became a notorious figure in 1990, the year he first openly aided terminally ill patients seeking to end their life. Kevorkian flouted the laws in Michigan and eventually was charged and convicted of murder. Kevorkian's actions brought new levels of attention to the issue of physician-assisted suicide, and lawmakers in several states initiated efforts to write laws that would make PAS a legally viable option for people facing terminal illness. In 1994, Oregon became the first, and for many years the only state, to legalize physician-assisted suicide.

In 1997, the Supreme Court unanimously declared that the Constitution did not guarantee Americans a right to commit suicide with the help of a physician. Assisted suicide thus became an issue for state legislatures to decide (Biskupic 1997). Washington became the second state to pass a referendum allowing physician-assisted suicide in 2008, and, one year later, the Montana Supreme Court upheld a PAS law that had been passed in that state. Vermont enacted legislation in 2013 allowing this practice, and a state judge in New Mexico declared this a right in early 2014. Since 2014, a dozen bills supporting PAS have been offered across the United States.

Democrats on the Right to Die

A majority of Democrats hold the position that people should have the right to die with dignity (Gallup 2007). They believe that the right to die should be understood as an important privacy right, similar to the right of same-sex couples to marry and for women to choose to terminate their pregnancy. This perspective coalesced into being during the Karen Ann Quinlan case in the 1970s. In 1976, the New Jersey Supreme Court created a new interpretation of the right of privacy by stating that Quinlan's interest in having her life support systems disconnected exceeded the state's interest in preserving life, so long as medical authorities saw "no reasonable possibility" that she would recover, reported Robert McFadden in a June 12, 1985, story for the *New York Times*. As a result of the decision many Democrats proposed and supported legislation to allow individuals facing terminal illness, rather than doctors and elected officials, to make end-of-life choices, which included the right to refuse care and, more recently, the right for terminally ill patients to choose a medically induced death. Nearly every state in the United States now has acknowledged the right of at least competent adults to refuse even basic, life-sustaining medical care, such as tubes supplying food and water.

As of 2015, right-to-die laws have been passed in five states where Democrats have successfully argued that adults have a right to choose death over a prolonged and painful illness that might lead to their loss of dignity and autonomy. Oregon passed the first death with dignity law by a ballot measure over the opposition by religious leaders and Republican lawmakers. Although passed in 1994, opponents of the law delayed its full enactment until 1998 by challenging the law in state court. Under the administration of President George W. Bush, the attorney general of the United States challenged the right of physicians in Oregon to dispense the medication used in assisted suicide, citing federal authority to revoke their licenses under the Controlled Substances Act of 1970. For many people, the case of *Gonzales v. Oregon* was another opportunity to debate PAS, and Oregon's five Democratic members of Congress filed a friend of the court brief supporting PAS. In a 6–3 decision, the Court upheld the right of states to enact laws allowing PAS.

Democrats continued to act on behalf of the right to die for terminally ill patients. Washington became the second state to support PAS through a referendum. The referendum was led by former Democratic governor Booth Gardner, who had long supported PAS legislation (Junge 2009). His Initiative 1000 was passed on November 4, 2008. In Vermont, Democratic Governor Peter Shumlin, first elected in 2010, worked with the state's Democrat-controlled legislature to craft a bill allowing physician-assisted suicide in 2013. When Shumlin signed the act into law, he emphasized that "this bill does not compel anyone to do anything they don't choose in sound mind to do. All it does is give those who are facing terminal illness and are facing excruciating pain a choice" (Barber 2013).

Democrats have also worked alongside nongovernmental organizations such as the ACLU, Compassion and Choices, and Death with Dignity National Center to enact PAS laws across the country. Democrats have tried to pass laws in California, Colorado, Maryland, New Jersey, and Pennsylvania but have faced stiff opposition from Republican lawmakers. Democrats in California who sought to enact legislation did so because they believe "that this voluntary option is a compassionate addition to the existing continuum of care that may be offered by modern medicine at the end of life," said Lois Wolk, Democrat and coauthor of the California bill. "SB 128 ensures that we honor the freedom to have end-of-life options . . . today, we are one step closer to ensuring that this fundamental right is protected for those in California who are coping with end-of-life issues," she said (Compassion and Choices 2015).

A New Mexico Judge Upholds the Legality of Physician-Assisted Suicide

In *Morris v. New Mexico* Judge Nan Nash, a Democrat appointee to New Mexico's Second Circuit Court, declared on January 13, 2014, that the right to die includes physician assisted suicide:

> Most fundamental rights have been attached to our system of government and an inherent concept of liberty. Some rights have been of a more personal nature such as the right of parents in the care, custody and control of their children . . . the freedom of personal choice in matters of family life . . . and the right to family integrity . . . This Court cannot envision a right more fundamental, more private or more integral to the liberty, safety and happiness of a New Mexican than the right of a competent, terminally ill patient to choose aid in dying. If decisions made in the shadow of one's imminent death regarding how they and their loved ones will face that death are not fundamental and at the core of these constitutional guarantees,. . . The Court therefore declares that the liberty, safety and happiness interest of a competent, terminally ill patient to choose aid in dying is a fundamental right under our New Mexico Constitution.

Source
Findings of Fact and Conclusions of Law, *Morris v. New Mexico,* January 13, 2014. Compassion and Choices Web site. Accessed July 5, 2015: http://www.compassionandchoices.org/userfiles/Morris-Trial-Court-Opinion.cc.pdf.

Democratic judges have been shown to be more supportive than their Republican colleagues of expanding the right of privacy to encompass the right to die. Opponents of PAS in the Supreme Court have been uniformly Republican. Judicial decisions in the states that allow PAS have been rendered by Democrats. The decision to allow physician-assisted suicide in New Mexico, for example, was written by Nan Nash of the Second District Court. Nash, who was appointed by Democratic Governor Bill Richardson, ruled in January 2014 that patients have a fundamental right to seek aid in dying, stating that the New Mexico Constitution prohibits the state from depriving a person from enjoying life and liberty or seeking and obtaining safety and happiness. "This court cannot envision a right more fundamental, more private or more integral to the liberty, safety and happiness of a New Mexican than the right of a competent, terminally ill patient to choose aid in dying," she wrote.

Some Democrats, though, have expressed strong opposition to physician-assisted suicide. Opposition among Democrats to PAS include members of the Catholic faith who adhere to Church teachings that condemn euthanasia. In states with large Catholic populations Democrats have had difficulty in mustering support for PAS. For example, when a "death with dignity" bill was introduced in Pennsylvania in 2015, its Democratic sponsor conceded that it would be difficult to get the bill to a floor vote because the measure was opposed by the state's Catholic leadership.

Republicans on the Right to Die

Republicans generally oppose right-to-die laws and physician-assisted suicide, although there are exceptions within their ranks. The Republicans added a plank to their official party platform in 2012 that stated that "faithful to the 'self-evident' truths enshrined in the Declaration of Independence, we assert the sanctity of human life . . . and we oppose the non-consensual withholding or withdrawal of care or treatment, including food and water, from people with disabilities, including newborns, as well as the elderly and infirm, just as we oppose active and passive euthanasia and assisted suicide" (Republican Party 2012).

Driven by these convictions, congressional Republicans have tried for many years to regulate end-of-life practices. After the 1997 Supreme Court decision that allowed the removal of artificial life support when the intent of a patient was known, Republican Senator John Danforth of Missouri introduced, and Congress passed, the Patient's Self Determination Act to regulate the practice of preparing a living will. This required that all patients receive informed consent and this be acknowledged in writing before they underwent surgery or other procedures that could lead to a coma (McDougall and Gorman 2008).

After Oregon became the first state to pass a referendum allowing for physician-assisted suicide, Republicans in Congress responded quickly. In 1999, Don Nickles (R OKLA), joined with other Republican cosponsors to propose the Pain Relief Promotion Act (PRPA). This bill would have criminalized physician-assisted suicide and nullified the Oregon law. The bill died in the Senate, however, after Democrats filibustered it.

Unable to pass legislation in Congress to nullify the actions in Oregon, Republicans within the administration of President George W. Bush, who served 2001 through 2009, challenged physician-assisted suicide in other ways. U.S. Attorney General John Ashcroft reinterpreted the Controlled Substances Act to criminalize the action of any doctor who prescribed life-ending drugs in Oregon. The plan was to undermine Oregon's death-with-dignity law and prevent other states from adopting similar measures. Proponents of assisted suicide sued the attorney general, and the case made its way to the Supreme Court, where, over the dissent of three Republican appointed judges, the Court ruled in *Washington v. Glucksberg* that Ashcroft's reinterpretation was not lawful.

Undeterred, Republicans around the country have continued to oppose state-level proposals to legalize PAS. For example, in Montana, where a judge ruled that there was a right to physician-assisted suicide, Republicans have introduced several bills to criminalize doctors who assisted in end-of-life measures. Governor Chris Christie of New Jersey threatened the New Jersey Assembly that if they passed a bill allowing physicians to prescribe life-ending drugs to terminally ill patients, he would veto it. Despite being outnumbered by Democrats in the California legislature, Republicans have successfully blocked death-with-dignity bills from going to the floor of the state assembly.

A Republican Senator Condemns a Supreme Court Ruling in Favor of Physician-Assisted Suicide

Tom Coburn was an Oklahoma Representative and later U.S. Senator who retired in 2014. In 2006, after the Supreme Court affirmed Oregon's Dignity in Death laws, he issued the following statement expressing deep disappointment with the Court's decision:

> Nowhere does our Constitution give doctors the right to take the lives of their patients. Deliberately causing death is never a legitimate medical purpose. By creating another class of human beings whose lives have no value, the Supreme Court has put all vulnerable persons at risk . . . In countries where euthanasia has been legalized, granting doctors the god-like power to decide at what point life has value and when it does not has led to the killing of babies, the elderly, depressed, and handicapped. I'm disturbed that the Supreme Court took our nation farther down that dark road today.

Source

"Dr. Coburn Troubled by U.S. Supreme Court Decision to Uphold Oregon's Physician-Assisted Suicide Law," January 17, 2006. Accessed July 5, 2015: VoteSmart.org Web site. http://votesmart.org/public-statement/146588/dr-coburn-troubled-by-us-supreme-court-decision-to-uphold-oregons-physician-assisted-suicide-law#.VdcuoZfiYgo.

Perhaps the best example of how this issue is both national and local in scope can be seen by the Republican response to the case of Terri Schiavo, a 26-year-old wife and mother who fell into a PVS in 1990. Schiavo had no living will, and the burden of proof as to her wishes came from a recollection by her husband years after she fell into the coma (Cote 2012). Citing her wishes, Michael Schiavo asked in 1998 that Terri be removed from life support. Terri's parents expressed disbelief about their son-in-law's account, however, and they took legal steps to prevent the withdrawal of the feeding tube keeping Terri alive. After a series of court cases, the Florida courts sided with Michael Schiavo in 2005 and her parents turned to conservative politicians, including Florida Governor Jeb Bush, who passed an emergency state law, "Terri's Law," that overturned the Florida court's decision. When that law was declared unconstitutional by the state court, Governor Jeb Bush urged Republicans in the U.S. House and Senate to intervene. Returning to Congress from Easter break, Republicans passed a special law granting federal courts jurisdiction in the case on Terri Schiavo's behalf. President George W. Bush noted upon signing the bill, "In cases like this one, where there are serious questions and substantial doubts, our society, our laws and our courts should have a presumption in favor of life" (Bush 2005).

Republican efforts failed, however, when federal courts refused to intervene in the case. Terri Schiavo's feeding tube was withdrawn, and she died two weeks later. This series of events sparked outrage from rank-and-file Republicans who saw the removal of artificial life support as immoral, unlawful, and against the will of the defenseless Schiavo. The fury was particularly palpable on conservative talk radio and social media. Tony Perkins, head of the conservative Christian policy group the Family Research Council, issued a statement that "as many in the nation mourn the passing of Terri Schiavo, we should remember that her death is a symptom of a greater problem: that the courts no longer respect human life" (Milbank 2005).

Further Reading

Barber, Melissa. 2013. "Vermont's Death with Dignity Signing Ceremony," Death with Dignity National Center, May 25. Accessed July 8, 2015: http://www.deathwithdignity .org/2013/05/25/vermonts-death-with-dignity-signing-ceremony#sthash.su85nOR1 .dpuf.

Biskupic, Joan. 1997. "Unanimous Decision Points to Tradition of Valuing Life," *Washington Post*, June 27. Accessed July 5, 2015: http://www.washingtonpost.com/wp-srv/national /longterm/supcourt/stories/die.htm.

Bush, George W. 2005. "Statement on Signing Legislation for the Relief of Theresa Marie Schiavo," March 21. *Public Papers of the Presidents of the United States, George W. Bush, 2005, Book 1, January 1 to June 30, 2005*. Washington, D.C.: Government Printing Office.

Caplan, Arthur, ed. 2006. *The Case of Terri Schiavo: Ethics at the End of Life*. Buffalo: Prometheus Books.

Compassion and Choices. 2015. "Medical Aid-in-Dying Bill Clears Senate Judiciary Committee in California," April 7. Accessed July 5, 2015: https://www.compassionandchoices .org/2015/04/07/medical-aid-in-dying-bill-clears-senate-judiciary-committee-in -california/.

Cote, Richard. 2012. *In Search of Gentle Death: The Fight for Your Right to Die with Dignity.* New York: Corinthian Books.

Cruzan v. Director, Missouri Dept. of Health. 1989. The Oyez Project at IIT Chicago-Kent College of Law. Accessed April 28, 2015: http://www.oyez.org/cases/1980-1989/1989 /1989_88_1503.

Dowbiggin, Ian. 2003. *A Merciful End: The Euthanasia Movement in Modern America.* New York: Oxford University Press.

Gallup. 2007. Accessed July 5, 2015: http://www.gallup.com/poll/27727/public-divided -over-moral-acceptability-doctorassisted-suicide.aspx.

Junge, Daniel, dir. 2009. *The Last Campaign of Governor Booth Gardner.* HBO Films.

McDougall, Jennifer Fecio, and Martha Gorman. 2008. *Euthanasia: A Reference Handbook.* Santa Barbara: ABC-CLIO.

McFadden, Robert. 1985. "Karen Ann Quilan, 31, Dies; Focus of '76 Right to Die Case," *New York Times*, June 12, 1985. Accessed February 9, 2016: http://www.nytimes .com/1985/06/12/nyregion/karen-ann-quinlan-31-dies-focus-of-76-right-to-die-case .html.

Milbank, Dana. 2005. "GOP, Democrats Look for Symbolism in Schiavo Case," *Washington Post*, April 1. Accessed July 6, 2015: http://www.washingtonpost.com/wp-dyn/articles /A15454-2005Mar31.html.

Republican Party. 2012. Accessed July 1, 2015: https://www.gop.com/platform/we-the -people/.

Sex Education

At a Glance

Do K-12 students need to know the mechanics as well as theories of sexuality? Should sex education be comprehensive and include discussions of sexual expression, contraceptives, and abortion? Is abstinence a viable solution to teenage pregnancy, sexually transmitted diseases, and abortion? Generally speaking, Democrats support comprehensive sexual education while Republicans are more apt to support a curriculum that emphasizes abstinence. Conservatives are also more likely to view some aspects of sex education as inappropriate subjects for school.

Many Democrats . . .

- Believe that sexuality is a fluid concept and runs the spectrum from heterosexual to homosexual, bisexual, and asexual expressions.
- Endorse comprehensive sexual education.
- Want children to know about the dangers of and ways to protect against sexually transmitted diseases.
- Want children to know their options when it comes to contraceptives.
- Reject abstinence-only education as unrealistic.

Many Republicans . . .

- Believe that some sex education programs risk promoting sexual activity and experimentation by children.
- Do not endorse sex education that deviates from promoting a heterosexual lifestyle.
- Express concern that comprehensive sex education is part of a liberal campaign to expose children to non-heterosexual lifestyles to further in order to confuse them about their sexual identity.
- Support abstinence-only messages that emphasize the psychological, emotional, and physical benefits of waiting until marriage to have sex.

––––––––––––

Overview

The debate about what this curriculum should look like and how it is funded has been a contentious part of the culture wars between conservatives, and their elected Republican allies, and liberals, and their elected Democratic allies. Many Democrats favor comprehensive sex education programs that cover a broad range of subjects but are often premised on the idea that sexuality is healthy and expected in teens who should, therefore, be informed about the risks of pregnancy and sexually transmitted diseases (STDs). Conservative Republicans, by contrast, are much more likely to support abstinence-based education programs. Abstinence-only programs teach that avoiding sexual intercourse until marriage has psychological, physical, and emotional benefits. Since the 1990s, the United States has funded states that adopt abstinence-only education plans in schools. States can reject this funds and, as of 2015, 23 states had rejected abstinence-only funds. Some states that have accepted abstinence-only educational funds have their own comprehensive sex education programs within schools in a situation called an "if then" law (Advocates for Youth n.d.).

In 1912 the National Education Association advocated for training teachers to provide sex education in the schools. However, the curriculum suggested was strongly informed by religious and moral values and included the idea that masturbation was a sin and that sexually transmitted diseases were punishment for immoral behavior. As high school education became compulsory in the 20th century, educators were faced with the task of dealing with sexuality in biology and health classes. Various organizations such as the National Education Association, the Public Health Service, and the American Medical Association worked to create a curriculum to educate students, which was offered to local schools.

The 1960s and early 1970s are sometimes referred to as the era of the sexual revolution since it was in this time period that the first birth control pill for women was created, that the Supreme Court ruled contraceptives were legal for all people, and that abortion was legalized. It was also during this time period that liberals and conservatives began contesting for control of the sex education curriculum. Under pressure from Planned Parenthood and a group created by Mary Calderone, the Sex Information and Education Council of the United States, Congress identified sex education as an important curricular reform in the 1965 Elementary and Secondary Education ACT (ESEA). This mobilized critics of sex education who were concerned that it encouraged sexual activity. Despite this opposition, however, the majority of schools in major cities began including some form of sex education in high school health or human development classes. In response, conservative opponents of sex education produced material calling for sexual abstinence and urged its inclusion in school curricula (Huber 2009).

In the 1980s public health concerns about the HIV/AIDS epidemic opened a new front in the debates over sex education. In 1981, Republican Senator Jeremiah Denton of Alabama proposed to discourage teen sex with the Adolescent Family

Life Act (AFLA), which funded school and community programs "to promote self-discipline and other prudent approaches" to adolescent sex (Mann 2010). Funding for this program continued until the present day and was supplemented by grants derived from the Personal Responsibility Work Opportunity Reform Act of 1996 that created the Temporary Assistance for Needy Families (TANF). This law added Title V of the Social Security Act, which established grants to states for abstinence-only-until-marriage programs. The program was originally administered by the Maternal and Child Health Bureau (MCHB) at the U.S. Department of Health and Human Services (HHS) and provided block grants to states that implemented Abstinence-Only programs that promoted chastity and minimal instruction on birth control and STD prevention. Under the law, HHS allocated $50 million in federal funds each year to the states. States that accepted the money matched every four federal dollars with three state-raised dollars. Every state except California has applied for this money (Mann 2010).

From the 1990s until the present, federal spending priorities on sex education have reflected partisan divisions. Republicans in Congress and the White House have funded abstinence-based programs, while Democrats in Congress and the White House have sought ways to counter this by providing alternate sources for comprehensive sexual education.

Both sides claim credit for the drop in teen pregnancy and decline of sexual activity among teens that has occurred since 2000. Teen birth rates have plunged in the past 20 years despite a drop in teen abortions. Drivers of that trend include an increase in the percentage of teens who are delaying having sex until later in life, as well as increased use of birth control among teenagers who are sexually active. However, racial and ethnic disparities in teen birth rates remain steady with the highest rates in 2012 among Hispanic girls aged 15–17, at 25.5 births per 1,000, compared to 21.9 for non-Hispanic blacks, 17 for American Indians or Alaska Natives, 8.4 for non-Hispanic whites, and 4.1 for Asian or Pacific Islanders. Advocates of comprehensive sex education also note that U.S. teen birth rates are still higher than in other developed countries (Valbrun 2013).

Democrats on Sex Education

Many Democrats believe that comprehensive sex education is superior to abstinence-only programs because many, if not most, young people will not wait until marriage to have sex and should, therefore, be taught about safe sex. They are especially concerned that school-age children learn how to prevent pregnancy and the transmission of sexually transmitted diseases. Supporters of comprehensive education often point to studies that show that giving teens more information about sex does not increase sexual activity or lower the age at which teens first start having sex (Taverner and Montfort 2005). They also cite research showing that abstinence-only programs are ineffective in lowering rates of teen pregnancy and STDs. "Young people need to know how to prevent unwanted pregnancies," said Representative Barbara Lee (D-Calif.) in a 2009 interview. "Young people need that information about sex education so that they don't get pregnant . . . until they marry. And I think this abstinence-only policy is not working. And you know I think it was under the Clinton administration and the welfare reform bill where abstinence-only was put into law. And I have been trying for many years now to repeal that. Federal funds could not be used in our public schools to teach comprehensive sex education. Federal funds could only be used to teach abstinence-only. And what I say and what many are saying is that, yes, abstinence, but we have to teach our young people comprehensive sex education, how to also prevent unwanted pregnancies, how to prevent the transmission of HIV and AIDS and sexually transmitted diseases and why we need to focus our resources and tax dollars on a comprehensive sex education strategy" (CNN 2009).

Despite their support for comprehensive sexual education, Democratic leaders have been unable to eliminate funding for abstinence-only sex education and fully fund comprehensive sex education. President Bill Clinton, who served from 1993 until 2001, signed into law the Personal Responsibility and Work Opportunity Reconciliation Act (PRWORA), or welfare reform act of 1996. The legislation contained a provision known as Title V, which provided funds to states for abstinence education if they agreed to bar teachers from discussing contraception and requiring all public school teachers to say that sex within marriage is the expected standard of sexual activity (Cornblatt 2009).

After the election of George W. Bush, who increased abstinence funding during his two terms in office, congressional Democrats fought to promote comprehensive sex education programs. In 2005, 2007, and again in 2009, Barbara Lee, a Democrat representing California's Ninth District, introduced the Responsible Education about Life (REAL) Act to provide funding for broadening sex education beyond abstinence. One of the cosponsors of the Senate version in 2007 was then senator Barack Obama, who as president worked to end abstinence-only education. Lee asserted that the REAL Act would help combat the spread of STDs and HIV/AIDS among young people, as well as prevent teen pregnancies. The goal of the REAL Act was to fund programs that promoted abstinence and provided information about the use of and access to contraception. Worried that the curriculum did not include male contraception the bill also included educational materials on condoms. Conservatives in Congress, however, blocked passage of the REAL Act every time it was introduced (Lee n.d.).

In 2007, after taking control of the House and Senate, congressional Democrats spoke out in favor of comprehensive sex education, or a curriculum that promoted abstinence as well as instruction about birth control and safe-sex methods. Democrats tried to rein in abstinence-only sex education by eliminating a $50 million grant. The president of the conservative Family Research Council, Tony Perkins, told supporters that Democrats were pushing a "radical agenda that few voters expected." Representative John Dingell, a Democrat from Michigan, dismissed Perkin's accusation by declaring abstinence-only education "a colossal failure." Dingell pointed to an eight-year study funded by the Department of Health and Human Services showing that students in four abstinence-only education programs first had sex at about 17 years of age, which was about the same as those not in abstinence programs (Finer 2007).

After President Barack Obama took office in 2009, he advocated for comprehensive sex education in his first budget proposal. Obama's budget responded to two key priorities of comprehensive sex education advocates: (1) eliminate support for the highly restrictive and harmful abstinence-until-marriage programs that denigrate the effectiveness of contraceptives and safe-sex behaviors; (2) redirect funding toward broader programs that are medically accurate and evidence-based. The administration planned to match dollar-for-dollar funding for both abstinence and comprehensive sex education. Obama's funding scheme aimed at providing $178 million for comprehensive sex education, which was equivalent to the money being spent on abstinence education. Obama's 2010 budget tried to eliminate the two discretionary federal funding streams for abstinence-only-until-marriage programs—the Community-Based Abstinence Education (CBAE) grant program and the abstinence-only-until-marriage portion of AFLA. In addition, Democrats in Congress wanted to allow the third funding source, the Title V abstinence-only-until-marriage program created in 1996, to expire (Advocates for Youth 2009). These efforts by the Obama administration were foiled when the House shifted to Republican control in the 2010 midterm election. In addition, a new source of abstinence-education money was included in the Affordable Care Act. Despite his inability to end these programs, President Obama made science-based sex education an issue during his reelection and in 2013 cut some funding for abstinence programs while working to eliminate all funding for Title V.

States have also been battlegrounds over sex education. Democrats in New York have unsuccessfully tried since 2006 to enact a sex education bill that promoted a comprehensive view of the subject. The 2006 Healthy Teens Act did not mandate sex education in public schools but gave districts a choice to offer such a curriculum paid for by the state. The bill passed the Democrat-controlled Assembly by a vote of 126 to 15, but the Republican-controlled state Senate refused to vote it out of committee. Advocates for comprehensive sex education unsuccessfully introduced similar bills in Hawaii, Arizona, Texas, and Missouri.

Republicans on Sex Education

Many conservative Republicans believe that sexual activity is normal and healthy but only when practiced by adults in a committed relationship. They believe premarital sex leads to STDs, pregnancy, and damaged self-esteem and could be avoided through both personal commitment and social pressure to wait until marriage to engage in sexual activity (Kim and Rector 2010). Many conservatives believe that comprehensive sex education, which includes discussion of sexual orientation, masturbation, contraceptives, sexually transmitted diseases, and abortion undermines traditional family values (Kendall 2012). Supporters of abstinence-only programs often cite a 1997 study that concluded that young people who pledged to remain virgins until marriage were more likely to start having sex at a later age than those who did not take such a pledge (Franklin et al. 1997). This perspective has led conservative groups such as the National Abstinence Education Association (NAEA) to extol the benefits of "sexual risk avoidance" (SRA) education programs. "SRA abstinence education, as funded by Congress . . . is decidedly more inclusive than 'just say no,'" according to the NAEA. "The term, 'abstinence only' is strategically attached to this funding by opponents to create the false perception that abstinence-centered education is a narrow and unrealistic approach. SRA abstinence education is overwhelmingly more comprehensive and holistic than other approaches and focuses on the real-life struggles that teens face as they navigate through the difficult adolescent years. SRA abstinence education realizes that 'having sex' can potentially affect not only the physical aspect of a teen's life but also, as research shows, can have emotional, psychological, social, economic, and educational consequences as well. That's why topics frequently discussed in an abstinence education class include how to identify a healthy relationship, how to avoid or get out of a dangerous, unhealthy, or abusive relationship, developing skills to make good decisions, setting goals for the future and taking realistic steps to reach them, understanding and avoiding STDs, information about contraceptives and their effectiveness against pregnancy and STDs, practical ways to avoid inappropriate sexual advances, and why saving sex until marriage is optimal" (National Abstinence Education Association n.d.).

Conservative Republicans were responsible for creating and maintaining the federal government's support for abstinence-based education by investing millions of dollars in such programs. AFLA was signed into law in 1981 as Title XX of the Public Health Service Act. In addition to providing comprehensive support services to pregnant and parenting teens and their families, AFLA was established to promote "chastity" and "self-discipline" (Huber 2009). They were also successful in creating a new program for abstinence-only in Clinton's welfare reform known as the Work Opportunity Reconciliation Act (WORA) of 1996. Ron Haskins and Carol Bevan, two congressional staff members who helped write the language for this provision, noted that while some people might think abstinence was outdated, it "was intended to align Congress with the social tradition . . . that sex should be confined to married couples" (Haskins and Bevan 1997).

President George W. Bush, who served from 2001 until 2009, promoted abstinence-based education and annually increased funding for the programs that supported this. Bush worked with congressional Republicans, who held majorities in both the House and Senate during his first six years in office, to increase annual funding for such programs from $80 million to $176 million. Working with conservatives in Congress, Bush fashioned the CBAE Program, which advanced additional funding for abstinence education geared to teens. The grant announcement for this money included the disclaimer that "sex education programs that promote the use of contraceptives are not eligible for funding" (Howell 2007). Conservatives were outraged when congressional Democrats, who took control of the House and Senate in the 2006 midterms, tried to strip funding away from abstinence education and advance their own comprehensive solution. As reported by Philip Turner in an article published in *USA Today*, May 18, 2007, Tony Perkins, head of the Family Research Council, derided the Democratic approach as one that amounted to little more than "provid[ing] more pills that prevent and abort pregnancies."

At the state level, conservative Republicans have likewise advanced abstinence-only education by regulating the kinds of topics schools can address when discussing sex education. On May 13, 2012, ABC News reported that Tennessee passed a law banning discussion of any "gateway sexual activity." The measure mandated state sex-education classes promote abstinence but includes a fine for teachers or guest speakers who promote activity that, according to conservatives, could "encourage" sexual activity, such as discussions of contraceptives and sexual orientation. In Kansas, legislators proposed a new policy requiring parents to "opt in" to sex education classes rather than allowing them to opt out. A sex education poster meant to promote abstinence in one school included the question "How do people express their sexual feelings?" and gave examples ranging from talking and kissing to oral sex and intercourse. Parents found the example of oral sex inappropriate and the resulting uproar led a state legislator to call for a law banning any such language from the classroom—and fining or jailing teachers or guest lecturers who used it (Brinker 2015). In 2014, a local school board in Arizona voted to redact pages from a biology textbook that included a discussion of contraceptives because this information contradicted their own abstinence-only sex education program.

Not all Republicans have opposed comprehensive sexual education. Public health officials in Republican administrations, for example, have run afoul of Republican lawmakers in several high-profile instances. C. Everett Koop, who served as surgeon general under Ronald Reagan, suggested schools adopt a sex education program that included information on preventing the transmission of the HIV virus through safe-sex practices. Conservatives balked at this proposal, however. Some even suggested that STDs and AIDS were punishments for immorality, and they cited the high rates of abortion, teen pregnancy, out of wedlock births, and the high rate of teenagers engaging in sexual intercourse as evidence that comprehensive sex education was failing and morals were crumbling (Solinger 2013). In 2001, Surgeon General David Satcher, who was appointed by President George W. Bush, issued *The Call to Action to Promote Sexual Health and Responsible Sexual Behavior*, which recommended providing adolescents with information on both abstinence and contraception. This proposal was rejected by congressional Republicans as well.

Further Reading

Advocates for Youth. n.d. Accessed October 12, 2015: http://www.advocatesforyouth.org /understanding-sex-education-policy-and-funding.

Advocates for Youth. 2009. "Comprehensive Sex Education: Research and Results." Accessed October 12, 2015: http://www.advocatesforyouth.org/publications/1487.

Brinker, Luke. 2015. "Kansas Could Put Teachers in Prison for Assigning Books Prosecutors Don't Like," Slate.com, February 27. Accessed October 12, 2015: http://www.salon .com/2015/02/27/kansas_could_put_teachers_in_prison_for_assigning_books _prosecutors_dont_like/.

CNN. 2009. "Q&A with Barbara Lee." Accessed October 12, 2015: http://www.c-span.org /video/?284170-1/qa-barbara-lee.

Cornblatt, Johannah. 2009. "A Brief History of Sex Ed in America," *Newsweek,* October 27. Accessed October 12, 2015: http://www.newsweek.com/brief-history-sex-ed-america -81001.

Finer, Lawrence B. 2007. "Trends in Premarital Sex in the United States, 1954–2003," *Public Health Reports*, 122, January–February. Accessed October 12, 2015: http://www .ncbi.nlm.nih.gov/pmc/articles/PMC1802108/.

Franklin, Cynthia, Darlene Grant, Jacqueline Corcoran, Pamela Miller, and Linda Bultman. 1997. "Effectiveness of Prevention Programs for Adolescent Pregnancy: A Meta-Analysis," *Journal of Marriage and the Family,* 59: 551–567.

Haskins, Ron, and Carol Statuto Bevan. 1997. "Abstinence Education under Welfare Reform," *Children and Youth Services Review*, 19 (5/6): 465–484.

Howell, Marcela. 2007. "The History of Federal Abstinence-Only Funding," *Advocates for Youth*. Accessed October 12, 2015: http://www.advocatesforyouth.org/storage/advfy /documents/fshistoryabonly.pdf.

Huber, Valerie. 2009. *A Historical Analysis of Public School Sex Education in America since 1900.* Unpublished Thesis, Cedarville University. Accessed October 12, 2015: http:// digitalcommons.cedarville.edu/cgi/viewcontent.cgi?article=1020&context=educat ion_theses.

Kendall, Nancy. 2012. *The Sex Education Debates.* Chicago: University of Chicago Press.

Kim, Christine, and Robert Rector. 2010. *Evidence on the Effectiveness of Abstinence Education: An Update.* Washington D.C.: The Heritage Foundation.

Lee, Barbara. n.d. "Education." Accessed October 12, 2015: https://lee.house.gov/issues /education.

Mann, Emily S. 2010. *The Politics of Teenage Sexualities: Social Regulation, Citizenship, and the U.S. State.* Dissertation: University of Maryland College Park. Accessed October 12, 2015: http://drum.lib.umd.edu/bitstream/handle/1903/10415/Mann_umd_0117E_11262 .pdf?sequence=1&isAllowed=y.

National Abstinence Education Association. n.d. "Frequently Asked Questions: Correcting Misinformation in the Sex Ed Debate." Accessed October 12, 2015: http://www .abstinenceassociation.org/faqs/.

Satcher, David. 2001. *The Surgeon General's Call to Action to Promote Sexual Health and Responsible Sexual Behavior.* Accessed February 9, 2016: http://www.ncbi.nlm.nih.gov /books/NBK44216/.

Solinger, Rickie. 2013. *Reproductive Politics: What Everyone Needs to Know.* New York: Oxford University Press.

Taverner, Bill, and Sue Montfort. 2005. *Making Sense of Abstinence: Lessons for Comprehensive Sex Education.* Planned Parenthood of Northern New Jersey.

Turner, Philip. 2007. "Democrats Say They Will End Abstinence Only Funding," USA TODAY, May 18. Accessed February 9, 2016: http://usatoday30.usatoday.com/news/religion/2007-05-17-abstinence-education_N.htm.

Valbrun, Marjorie. 2013. "Teen Sex," *CQ Researcher,* June 15. Accessed October 12, 2015: http://0-library.cqpress.com.libra.naz.edu/cqresearcher/cqr_ht_teen_sex_2013.

Unemployment Insurance

At a Glance

Republicans and Democrats frequently disagree over the benefits that workers should be eligible for when they lose their jobs, for instance, on what kind of benefits workers should be eligible for, how long benefits should be available to those out of work, and the expectations government should impose on job seekers who receive unemployment insurance.

Many Democrats . . .

- Believe that extending unemployment benefits assists hard-working families.
- Believe that unemployment insurance is an essential tool in protecting laid-off workers during times of economic recession.
- Assert that every dollar spent on unemployment programs generates over two dollars in economic activity.
- Would like to extend the length, diminish the eligibility requirements, and increase the amount of compensation available to workers

Many Republicans . . .

- Believe that the cost of unemployment insurance is exorbitant for small businesses.
- Believe that extending the length of time workers can get unemployment compensation is a disincentive to job seekers.
- Believe that the jobless rate in the United States would be lower if the length of time workers could receive unemployment compensation had not been extended during the 2008 recession.
- Believe that extended unemployment compensation pushes wages up and therefore keeps business and industry from hiring more workers.
- Favor mandates requiring those receiving unemployment benefits to participate in job retraining programs.

Overview

Unemployment insurance pays workers when they lose their job. Begun during the Great Depression, when jobs dried up for millions of American workers and unemployment rates reached 50 percent in some major cities, the program is financed by employers through their federal and state payroll taxes. Like other insurance programs, paid premiums go into a fund that is used when workers lose their jobs. The program was federalized in 1935 when President Franklin Roosevelt signed the Social Security Act into law and created the federal unemployment insurance program. The program requires employers and employees to pay premiums (Blaustein and Cohen1993). Republicans, state rights advocates, and businessmen challenged the program in court as unconstitutional, but the U.S. Supreme Court upheld the constitutionality of the program in 1937 (Tanner 2003).

The debate between Republicans and Democrats over unemployment compensation reflects differences in their philosophies and constituencies. The Democratic Party is often associated with the labor movement, whereas the Republican Party is often associated with the business community. Thus, most Democrats support unemployment insurance programs and would like to see more generous benefits for workers. Most Republicans, on the other hand, oppose expanding unemployment insurance benefits because these lead to new taxes or expenses for business owners (Garraty 1986).

The program remains unpopular among many small business owners who object to the fact that during hard economic times they are forced to cover the costs of the program. For example, during an economic recession, when the economy is shrinking many businesses, facing losses in profits lay off unnecessary workers. However, this creates more unemployment and a surge in claims to the program. During the recession of the 1970s, for example, Congress imposed an additional federal surtax on businesses to cover the rising cost of the program. Business owners complained that these new taxes were particularly onerous, coming at a time when they themselves were struggling to survive the economic downturn.

Although the business community has been unable to end the program, they have changed it substantially since it was first created. Initially, workers were eligible for payments if they quit their jobs or were fired and they were not required to actively seek work before receiving their benefits. The benefit was only available in companies with eight or more workers. Over the past eight years, amendments to the original bill now require all companies with one or more full-time employee to provide unemployment insurance. Workers are now required to actively seek work to obtain the funds, and they must be "available for work." Altogether this means that a person has to be ready, willing, and able to work. In most states, out-of-work individuals must register for work at a local employment office, and must show proof that they are making an effort to find a job. Individuals cannot refuse a suitable work offer. A suitable work offer is a job that matches the person's health, safety, and morals; the physical fitness and prior training, experience, and earnings of the person; the length of unemployment and prospects for securing local work in a customary occupation; and the distance of the available work from the claimant's residence. Generally, as the length of unemployment increases, the claimant is required to accept a wider range of jobs.

Many constituencies associated with the Democratic Party, from organized labor to antipoverty organizations, strongly support unemployment insurance. Historically, these and other advocates of unemployment insurance have lobbied to increase both the size and length of such compensation. Over time, they have had considerable success in this regard. For example, when the program first began in the 1930s, out-of-work individuals received unemployment benefits for only 16 weeks. During the recession of the 1970s this was extended to 26 weeks, and then again to

Applicants seeking work browse the job posting table at the 10,000 Best Jobs Expo at Angel Stadium in Anaheim, California, on March 21, 2013. The one-day job fair, organized by the National Employment Council, had hundreds of employers with more than 10,000 local jobs that matched qualified candidates to employment. (Photo by Mark Boster/Getty Images)

39 weeks, largely on the strength of Democratic support. And in response to the so-called Great Recession that began in 2008, Democrats in Congress joined with President Barack Obama to allow workers to collect up to 99 weeks of unemployment benefits. This legislation was passed over the strong objections of the GOP, which characterized it as fiscally irresponsible and counterproductive.

Democrats on Unemployment Insurance

Democrats generally envision unemployment compensation as a way of keeping people out of poverty, allowing them to lead lives of dignity, while also stimulating the economy during times of recession (Da Costa 2014). The Democratic Party controlled, with few exceptions, the House and Senate from 1933 to 1995, and they were able to strengthen unemployment benefits on several occasions during period. Democrats secured new benefits and extended the time period individuals could collect unemployment while also adding new taxes on businesses to pay for this expansion.

Before 1995 partisan divisions over unemployment compensation were relatively muted. Few Republicans openly opposed unemployment benefits. For example, Democrats worked together with Republican President George H. W. Bush in 1992 to extend unemployment benefits during that year's recession. A year later, Republicans in the Senate organized a filibuster to scuttle Democratic President Bill Clinton's stimulus bill designed to address ongoing recessionary conditions, but a bipartisan coalition of senators retained Clinton's call for an extension to unemployment benefits.

After Democrats regained control of the Senate in 2001 they were able to gain George W. Bush's support in extending unemployment benefits to assist workers in the recession of 2001. They later defeated a plan by Bush to take the federal government out of running the unemployment insurance program.

Democrats held a majority in the House and Senate in 2009 when the United States was faced with the worst recession since the Great Depression. With the support of newly elected President Barack Obama they secured passage of the American Recovery and Reinvestment Act, which increased the federal cost share of unemployment compensation to 100 percent until 2011. This legislation was designed to spare cash-strapped states, obligated by law to maintained balanced budgets, from cutting their unemployment programs and thus deepening the plight of laid-off workers within their borders.

Democrats working with Obama also extended unemployment benefits from 39 weeks to 99 weeks, thus giving laid-off workers more time to rejoin the workforce in a time of sluggish economic recovery. Democrats argued that these policies not only helped suffering families, they also gave a boost to overall economic activity.

When the special benefits program was set to end in 2013, Democrats urged renewal and cited data that they say showed how the program allowed millions of Americans to stay above the poverty line: 3.2 million in 2010, 2.3 million in 2011, and another 1.7 million in 2012. Democrats also condemned Republican lawmakers who wanted to stop the program. "I don't know if our colleagues who have opposed passing the unemployment-insurance legislation know or care about the impact on families," said Nancy Pelosi of California, the House minority leader.

After Democrats were unable to extend the program past 2013 due to Republican opposition, the liberal group Americans United for Change asserted that "Republicans stripped 1.3 million Americans of jobless benefits—folks who want to work, but cannot find a job—kicking them to the curb during Christmas" (Lowrey 2013). Condemnation was also heard from many liberal-leaning media outlets, including the editorial board of the *New York Times:* "Republicans see themselves as practicing tough love, jolting dependents into finding jobs. That . . . is not how it works. Long-term unemployment is high because there are not enough jobs, not because millions of Americans have suddenly lost their work ethic" (*New York Times* Editorial Board 2013).

Republicans on Unemployment Insurance

Many Republicans have been vocal critics of unemployment insurance in recent years. They claim that it creates a burden on businesses, which makes them less competitive in the global marketplace. They also are wary of extending unemployment insurance benefits beyond 39 weeks because they say it leads workers to become dependent on the government and debilitates their ability to find employment (Da Costa 2014). Republicans generally are strong advocates for restricting unemployment benefits. Many of the rules tightening eligibility for unemployment compensation were created during the presidency of Ronald Reagan, who served in the White House from 1981 to 1989. Reagan a conservative believed that "unemployment benefits were merely 'a prepaid vacation for freeloaders'" (Rampell 2009). Reagan signed legislation requiring that any state borrowing money from the federal unemployment insurance fund pay back the loans with interest.

The ideological battle over coverage, cost and purpose of the program have become sharper in the two decades since Republicans first captured the House and Senate in the 1994 elections and have been especially rancorous during times of recession. Republicans assert that overly generous benefits are a disincentive to look for a job and therefore prolong the amount of time people are out of work. This creates a moral hazard because the government policy encourages people to reduce their work habits. Business groups and their Republican allies are also upset that the payroll tax falls on business. They argue that the money spent on unemployment insurance could better be invested in ways that created new jobs.

President George W. Bush, who was in the White House from 2001 to 2009, proposed putting more power and responsibility for unemployment back onto the states. In 2003 his budget plan included eliminating the federal payroll taxes on business and placing management and benefit decision making back with the states so that the program would be more aligned with local and state labor markets and benefits more in line with other state-run entitlement programs. Democrats, believing that state lawmakers would not raise state benefits to match the loss of federal funds, rejected the idea, which they characterized as an underhanded scheme to gut the program.

Under President Obama, the program was extended for up to 99 weeks in some states and the cost was covered by the federal government. This decision was heavily criticized by the GOP and conservative media outlets. "The real problem is job creation," insisted the conservative editorial board at the *Wall Street Journal*. "Extended unemployment benefits create upward pressure on wages. The higher wage level reduces the employer's potential profits on any new job created, so naturally they don't create them" (*Wall Street Journal* Board of Editors, 2013).

The unemployment insurance extension expired in December 2013 and Congress returned to Washington in January 2014 to debate renewing the extension. "I do support unemployment benefits for the 26 weeks that they're paid for," said Senator Rand Paul of Kentucky on Fox News. "If you extend it beyond that, you do a disservice to these workers. When you allow people to be on unemployment insurance for 99 weeks, you're causing them to become part of this perpetual unemployed group in our economy." In 2014 debate raged between Republicans and Democrats over extending the benefits beyond the 99 weeks already in place with Republicans pointing out that the government spent $25 billion in unemployment benefits during the 2008 recession.

Some Republicans today would like to end or at least severely curtail the existing unemployment insurance program and replace it with one that places a greater emphasis on job training and returning unemployed people to the workforce. Newt Gingrich, a former Republican Speaker of the House of Representatives and unsuccessful candidate for the Republican presidential nomination in 2012, called for tying unemployment to mandatory job training. His idea was echoed by Senator Jeff Sessions, who agreed that job counseling would be beneficial for unemployed people. "I believe that will save money in the long run and make their lives more fulfilled" (Milligan 2014).

Further Reading

Blaustein, Saul, and Wilbur Cohen. 1993. *Unemployment Insurance in the United States: The First Half Century.* Kalamazoo, MI: W. E. Upjohn Institute.

Da Costa, Pedro Nicolaci. 2014. "Did Unemployment Benefits Boost Jobless Rate? Only Slightly, Fed Papers Says," *The Wall Street Journal,* September 5.

Ehrenreich, Barbara. 2011. *Nickel and Dimes: On Not Getting by in America.* New York: Picador.

Garraty, John. 1986. *Unemployment in History: Economic Thought and Public Policy.* New York: Harper Collins.

Lowrey, Annie. 2013. "Benefits Ending for One Million of Unemployed," *The New York Times,* December 28, A.1.

Milligan, Susan. 2014. "Fighting the Inequality Battle." *U.S. News Digital Weekly,* 6 (2), January 10: 4S.

New York Times Editorial Board. 2013. "No Cheer for the Jobless," *New York Times,* December 28. Accessed December 12, 2014: http://www.nytimes.com/2013/12/29/opinion/sunday/no-cheer-for-the-jobless.html?hpw&rref=opinion&_r=1&.

Rampell, Catherine. 2009. "Stimulus Bill Would Bestow New Aid to Many Workers," *New York Times,* February 13. Accessed December 19, 2014: http://www.nytimes.com/2009/02/14/business/economy/14benefits.html?module=Search&mabReward=relbias%3Aw%2C%7B%221%22%3A%22RI%3A9%22%7D.

Tanner, Jane. 2003. "Unemployment Benefits," *CQ Researcher,* 13 (16), April 25: 369–392.

Wall Street Journal Board of Editors. 2013. "The Wages of Unemployment," *The Wall Street Journal*, October 18: A.12.

Unions

At a Glance

Few if any Republicans are supportive of the collective bargaining power of unions. Most Republicans believe that errant union leadership creates more economic problems for business and workers than it resolves. Many Republicans would like to diminish the power of unions or eliminate them entirely. Democrats believe that without collective bargaining most workers are exploited by businesses. Most Democrats believe that historically, unions have provided the American worker with skills, workplace safety protections, and good wages, all of which contribute to a healthy, vibrant economy. They also believe that unions can continue to play an important role in protecting workers' rights and encouraging broad-based financial security for American families. Many Democrats also support unionization efforts in the fast-food service industry and in retail operations such as Walmart.

Many Democrats . . .

- Believe that unions benefit workers (both in and out of unions) by pushing for higher wages and benefits and stronger workplace safety laws.
- Describe unions as a hallmark of a healthy democracy.
- Believe that unions help keep industries from exploiting workers.
- Assert that unions provide needed training for unskilled workers entering the workforce.
- Believe that better-paid employees enhance the overall economy.
- Support the movement to organize fast-food workers and restaurant employees.
- Would like to see more unions in the public sector.
- Oppose right-to-work laws.

Many Republicans . . .

- See unions as corrupt relics of a bygone era.
- Assert that union membership dues are often used for political purposes not supported by rank-and-file members.

- Believe workers should have a choice to join a union.
- Believe workers should have the right to leave a union.
- Believe union leaders are counterproductive for business and workers.
- Oppose greater unionization.
- Think the United States could compete in the global economy better without unions.

Overview

Unions are organizations of workers that serve the interest of rank-and-file employees by negotiating with management on their behalf. Some unions are geared toward workers in specific industries such as the United Auto Workers (UAW) or United Mine Workers (UMW), other unions are geared toward general workers such as the American Federation of Labor–Congress of Industrial Organizations (AFL-CIO), which combined in 1955 to become the largest and most powerful union in the United States. There are even public sector unions, which are unions with memberships comprised of people who work for local, state, or federal governments. Public sector unions include the National Education Association (NEA), which represents over three million teachers. Modern unions are also political entities that advocate for state and federal laws to protect workers and regulate business conduct. Unions influence elections and policies by providing campaign contributions to candidates for office who support their agenda, assisting in voter registration, and mobilizing union members to vote.

Historically, labor unions have been a critical constituency of the Democratic Party ever since the New Deal, when Democratic President Franklin D. Roosevelt pursued a range of policies perceived as helping the "working man." Unions became wedded to the Democratic Party with the passage of the National Labor Relations Act (NLRA) in 1935. The legislation, also known as the Wagner Act, has been called the Magna Carta of Labor Unions. The law protects workers by recognizing the right of unions to exist, banning businesses from interfering in union activity, and securing the right of collective bargaining. Franklin Roosevelt's statement on signing the NLRA claimed that "by assuring the employees the right of collective bargaining [the law] fosters the development of the employment contract on a sound and equitable basis" (Roosevelt 1935).

Union support helped the Democratic Party dominate Congress from 1932 to 1994, and played a crucial role in delivering the White House to Democratic President Harry S. Truman in 1948. The alliance between the Democratic Party and labor unions has remained strong ever since, even as the political power of unions has waxed and waned over the decades. In 2012, for example, labor unions claimed that they played a pivotal role in Democratic President Barack Obama's reelection (Greenhouse 2012).

Republicans, who tend to favor business interests and are philosophically committed to individual over collective rights, are skeptical and often hostile to unions. Republicans have even suggested that union leaders are an elite group that serves their own interests and that of Democratic Party elites at the expense of ordinary working Americans. Industrialists and their Republican allies were unhappy with the gains made by unions during Franklin Roosevelt's presidency, 1933–1945. When the Cold War erupted in the mid-1940s, Republicans tried to tie unions to the Communist Party and the Red Scare of that period. Because the Cold War pitted the United States and its allies against the Communist-led USSR and its allies, anti-Communism was at an all-time high in the United States. The Republicans, who briefly controlled Congress, passed the Taft-Hartley Act in 1947. This legislation limited the power of unions by barring companies from only hiring union workers (a practice known as closed shop), punished unions that tolerated communist activity, and hindered union growth by allowing state laws regulating union organizing activity to supersede federal law. As a result many states, especially in the more politically conservative South, passed "Right to Work" laws that barred unions from requiring employees to join a union or face exclusion from collective bargaining agreement. This played a role in the decline of union power.

Union setbacks were worsened in the 1950s when some labor groups, most notably Jimmy Hoffa's Teamsters Union, became associated with organized crime. Thus, when economic decline beset the United States in the 1970s it was not difficult for business and industry to erode support for unions. Since then, the percentage of American workers belonging to unions dropped from a high of 1 out of every 3 workers at the height of organize labor's power to a low of 1 out 10 workers (National Conference of State Legislatures).

Even as national labor unions have been in decline, however, public sector and service sector unions have grown. Two examples include the American Federation of State, County, and Municipal Employees (AFSCME) and the Service Employees International Union (SEIU). These unions have become very powerful in negotiating with state governments and representing union members who work in health care and other key industries supported by the government. Their growth sparked a reaction by Republican governors in Wisconsin, Michigan, and Ohio to strip away collective bargaining rights. Union members in Ohio played a key role in a successful public referendum to restore their collective bargaining rights. Union leaders are also heartened by the increased number of Latinos and Asian Americans, a growing demographic in unions.

Democrats on Unions

Democrats generally have their origins in the working class. The Democratic Party was created in the 1830s when Andrew Jackson and Martin Van Buren pulled together Southern slaveholders and northern white working classmen (Watson

2006). Organized unions, meanwhile, arose in the late 19th century when workers had few rights in the fast-industrializing and rapidly expanding American economy. At that time, U.S. economic policy was bent toward a laissez-faire or hands-off view of business. Corporations were unregulated, income tax nonexistent, and there was no social safety net to assist workers who were fired, laid off, or injured on the job. Common law rules of that day stated that companies could not be sued for injuries but could fire workers who were hurt on the job and incapable of carrying out their duties. Nor were industries or judges sympathetic to collective bargaining rights. For many years neither of the two main political parties, Democrats and Republicans, looked upon unions favorably. For example, it was a Democratic president—Grover Cleveland—who issued an injunction and sent federal troops to Chicago to end the famous 1894 Pullman Strike led by the American Railway Union under the direction of Eugene Debs.

Unions became a critical component of the Democratic Party after the passage of the National Labor Relations Act of 1935. This landmark law, which had been championed by Franklin D. Roosevelt and his fellow "New Dealers" in the Democratic Party, recognized and protected the right of workers to form unions and to bargain collectively for better working conditions and pay. As a result of the law, union membership went from under 3 million to nearly 10 million workers by the end of the 1940s. In response to the rise of organized labor conservative Republicans attempted to curtail their power in the Taft-Hartley Act of 1947. President Harry Truman, a Democrat, vetoed the bill because he saw it as detrimental to workers and the economy (Truman 1947). The president's veto was overridden by pro-business Republicans and conservative Southern Democrats. Despite his failure to defeat the antiunion bill his actions signaled that the Democrats were not going to retreat from their New Deal social policy and unions showed their appreciation by playing a key role in lifting Truman to an upset victory in the 1948 presidential election (Busch 2012).

Although the Democratic Party has always enjoyed strong support from union leaders, a series of wedge issues such as the party support for affirmative action and the antiwar sentiment of some elected party leaders prompted some union members (especially white members) to stray from the Democratic Party during the 1960s. In addition, economic recession and inflation, which ran rampant in the 1970s, led some union members to believe that the Democratic Party no longer represented the interests of the middle class. This idea may have been hardened when union leadership persuaded Democratic President Jimmy Carter to bail out the Chrysler Corporation in 1979. The terms of this financial rescue included wage concessions by the union leaders. In the 1970s and 1980s growing numbers of white union members, stung by wage concessions and angered by affirmative action programs and other liberal policies that offended their social conservatism, swung their support to Republicans Richard Nixon in 1972 and Ronald Reagan in 1980 and 1984. Union workers as a percentage of all workers continued to decline in the 1990s and many were outraged by the successful

President Obama Praises American Labor Unions

Like many of his fellow Democrats, President Barack Obama regularly praises the value of organized labor and the importance of labor unions in U.S. history. Following is an excerpt from a 2012 Labor Day speech delivered by Obama.

The rights and benefits we enjoy today were not simply handed to working men and women; they had to be won. Brick by brick, America's labor unions helped raise the landmarks of middle-class security: the 40-hour workweek and weekends, paid leave and pensions, the minimum wage and health insurance, Social Security and Medicare. These are the victories that make our Nation's promise possible—the idea that if we work hard and play by the rules, we can make a better life for ourselves and our families.

I am committed to preserving the collective bargaining rights that helped build the greatest middle class the world has ever known. It is the fundamental right of every American to have a voice on the job, and a chance to negotiate for fair pay, safe working conditions, and a secure retirement. When we uphold these basic principles, our middle class grows and everybody prospers.

Our Nation faces tough times, but I have never stopped betting on the American worker. This is the labor force that revolutionized the assembly line and built the arsenal of democracy that defeated fascism in World War II. These are the workers who built our homes, highways, and rail lines, who educate our children and care for the sick. American workers have taken us through the digital revolution and into a 21st-century economy. As my Administration fights to create good jobs and restore the American dream, I am confident that, together, we will emerge from today's challenges as we always have—stronger than ever before.

Source

"Proclamation 8857—Labor Day, 2012," August 31, 2012. Online by Gerhard Peters and John T. Woolley, "The American Presidency Project." Accessed June 10, 2014: http://www.presidency.ucsb.edu/ws/?pid=101969.

effort by Bill Clinton to create the North American Free Trade agreement. NAFTA, as it was known, was rejected by union workers, some of whom voted for third-party candidate Ross Perot in the 1992 and 1996 elections. Some union members supported Pat Buchanan in his failed bid for the Republican nomination in 1992 (Levin 1992).

Unions and union workers found greater support when Barack Obama was elected president in 2008. President Obama found himself facing the worst economic decline since the Great Depression and the pending bankruptcy of General Motors and the Chrysler Corporation. When the president negotiated the terms of a financial bailout for these companies, which he characterized as an essential part of the nation's economic recovery, he insisted on protection of the union-members' benefits and demanded that unions receive an equity stake in the companies as a concession for government intervention. According to Obama and his fellow Democrats, it was the executives of these automakers—not the workers—who were responsible for their financial straits. Obama's action to help the automakers infuriated conservatives because other creditors were not given the same protections, but they proved beneficial to the incumbent president when they increased turnout nationwide and played a key role in delivering the state of Ohio to the Democratic president in 2012.

Republicans on Unions

The position of the Republican Party is that unions reduce the power of individual workers, protect incompetent workers from being fired, make U.S. industry less competitive globally, and serve as "slush funds" for the political campaigns of progressive Democrats. In response, Republicans have sought to pass legislation at the federal and state level to regulate and reduce the influence of unions. This was not always the case. In 1902, Republican President Teddy Roosevelt showed sympathy for unions when he brought the UAW and mining companies together to negotiate an end to a bitter strike rather than just throw the federal government's support behind the mine owners (Dray 2011). In subsequent administrations, however, Republican presidents Taft, Harding, Coolidge, and Hoover showed more sympathy for industry than workers and most Republicans were dismayed by the rise of unions after the passage of the Wagner Act in 1935.

Out of power since 1930, Republicans won control of Congress in the 1946 elections. After taking control of the 80th Congress in 1947, they immediately set out to dilute union power. The GOP led passage of the Labor Management Relations Act (a.k.a. Taft-Hartley) that year. President Truman vetoed the bill but Republicans allied with Southern Democrats easily overrode the president's veto. Robert Taft, whose father was the conservative president William Howard Taft, became Senate majority leader in the 1940s and was the chief sponsor of the bill to restore "justice and equality in labor management relations." Taft believed that the Wagner Act gave too much arbitrary power over industry, workers, and citizens to labor union leaders (Taft 1947).

Taft-Hartley forbids unions from secondary strikes, targeting suppliers of targeted businesses, forbid federal employees from striking, allowed the president to mandate an 80-day stay on strikes, allowed state labor laws to trump federal legislation, and forbid the closed shop, which required all employees to join a union as requisite for employment. The legislation weakened unions and encouraged 24 states, mostly located in the South and West, to pass "Right to Work" laws that made it more difficult for unions to organize by allowing workers to opt out of joining a union while still benefiting from union efforts to raise wages and improve working conditions (Varga 2014).

In the 1950s, labor unions were suspected of harboring ties to organized crime and being involved in racketeering, corruption, and other crimes. This led to the

Labor-Management Reporting and Disclosure Act, also known as the Landrum Griffin Act of 1959. This law expanded the Taft-Hartley restrictions on unions and regulated the conduct of union leadership including demanding scrupulous accounting practices and government oversight (National Labor Relations Board n.d.). As a result, workers in the South lacked union representation and received lower wages and fewer benefits. The textile industry, among others, took advantage of the cheaper and often nonunion labor and began moving their plants from the Northeast and Midwest to the sun belt in the 1960s and 1970s, reducing the number of union members nationwide (Patterson 1997; Montgomery 1989).

Ronald Reagan, who was president from 1981 to 1989, did not cause the decline of labor unions but his decision to invoke the Taft-Hartley Act and fire

---

Ronald Reagan Remarks on the Air Traffic Controllers Strike

In 1981, Republican President Ronald Reagan fired 11,000 unionized air traffic controllers across the nation. An excerpt from Reagan's announcement of this decision is reprinted below. Reagan's action has been described by scholars as one of the most significant setbacks suffered by organized labor in America in the past several decades.

> This morning at 7 a.m. the union representing those who man America's air traffic control facilities called a strike. This was the culmination of 7 months of negotiations between the Federal Aviation Administration and the union. At one point in these negotiations agreement was reached and signed by both sides, granting a $40 million increase in salaries and benefits . . . Now, however, the union demands are 17 times what had been agreed to—$681 million. This would impose a tax burden on their fellow citizens which is unacceptable.
>
> . . . Let me make one thing plain. I respect the right of workers in the private sector to strike. Indeed, as president of my own union, I led the first strike ever called by that union. I guess I'm maybe the first one to ever hold this office who is a lifetime member of an AFL-CIO union. But we cannot compare labor-management relations in the private sector with government. Government cannot close down the assembly line. It has to provide without interruption the protective services which are government's reason for being.
>
> It was in recognition of this that the Congress passed a law forbidding strikes by government employees against the public safety . . . It is for this reason that I must tell those who fail to report for duty this morning they are in violation of the law, and if they do not report for work within 48 hours, they have forfeited their jobs and will be terminated.

Source

"Ronald Reagan Remarks on the Air Traffic Controllers Strike (August 3, 1981)," Presidential Speech Archive Miller Center. Accessed January, 5, 2015: http://millercenter.org/president/speeches/speech-5452.

11,000 unionized air traffic controllers in 1981 is seen by many scholars as a pivotal moment in exposing the growing political vulnerability of unions. In 1981, members of the Professional Air Traffic Controllers Organization (PATCO) walked off the job demanding better pay and working conditions. Reagan invoked the Taft-Harley law that forbids federal employees from striking and ordered them back to work. When PATCO defied him, he fired them all and ordered the military to take on the role of coordinating U.S. airspace until new workers could be hired and trained (Bennett and Kaufman 1984).

Republicans generally have always seen unions as impediments to economic growth, but globalization and the demand for U.S. industries to compete worldwide has increased Republican hostility. Mitt Romney, the Republican candidate for president in 2012, angered union leaders with a *New York Times* editorial opposing a government bailout of General Motors (GM) and the Chrysler Corporation. Romney's editorial suggested that these companies were weakened by the UAW, which would not relent on the union's fringe benefits package for workers that included gold-plated health insurance and generous pension benefits. Romney claimed that these added another $2,000 cost to every car. According to Romney, the only way to free the automakers from the UAW was to allow them to go bankrupt.

Republicans within state governments were also keen on limiting the power of unions, in this case public sector unions that have grown as labor unions shrank (DiSalvo 2015). Conservative Republicans, many of whom are affiliated with the Tea Party movement, came to power in statehouses and governors' mansions across the United States in November 2010. Within a year 37, states had proposals aimed at curbing the power of public sector unions by limiting or eliminating collective bargaining and making strikes by government workers illegal (National Conference on State Legislatures n.d.). Scott Walker, the Republican governor of Wisconsin, came to national prominence in 2011 with his successful campaign to eliminate collective bargaining rights for all public-employee unions in the state except firefighters and police. Walker, like many Republicans, believes union leaders not workers are the problem (Walker 2014). Walker was quoted in a story published June 4, 2012, on Real Clear Politics: "My problem with public sector union leaders, the bosses, has been they stood in the way of protecting the taxpayer" (Huey-Burns 2012).

Walker's reforms included a provision requiring Wisconsin to hold an annual vote by members who may decide to leave the union. As a result, union membership in Wisconsin is falling. Walker's legislation outraged progressives and union leaders who failed to recall the governor, lost a Court challenge to his provisions, and then failed in their effort to oust Walker from office in his 2014 reelection. Following Wisconsin's lead, Republican lawmakers in Ohio, Tennessee, and Idaho passed laws that cut back bargaining rights for public sector unions, although the Ohio law was later removed through a public referendum (Greenhouse 2014). According to Mark Peters, in a story published in the *Wall Street Journal,* January 21, 2015, Republican-led states scored victories against unions by passing right-to-work laws in Indiana and Michigan in 2012.

Further Reading

Bennett, James T., and Bruce E. Kaufman. 1984. *What Do Unions Do? A Twenty-Year Perspective.* New York: Transaction Publishing.

Busch, Andrew. 2012. *Truman's Triumphs: The 1948 Election and the Making of Postwar America.* In *American Presidential Elections* series. Lawrence: University Press of Kansas.

DiSalvo, Daniel. 2015. *Government against Itself: Public Union Power and Its Consequences.* New York: Oxford University Press.

Dray, Philip. 2011. *There Is Power in a Union: The Epic Story of Labor in America.* New York: Anchor Books.

Greenhouse, Steven. 2012. "Labor Unions Claim Credit for Obama's Victory," *New York Times,* November 7. Accessed December 7, 2014: http://thecaucus.blogs.nytimes .com/2012/11/07/labor-unions-claim-credit-for-obamas-victory.

Greenhouse, Steven. 2014. "Wisconsin's Legacy for Unions," *New York Times*, February 23. Accessed August 10, 2014: http://www.nytimes.com/2014/02/23/business/wisconsins -legacy-for-unions.html?_r=0.

Huey-Burns, Caitlin. 2012. "Wisconsin Gov. Scott Walker Wins Recall Election," Real Clear Politics, June 6. Accessed February 9, 2016: http://www.realclearpolitics.com /articles/2012/06/06/wisconsin_gov_scott_walker_wins_recall_election_114387.html.

Levin, Doron. 1992. "The 1992 Campaign: Labor; Union Leaders Seek to Keep Auto Workers from the Arms of Perot," *New York Times*, June 18. Accessed December 15, 2014: http:// www.nytimes.com/1992/06/18/us/1992-campaign-labor-union-leaders-seek-keep-auto -workers-arms-perot.html.

Montgomery, David. 1989. *The Fall of the House of Labor: The Workplace, the State, and American Labor Activism, 1865–1925.* New York: Cambridge University Press.

National Conference of State Legislatures. n.d. "Collective Bargaining and Labor Union Legislation." Accessed December 17, 2014: www.ncsl.org/default.aspx?TabId=22275.

National Labor Relations Board. n.d. "Landrum Griffith Act 1959." Accessed December 13, 2014: http://www.nlrb.gov/who-we-are/our-history/1959-landrum-griffin-act.

Patterson, James T. 1997. *Grand Expectations: The United States, 1945–1974.* In *Oxford History of the United States* series. New York: Oxford University Press.

Peters, Mark. 2015. "Opting Out of Unions Gets Boost in States," Wall Street Journal, January 21. Accessed February 9, 2016: http://www.wsj.com/articles/opting-out-of -unions-gets-boost-in-states-1421365229.

Roosevelt, Franklin. 1935. "Signing Statement July 5." Accessed December 13, 2014: http://www.fdrlibrary.marist.edu/aboutfdr/wagneract.html.

Taft, Robert. 1947. "Sen. Robert Taft—1947 Taft-Hartley Speech." Accessed February 9, 2016: https://www.youtube.com/watch?v=ZJZvlCRxYHI.

Truman, Harry S. 1947. "Veto of the Taft-Hartley Labor Bill," June 20, by Gerhard Peters and John T. Woolley, "The American Presidency Project." Accessed December 15, 2014: http://www.presidency.ucsb.edu/ws/?pid=12675.

Varga, Joseph. 2014. "Dispossession Is Nine-tenths of the Law: Right-to-Work and the Making of the American Precariat," *Labor Studies Journal*, 39 (1): 25–45.

Walker, Scott, and Marc Thiessen. 2014. *Unintimidated: A Governor's Story and a Nation's Challenge.* New York: Sentinel Trade.

Watson, Harry L. 2006. *Liberty and Power: The Politics of Jacksonian America.* New York: Hill and Wang.

Voting Rights

At a Glance

Do historical patterns of voter discrimination in the South and Southwest require continued government oversight of elections held within certain states? Are voter identification laws merely a tool to strip the vote from poor and minority voters? Is voter fraud as rampant today as it was before Progressive Era regulation? Do people who committed serious crimes deserve to have their right to vote restored? Your answer to these questions may well depend on whether you are a Democrat or a Republican. Democrats often believe that without laws such as the Voting Rights Act of 1965, and renewed continually since, that poor and minority voters will lose their right to vote. Democrats oppose out-of-hand voting regulations, and especially voter ID laws that might hinder the ability of individuals to vote. Some Democrats also want to change laws to allow ex-convicts to have their voting rights restored. Democrats dismiss the idea that voter fraud is an issue in electoral politics and view Republican "solutions" to this nonexistent problem as a transparent bid to suppress votes from constituencies that are more likely to vote Democratic.

Republicans, on the other hand, claim that voter fraud is a serious and ongoing problem that would be addressed by voter ID laws. Republicans also say that federal oversight of local and state elections in the South and elsewhere is no longer necessary. Republicans dismiss the idea that voter suppression is a serious problem in contemporary elections. Members of the GOP reject the idea that people who willingly commit felonies should have their voting rights restored.

Many Democrats . . .

- Believe that voter suppression continues to be a problem in the United States.
- Believe the Voting Rights Act remains necessary to protect would-be voters.
- Oppose voter ID laws.
- Believe voter ID laws unfairly target low-income and minority voters who are less likely to have certain forms of identification.

- Believe that people convicted of crimes who have served their sentences should have their voting rights restored.
- Support the Department of Justice move to sue Republican-controlled states over perceived voting rights violations.
- Have criticized state laws that strip convicted felons from voting for life.
- Support easing voting registration through such things as a motor voter law and encouraging early voting.

Many Republicans . . .

- Believe that the Voting Rights Act of 1965 achieved its goals and is no longer necessary.
- Support voter ID laws.
- Believe voter ID laws ensure the integrity of elections.
- Reject the idea that felons should have a right to vote.
- Support reductions to early voting.

_____

Overview

Voting is a hallmark of full citizenship in the United States, and access to the ballot box has been at the core of civil rights struggles waged by women and minorities throughout American history. Under the Constitution the power to determine eligibility to vote—sometimes called "the franchise"—is given to the states. Each state has the power to determine the manner of election and eligibility for who may vote. This changed somewhat with the ratification of the Fifteenth Amendment, which granted all African American males the right to vote, the Nineteenth Amendment, which extended the franchise to include women, and the Twenty-Sixth Amendment, which expanded the franchise to those over the age of 18. After the passage of the Fifteenth Amendment, Southern states were resistant to granting black men the franchise. White lawmakers erected a variety of legal obstacles, such as the poll tax, literacy test, and understanding test to purposefully disenfranchise black voters (Lawson 1999). After nearly a century of struggle, the Twenty-Fourth Amendment, which made the poll tax unconstitutional, was passed in 1964. This was followed by the Voting Rights Act of 1965, which was signed into law by President Lyndon Johnson, a Democrat (May 2013). Johnson declared that "it is wrong—deadly wrong—to deny any of your fellow Americans the right to vote in this country" (Johnson 1965). Johnson urged Congress to give the federal government the power to oversee elections in the South to guarantee that elections were nondiscriminatory. The effect of the Voting Rights Act (VRA) was immediate and dramatic: Within months, over 250,000 African Americans were newly enrolled to vote. The VRA prohibited any voting regulation that had a discriminatory purpose and granted the Department of Justice unprecedented authority to reject

President Lyndon Johnson signs the Voting Rights Act as Martin Luther King Jr., with other Civil Rights leaders look on in the Capitol Rotunda, in Washington, D.C., on August 6, 1965. (PF-(usna)/Alamy Stock Photo)

changes to election laws that might keep minorities from voting. States with a history of discrimination were required to get preclearance from the federal government before election rules could change. Legal challenges to the VRA were turned aside by the Supreme Court, which upheld the legislation in a series of cases between 1965 and 1969. The VRA enjoyed bipartisan support for the next several decades. It was amended in the 1970s to extend protections to Native Americans and Latinos and to require bilingual ballots as appropriate, and renewed in 1982 and 2006 (Keyssar 2009).

Initially the Supreme Court upheld the right of voter ID laws in the 2008 case of *Crawford v. Marion County*. The Democratic Party and civil rights advocates brought suit against the state of Indiana, which required that potential voters produce a U.S. or state-issued ID before voting, claiming that many poor and minorities would be unable to produce these documents. The 6–3 decision upheld that the law as "neutral and nondiscriminatory" was written by John Paul Stevens. Just prior to the 2014 midterms, however, several lower federal courts struck down voter ID laws in some states, while the U.S. Supreme Court allowed a stringent Texas provision to stand. The split decision creates the strong likelihood that the Supreme Court will once again be called in to rule on voter ID laws.

A generation after the VRA, though, Democrats remained concerned that voter registration laws were still crafted in ways that hampered enrollment by the poor and minorities. They passed the National Voter Registration Act of 1993, a law

The Disputed Presidential Election of 2000

The 2000 presidential election led directly to the Help America Vote Act and raised the profile of voting rights for the next decade. That year, neither Democratic nominee Al Gore nor the Republican nominee had a clear majority of electoral votes on election night due to close election results in three states—Oregon, New Mexico, and Florida. Within days it became clear that the outcome of the election would be determined by which candidate was awarded the electoral votes from Florida, which was initially certified for Texas Governor George W. Bush. The Democratic candidate, Vice President Al Gore, sued for a selective recount of votes cast in four predominantly Democratic counties in Florida. Complicating the recount was the lack of uniform election standards in Florida, a state that allowed each county to determine the manner in which they held elections. Some counties used punch card ballots and the recount of these created a challenge because some voters had not completely penetrated the punch card. Those conducting the recount were asked to determine voter intent and to judge whether a dimple or a hanging chad was enough evidence to count the voter for one or another candidate. Citing the lack of uniformity, George W. Bush asked the federal courts to stop the recounts. The Supreme Court, split along partisan lines in their 5–4 decision to stop the recounts because of the lack of uniform standards and thereby ceded the election to George W. Bush. Democrats argued that the Republicans on the Supreme Court had given the election to George W. Bush and some sneered that he was the "selected president" not the elected one. Al Gore, who had insisted that every vote be counted, reminded potential voters of his loss by telling delegates at the 2004 Democratic National Convention that voting was power. "Don't let anyone take it away or talk you into throwing it away. And let's make sure that this time every vote is counted."

Sources

CNN. 2004. "Gore: Every Vote Counts—and Should Be Counted," July 27. Accessed December 3, 2015: http://www.cnn.com/2004/ALLPOLITICS/07/26/dems.gore/index.html?iref=mpstoryview.

Toobin, Jeffrey. 2001. *Too Close to Call: The Thirty-Six Day Battle to Decide the 2000 Election.* New York: Random House.

requiring states provide citizens with voter registration forms at all government offices (Abramowitz 2004). The law increased the number of registered voters between 1993 and 2000, but failed to increase turnout among the targeted populations (Crocker 2013). Democrats also sought reforms after the election of 2000, in which faulty voting equipment, confusing ballots, a lack of standards, and irregularities at polling sites generated a national debate on how votes were cast and counted. Congress subsequently passed the Help America Vote Act (HAVA) in October 2002 to establish uniform voting standards for all states. HAVA established a federal clearinghouse to assure that elections were fair, mandated that states adopt uniform standards for casting and counting ballots, required accessible technology in every voting district, set minimum standards for voter ID, and required that states provide provisional ballots for those who came to polling sites (Coleman and Fischer 2011).

While voting access was mainly addressed by Democrats in Congress or civil rights groups such as the NAACP, concerns about voter fraud led states with Republican legislative majorities to adopt voter ID laws requiring potential voters to show a state issued ID card before casting a ballot. Many of these Republicans insisted that voter fraud is widespread and part of an attempt by supporters of the Democratic Party to carry close elections. Voter ID laws were upheld as constitutional by the Supreme Court in 2008, but they outraged Democrats.

The number of states with stringent voter ID laws increased after the Supreme Court struck down Section 4 of the VRA in the case of *Shelby County v. Holder*

Voting Rights Advocate Eric Holder

Eric Holder was appointed the first African American attorney general in U.S. history by Barack Obama in 2009. Previously, Holder had served under President Bill Clinton as deputy attorney general and prior to that he had been appointed by President Ronald Reagan to the Superior Court of the District of Columbia. Born in New York City, Holder was an American History major at Columbia College and then went on to law school, graduating from Columbia Law in 1976. In law school he clerked for the NAACP Legal Defense Fund and the Department of Justice's Criminal Division. After graduation Holder worked for the Department of Justice in Washington D.C.

Holder's tenure as attorney general, which concluded in April 2015 when he was succeeded by Loretta Lynch, was often criticized by Republicans. But Holder was also defended as a zealous advocate for voter rights. Civil rights groups praised him for challenging redistricting plans, voter ID laws, and attempts by Republican governors and legislatures to end early voting and other mechanisms that afforded potential voters more time to cast their ballot. Holder also challenged 11 states to restore voting rights to 5.8 million convicted felons, a disproportionate number of whom are African American males, who lost their franchise under state law. When it was announced that Holder would leave office after six years, President Barack Obama singled out his actions to uphold voting rights for particular praise: "He has been relentless against attacks on the Voting Rights Act—because no citizen, including our service members, should have to jump through hoops to exercise their most fundamental right."

Sources

Barrett, Devlin. 2014. "Eric Holder Takes Voting Rights Battle to Ohio, Wisconsin Attorney General Challenges States' Election Laws, Calling Them Discriminatory," *Wall Street Journal,* July 30. Accessed May 10, 2015: http://online.wsj.com/articles/eric-holder-takes -voting-rights-battle-to-ohio-wisconsin-1406752699.

Popper, Robert D. 2014. "Political Fraud about Voter Fraud," *Wall Street Journal,* April 28, A13.

White House Profile: Eric Holder. Accessed April 5, 2015: http://www.whitehouse.gov/blog/ author/Eric%20Holder.

(2013). This effectively nullified the VRA requirement that states get preclearance for changes in election law. However, Attorney General Eric Holder filed suit on behalf of the Obama administration to prevent voter ID laws from taking effect. Holder's lawsuit reflected a widely held Democratic conviction that the voter ID laws were aimed at preventing minorities and those in poverty from voting. During his tenure as attorney general under President Obama, Eric Holder also suggested there was racial motivation in laws that disenfranchised convicted felons from voting, because these laws disproportionately affected African American males (Johnson 2014).

Democrats on Voting Rights

The Voting Rights Act of 1965, along with the Civil Rights Act of 1964, created a wedge between elected Democrats and the Democratic base in the South, which set Southern voters on a path toward realignment with the Republican Party. Prior to the 1965 Voting Rights Act, many of the states that discriminated against African Americans were controlled by members of the Democratic Party, which from the Civil War through 1964 counted on the solid South to provide electoral votes to Democratic presidential candidates. One presidential aide remembers that after signing the Voting Rights Act, President Johnson remarked "we just delivered the South to the Republican Party for a long time to come" (Wilson Quarterly 2000).

Democrats have sought to protect and strengthen the VRA to bolster the civil rights of citizens, and to enhance their own election fortunes, which benefited from the enrollment of African Americans, Hispanics, and individuals below the poverty level. Democrats sought not only equal access to the ballot box but also an election system that would guarantee that minorities have accessed to elected office. To fulfill this ideal the Democrats and civil rights organizations waged battle against states that created election districts that diminished the capacity of minorities to be elected. In 1978, for example, civil rights advocates sued the city of Mobile, Alabama, for creating multiple member at-large voting districts for elections, which they claimed "unfairly diluted the voting strength of Negroes" in violation of the VRA (Boyd and Markman 1983). The Supreme Court ruled in the case of *Mobile v. Boland* that neither the Fifteenth Amendment nor the VRA were created to guarantee the election of African American politicians. Civil rights leaders were outraged and persuaded Democrats in the House and Senate to support legislation to strengthen the VRA and to extend its provisions to 1992. The 1982 amendments required that election laws be nondiscriminatory in both intent and in their effect, to better allow minorities the opportunity to elect candidates of their choice. After the 1982, VRA amendments, state legislatures created majority-minority voting districts, which grouped members of minority populations in a manner to ensure that they had an electoral majority (Boyd and Markman 1983). This trend increased the number of minority candidates elected to office but may have diminished the overall number of elected Democrats who were effectively packed into one election district rather than spread through several.

Congressional Democrats sought to expand voter enrollment and turnout in the National Voter Registration Act of 1993. Sometimes called the motor voter bill, the measure mandated that states allow voter registration at convenient locations such as vehicle registration sites and state offices where people applied for public assistance. Republicans generally were unconvinced that such actions would increase turnout and warned that it might instead increase voter fraud. The 1993 act was passed by a Democrat-controlled Congress and signed into law by Democratic President Bill Clinton, who described it as the next step in a long effort to "enfranchise women and minorities, the disabled and the young."

The 2006 extension and amendments to the VRA were also generated by Supreme Court decisions pertaining to the drawing of legislative districts. The Supreme Court held that changes in the size and placement of election districts were legal under the VRA if the effect of changes led to a form of discrimination that was not retrogressive (Overton 2013). Democrats were urged to pass the 2006 VRA to end the second-generation barriers constructed to prevent minority voters from fully participating in the electoral process.

Attorney General Eric Holder, head of President Barack Obama's Justice Department from January 2009 to April 2015, was vigilant in his attempts to uphold the VRA. After the Supreme Court struck down a key provision of the VRA, Holder filed suit against Texas, Wisconsin, and North Carolina under Section 2 of the VRA, which bars discriminatory effects on minority voters. "We will not allow political pretexts to disenfranchise American citizens," Holder told a gathering of the NAACP (Savage 2012). Republicans, though, criticized Holder's actions as an exercise in racial politics that cast unfair doubts about genuine state efforts to ensure honest elections.

Republicans on Voting Rights

For much of its history, the Republican Party supported extending the right to vote as part of their ideology that everyone should have an equal opportunity. It was a Republican-led Congress that sent the Fifteenth Amendment to the states for ratification, and the call for women's right to vote was led by Republican Susan B. Anthony and was part of the Republican Party platform even before Democrats adopted it. The Voting Rights Act of 1965 was opposed by Southern Democrats and supported by the majority of Republicans in Congress. Republicans also generally supported the 1982 amendments, and the 2006 revisions were introduced by Republican Representative James Sensenbrenner of Wisconsin.

While embracing the ideal of equality of opportunity, many Republicans reject the concept of equality of outcome and have strongly criticized any interpretation of the VRA they believe grants preferential treatment to a particular group. This can be seen in the written decisions of Supreme Court justices appointed by

Republican presidents who have sought to apply the VRA in a race-neutral fashion. In the 1978 case of *Mobile v. Boland*, Justice Potter Stewart, an Eisenhower appointee, ruled that only purposeful discrimination was subject to the VRA and that the Fifteenth Amendment did not grant "the right to have Negro candidates elected."

After Bill Clinton's attorney general, Janet Reno, sued North Carolina for a redistricting plan that created only one minority district, legislatures across the United States responded by creating majority-minority districts. To create these meant that one of the districts was drawn in a narrow serpentine manner that led white residents to claim that their rights were being violated. Writing for the majority in *Shaw v. Reno* (1993), Sandra Day O'Connor, a Reagan appointee, held that any redistricting based on race must be held to a standard of strict scrutiny under the Equal Protection Clause and sent the case back to the District Court for implementing a less overtly racial district. O'Connor also authored the decision in *Georgia v. Ashcroft* (2003), which upheld the right of the state legislature to divide minorities into several election districts. While O'Connor was cautious in her view of the VRA, her colleague on the Court, Associate Justice Antonin Scalia, who was also appointed by Ronald Reagan, was a vocal critic of the VRA. He charged that key provisions of the act are motivated by a "perpetuation of racial entitlement" and "an embedded form of racial preferment."

A key provision of the VRA was struck down by the Supreme Court in 2013 in the case of *Shelby County v. Holder*. The Court ruled that the existing formula used to impose federal oversight of elections was outdated and failed to reflect demographic change since 1965. The immediate effect of this was to allow state governments to move ahead with elections laws, such as adding more stringent voter ID laws or creating election districts, without first seeking federal authorization.

Many Republicans cite voting integrity as a key aspect of their support for voter ID measures. Republicans, who have a smaller nationwide enrollment than Democrats, fear that voter fraud might swing close elections to Democratic candidates. Voter fraud occurs when someone who is ineligible to vote because they do not legally reside in the election district, or are ineligible to vote due to citizen status or criminal record, casts a ballot. Fraud also occurs when someone votes more than once. James Sensenbrenner, a strong proponent of the VRA, is also a vocal supporter of voter ID laws, which he sees as "a useful tool to prevent fraud." Democrats and civil rights leaders reject this claim and believe that the real intent of voter ID laws is to prevent or suppress the number of minority or poor voters who generally vote for Democratic candidates.

Further Reading

Abramowitz, Alan. 2004. *Voice of the People: Elections and Voting in the United States*. Boston: McGraw Hill.

Boyd, Thomas M., and Stephen J. Markman. 1983. "The 1982 Amendments to the Voting Rights Act: A Legislative History," *Washington & Lee Legal Review*, 1347, (40). Accessed October 16, 2014: http://scholarlycommons.law.wlu.edu/wlulr/vol40/iss4/3.

Coleman, Kevin J., and Eric A. Fischer. 2011. *The Help America Vote Act and Elections Reform: Overview and Issues.* Washington: Congressional Research Services, January 13. Accessed October 15, 2014: http://fpc.state.gov/documents/organization/155625 .pdf.

Crocker, Royce. 2013. *The National Voter Registration Act of 1993: History, Implementation, and Effects.* Washington, D.C.: Congressional Research Services.

Johnson, Carrie. 2014. "Holder Calls for Restoring Felons' Voting Rights," NPR. Accessed October 15, 2014: http://www.npr.org/blogs/itsallpolitics/2014/02/11/275270711 /holder-calls-for-restoring-felons-voting-rights.

Johnson, Lyndon. 1965. "Speech before Congress on Voting Rights," March 15. Miller Center. Accessed October 15, 2015: http://millercenter.org/president/speeches/ speech-3386.

Keyssar, Alexander. 2009. *The Right to Vote: The Contested History of Democracy in the United States.* New York: Basic Books.

Lawson, Steven. 1999. *Black Ballots: Voting Rights in the South, 1944–1969.* New York: Lexington Books.

May, Gary. 2013. *Bending toward Justice: The Voting Rights Act and the Transformation of American Democracy.* New York: Basic Books.

Overton, Spencer. 2013. *Stealing Democracy: The New Politics of Voter Suppression.* New York: W. W. Norton.

Savage, Charlie. 2012. "Holder, at N.A.A.C.P. Event, Criticizes Voter ID Laws," *New York Times,* July 10. Accessed October 17, 2014: http://thecaucus.blogs.nytimes.com/2012 /07/10/holder-at-n-a-a-c-p-event-criticizes-voter-id-laws/?module=Search&mabRewa rd=relbias%3Aw%2C%7B%222%22%3A%22RI%3A17%22%2C%221%22%3A%22 RI%3A8%22%7D.

Wilson Quarterly. 2000. "Achilles in the White House: A Discussion with Harry McPherson and Jack Valenti," *Wilson Quarterly,* 24, Spring.

Glossary

ACLU: The American Civil Liberties Union; a nonprofit organization that seeks to protect the civil rights and civil liberties of U.S. citizens from government intrusion.

ACT UP: Nonpartisan organization committed to direct action to end the AIDS crisis.

AFDC (Aid to Families with Dependent Children): A government program from 1935 until 1996 administered and funded by federal and state governments to provide financial assistance to needy families.

Affirmative Action: Affirmative action policies are those in which an institution or organization actively engages in efforts to improve opportunities for historically excluded groups in American society. Affirmative action policies often focus on employment and education.

Affordable Care Act (also called Obamacare): A universal health care act passed under President Barack Obama in 2009 requiring U.S. citizens to have access to health insurance.

Americans with Disabilities Act: Act passed in 1990 under President George H. W. Bush that barred discrimination against disabled persons in hiring and education.

Amicus Curie Brief: A brief filed by a third party, "friend of the court," who is not directly involved in the litigation but who has an interest in the outcome of the case.

At-Will Employment: When an employer can terminate or dismiss an employee at any time, for any cause or reason, except for an illegal one. The employer does not incur legal liability. At the same time, an employee is free to separate him- or herself from work at any time for any reason without incurring adverse legal actions.

Bill of Rights: The first 10 amendments to the U.S. Constitution.

Body Mass Index: Body mass index (BMI) is a person's weight in kilograms divided by the square of height in meters. A high BMI can be an indicator of high body fatness.

Brady Bill: Name often given to the Brady Handgun Violence Prevention Act, passed in 1994 during the administration of Bill Clinton. The law imposed as an interim measure a waiting period of five days before a licensed importer, manufacturer, or dealer may sell, deliver, or transfer a handgun to an unlicensed individual.

The Brady Handgun Violence Prevention Act: See Brady Bill.

Broken Windows Theory: A theory created by political scientist James Q. Wilson that disorganization in communities (typified by the broken windows metaphor) created situations that invite crime. Therefore, communities and police should pay attention to crimes of disorder, help clean up neighborhoods, and work toward reducing levels of fear in communities.

Capitalism: An economic system characterized by private or corporate ownership of capital goods, by investments that are determined by private decision, and by prices, production, and the distribution of goods that are determined mainly by competition in a free market.

Centers for Disease Control and Prevention: Also known as the CDC, the federal agency is part of the Department of Health and Human Services. The CDC's mission is the promotion of health, prevention of chronic and infectious diseases, and preparedness against epidemics and pandemics.

Child Tax Credit: A federal tax benefit that provides a tax credit for families with children younger than 17 years of age.

Civil Rights: The rights derived from the Fourteenth Amendment's guarantee of equal protection under the law.

The Clean Air Act: Is a comprehensive federal law that regulates air emissions from stationary and mobile sources. Initially passed during the presidency of Richard Nixon it was amended during the administration of George H. W. Bush.

The Clean Water Act: In 1972, Congress passed the Clean Water Act to protect all "waters of the United States." It is the primary tool whereby the U.S. government controls water pollution.

Cold War: The historical period between 1947 and 1991 characterized by tension and conflict between the United States and its allies and the Soviet Union and other communist countries.

Collective Bargaining: Bargaining over terms and conditions of service is governed by law and involves unions, on behalf of employees and management, represented by authorized representatives.

Common Core: A set of academic standards in mathematics and English language arts/literacy (ELA). These learning goals outline what a student should know and be able to do at the end of each grade. During the Obama administration, 33 states adopted these standards.

Community Policing: Philosophy and practice of integrating police into local communities. A sometimes controversial practice when combined with the "broken windows theory" of policing in which police crackdown on minor offenses as a strategy to stop major crimes from developing.

Conservativism: A set of belief that include a limited role for the national government in assisting people, and support for traditional values and lifestyles.

Constituent: One of the people represented by a legislator or other elected or appointed official.

Contract with America: Document presented by congressional Republicans during the 1994 midterm elections providing a blueprint for the 104th congressional legislative agenda. Principles include return of program authority to states, a balanced budget, and emphasis on strengthening two-parent families, reduced spending on welfare, and capping federal entitlement programs.

Controlled Substances Act: This law was passed during the administration of Richard Nixon and regulated drugs that could not be manufactured, imported, possessed, used, or distributed.

DARE Program: Program to connect police and other social agencies with K-12 students to create Drug Abuse Resistance Education.

Defense of Marriage Act (DOMA): The Defense of Marriage Act was passed during the administration of President Bill Clinton in 1996. The federal law defined marriage for federal purposes as the union of one man and one woman. In 2013, the Supreme Court ruled the law was unconstitutional.

Deficit: The difference between budgeted government revenues and obligations.

Democratic National Committee: The Democratic National Committee or DNC provides national leadership for the Democratic Party and is responsible for creating the Democratic political platform, as well as coordinating fund-raising and election strategy.

Department of Homeland Security: Government bureaucracy created after the September 11, 2001, terrorist attacks designed to coordinate with other intelligence agencies in order to intercept terrorist threats.

Depression: prolonged period of increased high unemployment, diminished trade and commerce, volatility in currency values, and credit squeeze. A term used to refer to the Great Depression, 1929–1938.

Dissenting Opinion: A separate opinion in which a judge dissents, or disagrees, with the conclusion reached by the majority of the court.

Driving While Black: Term coined during the 1990s to indicate that a motorist might be pulled over by a police officer simply because he or she is black, and then questioned, searched, and/or charged with a trivial offense.

Earned Income Tax Credit: A federal tax credit given to low- to moderate-income working individuals and families. The amount of EITC depends on a recipient's income and number of children.

Elementary and Secondary Education Act (ESEA) of 1965: Was initially part of Lyndon Johnson's War on Poverty. This act recognized the needs of lower income children in public and private education and sought to provide assistance to local school districts to enhance education and break the cycle of poverty. Reauthorization of this act in 2001 led to the No Child Left Behind policy.

Endangered Species Act: The purpose of the ESA is to protect and recover imperiled species and the ecosystems upon which they depend. It is administered by the U.S. Fish and Wildlife Service and the Commerce Department's National Marine Fisheries Service (NMFS). The FWS has primary responsibility for terrestrial and freshwater organisms, while the responsibilities of NMFS are mainly marine wildlife such as whales and anadromous fish such as salmon.

Entitlement: Government programs targeted to specific individuals who meet program eligibility criteria. Normally federal funds flow to states in accordance with the number of people in need.

Environmental Racism: Environmental racism is the disproportionate impact of environmental hazards on people of color, either intentionally or through neglect.

Equal Employment Opportunity Commission: Federal agency responsible for enforcing federal laws that make it illegal to discriminate against a job applicant or an employee because of the person's race, color, religion, sex (including pregnancy), national origin, age (40 or older), disability, or genetic information.

Equal Pay Act: Passed during the administration of John F. Kennedy, the law prohibits sex-based wage discrimination between men and women in the same establishment who perform jobs that require substantially equal skill, effort, and responsibility under similar working conditions. Advocates for equal pay have called for passage of the Paycheck

Fairness Act, which would amend the Equal Pay Act to add enforcement procedures to the bill.

Establishment Clause: Section of the First Amendment of the U.S. Constitution prohibiting the establishment of a church supported by the national government.

Euthanasia: Literally means "good death." The term is associated with the right to die, or death with dignity, movement.

Evangelicals: A group of Christians of various denominations who believe that they have been "Born Again" through salvation through Christ. They place an emphasis on obedience to the Bible and on sharing the "good news" of Jesus Christ. Politically the term has been used to describe conservative and right-wing Christians of all backgrounds, even fundamentalists.

Executive Order: Directives issued by the president and other legal heads of executive branches. Although executive orders have the force of law, there is no expectation for legislative approval.

Family Medical Leave Act (FMLA): A federal law first passed under President Bill Clinton regulating employee medical leave. Reasons for medical leave include: military leave, pregnancy, childbirth, and serious illness.

Farm Bill: An overarching piece of legislation that provides the funding for many of the programs run by the U.S. Department of Agriculture, including farm subsidies and food stamps.

Fast-Food Industry: A sector of the restaurant industry that serves food that can be prepared quickly and easily and is sold as a quick meal or as take out.

Federal Insurance Contributions Act (FICA): Originally Title II of the Social Security Act of 1935, legislated payroll taxes paid by employers and employees to fund the Social Security system. Subsequent amendments assigned taxation provisions to the Internal Revenue Code under the Federal Insurance Contributions Act in 1939.

Feminism: The movement that supports political, economic, and social equality for women.

Filibuster: The use of the Senate's tradition of unlimited debate to delay or block a vote in that body.

Food Desert: The U.S. Department of Agriculture (USDA) defines food deserts as urban neighborhoods and rural towns that lack supermarkets and grocery stores that sell fresh, healthy, and affordable food. Instead, they are served by small business such as fast-food restaurants, convenience stores, and liquor stores, etc., that offer few healthy, affordable food options.

Food Stamp Program: The permanent nutritional program established by the Food Stamp Act of 1964.

Fracking: Process of extracting gas that uses a high-pressure mixture to release the gas.

Free Exercise Clause: The provision of the First Amendment that guarantees Americans the free exercise of their religion.

Fundamentalists: A group of Christians of various denominations who believe in the inerrancy and literal interpretation of the Bible. Often resistant to cultural or social change that they believe challenges biblical authority, they may be lumped together with conservative evangelicals.

Glass Ceiling: Usually associated with women, this is a system or set of attitudes that prevents women from getting hired for certain jobs or promotions.

GOP: Grand Old Party is a nickname for the Republican Party and a synonym for that political party.

Great Recession of 2008–2009: The economic crisis that threatened the collapse of many of the world major financial institutions considered by many economists to be the most significant economic downturn in the United States since the Great Depression.

Green Energy: A type of energy that is naturally replenished, for example, solar power, wind, hydropower, geothermal, tidal, and biomass.

Greenhouse Gases (GHGs): Greenhouse gases include carbon dioxide, methane, chlorofluorocarbons, and nitrous oxide, which collectively trap the sun's energy in the stratosphere, preventing infrared energy from escaping the Earth's surface and slowly increasing the global temperature.

Hart-Cellar Act: Also known as the Immigration and Nationality Act. The law was passed in 1965 during the administration of Lyndon Johnson abolishing the national origins quota system that had regulated American immigration policy since the 1920s, replacing it with a preference system that focused on immigrants' skills and family relationships with citizens or residents of the United States. Numerical restrictions on visas were set at 170,000.

Help America Vote Act: Also known by the acronym HAVA, legislation passed after the election of 2000 to upgrade and ensure election integrity across the United States.

HIV/AIDS: Human immunodeficiency virus and acquired immunodeficiency syndrome were first identified in the 1980s.

Homeschool Legal Defense Fund: A nonprofit advocacy organization established to defend and advance the constitutional right of parents to direct the upbringing and education of their children and to protect family freedoms. HLDF promotes homeschool-friendly legislation at the state and federal levels and offers information and resources to encourage and support all homeschoolers.

Hydraulic Fracturing: Extraction process for underground resources such as oil, natural gas, geothermal, or water. Often referred to as "fracking." It is an extraction method commonly used by companies in the oil and gas industry to bring oil or natural gas to the surface by drilling deep production wells in either horizontal or vertical directional sections and creating fractures in the geologic formations containing the desired resources.

Immigration Reform and Control Act (IRCA) of 1986: Passed to deal with the rise of unauthorized immigrants during the Reagan administration, the bill gave unauthorized aliens the opportunity to apply and gain legal status if they met mandated requirements. Applicants had to prove that they lived and maintained a continuous physical presence in the United States since January 1, 1982, possessed a clean criminal record, and provided proof of registration within the Selective Service. Moreover, applicants had to meet minimal knowledge requirements in U.S. history, government, and the English language or be pursuing a course of study approved by the attorney general.

Incarceration: The state of being confined to jail or prison.

Incarceration Rate: The number of persons imprisoned for every 100,000 persons in a particular population or group.

Income Inequality: A term used to address the distribution of income among a population. In the United States, income inequality is often discussed as the gap between the wealthiest earners, the top 1 percent, and everyone else.

Income Redistribution: the transfer of wealth from some members of society to other members through some form of government process such as taxation.

Individuals with Disabilities Education Act (IDEA): The Individuals with Disabilities Education Act (IDEA) is a law ensuring educational services to disabled children.

Internet Service Providers: Also known by the acronym ISPs. These are companies that provide customers with access to the Internet. There are two main methods used by ISPs to connect clients to the Internet, one is using a phone line called dial-up, the other is to use cable or DSL, called broadband.

Keynesian Economics: Belief that it is the responsibility of the government to assist in stabilizing the economy of the nation that it governs through manipulation of the value of currency and public sector job creation.

Labor Movement: An organized effort to express the interests of working-class Americans.

Landrum Griffin Act of 1959: A bill passed during the administration of Dwight Eisenhower to regulate the internal affairs of unions and their conduct with employers.

Latino: A term used interchangeably with Hispanic to designate individuals who can claim heritage from a Spanish-speaking country other than Spain. The term is only used in the United States.

Liberalism: A set of belief that includes advocating for positive government action to improve the welfare of individuals, support for civil rights, and an openness to political and social change.

Lobbyist: An organization or individual that attempts to influence legislative and administrative decision making in government.

Majority Opinion: A court opinion reflecting the views of the majority of the judges.

Medicaid: A joint state–federal program created during the administration of Lyndon Johnson that provides medical care to the poor, including indigent elderly persons in nursing homes. The program is funded from general government revenues.

Medicare: A federal health insurance program created during the administration of Lyndon Johnson that covers U.S. residents over the age of 65. The program is paid for by a tax on wages and salaries.

Minimum Wage: The lowest hourly wage that a state or federal government can pay employees.

NAACP: The National Association for the Advancement of Colored People, or NAACP, is a civil rights organization dedicated to protecting and promoting the civil rights of people of color.

National Council on Disability: NCD is an independent federal agency charged with advising the president, Congress, and other federal agencies regarding policies, programs, practices, and procedures that affect people with disabilities.

National Environmental Policy Act: A United States environmental law passed during the administration of President Richard Nixon that promotes the enhancement of the environment and established the president's Council on Environmental Quality (CEQ).

National Federation of Independent Businesses: Organization created to support the efforts of small businesses across the United States. They advocate for pro-business policies and oppose legislation or rulings that hurt small business. They may also support candidates for office.

National Labor Relations Act in 1935: Also known as the Wagner Act, the law was created during the presidency of Franklin Roosevelt and recognized and protected the right of workers to have collective bargaining with employers.

National Organization for Women: Also known by the acronym NOW, the National Organization for Women advocates for feminism.

National Restaurant Association: A trade association that advocates, or lobbies, for policies favorable to their industry and opposes legislation or rulings that hurt their industry. They may also support candidates for political office.

National Rifle Association: Nonprofit organization dedicated to protecting the rights of gun owners. The organization advocates for policy favorable to gun ownership and opposes laws or regulation that restrict ownership or access to firearms or ammunition.

National Security Agency: The agency was created under Harry Truman during the Cold War to assist all intelligence services by breaking coded transmissions of information. After the September 11 terrorist attacks the agency played a key role in gathering intelligence, including wire-tapping, and gathering information from domestic telecommunications companies.

Net Neutrality: The principle that Internet service providers should enable access to all content and applications regardless of the source, and without favoring or blocking particular products or Web sites.

New Deal: Economic policies initiated in the early days of Franklin Delano Roosevelt's administration in 1933 with the intent of mitigating the effects of the Great Depression.

No Child Left Behind: Passed during the administration of George W. Bush, NCLB replaced the Elementary and Secondary Education Act (ESEA) with a set of standards in mathematics and literacy. The law required that schools test students to measure whether they were meeting required standards. If schools failed to meet the standards, the legislation authorized the Department of Education to cut Federal funds.

NOW: See National Organization for Women.

Obamacare: Also known as the Affordable Care Act of 2010. The centerpiece of President Barack Obama's first presidential term, designed to comprehensively reform the system of health insurance in the United States.

Opinion: The statement by a judge of the decision reached in a case.

Personal Responsibility and Work Opportunity Act: A major reform of the American welfare system passed during the administration of President Bill Clinton. The purpose of the act was to move individuals from government programs to gainful employment.

Political Action Committee (PAC): A committee set up by and representing a corporation, labor union, or special interest group to raise and give campaign contributions to candidates running for office.

Poverty: A general term for a condition in which people's basic needs for food, clothing, and shelter are not being met. In the United States, the term is equated with an income that places individuals and families above or below the poverty line. Different agencies of the U.S. government have different standards for what meets the income threshold of poverty.

Privatization: Replacing government services, such as prisons, with services provided by private firms.

Profiling: In criminal justice, profiling is the use of an individual's psychological and behavioral characteristics to determine their likelihood to commit a crime. A controversial practice often associated with discrimination against religious, ethnic, and racial minorities.

Recession: Two or more successive quarters in which the economy shrinks rather than grows.

Rehabilitation Act of 1973: The Rehabilitation Act of 1973 (often just called the "Rehab Act") prohibits discrimination on the basis of disability in programs run by federal agencies; programs that receive federal financial assistance; in federal employment; and in the employment practices of federal contractors.

Religious Freedom Restoration Act: Law that requires the U.S. government to give stricter scrutiny to any laws that deny a person's right to worship. The bill was passed in 1993 with strong bipartisan support. It later became the basis of a Supreme Court decision that struck down provisions of the Affordable Care Act mandating employers provide contraceptives and abortion services in health insurance offered to employees.

Reparations: The making of amends for a wrong that has been done in the past, by paying money to or otherwise helping those who have been wronged. In the U.S., Japanese Americans who were forcibly evacuated to detention camps in World War II received reparations, as did native Hawaiians. This has led African Americans to call for reparations for centuries of enslavement.

Republican National Committee: The Republican National Committee or RNC provides national leadership for the Republican Party and is responsible for creating the Republican political platform, as well as coordinating fund-raising and election strategy.

Reverse Discrimination: The claim by a member or members of a majority group that they are discriminated against on the basis of a protected factor, such as race or gender. Thus, a Caucasian individual who claims they were denied employment or admission to a college in favor of a racial minority.

Right-to-Work States: States that prohibit union collective bargaining. No worker need join or pay dues to a union as a condition of employment.

Rockefeller Drug Laws: Named for New York Governor Nelson Rockefeller who championed strict sentencing guidelines for possession and sale of narcotic drugs that put even minor drug offenders behind bars for decades.

RU486: Also known as mifepristone, or the "morning after pill," it chemically hinders the implantation of the sperm into the egg.

Safety Net: Public assistance programs for the poor, such as food stamps, unemployment benefits, etc.

Same-Sex Marriage: Marriage between two persons of the same sex.

Sexual Harassment: The unwanted physical or verbal conduct or abuse of an unwanted nature that interferes with the recipient's job performance or creates a hostile working environment.

Sexually Transmitted Diseases: Sexually transmitted diseases (STDs) are caused by infections that are passed from one person to another during sexual contact.

Social Security Administration (SSA): Created in 1935 as the Social Security Board to administer Social Security benefits, the Social Security Administration was established in 1946 under the direction of the Federal Security Agency and later the Department of Health, Education, and Welfare. The SSA became an independent federal agency in 1994.

Stimulus: More than $700 billion in funding allocated in 2009 by the federal government to stimulate the economy to help recover from the 2008 economic crash.

Supplemental Nutrition Assistance Program (SNAP): As of 2008, the new name of the food stamp program.

Taft-Hartley Act: A law passed over the veto of President Harry S. Truman, the legislation allowed employees to refrain from participating in union or mutual aid activities unless it was a condition of employment.

TANF (Temporary Assistance to Needy Families): TANF replaced the AFDC program in 1996 with passage of the Personal Responsibility and Work Opportunity Act signed into law by President Bill Clinton in 1996.

"Three-Strikes" Law: Provision in the Violent Crime Control and Law Enforcement Act of 1994, passed during the administration of Bill Clinton, that mandatory life imprisonment can be handed out if a person is convicted in federal court of a "serious violent felony" and already has two or more previous convictions in federal or state courts, at least one of which is a "serious violent felony."

Troubled Asset Relief Program: A program initiated during the recession of 2008–2009 to purchase assets and equity from financial institutions to strengthen the financial sector of the U.S. economy. Begun under President George W. Bush to assist financial institutions, it was expanded under President Barack Obama to include the automobile industry.

Unemployment: Refers to general joblessness. Persons are considered unemployed if they are actively seeking employment at prevailing wages. The unemployment rate is a metric calculated as a percentage of the unemployed to the number of persons in the labor force.

Unemployment Insurance: Income provided to persons who have lost jobs through no fault of their own.

U.S. Chamber of Commerce: A nonprofit advocacy organization formed to protect the interest of businesses. With state and local branches across the United States, the Chamber of Commerce advocates for policies favorable to business or opposes legislation or rulings that hurt their industry. They may also support candidates for political office.

USA Patriot Act: Passed after the terrorist attacks on the United States in 2001, Congress passed the Patriot Act by overwhelming, bipartisan margins with an aim to providing new tools to law enforcement agencies new to better detect and prevent acts of terrorism.

War on Poverty: The Kennedy–Johnson Administration's 13-point program that declared an "unconditional war on poverty" via creation of new social safety-net programs such as Head Start.

Bibliography

Abramowitz, Alan. 2004. *Voice of the People: Elections and Voting in the United States*. Boston: McGraw Hill.

Alexander, Michelle. 2012. *The New Jim Crow: Mass Incarceration in the Age of Colorblindness*. New York: The New Press.

Allen, Louise. 2005. *Sexual Subjects: Young People, Sexuality and Education*. Basingstoke: Palgrave Macmillan.

Ankarlo, Darrell. 2010. *Illegals: The Unacceptable Cost of America's Failure to Control Its Borders*. New York: Thomas Nelson.

Babcock, Linda, and Sara Laschever. 2003. *Women Don't Ask: Negotiation and the Gender Divide*. Princeton: Princeton University Press.

Bade, Rachael. 2015. "Criminal Justice Reform Gains Bipartisan Momentum," Politico, July 15. Accessed October 5, 2015: http://www.politico.com/story/2015/07/criminal -justice-reform-gains-bipartisan-momentum-120125.

Balko, Radley. 2014. *Rise of the Warrior Cop: The Militarization of America's Police Forces*. New York: Public Affairs.

Ball, Carlos, and Michael Bronski. 2011. *From the Closet to the Courtroom: Five LGBT Rights Lawsuits That Have Changed Our Nation*. Boston: Beacon Press.

Ball, Tim. 2014. *The Deliberate Corruption of Climate Science*. Mount Vernon, WA: Stairway Press.

Banner, Stuart. 2003. *The Death Penalty: An American History*. Cambridge: Harvard University Press.

Barkan, Elliot Robert, ed. 2013. *Immigrants in American History Arrival, Adaptation, and Integration*. Santa Barbara: ABC-CLIO.

Bartol, Curtis, and Anne M. Bartol. 2012. *Criminal & Behavioral Profiling: Theory Research and Practice*. New York: SAGE.

Baum, Dan. 1997. *Smoke and Mirrors: The War on Drugs and the Politics of Failure*. Boston: Back Bay Books.

Bazelon, Emily. 2014. *Sticks and Stones: Defeating the Culture of Bullying and Rediscovering the Power of Character and Empathy*. New York: Random House.

Bedau, Hugo Adam, and Paul Cassell, eds. 2005. *Debating the Death Penalty: Should America Have Capital Punishment? The Experts on Both Sides Make Their Case*. New York: Oxford University Press.

Bergmann, Barbara. 1997. *In Defense of Affirmative Action*. New York: Basic Books.

Berkowitz, Edward D. 1987. *Disabled Policy: America's Programs for the Handicapped—A Twentieth Century Fund Report*. New York and London: Cambridge University Press.

Berkowitz, Edward D. 1991. *America's Welfare State: From Roosevelt to Reagan*. Baltimore: Johns Hopkins University Press.

Berlatsky, Noah. 2012. *The Minimum Wage*. New York: Greenhaven Press.

Berry, Mary Frances. 2006. *My Face Is Black Is True: Callie House and the Struggle for Ex-Slave Reparations*. New York: Random House.

Biondi, Martha. 2003. "The Rise of the Reparations Movement," *Radical History Review*, 87, Fall: 5–18.

Blaustein, Saul, and Wilbur Cohen. 1993. *Unemployment Insurance in the United States: The First Half Century.* Kalamazoo, MI: W. E. Upjohn Institute.

Brady, Sara. 2002. *A Good Fight.* New York: Public Affairs.

Bronski, Michael. 2012. *A Queer History of the United States.* Boston: Beacon Press.

Brophy, Alfred L. 2008. *Reparations: Pro and Con.* New York: Oxford.

Brownell, Kelly. 2004. *Food Fight: The Inside Story of the Food Industry, America's Obesity Crisis, and What We Can Do about It.* New York: McGraw Hill.

Bumgarner, Jeff. 2014. *Profiling and Criminal Justice in America: A Reference Handbook,* 2nd edition. In *Contemporary World Issues* series. Santa Barbara: ABC-CLIO.

Caplan, Arthur, ed. 2006. *The Case of Terri Schiavo: Ethics at the End of Life.* Buffalo: Prometheus Books.

Carney, Eliza Newlin. 2015. "Left Meets Right in Prison Politics," *CQ Weekly*, April 13: 20–23. Accessed July 20, 2015: http://0-library.cqpress.com.libra.naz.edu/cqweekly /weeklyreport114-000004660482.

Carter, Gregg Lee. 2012. *Guns in American Society: An Encyclopedia of History, Politics, Culture, and the Law.* Santa Barbara: ABC-CLIO.

Clemmitt, Marcia. 2012. "Internet Regulation," *CQ Researcher*, April 13, 22. Accessed June 12, 2014: http://0-library.cqpress.com.libra.naz.edu/cqresearcher/.

Clendinen, Dudley, and Nagourney, Adam. 1999. *Out for Good: The Struggle to Build a Gay Rights Movement in America.* New York: Simon and Schuster.

Clinton, Hillary. 2006. *It Takes a Village,* 10th anniversary edition. New York: Simon and Schuster.

Coates, Ta-Nehisi. 2014. "The Case for Reparations," *The Atlantic,* May 21.

Coll, Blanche D. 1995. *Safety Net: Welfare and Social Security, 1929–1979.* New Brunswick: Rutgers University Press.

Coloroso, Barbara. 2009. *The Bully, the Bullied, and the Bystander: From Preschool to High School—How Parents and Teachers Can Help Break the Cycle.* New York: William Morrow.

Connerly, Ward. 2007. *Creating Equal: My Fight against Race Preferences,* 2nd edition. New York: Encounter Books.

Cook, Phillip, and Kim Goss. 2014. *The Gun Debate: What Everyone Needs to Know* New York: Oxford University Press.

Corlett, Angelo J. 2010. *Heirs of Oppression: Racism and Reparations. Studies in Social, Political, and Legal Philosophy* series. Lanham, MD: Rowman and Littlefield.

Cote, Richard. 2012. *In Search of Gentle Death: The Fight for Your Right to Die with Dignity.* New York: Corinthian Books.

Crawford, Susan. 2014. *Captive Audience: The Telecom Industry and Monopoly Power in the New Gilded Age.* New Haven: Yale University Press.

DiSalvo, Daniel. 2015. *Government against Itself: Public Union Power and Its Consequences.* New York: Oxford University Press.

Dowbiggin, Ian. 2003. *A Merciful End: The Euthanasia Movement in Modern America.* New York: Oxford University Press.

Downes, Larry, and Paul Nunes. 2014. *Big Bang Disruption: Strategy in the Age of Devastating Innovation.* New York: Portfolio.

Downie, David L., Kate Brash, and Catherine Vaughan. 2009. *Climate Change: A Reference Handbook.* Santa Barbara: ABC-CLIO.

Dray, Philip. 2011. *There Is Power in a Union: The Epic Story of Labor in America.* New York: Anchor Books.

Drucker, Ernest. 2013. *A Plague of Prisons: The Epidemiology of Mass Incarceration in America.* New York: The New Press.

Duerst-Lahti, Georgia. 1989. "The Government's Role in Building the Women's Movement," *Political Science Quarterly*, 104 (2): 249–268, 251.

Early, Steve. 2013. *Save Our Unions: Dispatches from a Movement in Distress.* New York: Monthly Review Press.

Ehrenreich, Barbara. 2011. *Nickel and Dimed: On (Not) Getting by in America.* New York: Picador Press.

Endean, Steve. 2006. *Bringing Lesbian and Gay Rights into the Mainstream: Twenty Years of Progress.* New York: Harrington Park.

Engelmann, Peter. 2011. *A History of the Birth Control Movement in America.* In *Healing Society: Disease, Medicine, and History* series. New York: Praeger.

Farrel, Warren. 2005. *Why Men Earn More: The Startling Truth behind the Pay Gap—and What Women Can Do about It.* New York: AMACOM Press.

Fisher, Gary L. 2006. *Rethinking Our War on Drugs.* Santa Barbara: Praeger.

Fleischer, Doris, and Frieda Zames. 2011. *Disability Rights Movement: From Charity to Confrontation,* 2nd edition. Philadelphia: Temple University Press.

Fuller, Edwin Torrey. 2013. *American Psychosis: How the Federal Government Destroyed the Mental Illness Treatment System.* New York: Oxford University Press.

Gellman, Robert. 2011. *Online Privacy: A Reference Handbook.* In *Contemporary World Issues* series. Santa Barbara: ABC-CLIO.

Gerdes, Louise. 2012. *The Columbine School Shooting.* New York: Greenhaven Press.

Giddens, Anthony. 2011. *The Politics of Climate Change,* 2nd edition. Malden, MA: Polity.

Giffords, Gabby. 2014. *Enough: Our Fight to Keep America Safe from Gun Violence.* New York: Scribner.

Glaser, Jack. 2014. *Suspect Race: Causes and Consequences of Racial Profiling.* New York: Oxford University Press.

Glazer, Nathan. 1987. *Affirmative Discrimination: Ethnic Inequality and Public Policy.* Cambridge: Harvard University Press.

Glazer, Sarah. 2014. "Sentencing Reform. Are Mandatory Sentences Too Harsh?" *CQ Researcher,* 24 (2), January 10: 25–48.

Glen, Richard A. *2003. The Right to Privacy: Rights and Liberties under the Law.* In *America's Freedoms* series. Santa Barbara: ABC-CLIO.

Goldstein, Dana. 2014. *The Teacher Wars: A History of America's Most Embattled Profession.* New York: Doubleday.

Gordon, Linda. 2007. *The Moral Property of Women: A History of Birth Control Politics in America.* Urbana: University of Illinois.

Gould, Lewis. 2003. *Grand Old Party: A History of the Republicans.* New York: Random House.

Gouwens, Judith A. 2009. *Education in Crisis: A Reference Handbook.* Santa Barbara: ABC-CLIO.

Greenhouse, Linda. 2006. *Becoming Justice Blackmun: Harry Blackmun's Supreme Court Journey.* New York: New York Times Books.

Greenwald, Glenn. 2014. *No Place to Hide: Edward Snowden, the NSA, and the U.S. Surveillance State.* New York: Metropolitan Books.

Grob, Gerald, and Howard H. Goldman. 2006. *The Dilemma of Federal Mental Health Policy: Radical Reform or Incremental Change?* New Brunswick: Rutgers University Press.

Haider-Markel, Donald P. 2010. *Out and Running: Gay and Lesbian Candidates, Elections, and Policy Representation.* Washington, D.C.: Georgetown University Press.

Harden, Victoria. 2012. *AIDS at 30: A History.* Washington, D.C.: Potomac Books.

Hardisty, Jean. 1999. *Mobilizing Resentment: Conservative Resurgence from the John Birch Society to the Promise Keepers.* Boston: Beacon Press.

Hari, Johann. 2015. *Chasing the Scream: The First and Last Days of the War on Drugs.* New York: Bloomsbury.

Harrington, Michael. 1997. *The Other America: Poverty in the United States.* New York: Touchstone.

Hasen, Richard. 2012. *The Voting Wars: From Florida 2000 to the Next Election Meltdown.* New Haven: Yale University Press.

Hays, Sharon. 2004. *Flat Broke with Children: Women in the Age of Welfare Reform.* New York: Oxford University Press.

Hazlett, Thomas. 2011. *The Fallacy of Net Neutrality.* New York: Encounter Books.

Hendershott, Anne. 2006. *The Politics of Abortion.* New York: Encounter Books.

Henry, Charles P. 2003. "The Politics of Racial Reparations," *Journal of Black Studies,* 34 (2), November: 131–152.

Hess, Frederick. 2007. *No Remedy Left Behind: Lessons from a Half-Decade of NCLB.* Washington, D.C.: American Enterprise Institute.

Hillstrom, Kevin. 2014. *Medical Marijuana.* Farmington Hills, MI: Gale Cengage Learning.

Hull, N. E. H., and Peter Charles Hoffer. 2010. *Roe v. Wade: The Abortion Rights Controversy in American History,* 2nd edition. In *Landmark Law Cases and American Society* Charles Peter Hoffer, Ed., series. Lawrence: University Press of Kansas.

Ifill, Gwen. 2007. *The Breakthrough: Politics and Race in the Age of Obama.* New York: Anchor Books.

Inhofe, James D. 2012. *The Greatest Hoax: How the Global Warming Conspiracy Threatens Your Future.* Medford, OR: WND Books.

Johnson, Michelle. 2014. "Legalizing Marijuana," *CQ Researcher,* March 25.

Jutte, Robert. 2008. *Contraception: A History.* New York: Polity.

Karger, Howard Jacob, and David Stoesz. 2013. *American Social Welfare Policy: A Pluralist Approach,* 7th edition. New York: Pearson.

Katz, Michael. 2013. *The Undeserving Poor: America's Enduring Confrontation with Poverty,* 2nd edition. New York: Oxford University Press.

Keefe, William J., and Marc J. Hetherington. 2013. *Parties, Politics, and Public Policy in America,* 9th edition. Washington, D.C.: CQ Press.

Kendall, Nancy. 2012. *The Sex Education Debates.* Chicago: University of Chicago Press.

Keynes, John Maynard. 2011. *The General Theory of Employment, Interest, and Money.* Create Space Independent Publishing Platform.

Keyssar, Alexander. 2009. *The Right to Vote: The Contested History of Democracy in the United States.* New York: Basic Books.

Kim, Christine, and Robert Rector. 2010. *Evidence on the Effectiveness of Abstinence Education: An Update.* Washington D.C.: The Heritage Foundation.

Klarman, Michael J. 2013. *From the Closet to the Altar: Courts, Backlash and the Struggle for Same-Sex Marriage.* New York: Oxford University Press.

Knowles, Helen. 2009. *The Tie Goes to Freedom: Justice Anthony M. Kennedy on Liberty.* Lanham, MD: Rowman and Littlefield.

Krieger, Linda Hamilton. 2003. *Backlash against the ADA: Reinterpreting Disability Rights.* Ann Arbor: University of Michigan Press.

Kronenwetter, Michael John. 1993. *Capital Punishment: A Reference Handbook.* In *Contemporary World Issues* series. Santa Barbara: ABC-CLIO.

Latzler, Barry. 2010. *Death Penalty Cases: Leading U.S. Supreme Court Cases on Capital Punishment,* 3rd edition. New York: Butterworth-Heinemann.

Lawson, Steven. 1999. *Black Ballots: Voting Rights in the South, 1944–1969.* New York: Lexington Books.

Layzer, Judith A. 2011. *The Environmental Case: Translating Values into Policy.* Washington, D.C.: CQ Press.

Ledbetter, Lilly. 2013. *Grace and Grit: My Fight for Equal Pay and Fairness at Goodyear and Beyond.* New York: Three Rivers Press.

Lee, Martin A. 2012. *Smoke Signals: A Social History of Marijuana—Medical, Recreational, and Scientific.* New York: Scribner.

Leiter, William. 2011. *Affirmative Action in Antidiscrimination Law and Policy: An Overview and Synthesis.* Albany: State University of New York Press.

LeMay, Michael. 2006. *Illegal Immigration: A Reference Handbook.* In *Contemporary World Issues* series. Santa Barbara: ABC-CLIO.

Lipinski, John. 2013. *Bullying in the Workplace: Causes, Symptoms, and Remedies.* New York: Routledge.

Lopoo, Leonard M., and Kerri M. Raissan. 2014. "U.S. Social Policy and Family Complexity," *The Annals of the American Academy of Political and Social Science,* July, 654 (1): 213–230.

Mantel, Barbara. 2014. "Minimum Wage," *CQ Researcher,* 24 (4), January 24: 73–96.

Marquardt, Maria Freidmann, Timothy J. Steigenga, and Philip J. Williams. 2011. *Living "Illegal": The Human Face of Unauthorized Immigration.* New York: New Press.

Martin, Alyson, and Nushin Rashidian. 2014. *A New Leaf: The End of the Cannabis Prohibition e-Book.* New York: Free Press.

Martin, Shannan, Robert Rector, and Melissa Pardue. 2004. *Comprehensive Sex Education vs. Authentic Abstinence: A Study of Competing Curricula.* Washington, D.C.: The Heritage Foundation.

Martin, Waldo E., Jr. 1998. *Brown v. Board of Education: A Brief History with Documents.* New York: St. Martin's/Bedford.

May, Gary. 2013. *Bending Toward Justice: The Voting Rights Act and the Transformation of American Democracy.* New York: Basic Books.

McBride, Dorothy. 2008. *Abortion in the United States: A Reference Handbook.* Santa Barbara: ABC-CLIO.

McDougall, Jennifer Fecio, and Martha Gorman. 2008. *Euthanasia: A Reference Handbook.* Santa Barbara: ABC-CLIO.

McKibben, Bill. 2012. *The Global Warming Reader: A Century of Writing about Climate Change.* New York: Penguin Books.

Melusky, Joseph, and Keith Alan Pesto. 2014. *The Death Penalty: Documents Decoded.* Santa Barbara: ABC-CLIO.

Merrick, Janna C., and Robert H. Blank. 2003. *Reproductive Issues in America: A Reference Handbook.* Santa Barbara: ABC-CLIO.

Milkis, Sidney M., and Jerome M. Mileur, eds. 2005. *The Great Society and the High Tide of Liberalism.* Boston: University of Massachusetts Press.

Miller, Linda S., Karen Hess, and Christine M.H. Orthmann. 2013. *Community Policing: Partnerships for Problem Solving.* New York: Cengage.

Montgomery, David. 1989. *The Fall of the House of Labor: The Workplace, the State, and American Labor Activism, 1865–1925*. New York: Cambridge University Press.

Mooney, Chris. 2012. *The Republican Brain: The Science of Why They Deny Science—and Reality*. New York: Wiley.

Morone, James A., and Dan Ehlke. 2014. *Health Politics and Policy*. New York: Cengage Learning.

Murray, Charles. 2015. *Losing Ground: American Social Policy, 1950–1980*. New York: Basic Books.

Nathan, Randy. 2014. *Bullying in Sports: A Guide to Identifying the Injuries We Don't See*. New York: Pearson.

Newton, David E. 2009. *Environmental Justice: A Reference Handbook*. Santa Barbara: ABC-CLIO.

Newton, David E. 2010. *Same-Sex Marriage: A Reference Handbook*. Santa Barbara: ABC-CLIO.

Newton, David E. 2013. *Marijuana: A Reference Handbook*. In *Contemporary World Issues* series. Santa Barbara: ABC-CLIO.

Newton, David E. 2015. *Fracking. A Reference Handbook*. Santa Barbara: ABC-CLIO.

Ngai, Mae. 2014. *Impossible Subjects: Illegal Aliens and the Making of Modern America*. In *Politics and Society in Twentieth-Century America* series. Princeton: Princeton University Press.

Nuemark, David, and William Waschler. 2010. *Minimum Wages*. Boston: MIT Press.

Obama, Michelle. 2009. *Michelle Obama in Her Own Words: The Views and Values of America's First Lady*, edited by Lisa Rogan. New York: Public Affairs.

Obama, Michelle. 2012. *American Grown: The Story of the White House Kitchen Garden and Gardens across America*. New York: Crown.

O'Connor, Brendan. 2004. *A Political History of the American Welfare System: When Ideas Have Consequences*. Lanham, MD: Rowman and Littlefield.

Ogletree, Charles, and Austin Sarat, eds. 2006. *From Lynch Mobs to the Killing State: Race and the Death Penalty in America*. In *the Charles Hamilton Houston Institute Series on Race and Justice*. New York: NYU Press.

Oleary, Christopher J., and Stephen Wandner. 1987. *Unemployment Insurance in the United States: Analysis of Policy Issues*. Kalamazoo, MI: W. E. Upjohn Institute.

Overston, Spencer. 2013. *Stealing Democracy: The New Politics of Voter Suppression*. New York: W. W. Norton.

Palmer, Louis. 2013. *The Death Penalty in the United States: A Complete Guide to Federal and State Laws*, 2nd edition. Jefferson, NC: McFarland.

Pielke, Roger, Jr. 2014. *The Rightful Place of Science: Disasters and Climate Change*. Tempe, AZ: Consortium for Science, Policy and Outcomes.

Piven, Frances Fox, and Richard Cloward. 1993. *Regulating the Poor: The Functions of Public Welfare*. New York: Knopf.

Prejean, Helen. 1994. *Dead Man Walking: The Eyewitness Account of the Death Penalty That Sparked a National Debate*. New York: Vintage.

Price, Byron Eugene, and John Charles Morris, eds. 2012. *Prison Privatization: The Many Facets of a Controversial Industry*. Santa Barbara: Praeger.

Provine, Doris Marie. 2007. *Unequal under Law: Race in the War on Drugs*. Chicago: University of Chicago Press.

Quadagno, Jill. 2004. *The Color of Welfare: How Racism Undermined the War on Poverty*. New York: Oxford University Press.

Rafter, Nicole Hahn, and Debra L. Stanley. 1999. *Prisons in America: A Reference Handbook.* Santa Barbara: ABC-CLIO.

Rasmussen, Scott, and Douglas Schoen. 2010. *Mad as Hell: How the Tea Party Movement Is Fundamentally Remaking Our Two-Party System.* New York: HarperCollins.

Ravitch, Diana. 2011. *The Death and Life of the Great American School System: How Testing and Choice Are Undermining Education.* New York: Basic Books.

Reese, Ellen. 2013. *They Say Cutback, We Say Fight Back! Welfare Activism in an Era of Retrenchment.* New York: Russell Sage Foundation.

Roberts, Kevin D. 2005. *African American Issues.* Westport: Greenwood Press.

Robinson, Randall. 2001. *The Debt: What America Owes to Blacks.* New York: Plume.

Rosenbaum, Walter A. 2013. *Environmental Politics and Policy,* 9th edition. New York: CQ Press.

Ryan, Paul. 2014. *The Way Forward: Renewing the American Idea.* New York: Twelve.

Sandberg, Sherry. 2013. *Lean In: Women, Work, and the Will to Lead.* New York: Knopf.

Scheer, Robert. 2015. *They Know Everything about You: How Data-Collecting Corporations and Snooping Government Agencies Are Destroying Democracy.* New York: Nation Books.

Schlosser, Eric. 2012. *Fast Food Nation: The Dark Side of the All-American Meal.* Reprint, Boston, MA: Mariner Books.

Schneir, Bruce. 2015. *Data and Goliath: The Hidden Battles to Collect Your Data and Control Your World.* New York: W. W. Norton.

Schwab, William A. 2013. *Right to DREAM: Immigration Reform and America's Future.* Little Rock: University of Arkansas Press.

Shilts, Randy. 2007. *And the Band Played On: Politics, People, and the AIDS Epidemic,* 20th anniversary edition. New York: St. Martin's.

Smith, Raymond A. 2013. *Global HIV/AIDS Politics, Policy, and Activism,* in 3 volumes. Santa Barbara: Praeger.

Solinger, Rickie. 2013. *Reproductive Politics: What Everyone Needs to Know.* New York: Oxford University Press.

Spring, Joel. 2013. *Political Agendas for Education: From Race to the Top to Saving the Planet.* New York: Routledge.

Sterling, Terry. 2010. *Illegal: Life and Death in Arizona's Immigration War Zone.* New York: Lyons Press.

Stern, Judith, and Alexandra Kazaks. 2009. *Obesity: A Reference Handbook.* Santa Barbara: ABC-CLIO.

Steverson, Leonard A. 2008. *Policing in America: A Reference Handbook,* 2nd edition. Santa Barbara: ABC-CLIO.

Stewart, Chuck. 2014. *Proud Heritage: People, Issues, and Documents of the LGBT Experience,* 3rd edition. Santa Barbara: ABC-CLIO.

Swartz, James. 2012. *Substance Abuse in America: A Documentary and Reference Guide.* Santa Barbara: Greenwood.

Tanner, Jane. 2003. "Unemployment Benefits," *CQ Researcher,* 13 (16), April 25: 369–392.

Taverner, Bill, and Sue Montfort. 2005. *Making Sense of Abstinence: Lessons for Comprehensive Sex Education.* Planned Parenthood of Northern New Jersey.

Taylor, Jami Kathleen, and Donald P. Haider-Markel. 2014. *Transgender Rights and Politics: Groups, Issue Framing, and Policy Adoption.* Ann Arbor: University of Michigan Press.

Thompson, Janna. 2002. *Taking Responsibility for the Past: Reparation and Historical Injustice.* New York: Polity.

Thurman, Quint, and Andrew Giacomazzi. 2014. *Controversies in Policing.* New York: Routledge.

Turner, Jeffrey Scott. 2002. *Families in America: A Reference Handbook*. Santa Barbara: ABC-CLIO.

Urban, Wayne, and Jennings L. Wagoner. 2013. *American Education: A History*. New York: Routledge.

Varga, Joseph. 2014. "Dispossession Is Nine-tenths of the Law: Right-to-Work and the Making of the American Precariat," *Labor Studies Journal*, 39 (1): 25–45.

Waldman, Michael. 2014. *The Second Amendment: A Biography*. New York: Simon and Schuster.

Walker, Scott, and Marc Thiessen. 2014. *Unintimidated: A Governor's Story and a Nation's Challenge*. New York: Sentinel Trade.

Waltman, Jerrald. 2000. *The Politics of the Minimum Wage*. Urbana: University of Illinois Press.

Weingarten, Karen. 2014. *Abortion in the American Imagination: Before Life and Choice, 1880–1940*. Rutgers: Rutgers University Press.

White, Edward G. 2002. *The Constitution and the New Deal*. Cambridge: Harvard University Press.

Wilson, James. Q. 1978. *Varieties of Police Behavior*. Cambridge: Harvard University Press.

Winkler, Adam. 2013. *Gunfight: The Battle over the Right to Bear Arms in America*. New York: W. W. Norton.

Witcover, Jules. 2003. *Party of the People: A History of the Democrats*. New York: Random House.

Withrow, Brian. 2010. *The Racial Profiling Controversy: What Every Police Leader Should Know*. New York: Looseleaf Law Publications.

Woods, Dorian. 2012. *Family Policy in Transformation: US and UK Policies*. New York: Macmillan.

Wu, Tim. 2011. *The Master Switch: The Rise and Fall of Information Empires*. New York: Vintage.

Index

About the Author

Timothy W. Kneeland, full professor and chair, History and Political Science Department, Nazareth College, received his PhD from the University of Oklahoma in 1996. Publications include *Pushbutton Psychiatry: A Cultural History of Electroshock in America* (Praeger, 2002); chapter length studies of "Presidents and Radio" in *American Presidents in Popular Culture*, ed. John Matviko (Greenwood, 2005); "FDR's Pre-Presidential Career" in *A Companion to Franklin D. Roosevelt*, ed. William Pederson (2011); "Millard Fillmore and the Crisis of 1850" in *Chronology of the U.S. Presidency*, ed. Matthew Manweller (ABC-CLIO, 2012); and "George H. W. Bush" in *Encyclopedia of U.S. Presidency*, ed. Nancy Beck Young (2013).